John William Draper

**History of the intellectual Development of Europe VOL. 2**

John William Draper

**History of the intellectual Development of Europe VOL. 2**

ISBN/EAN: 9783741171864

Manufactured in Europe, USA, Canada, Australia, Japa

Cover: Foto ©ninafisch / pixelio.de

Manufactured and distributed by brebook publishing software (www.brebook.com)

John William Draper

**History of the intellectual Development of Europe VOL. 2**

# THE
# INTELLECTUAL DEVELOPEMENT
# OF EUROPE.

# HISTORY

OF THE

# INTELLECTUAL DEVELOPEMENT

OF

# EUROPE.

BY

JOHN WILLIAM DRAPER, M.D., LL.D.,

PROFESSOR OF CHEMISTRY AND PHYSIOLOGY IN THE UNIVERSITY OF NEW YORK;
AUTHOR OF A 'TREATISE ON HUMAN PHYSIOLOGY,' ETC. ETC.

IN TWO VOLUMES.

VOL. II.

LONDON:
BELL AND DALDY, FLEET STREET.
1864.

# CONTENTS.

## CHAPTER XV.

### THE AGE OF FAITH IN THE WEST. THE THREE ATTACKS; NORTHERN OR MORAL, WESTERN OR INTELLECTUAL; EASTERN OR MILITARY.

#### THE NORTHERN OR MORAL ATTACK ON THE ITALIAN SYSTEM, AND ITS TEMPORARY REPULSE.

Page

Geographical Boundaries of Italian Christianity.—Attacks upon it.
The Northern or moral Attack.—The Emperor of Germany insists on a reformation in the Papacy.—Gerbert, the representative of these Ideas, is made Pope.—They are both poisoned by the Italians.
Commencement of the Intellectual Rejection of the Italian System.—Originates in the Arabian doctrine of the supremacy of Reason over Authority.—The question of Transubstantiation.—Rise and Development of Scholasticism.—Mutiny among the Monks.
Gregory VII. spontaneously accepts and enforces a Reform in the Church.—Overcomes the Emperor of Germany.—Is on the point of establishing a European Theocracy.—The Popes seize the military and monetary Resources of Europe through the Crusades . . . . . . . . . . . . 1

## CHAPTER XVI.

### THE AGE OF FAITH IN THE WEST—(Continued).

#### THE WESTERN OR INTELLECTUAL ATTACK ON THE ITALIAN SYSTEM.

The intellectual Condition of Christendom contrasted with that of Arabian Spain.
Diffusion of Arabian intellectual Influences through France and Sicily.—Example of Saracen Science in Alhazen, and of Philosophy in Algazzali.—Innocent III. prepares to combat these Influences.—Results to Western Europe of the Sack of Constantinople by the Catholics.

The spread of Mohammedan light Literature is followed by Heresy.—The crushing of Heresy in the South of France by armed Force, the Inquisition, mendicant Orders, auricular Confession, and Casuistry.
The rising sentiment is embodied in Frederick II. in Sicily.—His Conflict with and Overthrow by the Pope.—Spread of Mutiny among the mendicant Orders . . . . . . . . . . . . . . . . 26

## CHAPTER XVII.

### THE AGE OF FAITH IN THE WEST—(Continued).

#### OVERTHROW OF THE ITALIAN SYSTEM BY THE COMBINED INTELLECTUAL AND MORAL ATTACK.

Progress of Irreligion among the mendicant Orders.—Publication of heretical Books.—The 'Everlasting Gospel' and the Comment on the Apocalypse.
Conflict between Philip the Fair and Boniface VIII.—Outrage upon and Death of the Pope.
The French King removes the Papacy from Rome to Avignon.—Postmortem Trial of the Pope for Atheism and Immorality.—Causes and Consequences of the Atheism of the Pope.
The Templars fall into Infidelity.—Their Trial, Conviction, and Punishment.
Immoralities of the Papal Court at Avignon.—Its return to Rome.—Causes of the great Schism.—Disorganization of the Italian System.—Decomposition of the Papacy.—Three Popes.
The Council of Constance attempts to convert the Papal Autocracy into a constitutional Monarchy.—It murders John Huss and Jerome of Prague.—Pontificate of Nicholas V.—End of the Intellectual Influence of the Italian System . . . . . . . . . . . . . . . 78

## CHAPTER XVIII.

### THE AGE OF FAITH IN THE WEST—(Concluded).

#### EFFECT OF THE EASTERN OR MILITARY ATTACK.—GENERAL REVIEW OF THE AGE OF FAITH.

The Fall of Constantinople.—Its momentary Effect on the Italian System.
GENERAL REVIEW OF THE INTELLECTUAL CONDITION IN THE AGE OF FAITH.—Supernaturalism and its Logic spread all over Europe.—It is destroyed by the Jews and Arabians.—Its total Extinction.
The Jewish Physicians.—Their Acquirements and Influence.—Their Collision with the Imposture-medicine of Europe.—Their Effect on the higher Classes.—Opposition to them.
Two impostors, the Intellectual and Moral, operating against the Mediæval state of Things.—Downfall of the Italian System through the intellectual

Impulse from the West and the moral from the North.—Action of the former through Astronomy.—Origin of the moral Impulse.—Their conjoint irresistible Effect.—Discovery of the state of Affairs in Italy.—The Writings of Machiavelli.—What the Church had actually done.
Entire Movement of the Italian System determined from a consideration of the four Revolts against it . . . . . . . . . . . . . . . 102

## CHAPTER XIX.

### APPROACH OF THE AGE OF REASON IN EUROPE.

#### IT IS PRECEDED BY MARITIME DISCOVERY.

Consideration of the definite Epochs of social Life.
Experimental Philosophy emerging in the Age of Faith.
The Age of Reason ushered in by Maritime Discovery and the rise of European Criticism.
MARITIME DISCOVERY.—The three great Voyages.
COLUMBUS discovers America.—DE GAMA doubles the Cape and reaches India.—MAGELLAN circumnavigates the Earth.—The material and intellectual Results of each of these Voyages.
DIGRESSION ON THE SOCIAL CONDITION OF AMERICA.—In isolated human Societies the Process of Thought and of Civilization is always the same.—Man passes through a determinate succession of Ideas and embodies them in determinate Institutions.—The state of Mexico and Peru proves the Influence of Law in the developement of Man . . . . . . . 117

## CHAPTER XX.

### APPROACH OF THE AGE OF REASON IN EUROPE.

#### IT IS PRECEDED BY THE RISE OF CRITICISM.

Restoration of Greek Literature and Philosophy in Italy.—Developement of Modern Languages and Rise of Criticism.—Imminent danger to Latin Ideas.
Invention of Printing.—It revolutionizes the Communication of Knowledge, especially acts on Public Worship, and renders the Pulpit secondary.
THE REFORMATION.—Theory of Supererogation and use of Indulgences.—The Right of Individual Judgment asserted.—Political History of the Origin, Culmination, and Check of the Reformation.—Its Effects in Italy.
Causes of the Arrest of the Reformation.—Internal Causes in Protestantism.—External in the Policy of Rome.—The Counter-Reformation.—Inquisition.—Jesuits.—Secession of the great Critics.—Culmination of the Reformation in America.—Emergence of Individual Liberty of Thought. 163

## CHAPTER XXI.

### DIGRESSION ON THE CONDITION OF ENGLAND AT THE END OF THE AGE OF FAITH

#### RESULTS PRODUCED BY THE AGE OF FAITH.

Page

Condition of England at the Suppression of the Monasteries.
Condition of England at the close of the Seventeenth Century.—Locomotion, Literature, Libraries.—Social and Private Life of the Laity and Clergy.—Brutality in the Administration of Law.—Profligacy of Literature.—The Theatre, its three Phases.—Miracle, Moral, and Real Plays. Estimate of the Advance made in the Age of Faith.—Comparison with that already made in the Age of Reason . . . . . . . . . . . . . 222

## CHAPTER XXII.

### THE EUROPEAN AGE OF REASON.

#### REJECTION OF AUTHORITY AND TRADITION, AND ADOPTION OF SCIENTIFIC TRUTH.—DISCOVERY OF THE TRUE POSITION OF THE EARTH IN THE UNIVERSE.

Ecclesiastical Attempt to enforce the GEOCENTRIC DOCTRINE that the Earth is the Centre of the Universe, and the most important Body in it. The HELIOCENTRIC DOCTRINE that the Sun is the Centre of the Solar System, and the Earth a small Planet, comes gradually into Prominence. Struggle between the Ecclesiastical and Astronomical Parties.—Activity of the Inquisition.—Burning of Bruno.—Imprisonment of GALILEO.
INVENTION OF THE TELESCOPE.—Complete Overthrow of the Ecclesiastical Idea.—Rise of Physical Astronomy.—NEWTON.—Rapid and resistless Developement of all Branches of Natural Philosophy.
Final Establishment of the Doctrine that the Universe is under the Dominion of Mathematical, and, therefore, necessary Laws.
Progress of Man from Anthropocentric Ideas to the Discovery of his true Position and Insignificance in the Universe . . . . . . . . . . . 251

## CHAPTER XXIII.

### THE EUROPEAN AGE OF REASON—(Continued).

#### HISTORY OF THE EARTH.—HER SUCCESSIVE CHANGES IN THE COURSE OF TIME.

Oriental and Occidental Doctrines respecting the Earth in Time.—Gradual Weakening of the latter by Astronomical Facts, and the Rise of Scientific Geology.
Impersonal Manner in which the Problem was eventually solved, chiefly through Facts connected with Heat.

Proofs of Limitless Duration from Inorganic Facts.—Igneous and Aqueous Rocks.

Proofs of the same from Organic Facts.—Successive Creations and Extinctions of Living Forms, and their contemporaneous Distribution.

Evidences of a slowly declining Temperature, and, therefore, of a long Time.—The Progress of Events by Catastrophe and by Law.—Analogy of Individual and Race Development.—Both are determined by unchangeable Law.

Conclusion that the Plan of the Universe indicates a Multiplicity of Worlds in Infinite Space, and a Succession of Worlds in Infinite Time . . . 281

## CHAPTER XXIV.

### THE EUROPEAN AGE OF REASON.—(Continued).

#### THE NATURE AND RELATIONS OF MAN.

Position of Man according to the Heliocentric and Geocentric Theories.

Of Animal Life.—The transitory Nature of Living Forms.—Relations of Plants and Animals.—Animals are Aggregates of Matter expending Force originally derived from the Sun.

The Organic Series.—Man a Member of it.—His Position determined by Anatomical and Physiological Investigation of his Nervous System.—Its triple Form: Automatic, Instinctive, Intellectual.

The same progressive Development is seen in individual Man, in the entire Animal Series, and in the Life of the Globe.—They are all under the Control of an eternal, universal, irresistible Law.

The Aim of Nature is Intellectual Development, and Human Institutions must conform thereto.

Summary of the Investigation of the Position of Man.—Production of Inorganic and Organic Forms by the Sun.—Nature of Animals and their Series.—Analogies and Differences between them and Man.—the Soul.—The World . . . . . . . . . . . . . . . . 320

## CHAPTER XXV.

### THE EUROPEAN AGE OF REASON.—(Continued).

#### THE UNION OF SCIENCE AND INDUSTRY.

European Progress in the Acquisition of exact Knowledge.—Its Resemblance to that of Greece.

Discoveries respecting the Air.—Its Mechanical and Chemical Properties.—Its Relation to Animals and Plants.—The Winds.—Meteorology.—Sounds.—Acoustic Phenomena.

Discoveries respecting the Ocean.—Physical and Chemical Phenomena.—Tides and Currents.—Clouds.—Decomposition of Water.

Discoveries respecting other material Substances.—Progress of Chemistry.
Discoveries respecting Electricity, Magnetism, Light, Heat.
Mechanical Philosophy and Inventions.—Physical Instruments.—The Result illustrated by the Cotton Manufacture—Steam-Engine—Bleaching—Canals—Railways.—Improvements in the Construction of Machinery.—Social Changes produced.—Its Effect on Intellectual Activity.
The scientific Contributions of various Nations, and especially of Italy . . 351

## CHAPTER XXVI.

### CONCLUSION.—THE FUTURE OF EUROPE.

Summary of the Argument presented in this Book respecting the Mental Progress of Europe.
Intellectual Development is the Object of Individual Life.—It is also the Result of Social Progress.
Nations arriving at Maturity instinctively attempt their own Intellectual Organization.—Example of the manner in which this has been done in China.—Its Imperfection.—What it has accomplished.
The Organization of Public Intellect is the end to which European Civilization is tending . . . . . . . . . . . . . . . . . . . . . 380

# THE INTELLECTUAL DEVELOPEMENT OF EUROPE.

## CHAPTER XV.

THE AGE OF FAITH IN THE WEST. THE THREE ATTACKS: NORTHERN OR MORAL, WESTERN OR INTELLECTUAL, EASTERN OR MILITARY.

THE NORTHERN OR MORAL ATTACK ON THE ITALIAN SYSTEM, AND ITS TEMPORARY REPULSE.

THE realm of an idea may often be defined by geometrical lines. *The geographical boundaries of Latin Christianity.*

If from Rome, as a centre, two lines be drawn, one of which passes eastward, and touches the Asiatic shore of the Bosphorus, the other westward, and crosses the Pyrenees, nearly all those Mediterranean countries lying to the south of these lines were living, at the time of which we speak, under the dogma, "There is but one God, and Mohammed is his prophet;" but the countries to the north had added to the orthodox conception of the Holy Trinity the adoration of the Virgin, the worship of images, the invocation of saints, and a devout attachment to relics and shrines.

I have now to relate how these lines were pushed forward on Europe, that to the east by military, that to the west by intellectual force. On Rome, as on a pivot, they worked; now opening, now closing, now threatening to curve round at their extremes and compress paganizing Christendom in their *Forces acting upon it.*

clasp; then, through the convulsive throes of the nations they had enclosed, receding from one another and quivering throughout their whole length, but receding only for an instant, to shut more closely again.

It was as if from the hot sands of Africa invisible arms were put forth, enfolding Europe in their grasp, and struggling to join their hands to give to paganizing Christendom a fearful and mortal compression. There were struggles and resistances, but the portentous hands clasped at last. Historically, we call the pressure that was then made the Reformation.

Not without difficulty can we describe the convulsive struggles of nations so as to convey a clear idea of the forces acting upon them. I have now to devote many, perhaps not uninteresting, certainly not uninstructive, pages to these events.

In this Chapter I begin that task by relating the consequences of the state of things heretofore described—the earnestness of converted Germany and the immoralities of the Popes.

*The Germans insist on a reform of the Papacy.*

The Germans insisted on a reformation among ecclesiastics, and that they should lead lives in accordance with religion. This moral attack was accompanied also by an intellectual one, arising from another source, and amounting to a mutiny in the Church itself. In the course of centuries, and particularly during the more recent evil times, a gradual divergence of theology from morals had taken place, to the dissatisfaction of that remnant of thinking men who here and there, in the solitude of monasteries, compared the dogmas of theology with the dictates of reason. Of those, and the number was yearly increasing, who had been among the Arabs in Spain, not a few had become infected with a love of philosophy.

*Reappearance of philosophy.*

Whoever compares the tenth and twelfth centuries together cannot fail to remark the great intellectual advance which Europe was making. The ideas occupying the minds of Christian men, their very turn of thought, had altogether changed. The earnestness of the Germans, commingling with the knowledge of the Mohammedans, could no longer be diverted from the misty clouds of theological discussion out of which Philosophy emerged, not in the Grecian classical vesture in which she had disappeared at Alexandria, but in the grotesque garb of the cowled and mortified monk. She timidly came back to the world as Scholasticism, persuading men to consider, by the light of their own reason, that dogma which seemed to put common sense at defiance—transubstantiation. Scarcely were her whispers heard in the ecclesiastical ranks when a mutiny against authority arose; and since it was necessary to combat that mutiny with its own weapons, the Church was compelled to give her countenance to Scholastic Theology.

Lending himself to the demand for morality, and not altogether refusing to join in the intellectual progress, a great man, Hildebrand, brought on an ecclesiastical reform. He raised the Papacy to its maximum of power, and prepared the way for his successors to seize the material resources of Europe through the Crusades.

Such is an outline of the events with which we have now to deal. A detailed analysis of those events shows that there were three directions of pressure upon Rome. The pressure from the West and that from the East were Mohammedan. Their resultant was a pressure from the North: it was essentially Christian. While those were foreign, this was domestic. It is almost immaterial in what order we consider them; the manner in which I am handling the subject leads me, however, to treat of the Northern pressure first, then of that of the West, and on subsequent pages of that of the East. *The three pressures upon Rome.*

It had become absolutely necessary that something should be done for the reformation of the Papacy. Its crimes, such as we have related in Chapter XII., outraged religious men. To the master-spirit of the movement for accomplishing this end we must closely look. He is the representative of influences that were presently to exert a most important agency. In the train of the Emperor Otho III., when he resolved to put a stop to all this wickedness, was Gerbert, a French ecclesiastic, born in Auvergne. In his boyhood, while a scholar in the Abbey of Avrillac, he attracted the attention of his superiors; among others, of the Count of Barcelona, who took *Foreign influence for reforming the Papacy. Life of Gerbert.*

him into Spain. There he became a proficient in the mathematics, astronomy, and physics of the Mohammedan schools. He spoke Arabic with the fluency of a Saracen. His residence at Cordova, where the khalif patronized all the learning and science of the age, and his subsequent residence in Rome, where he found an inconceivable ignorance and immorality, were not lost upon his future life. He established a school at Rheims, where he taught logic, music, astronomy, explained Virgil, Statius, Terence, and introduced what were at that time regarded as wonders, the globe and the abacus. He laboured to persuade his countrymen that learning is far to be preferred to the sports of the field. He observed the stars through tubes, invented a clock, and an organ played by steam. He composed a work on Rhetoric. Appointed Abbot of Bobbio, he fell into a misunderstanding with his monks, and had to retire first to Rome, and then to resume his school at Rheims. In the political events connected with the rise of Hugh Capet, he was again brought into prominence. The speech of the Bishop of Orleans at the Council of Rheims, which was his composition, shows us how his Mohammedan education had led him to look upon the state of things in Christendom: "There is not one at Rome, it is notorious, who knows enough of letters to qualify him for a door-keeper; with what face shall he presume to teach who has never learned?" He does not hesitate to allude to Papal briberies and Papal crimes: "If King Hugh's ambassadors could have bribed the Pope and Crescentius, his affairs had taken a different turn." He recounts the disgraces and crimes of the pontiffs,—how John XII. had cut off the nose and tongue of John the Cardinal; how Boniface had strangled John XIII.; how John XIV. had been starved to death in the dungeons of the Castle of St. Angelo. He demands, "To such monsters, full of all infamy, void of all knowledge, human and divine, are all the priests of God to submit—men distinguished throughout the world for their learning and holy lives? The pontiff who so sins against his brother—who, when admonished, refuses to hear the voice of counsel—is as a publican and a sinner." With a prophetic inspiration of the accusations of the Refor-

*His Saracen education.*

*His reproaches against the Church.*

mation, he asks, "Is he not Anti-Christ?" He speaks of him as "the Man of Sin," "the Mystery of Iniquity." Of Rome he says, with an emphasis doubtless enforced by his Mohammedan experiences, "She has already lost the allegiance of the East; Alexandria, Antioch, Africa, and Asia are separate from her; Constantinople has broken loose from her; the interior of Spain knows nothing of the Pope." He says, "How do your enemies say that, in deposing Arnulphus, we should have waited for the judgment of the Roman bishop? Can they say that his judgment is before that of God which our synod pronounced? The Prince of the Roman bishops and of the apostles themselves proclaimed that God must be obeyed rather than men; and Paul, the teacher of the Gentiles, announced anathema to him, though he were an angel, who should preach a doctrine different from that which had been delivered. Because the pontiff Marcellinus offered incense to Jupiter, must therefore all bishops sacrifice?" In all this there is obviously an insurgent spirit against the Papacy, or rather against its iniquities.

In the progress of the political movements Gerbert was appointed to the archbishopric of Rheims. On this occasion, it is not without interest that we observe his worldly wisdom. It was desirable to conciliate the clergy,—perhaps it might be done by the encouragement of marriage. He had lived in the polygamic court of the khalif, whose family had occasionally boasted of more than forty sons and forty daughters. Well then may he say, "I prohibit not marriage. I condemn not second marriages. I do not blame the eating of flesh." His election not only proved unfortunate, but, in the tortuous policy of the times, he was removed from the exercise of his episcopal functions and put under interdict. The speech of the Roman legate, Leo, who presided at his condemnation, gives us an insight into the nature of his offence, of the intention of Rome to persevere in her ignorance and superstition, and is an amusing example of ecclesiastical argument: "Because the vicars of Peter and their disciples will not have for their teachers a Plato, a Virgil, a Terence, and the rest of the herd of philosophers, who soar aloft like the birds of the air,

*His ecclesiastical advancement.*

and dive into the depths like the fishes of the sea, ye say that they are not worthy to be door-keepers, because they know not how to make verses. Peter is, indeed, a door-keeper — but of heaven!" He does not deny the systematic bribery of the pontifical government, but justifies it: "Did not the Saviour receive gifts of the wise men?" Nor does he deny the crimes of the pontiffs, though he protests against those who would expose them, reminding them that "Ham was cursed for uncovering his father's nakedness." In all this we see the beginnings of that struggle between Mohammedan learning and morals and Italian ignorance and crime, at last to produce such important results for Europe.

Once more Gerbert retired to the court of the emperor. It was at the time that Otho III. was contemplating a revolution in the empire and a reformation of the Church. He saw how useful Gerbert might be to his policy, and had him appointed Archbishop of Ravenna, and, on the death of Gregory V., issued his decree for the election of Gerbert as Pope. The low-born French ecclesiastic, thus attaining to the utmost height of human ambition, took the name of Sylvester II., a name full of meaning.

*Gerbert the Pope.*

But Rome was not willing thus to surrender her sordid interests; she revolted. Tusculum, the disgrace of the Papacy, rebelled. It required the arms of the emperor to sustain his pontiff. For a moment it seemed as if the Reformation might have been anticipated by many centuries — that Christian Europe might have been spared the abominable Papal disgraces awaiting it. There was a learned and upright Pope, an able and youthful emperor; but Italian revenge, in the person of Stephania, the wife of the murdered Crescentius, blasted all these expectations. From the hand of that outraged but noble criminal, who with more than Roman firmness of purpose, could deliberately barter her virtue for vengeance, the unsuspecting emperor took the poisoned cup, and left Rome only to die. He was but twenty-two years of age. Sylvester, also, was irretrievably ruined by the drugs that had been stealthily mixed with his food. He soon followed his patron to the grave. His steam organs, physical experiments,

*Poisoning of the Emperor and Pope.*

mechanical inventions, foreign birth, and want of orthodoxy, confirmed the awful imputation that he was a necromancer. The mouth of every one was full of stories of mystery and magic in which Gerbert had borne a part. Afar off in Europe, by their evening firesides, the goblin-scared peasants whispered to one another that in the most secret apartment of the palace at Rome there was concealed an impish dwarf, who wore a turban, and had a ring that could make him invisible, or give him two different bodies at the same time; that, in the midnight hours, strange sounds had been heard, when no one was within but the Pope; that while he was among the infidels in Spain, the future pontiff had bartered his soul to Satan, on condition that he would make him Christ's vicar upon earth, and now it was plain that both parties had been true to their compact. In their privacy, hollow-eyed monks muttered to one another under their cowls, "Homagium diabolo fecit et male finivit."

To a degree of wickedness almost irremediable had things thus come. The sins of the pontiffs were repeated, without any abatement, in all the clerical ranks. Simony and concubinage prevailed to an extent that threatened the authority of the Church over the coarsest minds. Ecclesiastical promotion could in all directions be obtained by purchase; in all directions there were priests boasting of illegitimate families. But yet, in the Church itself, there were men of irreproachable life, who, like Peter Damiani, lifted up their voices against the prevailing scandal. He it was who proved that nearly every priest in Milan had purchased his preferment and lived with a concubine. The immoralities thus forced upon the attention of pious men soon began to be followed by the consequences that might have been expected. It is but a step from the condemnation of morals to the criticism of faith. The developing intellect of Europe could no longer bear the acts or the thoughts that it had heretofore submitted to. The dogma of transubstantiation led to revolt. Commencing protest in the Church against its sins.

The early Fathers delighted to point out the agreement of doctrines flowing from the principles of Christianity with those of Greek philosophy. For long it was asserted that a corre- Primitive agreement of philosophy and theology.

*Their gradual alienation.*

spondence between faith and reason exists; but by degrees, as one dogma after another of a mysterious and unintelligible kind was introduced, and matters of belief could no longer be co-ordinated with the conclusions of the understanding, it became necessary to force the latter into a subordinate position. The great political interests involved in these questions suggested the expediency and even necessity of compelling such a subordination by the application of civil power. In this manner, as we have described, in the reign of Constantine the Great, philosophical discussions of religious things came to be discountenanced, and implicit faith required in the decisions of existing authority. Philosophy was subjugated and enslaved by theology. We shall now see what were the circumstances of her revolt.

*The mutiny against theology commences among the monks.*

In the solitude of monasteries there was every inducement for those who had become weary of self-examination to enter on the contemplation of the external world. Herein they found a field offering to them endless occupation, and capable of worthily exercising their acuteness. But it was not possible for them to take the first step without offending against the decisions established by authority. The alternative was stealthy proceeding or open mutiny; but before mutiny there occurs a period of private suggestion and another of more extensive discussion.

*Persecution of Gotschalk.*

It was thus that the German monk Gotschalk, in the ninth century, occupied himself in the profound problem of predestination, enduring the scourge and death in prison for the sake of his opinion. The presence of the Saracens in Spain offered an incessant provocation to the restless intellect of the West, now rapidly expanding, to indulge itself in such forbidden exercises. Arabian philosophy, unseen and silently, was diffusing itself throughout France and Europe, and churchmen could sometimes contemplate a refuge from their enemies among the infidel. In his extremity, Abelard himself expected a retreat among the Saracens—a protection from ecclesiastical persecution.

*Who sets up reason against authority.*

In the conflict with Gotschalk on the matter of predestination was already foreshadowed the attempt to set up reason against authority. John Erigena, who was employed by Hincmar, the Archbishop of Rheims, on that occasion, had already made a pilgrimage to the birthplaces of Plato and Aristotle, A.D. 825, and indulged the hope of uniting philosophy and religion in the manner proposed by the ecclesiastics who were studying in Spain.

From Eastern sources John Erigena had learned the doctrines of the eternity of matter, and even of the creation, with which, indeed, he confounded the Deity himself. He was, therefore, a Pantheist; accepting the Oriental ideas of emanation and absorption not only as respects the soul of man, but likewise all material things. In his work 'On the Nature of Things,' his doctrine is, "That, as all things were originally contained in God, and proceeded from him into the different classes by which they are now distinguished, so shall they finally return to him and be resolved into the source from which they came; in other words, that as, before the world was created, there was no being but God, and the causes of all things were in him, so, after the end of the world, there will be no being but God, and the causes of all things in him." This final resolution he denominated deification, or theosis. He even questioned the eternity of hell, saying, with the emphasis of a Saracen, "There is nothing eternal but God." It was impossible, under such circumstances, that he should not fall under the rebuke of the Church. *John Erigena falls into Pantheism.*

Transubstantiation, as being, of the orthodox doctrines, the least reconcilable to reason, was the first to be attacked by the new philosophers. What was perhaps, in the beginning, no more than a jocose Mohammedan sarcasm, became a solemn subject of ecclesiastical discussion. Erigena strenuously upheld the doctrine of the Stercorists, who derived their name from the fact that they asserted a part of the consecrated elements to be voided from the body in the manner customary with other relics of food; a doctrine which was denounced by the orthodox, who declared that the priests could "make God," and that the eucharistic elements were not liable to digestion. *The conflict begins on transubstantiation.*

And now, A.D. 1050, Berengar of Tours prominently brought forward the controversy respecting the real presence. The *Opinions of Berengar of Tours.*

question had been formularized by Radbert under the term transubstantiation, and the opinions entertained respecting the sacred elements greatly differed; mere fetich notions being entertained by some, by others the most transcendental ideas. In opposition to Radbert and the orthodox party, who asserted that those elements ceased to be what to the senses they appeared, and actually became transformed into the body and blood of the Saviour, Berengar held that, though there is a real presence in them, that presence is of a spiritual nature. These heresies were condemned by repeated councils, Berengar himself being offered the choice of death or recantation. He wisely preferred the latter, but more wisely resumed his offensive doctrines as soon as he had escaped from the hands of his persecutors. As might be supposed from the philosophical indefensibility of the orthodox doctrine, Berengar's opinions, which, indeed, issued from those of Erigena, made themselves felt in the highest ecclesiastical regions, and, from the manner in which Gregory VII. dealt with the heresiarch, there is reason to believe that he himself had privately adopted the doctrines thus condemned.

*The Pope privately adopts them.*

But it is in Peter Abelard that we find the representative of the insurgent spirit of those times. The love of Heloisa seems in our eyes to be justified by his extraordinary intellectual power. In his oratory, "The Paraclete," the doctrines of faith and the mysteries of religion were without any restraint discussed. No subject was too profound or too sacred for his contemplation. By the powerful and orthodox influence of St. Bernard, "a morigerous and mortified monk," the opinions of Abelard were brought under the rebuke of the authorities. In vain he appealed from the Council of Sens to Rome; the power of St. Bernard at Rome was paramount. "He makes void the whole Christian faith by attempting to comprehend the nature of God through human reason. He ascends up into heaven; he goes down into hell. Nothing can elude him either in the height above or in the nethermost depths. His branches spread over the whole earth. He boasts that he has disciples in Rome itself, even in the College of Cardinals. He draws the whole earth after him. It is time, therefore, to

*Peter Abelard among the insurgents.*

*St. Bernard attacks him.*

silence him by apostolic authority." Such was the report of the Council of Sens to Rome, A.D. 1140.

Perhaps it was not so much the public accusation that Abelard denied the doctrine of the Trinity, as his assertion of the supremacy of reason—which clearly betrayed his intention of breaking the thraldom of authority—that insured his condemnation. It was impossible to restrict the rising discussions within their proper sphere, or to keep them from the perilous ground of ecclesiastical history. Abelard, in his work entitled 'Sic et Non,' sets forth the contradictory opinions of the Fathers, and exhibits their discord and strifes on great doctrinal points, thereby insinuating how little of unity there was in the Church. It was a work suggesting a great deal more than it actually stated, and was inevitably calculated to draw down upon its author the indignation of those whose interests it touched. *The book 'Sic et Non.'*

Out of the discussions attending these events sprang the celebrated doctrines of Nominalism and Realism, though the terms themselves seem not to have been introduced till the end of the twelfth century. The Realists thought that the general types of things had a real existence; the Nominalists, that they were merely a mental abstraction expressed by a word. It was therefore the old Greek dispute revived. Of the Nominalists, Roscelin of Compiègne, a little before A.D. 1100, was the first distinguished advocate; his materializing views, as might be expected, drawing upon him the reproof of the Church. In this contest, Anselm, the Archbishop of Canterbury, attempted to harmonize reason in subordination to faith, and again, by his example, demonstrated the necessity of submitting all such questions to the decision of the human intellect. *Scholastic philosophy, rise of. Nominalism and Realism.*

The developement of scholastic philosophy, which dates from the time of Erigena, was accelerated by two distinct causes: the dreadful materialization into which, in Europe, all sacred things had fallen, and the illustrious example of the Mohammedans, who already, by their physical inquiries, had commenced a career destined to end in brilliant results. The Spanish universities were filled with ecclesiastics from many parts of Europe. Peter the Venerable, the friend and protector of Abe- *The Arabs in Spain promote these discussions.*

land, who had spent much time in Cordova, and not only spoke Arabic fluently, but actually translated the Koran into Latin, mentions that, on his first arrival in Spain, he found many learned men, even from England, studying astronomy. The reconciliation of many of the dogmas of authority with common sense was impossible for men of understanding. Could the clear intellect of such a statesman as Hildebrand be for a moment disgraced by accepting the received view of a doctrine like that of transubstantiation? His great difficulty was to reconcile what had been rendered orthodox by the authority of the Church with the suggestions of reason, or even with that reverence for holy things which is in the heart of every intelligent man. In such sentiments we find an explanation of the lenient dealings of that stern ecclesiastic with the heretic Berengar. He saw that it was utterly impossible to offer any defence of many of the materialized dogmas of the age, but then those dogmas had been put forth as absolute truth by the Church. Things had come to the point at which reason and theology must diverge; yet the Italian statesmen did not accept this issue without an additional attempt, and under their permission, Scholastic Theology, which originated in the scholastic philosophy of Erigena and his followers, sought, in the strange union of the Holy Scriptures, the Aristotelian Philosophy, and Pantheism, to construct a scientific basis for Christianity. Heresy was to be combated with the weapons of the heretics, and a co-ordination of authority and reason effected. Under such auspices scholastic philosophy pervaded the schools, giving to some of them, as the University of Paris, a fictitious reputation, and leading to the foundation of others in other cities. It answered the object of its politic promoters in a double way, for it raised around the orthodox theology an immense and impenetrable bulwark of what seemed to be profound learning, and also diverted the awakening mind of Western Europe to occupations which, if profitless, were yet exciting, and without danger to the existing state of things. In that manner was put off for awhile the inevitable day in which philosophy and theology were to be brought in mortal conflict with each other. It was doubtless seen by Hildebrand

*Rise of Scholastic Theology.*

and his followers that, though Berengar had set the example
of protesting against the principle that the decision of a majority of voters in a council or other collective body should ever
be received as ascertaining absolute truth, yet so great was the
uncertainty of the principles on which the scholastic philosophy was founded, so undetermined its mental exercise, so ineffectual the results to which it could attain, that it was unlikely for a long time to disturb the unity of doctrine in the
Church. While men were reasoning round and round again
in the same vicious circle without finding any escape, and indeed without seeking any, delighted with the dexterity of their
movements, but never considering whether they were making
any real advance, it was unnecessary to anticipate inconvenience from their progress.

*Its advan-
tage in the
existing
state of the
Church.*

He stood the difficulty. The decisions of the Church were
asserted to be infallible and irrevocable; her philosophy,—if
such it can be called,—as must be the case with any philosophy
reposing upon a final revelation from God, was stationary.
But the awakening mind of the West was displaying, in an
unmistakable way, its propensity to advance. As one who
rides an unruly horse will sometimes divert him from a career
which could not be checked by main force, by reining him round
and round, and thereby exhausting his spirit and strength, and
keeping him in a narrow space, so the wanton efforts of the
mind may be guided, if they cannot be checked. These principles of policy answered their object for a time, until metaphysical were changed for physical discussions. Then it became
impossible to divert the onward movement, and on the first
question arising,—that of the figure and place of the earth,—
a question dangerous to the last degree, since it inferentially
included the determination of the position of man in the universe, theology suffered an irretrievable defeat. Between her
and philosophy there was thenceforth no other issue than a
mortal duel.

*The philo-
sophical di-
lemma of
the Church*

Though Erigena is the true founder of Scholasticism, Roscelin, already mentioned as renewing the question of Platonic Universals, has been considered by some to be entitled to
that distinction. After him, William of Champeaux opened

*Course of
Scholasti-
cism.*

a school of logic in Paris, A.D. 1109, and from that time the University made it a prominent study. On the rise of the mendicant orders, Scholasticism received a great impulse, perhaps, as has been affirmed, because its disputations suited their illiterate state; Thomas Aquinas, the Dominican, and Duns Scotus, the Franciscan, founding rival schools, which wrangled for three centuries. In Italy, Scholasticism never prevailed as it did in France and elsewhere, and at last it died away, its uselessness, save in the political result before mentioned, having been detected.

*Reaction in the Papacy against these pressures.* The middle of the eleventh century ushers in an epoch for the Papacy and for Europe. It is marked by an attempt at a moral reformation of the Church,—by a struggle for securing the independence of the Papacy both of the Emperors of Germany and of the neighbouring Italian nobles—thus far the Pope being the mere officer of the emperor, and often the creature of the surrounding nobility,—by the conversion of the temporalities of the Church, heretofore indirect, into absolute possessions, by securing territories given "to the Church, the blessed Peter, and the Roman republic" to the first of those beneficiaries, excluding the last. *Preparation for a concentration of the Papal power.* As events proceeded, these minor affairs converged, and out of their union arose the great conflict of the Imperial and Papal powers for supremacy. The same policy which had succeeded in depriving the Roman people of any voice in appointments of Popes,—which had secularized the Church in Italy,—for awhile seized all the material resources of Europe through the device of the Crusades, and nearly established a Papal autocracy in all Europe. These political events demand from us a notice, since from them arose intellectual consequences of the utmost importance.

The second Lateran Council, under Nicholas II., accomplished the result of vesting the elective power to the Papacy in the Cardinals. That was a great revolution. It was this council which gave to Berengar his choice between death and recantation. *Three parties in Italy.* There were at this period three powers engaged in Italy,—the Imperial, the Church party, and the Italian nobles. It was for the sake of holding the last in check,—for, since it was the nearest, it required the most unremitting attention,—

that Hildebrand had advised the Popes who were his immediate predecessors to use the Normans, who were settled in the south of the peninsula, by whom the lands of the nobles were devastated. Thus the difficulties of their position led the Popes to a repetition of their ancient policy; and as they had, in old times, sought the protection of the Frankish kings, so now they sought that of the Normans. But in the midst of the dissensions and tumults of the times, a great man was emerging,—Hildebrand, who, with almost superhuman self-denial, again and again abstained from making himself Pope. On the death of Alexander II. his opportunity came, and, with acceptable force, he was raised to that dignity, A.D. 1073.

*Hildebrand becomes Pope.*

Scarcely was Hildebrand Pope Gregory VII. when he vigorously proceeded to carry into effect the policy he had been preparing during the pontificates of his predecessors. In many respects, the times were propitious. The blameless lives of the German Popes had cast a veil of oblivion over the abominations of their Italian predecessors. Hildebrand addressed himself to tear out every vestige of simony and concubinage with a remorseless hand. The task must be finished before he could hope to accomplish his grand project of an ecclesiastical autocracy in Europe, with the Pope at its head, and the clergy, both in their persons and property, independent of the civil power; and it was plain that, apart from all moral considerations, the supremacy of Rome in such a system altogether turned on the celibacy of the clergy. If marriage was permitted to the ecclesiastic, what was to prevent him from handing down, as an hereditary possession, the wealth and dignities he had obtained? In such a state of things, the central government at Rome necessarily stood at every disadvantage against the local interests of an individual, and still more so if many individuals should combine together to promote, in common, similar interests. But very different would it be if the promotion must be looked for from Rome,—very different as regards the hold upon public sentiment, if such a descent from father to son was absolutely prevented, and a career fairly opened to all irrespective of their station in life. To the Church it was to the last degree important that a man should derive his advancement from her,

*Hildebrand resolves on a reform.*

*Necessity of celibacy of the clergy.*

not from his ancestor. In the trials to which she was perpetually exposed, there could be no doubt that by such persons her interest would be best served.

In these circumstances, Gregory VII. took his course. The synod held at Rome in the first year of his pontificate denounced the marriage of the clergy, enforcing its decree by the doctrine that the efficacy of the sacraments altogether depended on their being administered by hands sinless in that respect, and made all communicants partners in the pastoral crime. With a provident foresight of the coming opposition, he carried out the policy he had taught his predecessors of conciliating the Normans in the south of Italy, though he did not hesitate to resist them, by the aid of the Countess Matilda, when they dared to touch the possessions of the Church. It was for the sake of this that the Norman invasion of England under William the Conqueror had already been approved of, a consecrated standard and a ring containing a hair from the head of St. Peter sent him, and permission given for the replacement of Saxon bishops and other dignitaries by Normans. It was not forgotten how great had been the gains to the Papacy, three centuries before, by changing the dynasty of the Franks; and thus the policy of an Italian town gave a permanent impress to the history of England. Hildebrand foresaw that the sword of the Italian-Norman would be wanted to carry out his projected ends. He did not hesitate to authorize the overthrow of a Saxon dynasty by the French-Norman, that he might be more sure of the fidelity of that sword. Without the countenance of the Pope, the Norman could never have consolidated his power, nor even held his ground in England.

From these movements of the Papacy sprang the conflict with the Emperors of Germany respecting investitures. The Bishop of Milan—who, it appears, had perjured himself in the quarrel respecting concubinage—had been excommunicated by Alexander II. The imperial council appointed as his successor one Godfrey; the Pope had nominated Atto. Hereupon Alexander had summoned the emperor to appear before him on a charge of simony, and granting investitures without his approbation. While the matter was yet in abeyance, Alexander died; but Gregory took up the contest. A synod he had assembled ordered that, if any one should accept investiture from a layman, both the giver and receiver should be excommunicated. The pretence against lay-investiture was that it was a usurpation of a Papal right, and that it led to the appointment of evil and ignorant men; the reality was a determination to extend Papal power, by making Rome the fountain of emolument. Gregory, by his movements, had thus brought upon himself three antagonists—the imperial power, the Italian nobles, and the married clergy. The latter, unscrupulous and exasperated, met him with his own weapons, not hesitating to calumniate his friendship with the Countess Matilda. It was also suspected that they were connected with the outrage perpetrated by the nobles that took place in Rome. On Christmas night, A.D. 1075, in the midst of a violent rain, while the Pope was administering the communion, a band of soldiers burst into the church, seized Gregory at the altar, stripped and wounded him, and haling him on horseback behind one of the soldiers, carried him off to a stronghold, from which he was rescued by the populace by force. But, without wavering for a moment, the undaunted pontiff pressed on his conflict with the imperial power, summoning Henry to Rome to account for his delinquencies, and threatening his excommunication if he should not appear before an appointed day. In haste, under the auspices of the king, a synod was assembled at Worms; charges against the Pope of licentious life, bribery, necromancy, simony, murder, atheism, were introduced, and sentence of deposition pronounced against him. On his side, Gregory assembled the third Lateran Council, A.D. 1076, placed King Henry under interdict, absolved his subjects from allegiance, and deposed him. A series of constitutions, clearly defining the new bases of the Papal system, was published. They were to the following effect:—"That the Roman pontiff can alone be called universal; and he alone has a right to depose bishops; that his legates have a right to preside over all bishops in a general council; that he can depose absent prelates; that he alone has a right to use imperial ornaments; that princes are bound to kiss his feet, and his only; that he has a right to de-

*Outrage on Hildebrand.*

*He defines the position of the Church.*

pose emperors; that no synod or council summoned without his commission can be called general; that no book can be called canonical without his authority; that his sentence can be annulled by none, but that he may annul the decrees of all; that the Roman Church has been, is, and will continue to be infallible; that whoever dissents from it ceases to be a Catholic Christian, and that subjects may be absolved from their allegiance to wicked princes." The power that could assert such resolutions was near its culmination.

*And overcomes the King of Germany.*
And now was manifest the superiority of the spiritual over the temporal power. The quarrel with Henry went on, and, after a hard struggle and many intrigues to draw the Normans over to him, that monarch was compelled to submit, and in the depth of winter to cross the snowy Alps, under circumstances of unparalleled hardship, to seek absolution from his adversary. Then ensued the scene at Canosa,—a penitent in white raiment standing in the dreary snow of three winter days, January, 1077, cold and fasting at the gate, seeking pardon and reconciliation of the inexorable pontiff; that penitent was King of Germany. Then ensued the dramatic scene at the sacrament, in which the grey-haired pontiff called upon Heaven to strike him dead upon the spot if he were not innocent of the crimes of which he had been accused, and dared the guilty monarch to do the same.

*Conclusions from these events.*
Whoever will reflect on these interesting events cannot fail to discern two important conclusions. The tone of thought throughout Europe had changed within the last three ages; ideas were entertained, doctrines originated or controverted, a policy conceived and attempted altogether in advance of the old times. Intellect, both among the clergy and the laity, had undergone a great developement. But the peculiar character of the Papal power is also ascertained,—that it is worldly, and the result of the policy of man. The outrage on Hildebrand shows how that power had diminished at its centre, but the victory over Henry, that it maintained its strength at a distance. Natural forces diminish as the distance increases; this unnatural force displayed an opposite quality.

Gregory had carried his point. He had not only beaten

back the Northern attack, but had established the supremacy of the ecclesiastical over the temporal power, and that point, with inflexible resolution, he maintained, though in its consequences it cost Germany a civil war. But, while he was thus unyielding in his temporal policy, there is reason to suppose that he was not without misgivings in his theological belief. In the war between Henry and his rival Rodolph, Gregory was compelled by policy to be at first neutral. He occupied himself with the Eucharistic controversy. This was at the time that he was associated with Berengar, who lived with him for a year. Nor did the Pope think it unworthy of himself to put forth, in excuse of the heretic, a vision, in which the Virgin Mary had asserted the orthodoxy of Berengar; but, as his quarrel with King Henry went on to new excommunications and depositions, a synod of bishops presumed to condemn him as a partisan of Berengar and a necromancer. On the election of Gilbert of Ravenna as Antipope, Gregory, without hesitation, pushed his principles to their consequences, denouncing kingship as a wicked and diabolical usurpation, an infraction of the equal rights of man. Hereupon Henry determined to destroy him or to be destroyed; and descending again into Italy, A.D. 1081, for three successive years laid siege to Rome. In vain the amorous Matilda, with more than the devotion of an ally, endeavoured to succour her beleaguered friend. The city surrendered to Henry at Christmas, A.D. 1084. With his Antipope he entered it, receiving from his hands the imperial crown. The Norman allies of Hildebrand at last approached in strength. The emperor was compelled to retreat. A feeble attempt to hold the city was made. The Normans took it by surprise, and released Gregory from his imprisonment in the Castle of St. Angelo. An awful scene ensued. Some conflicts between the citizens and the Normans occurred, a battle in the streets was the consequence, and Rome was pillaged, sacked, and fired. Streets, churches, palaces, were left a heap of smoking ashes. The people by thousands were massacred. The Saracens, of whom there were multitudes in the Norman army, were in the Eternal City at last, and, horrible to be said, were there as the hired supporters of the Vicar of Christ.

*Culmination of the ecclesiastical power.*

*Friendship of Hildebrand and Berengar.*

*The German contest renewed.*

*The Mohammedans support Hildebrand.*

Matrons, nuns, young women, were defiled. Crowds of men, women, and children were carried off and sold as slaves. It was the treatment of a city taken by storm. In consternation, the blasted pontiff retired, with his infidel deliverers, from the ruined capital to Salerno, and there he died, A.D. 1085.

*Sack of Rome, and death of the Pope.*

He had been dead ten years, when a policy was entered upon by the Papacy which imparted to it more power than all the exertions of Gregory. The Crusades were instituted by a French Pope, Urban II. Unpopular in Italy, perhaps by reason of his foreign birth, he aroused his native country for the recovery of the Holy Land. He began his career in a manner not now unusual, interfering in a quarrel between Philip of France and his wife, taking the part of the latter, as experience had shown it was always advisable for a Pope to do. Soon, however, he devoted his attention to something more important than these matrimonial broils. It seems that a European crusade was first distinctly conceived of and its value most completely comprehended by Gerbert, to whom, doubtless, his Mohammedan experiences had suggested it. In the first year of his pontificate, he wrote an epistle, in the name of the Church of Jerusalem, to the Church throughout the world, exhorting Christian soldiers to come to her relief either with arms or money. It had been subsequently contemplated by Gregory VII. For many years, pilgrimages to Palestine had been on the increase; a very valuable export trade in relics from that country had risen; crowds from all parts of Europe had of late made their way to Jerusalem, for the singular purpose of being present at the great assize which the Scriptures were supposed to prophesy would soon take place in the Valley of Jehoshaphat. The Mohammedans had inflicted on these pious persons much maltreatment, being unable to comprehend the purport of their extraordinary journey, and probably perceiving the necessity of putting some restriction upon the apparition of such countless multitudes. Peter the Hermit, who had witnessed the barbarities to which his Christian brethren were exposed, and the abominations of the holy places now in the hands of the infidel, roused Europe, by his preaching, to a frantic state; and Urban, at the Council of Clermont,

*The Crusades.*

A.D. 1095, gave authority to the Holy War. "It is the will of God," was the unanimous shout of the council and populace. The periodical shower of shooting stars was seen with remarkable brilliancy on April 25th, and mistaken by the Council for a celestial monition that the Christians must precipitate themselves in like manner on the East. From this incident we may perceive how little there was of inspiration in these blundering and violent ecclesiastical assemblages; the moment that they can be brought to a scientific test, their true nature is detected. As a preliminary exercise, a ferocious persecution of the Jews of France had burst forth, and the blood and tortures of multitudes offered a tardy expiation for the crimes that their ancestors had committed at the Crucifixion in Jerusalem, more than a thousand years before.

*The Council of Clermont authorizes a crusade.*

It does not fall within my plan to give a detailed description of the Crusades. It is enough to say that, though the clergy had promised the protection of God to every one who would thus come to his assistance,—an ample reward for their pious work in this life, and the happiness of heaven in the next,— Urban's crusade failed not only disastrously, but hideously, so far as the ignorant rabbles, under Peter the Hermit and Walter the Penniless, were concerned. Nevertheless, under the better-organized expeditions that soon followed, Jerusalem was captured, July 15th, A.D. 1099. The long and ghastly line of bones whitening the road through Hungary to the East showed how different a thing it was for a peaceable and solitary pilgrim to beg his way, with his staff and wallet and scallop-shell, and a disorderly riot of thousands upon thousands to rush forward without any subordination, any organization, trusting only to the providence of God. The van of the Crusades consisted of two hundred and seventy-five thousand men, accompanied by eight horses, and preceded by a goat and a goose, into which some one had told them that the Holy Ghost had entered. Driven to madness by disappointment and famine,—expecting, in their ignorance, that every town they came to must be Jerusalem,—in their extremity they laid hands on whatever was in their way. Their track was marked by robbery, bloodshed, and fire. In the first Crusade

*The first Crusade.*

22    *Results of the Crusades.*

more than half a million of men died. It was far more disastrous than the Moscow retreat.

*Storming of Jerusalem.*    But still, in a military sense, the first Crusade accomplished its object. The capture of Jerusalem, as might be expected under such circumstances, was attended by the perpetration of atrocities almost beyond belief. What a contrast to the conduct of the Arabs! When the Khalif Omar took Jerusalem, A.D. 637, he rode into the city by the side of the Patriarch Sophronius, conversing with him on its antiquities. At the hour of prayer, he declined to perform his devotions in the Church of the Resurrection, in which he chanced to be, but prayed on the steps of the Church of Constantine; "for," said he to the patriarch, "had I done so, the Mussulmans in a future age would have infringed the treaty, under colour of imitating my example." But, in the capture by the Crusaders, the brains of young children were dashed out against the walls; infants were pitched over the battlements; every woman that could be seized was violated; men were roasted at fires; some were ripped up, to see if they had swallowed gold; the Jews were driven into their synagogue, and there burnt; a massacre of nearly 70,000 persons took place; and the Pope's legate was seen "partaking in the triumph."

*Political results of the Crusades.*    It had been expected by the politicians who first projected these wars that they would heal the divisions of the Latin and Greek Churches, and give birth to a European republic, under the spiritual presidency of the Pope. In these respects they proved a failure. It does not appear that the Popes themselves personally had ever any living faith in the result. Not one of them ever joined a Crusade; and the Church, as a corporation, took care to embark very little money in these undertakings. But, though they did not answer to the original intention, they gave, in an indirect way, a wonderful stimulus to the Papal power. Under the plausible pretences offered by them, the Pope obtained control over the person of every Christian man from the highest to the lowest. The cross once taken, all civil control over the Crusader ceased,—he became the man of the Church. Under those pretences also, a right was imperceptibly acquired of raising revenue in all parts of Europe; even the

*Give to Rome the control of men and money in Europe.*

clergy might be assessed. A drain was thus established on the resources of distant nations for an object which no man dared to gainsay; if he adventured on any such thing, he must encounter the odium of being an infidel—an atheist. A steady stream of money flowed into Italy. Nor was it alone by this taxation of every Christian nation without permission of its government—this empire within every empire; immense wealth accrued to the projectors, while the infatuation could be kept up, by the diminished rate at which land could be obtained. Domains were thrown into the market; there were few purchasers except the Church. Immense domains were also given away by weak-minded sinners, and those on the point of death, for the salvation of their souls. Thus, all things considered, the effect of the Crusades, though not precisely that which was expected, was of singular advantage to the Church, giving it a commanding strength it had never possessed before.

In their resistance to the German attack the Popes never hesitated at any means. They prompted Prince Henry to revolt against their great antagonist, his father; they intervened, not to rebuke, but to abet him, when he threw his father into prison and deprived him of the necessaries of life. They carried their vengeance beyond the grave. When the aged emperor, broken in heart, escaped from their torment, and was honourably buried by the Bishop of Liége, that prelate was forthwith excommunicated and compelled to disinter the corpse. But crimes like these, against which human nature revolts, meet with a retribution. This same Prince Henry, becoming Henry V., was forced by circumstances to resume his father's quarrel, and to refuse to yield his right of granting investitures. He marched upon Rome, and at the point of the sword compelled his adversary, Pope Paschal II., to surrender all the possessions and royalties of the Church,—compelled him to crown him emperor,—not, however, until the pontiff had been subjected to the ignominy of imprisonment, and brought into condemnation among his own party. *Resistance of Henry V.*

Things seemed to be going to ruin in Rome, and such must inevitably have been the issue, had not an extraneous influence arisen in Bernard of Clairvaux, to whom Europe learned to *Bernard of Clairvaux stimulates the second Crusade.*

look up as the beaten down of heresies, theological and political. He had been a pupil of William of Champeaux, the vanquished rival of Abelard, and Abelard he hated with a religious and personal hate. He was a wonder-worker, though some of his miracles now only excite a smile; as when he excommunicated the flies which infested a church, and they all fell down dead and were swept out by the basketful. He has been described as "the mellifluous doctor, whose works are not scientific, but full of unction." He could not tolerate the principle at the basis of Abelard's philosophy—the assertion of the supremacy of reason. Of Arnold of Brescia—who carried that principle to its political consequences, and declared that the riches and power of the clergy were inconsistent with their profession—he was the accuser and punisher. Bernard preached a new crusade, authenticating his power by miracles, affirmed to be not inferior to those of our Saviour; promising to him who should slay an unbeliever happiness in this life and Paradise in the life to come. This second Crusade was conducted by kings, and included fanatic ladies, dressed in the armour of men; but it ended in ruin.

*Its failure.*

It was reserved for the only Englishman who ever attained to the Papacy to visit Rome with the punishment she had so often inflicted upon others. Nicholas Breakspear—Adrian IV.—put the Eternal City under interdict, thereby ending the republic which the partisans of Arnold of Brescia had set up. But herein he was greatly aided by a change of sentiment in many of the inhabitants of Rome, who had found to their cost that it was more profitable for their city to be the centre of Christianity than the seat of a phantom republic. As an equivalent for his coronation by Adrian, Frederick Barbarossa agreed to surrender to the Church Arnold of Brescia. With indecent haste, the moment she had obtained possession of her arch-enemy she put him to death,—not delivering him over to the secular arm, as the custom had been, but murdering him with her own hand. Seven centuries have elapsed, and the blood of Arnold is still crying from the ground for retribution. Notwithstanding a new—the third—crusade, things went from bad to worse in the Holy Land. Saladin had retaken

*Murder of Arnold of Brescia.*

## Summary of the Foregoing Events.

Jerusalem, A.D. 1187. Barbarossa was drowned in a river in Pisidia. Richard of England was treacherously imprisoned; nor did the Pope interfere for this brave soldier of the Cross. In the meantime, the Emperors of Germany had acquired Sicily by marriage,—an incident destined to be of no little importance in the history of Europe; for, on the death of the Emperor Henry VI. at Messina, his son Frederick, an infant not two years old, was left to be brought up in that island. *Birth of Frederick II.*

What the consequences were we shall soon see.

If we review the events related in this Chapter, we find that the idolatry and immorality into which Rome had fallen had become connected with material interests sufficiently powerful to cause their perpetuation; that converted Germany insisted on a reform, and therefore made a moral attack upon the Italian system, attempting to carry it into effect by civil force. This attack was, properly speaking, purely moral, the intellectual element accompanying it being derived from Western or Arabian influences, as will be shown in the next Chapter; and in its resistance to this, the Papacy was not only successful, but actually was able to retaliate, overthrowing the Emperors of Germany, and being even on the point of establishing a European autocracy, with the Pope at its head. It was in these events that the Reformation began, though circumstances intervened to postpone its completion to the era of Luther. Henceforth we see more and more plainly the attitude in which the Papacy, through its material interests, was compelled to stand, as resisting all intellectual advancement. Our subject has therefore here to be left unfinished until we shall have described the Mohammedan influences making pressures on the West and the East. *Review of the preceding events.*

## CHAPTER XVI.

### THE AGE OF FAITH IN THE WEST—(*Continued*).

#### THE WESTERN OR INTELLECTUAL ATTACK ON THE ITALIAN SYSTEM.

*The pressure from the West upon Rome.*

A PRESSURE upon the Italian system had meantime been arising in the West. It was due to the presence of the Arabs in Spain. It is necessary, therefore, to relate the circumstances of their invasion and conquest of that country, and to compare their social and intellectual condition with the contemporary state of Christendom.

*Barbarism of Europe.*

From the barbarism of the native people of Europe, who could scarcely be said to have emerged from the savage state, unclean in person, benighted in mind, inhabiting huts in which it was a mark of wealth if there were bulrushes on the floor and straw mats against the wall; miserably fed on beans, vetches, roots, and even the bark of trees; clad in garments of untanned skin, or, at the best, of leather—perennial in durability, but not conducive to personal purity,—a state in which the pomp of royalty was sufficiently and satisfactorily manifested in the equipage of the sovereign, an ox-cart, drawn by not less than two yokes of cattle, quickened in their movements by the goads of pedestrian serfs, whose legs were wrapped in wisps of straw; from a people, devout believers in all the wild fictions of shrine-miracles and preposterous relics; from the degradation of a base theology, and from the disputes of ambitious ecclesiastics for power,—it is pleasant to turn to the south-west corner of the Continent, where, under auspices of a very different kind, the irradiations of light were to break forth. The crescent in the West was soon to pass eastward to its full.

But I must retrace my steps through four centuries, and resume the description of the Arabian movement after the subjugation of Africa, as related in Vol. I. p. 323.

These were the circumstances of the Arab conquest of Spain. In that country the Arian Creed had been supplanted by the orthodox, and the customary persecutions had set in. From the time of the Emperor Hadrian, who had transported 50,000 Jewish families into Spain, that race had singularly increased, and, as might be expected, had received no mercy at the hands of the orthodox. Ninety thousand individuals had recently suffered compulsory baptism, and so had been brought under the atrocious Catholic law that whoever has been baptized shall be compelled to continue the observances of the Church. The Gothic monarchy was elective, and Roderic had succeeded to the throne, to the prejudice of the heirs of his predecessor. Though a very brave soldier, he was a luxurious and a licentious man. It was the custom of the Goths to send their children to Toledo to be educated, and, under these circumstances, a young girl of extraordinary beauty, the daughter of Count Julian, governor of Ceuta in Africa, was residing there. King Roderic fell passionately in love with her, and, being unable to overcome her virtuous resolution by persuasion, resorted to violence. The girl found means to inform her father of what had occurred. "By the living God!" exclaimed the count, in a paroxysm of rage, "I will be revenged." But, dissembling his wrath, he crossed over into Spain, had an understanding with Oppas, the Archbishop of Toledo, and other disaffected ecclesiastics, and, under specious pretences, lulled the suspicions of Roderic, and brought his daughter away. And now he opened communications with the Emir Musa, prevailing upon him to attempt the conquest of the country, and offering that he himself would take the lead. The conditions were settled between them, and the consent of the khalif to the expedition obtained. Tarik, a lieutenant of the emir, was sent across the Straits with the van of the army. He landed on the rock called in memory of his name, Gibraltar, April, A.D. 711. In the battle that ensued, a part of Roderic's troops, together with the Archbishop of Toledo, con-

*Arab invasion of Spain.*

summated their treasonable compact, and deserted to the Arabs; the rest were panic-stricken. In the rout, Roderic himself was drowned in the waters of the Guadalquivir.

*Its conquest.*

Tarik now proceeded rapidly northward, and was soon joined by his superior, the Emir Musa, who was not perhaps without jealousy at his success. As the Arab historians say, the Almighty delivered the idolaters into their hand, and gave them one victory after another. As the towns successively fell, they left them in charge of the Jews, to whose revenge the conquest was largely due, and who could be thoroughly trusted; nor did they pause in their march until they had passed the French frontier and reached the Rhone. It was the intention of Musa to cross the European continent to Constantinople, subjugating the Frank, German, and Italian barbarians by the way. At this time it seemed impossible that France could escape the fate of Spain; and if she fell, the threat of Musa would inevitably have come to pass, that he would preach the Unity of God in the Vatican. But a quarrel had arisen between him and Tarik, who had been imprisoned and even scourged. The friends of the latter, however, did not fail him at the court of Damascus. An envoy from the Khalif Alwalid appeared, ordering Musa to desist from his enterprise, to return to Syria, and exonerate himself of the things laid to his charge. But Musa bribed the envoy to let him advance. Hereupon the angry khalif dispatched a second messenger, who, in face of the Moslems and Christians, audaciously arrested him, at the head of his troops, by the bridle of his horse. The conqueror of Spain was compelled to return. He was cast into prison, fined 200,000 pieces of gold, publicly whipped, and his life with difficulty spared. As is related of Belisarius, Musa was driven as a beggar to solicit charity, and the Saracen conqueror of Spain ended his days in grief and absolute want.

*Arrest of Mohammedanism in Western Europe.*

These dissensions among the Arabs, far more than the sword of Charles Martel, prevented the Mohammedanization of France. Their historians admit the great check received at the battle of Tours, in which Abderrahman was killed; they call that field the Place of the Martyrs; but their accounts by no means correspond to the relations of the Christian authors, who affirm that 375,000 Mohammedans fell, but only 1500 Christians. The defeat was not so disastrous but that in a few months they were able to resume their advance, and their progress was arrested only by renewed dissensions among themselves—dissensions not alone among the leaders in Spain, but also more serious ones of aspirants for the khalifate in Asia. On the overthrow of the Ommiade house, Abderrahman, one of that family, escaped to Spain, which repaid the patronage of its conquest by acknowledging him as its sovereign. He made Cordova the seat of his government. Neither he nor his immediate successors took any other title than that of Emir, out of respect to the khalif, who resided at Bagdad, the metropolis of Islam, though they maintained a rivalry with him in the patronage of letters and science. Abderrahman himself strengthened his power by an alliance with Charlemagne.

Scarcely had the Arabs become firmly settled in Spain before they commenced a brilliant career. Adopting what had now become the established policy of the Commanders of the Faithful in Asia, the Khalifs of Cordova distinguished themselves as patrons of learning, and set an example of refinement strongly contrasting with the condition of the native European princes. Cordova, under their administration, at its highest point of prosperity, boasted of more than two hundred thousand houses, and more than a million of inhabitants. After sunset, a man might walk through it in a straight line for ten miles by the light of the public lamps. Seven hundred years after this time there was not so much as one public lamp in London. Its streets were solidly paved. In Paris, centuries subsequently, whoever stepped over his threshold on a rainy day stepped up to his ankles in mud. Other cities, as Granada, Seville, Toledo, considered themselves rivals of Cordova. The palaces of the khalifs were magnificently decorated. Those sovereigns might well look down with supercilious contempt on the dwellings of the rulers of Germany, France, and England, which were scarcely better than stables,—chimneyless, windowless, and with a hole in the roof for the smoke to escape,

*Civilization and splendour of the Spanish Arabs.*

*Their palaces and gardens.*

like the wigwams of certain Indians. The Spanish Mohammedans had brought with them all the luxuries and prodigalities of Asia. Their residences stood forth against the clear blue sky, or were embosomed in woods. They had polished marble balconies, overhanging orange-gardens; courts with cascades of water; shady retreats provocative of slumber in the heat of the day; retiring-rooms vaulted with stained glass, speckled with gold, over which streams of water were made to gush; the floors and walls were of exquisite mosaic. Here, a fountain of quicksilver shot up in a glistening spray, the glittering particles falling with a tranquil sound like fairy bells; there, apartments into which cool air was drawn from the flower-gardens, in summer, by means of ventilating towers, and in the winter through earthen pipes or caleducts, embedded in the walls,—the hypocaust, in the vaults below, breathing forth volumes of warm and perfumed air through these hidden passages. The walls were not covered with wainscot, but adorned with arabesques, and paintings of agricultural scenes and views of Paradise. From the ceilings, corniced with fretted gold, great chandeliers hung, one of which, it is said, was so large that it contained 1084 lamps. Clusters of frail marble columns surprised the beholder with the vast weights they bore. In the boudoirs of the sultanas they were sometimes of verd-antique, and incrusted with lapis lazuli. The furniture was of sandal and citron wood, inlaid with mother-of-pearl, ivory, silver, or relieved with gold and precious malachite. In orderly confusion were arranged vases of rock crystal, Chinese porcelains, and tables of exquisite mosaic. The winter apartments were hung with rich tapestry; the floors were covered with embroidered Persian carpets. Pillows and couches, of elegant forms, were scattered about the rooms, which were perfumed with frankincense. It was the intention of the Saracen architect, by excluding the view of the external landscape, to concentrate attention on his work; and since the representation of the human form was religiously forbidden, and that source of decoration denied, his imagination ran riot with the complicated arabesques he introduced, and sought every opportunity of replacing the prohibited works of art by the trophies and rarities of the garden. For this reason, the Arabs never produced artists; religion turned them from the beautiful, and made them soldiers, philosophers, and men of affairs. Splendid flowers and rare exotics ornamented the courtyards and even the inner chambers. Great care was taken to make due provision for the cleanliness, occupation, and amusement of the inmates. Through pipes of metal, water, both warm and cold, to suit the season of the year, ran into baths of marble; in niches, where the current of air could be artificially directed, hung dripping alcarazzas. There were whispering-galleries for the amusement of the women; labyrinths and marble play-courts for the children; for the master himself, grand libraries. The Khalif Alhakem's was so large that the catalogue alone filled forty volumes. He had also apartments for the transcribing, binding, and ornamenting of books. A taste for calligraphy and the possession of splendidly-illuminated manuscripts seems to have anticipated in the khalifs, both of Asia and Spain, the taste for statuary and paintings among the later Popes of Rome. *Libraries and works of taste.*

Such were the palace and gardens of Zehra, in which Abderrahman III. honoured his favourite sultana. The edifice had twelve hundred columns of Greek, Italian, Spanish, and African marble. Its hall of audience was incrusted with gold and pearls. Through the long corridors of its seraglio black eunuchs silently glided. The ladies of the harem, both wives and concubines, were the most beautiful that could be found. To that establishment alone 6300 persons were attached. The body-guard of the sovereign was composed of 12,000 horsemen, whose scimitars and belts were studded with gold. This was that Abderrahman who, after a glorious reign of fifty years, sat down to count the number of days of unalloyed happiness he had experienced, and could only enumerate fourteen. "O man," exclaimed the plaintive khalif, "put not thy trust in this present world." *The court of Abderrahman III.*

No nation has ever excelled the Spanish Arabs in the beauty and costliness of their pleasure-gardens. To them, also, we owe the introduction of very many of our most valuable cultivated fruits, such as the peach. Retaining the love of their *Social habits of the Moors.*

ancestors for the cooling effect of water in a hot climate, they spared no pains in the superfluity of fountains, hydraulic works, and artificial lakes in which fish were raised for the table. Into such a lake, attached to the palace of Cordova, many loaves were cast each day to feed the fish. There were also menageries of foreign animals; aviaries of rare birds; manufactories in which skilled workmen, obtained from foreign countries, displayed their art in textures of silk, cotton, linen, and all the miracles of the loom; in jewellery and filigree-work, with which they ministered to the female pride of the sultanas and concubines. Under the shade of cypresses cascades disappeared; among flowering shrubs there were winding walks, bowers of roses, seats cut out of the rock, and crypt-like grottoes hewn in the living stone. Nowhere was ornamental gardening better understood; for not only did the artist try to please the eye as it wandered over the pleasant gradation of vegetable colour and form—he also boasted his success in the gratification of the sense of smell by the studied succession of perfumes from beds of flowers.

*Their domestic life.*

To these Saracens we are indebted for many of our personal comforts. Religiously cleanly, it was not possible for them to clothe, according to the fashion of the natives of Europe, in a garment unchanged till it dropt to pieces of itself, a loathsome mass of vermin, stench, and rags. No Arab who had been a minister of state, or the associate or antagonist of a sovereign, would have offered such a spectacle as the corpse of Thomas à Becket when his haircloth shirt was removed. They taught us the use of the often-changed and often-washed under-garment of linen or cotton, which still passes among ladies under its old Arabic name. But to cleanliness they were not unwilling to add ornament. Especially among women of the higher classes was the love of finery a passion. Their outer garments were often of silk, embroidered and decorated with gems and woven gold. So fond were the Moorish women of gay colours, and the lustre of chrysolites, hyacinths, emeralds, and sapphires, that it was quaintly said that the interior of any public building in which they were permitted to appear, looked like a flower meadow in the spring besprinkled with rain.

In the midst of all this luxury, which cannot be disregarded by the historian, since in the end it produced a most important result in the south of France, the Spanish khalifs, emulating the example of their Asiatic compeers, and in this strongly contrasting with the Popes of Rome, were not only the patrons, but the personal cultivators of all the branches of human learning. One of them was himself the author of a work on polite literature in not less than fifty volumes; another wrote a treatise on algebra. When Zaryab the musician came from the East to Spain, the Khalif Abderrahman rode forth to meet him in honour. The College of Music in Cordova was sustained by ample government patronage, and is said to have produced many illustrious professors.

*They cultivate literature, music,*

The Arabs never translated into their own tongue the great Greek poets, though they so sedulously collected and translated the Greek philosophers. Their religious sentiments and sedate character caused them to abominate the lewdness of our classical mythology, and to denounce indignantly any connection between the licentious, impure Olympian Jove and the Most High God, as an insufferable and unpardonable blasphemy. Haroun al Raschid had gratified his curiosity by causing Homer to be translated into Syriac, but he did not adventure on rendering the great epics into Arabic. Notwithstanding this aversion to our graceful but not unobjectionable ancient poetry, among them originated the Tensons, or poetic disputations, carried afterward to perfection among the Troubadours; from them, also, the Provençals learned to employ jongleurs. Across the Pyrenees, literary, philosophical, and military adventurers were perpetually passing; and thus the luxury, the taste, and above all, the chivalrous gallantry and elegant courtesies of Moorish society found their way from Granada and Cordova to Provence and Languedoc. The French and German and English nobles imbibed the Arab admiration of the horse; they learned to pride themselves on skilful riding. Hunting and falconry became their fashionable pastimes; they tried to emulate that Arab skill which had produced the celebrated breed of Andalusian horses. It was a scene of grandeur and gallantry; the pastimes were tilts and tournaments. The

*But disapprove of European mythology.*

*The South of France contracts their tastes.*

refined society of Cordova prided itself on its politeness. A gay contagion also spread from the beautiful Moorish miscreants to their sisters beyond the mountains; the south of France was full of the witcheries of female fascinations, and of dancing to the lute and mandolin. Even in Italy and Sicily the love-song became the favourite composition; and out of these genial but not orthodox beginnings the polite literature of modern Europe arose. The pleasant epidemic spread by degrees along every hillside and valley. In monasteries, voices that had vowed celibacy might be heard carolling stanzas of which St. Jerome would hardly have approved; there was many a juicy abbot, who could troll forth, in jocund strains, like those of the merry sinners of Malaga and Xeres, the charms of women and wine, though one was forbidden to the Moslem and one to the monk. The sedate greybeards of Cordova had already applied to the supreme judge to have the songs of the Spanish Jew, Abraham Ibn Sahal, prohibited; for there was not a youth, nor woman, nor child in the city who could not repeat them by heart. Their immoral tendency was a public scandal. The light gaiety of Spain was reflected in the coarser habits of the northern countries. It was an archdeacon of Oxford who some time afterward sang—

*Light literature spreads in to Sicily and Italy.*

"Mihi sit propositum in tabernâ mori,
Vinum sit appositum morientis ori,
Ut dicant, cum venerint angelorum chori,
'Deus sit propitius huic potatori,'" etc.

Even as early as the tenth century, persons having a taste for learning and for elegant amenities found their way into Spain from all adjoining countries; a practice in subsequent years still more indulged in, when it became illustrated by the brilliant success of Gerbert, who, as we have seen, passed from the infidel university of Cordova to the Papacy of Rome.

The khalifs of the West carried out the precepts of Ali, the fourth successor of Mohammed, in the patronage of literature. They established libraries in all their chief towns; it is said that not fewer than seventy were in existence. To every mosque was attached a public school, in which the children of the poor were taught to read and write, and instructed in the pre-

*The Arabian school system.*

cepts of the Koran. For those in easier circumstances there were academies, usually arranged in twenty-five or thirty apartments, each calculated for accommodating four students; the academy being presided over by a rector. In Cordova, Granada, and other great cities, there were universities, frequently under the superintendence of Jews; the Mohammedan maxim being that the real learning of a man is of more public importance than any particular religious opinions he may entertain. In this they followed the example of the Asiatic khalif, Haroun al Raschid, who actually conferred the superintendence of his schools on John Masué, a Nestorian Christian. The Mohammedan liberality was in striking contrast with the intolerance of Europe. Indeed, it may be doubted whether at this time any European nation is sufficiently advanced to follow such an example. In the universities, the professors of polite literature gave lectures upon Arabic classical works; others taught rhetoric, or composition, or mathematics, or astronomy, or other sciences. From these institutions many of the practices observed in our colleges were derived. They held Commencements as we do, at which poems were read and orations delivered in presence of the public. They had also, in addition to these schools of general learning, professional ones, particularly for medicine.

With a pride perhaps not altogether inexcusable, the Arabians boasted of their language as being the most perfect spoken by man. Mohammed himself, when challenged to produce a miracle in proof of the authenticity of his mission, uniformly pointed to the composition of the Koran, its unapproachable excellence vindicating its inspiration. The orthodox Moslems —the Moslems are those who are submissively resigned to the Divine will—are wont to assert that every page of that book is indeed a conspicuous miracle. It is not then surprising that, in the Arabian schools, great attention was paid to the study of language, and that so many celebrated grammarians were produced. By these scholars, dictionaries, similar to those now in use, were composed; their copiousness is indicated by the circumstance that one of them consisted of sixty volumes, the definition of each word being illustrated or sustained by

*Cultivation of grammar, rhetoric, composition.*

quotations from Arab authors of acknowledged repute. They had also lexicons of Greek, Latin, Hebrew; and cyclopædias such as the Historical Dictionary of Sciences of Mohammed Ibn Abdallah, of Granada. In their highest civilization and luxury they did not forget the amusements of their forefathers —listening to the tale-teller, who never failed to obtain an audience in the midst of Arab touts. Around the evening fires in Spain the wandering literati exercised their wonderful powers of Oriental invention, edifying the eager listeners by such narrations as those that have descended to us in the Arabian Nights' Entertainments. The more sober and higher efforts of the educated were, of course, directed to pulpit eloquence, in conformity to the example of all the great Oriental khalifs, and sanctified by the practice of the Prophet himself. Their poetical productions embraced all the modern minor forms— satires, odes, elegies, etc.; but they never produced any work in the higher walks of poetry,—no epic, no tragedy. Perhaps this was due to their false fashion of valuing the mechanical execution of a work. They were the authors and introducers of rhyme; and such was the luxuriance and abundance of their language, that, in some of their longest poems, the same rhyme is said to have been used alternately from the beginning to the end. Where such mechanical triumphs were popularly prized, it may supposed that the conception and spirit would be indifferent. Even among the Spanish women there were not a few who, like Velada, Ayesha, Labana, Algasania, achieved reputation in these compositions; and some of them were daughters of khalifs. And this is the more interesting to us, since it was from the Provençal poetry, the direct descendant of these efforts, that European literature arose. Sonnets and romances at last displaced the grimly-orthodox productions of the wearisome and ignorant Fathers of the Church.

*Defects of their literature.*

If fiction was prized among the Spanish Arabs, history was held in not less esteem. Every khalif had his own historian. The instincts of the race are perpetually peeping out; not only were there historians of the Commanders of the Faithful, but also of celebrated horses and illustrious camels. In connection with history, statistics were cultivated; this having been, it may be said, a necessary study from the first, enforced on the Saracen officers in their assessment of tribute on conquered misbelievers, and subsequently continued as an object of taste. It was, doubtless, a similar necessity, arising from their position, that stamped such a remarkably practical aspect on the science of the Arabs generally. Many of their learned men were travellers and voyagers, constantly moving about for the acquisition or diffusion of knowledge, their acquirements being a passport to them wherever they went, and a sufficient introduction to any of the African or Asiatic courts. They were thus continually brought in contact with men of affairs, soldiers of fortune, statesmen, and became imbued with much of their practical spirit; and hence the singularly romantic character which the biographies of many of these men display,—wonderful turns of prosperity, violent deaths. The scope of their literary labours offers a subject well worthy of meditation; it contrasts with the contemporary ignorance of Europe. Some wrote on chronology; some on numismatics; some, now that military eloquence had become objectless, wrote on pulpit oratory; some on agriculture and its allied branches, as the art of irrigation. Not one of the purely mathematical, or mixed, or practical sciences was omitted. Out of a list too long for detailed quotation, I may recall a few names: Assamh, who wrote on topography and statistics, a brave soldier, who was killed in the invasion of France, A.D. 702; Avicenna, the great physician and philosopher, who died A.D. 1037; Averrhoes, of Cordova, the chief commentator on Aristotle, A.D. 1198. It was his intention to unite the doctrines of Aristotle with those of the Koran. To him is imputed the discovery of spots upon the sun. The leading idea of his philosophy was the numerical unity of the souls of mankind, though parted among millions of living individuals. He died at Morocco. Abu Othman wrote on zoology; Alberuni, on gems,—he had travelled to India to procure information; Rhazes, Al Abbas, and Al Beithar, on botany,—the latter had been in all parts of the world for the purpose of obtaining specimens. Ebn Zoar, better known as Avenzoar, may be looked upon as the authority in Moorish pharmacy. Pharmacopœias were published by the schools, improvements on the old ones of the Nestorians; to them may be traced the introduction of many Arabic words, such as syrup, julep, elixir, still used among our apothecaries. A competent scholar might furnish not only an interesting, but valuable book, founded on the remaining relics of the Arab vocabulary; for, in whatever direction we may look, we meet, in the various pursuits of peace and war, of letters and of science, Saracenic vestiges. Our dictionaries tell us that such is the origin of admiral, alchemy, alcohol, algebra, chemise, cotton, and hundreds of other words. The Saracens commenced the application of chemistry both to the theory and practice of medicine, in the explanation of the functions of the human body and in the cure of its diseases. Nor was their surgery behind their medicine. Albucasis, of Cordova, shrinks not from the performance of the most formidable operations in his own and in the obstetrical art; the actual cautery and the knife are used without hesitation. He has left us ample descriptions of the surgical instruments then employed; and from him we learn that, in operations on females in which considerations of delicacy intervened, the services of properly instructed women were secured. How different was all this from the state of things in Europe: the Christian peasant, fever-stricken or overtaken by accident, hied to the nearest saint-shrine and expected a miracle; the Spanish Moor relied on the prescription or lancet of his physician, or the bandage and knife of his surgeon.

In mathematics the Arabians acknowledged their indebtedness to two sources, Greek and Indian, but they greatly improved upon both. The Asiatic khalifs had made exertions to procure translations of Euclid, Apollonius, Archimedes, and other Greek geometers. Almaimon, in a letter to the Emperor Theophilus, expressed his desire to visit Constantinople if his public duties would have permitted. He requests of him to allow Leo the mathematician to come to Bagdad to impart to him a portion of his learning, pledging his word that he would restore him quickly and safely again. "Do not," says the high-minded khalif, "let diversity of religion or of country cause you to refuse my request. Do what friendship would concede to a friend. In return I offer you a hundredweight of gold, a perpetual alliance and peace." True to the instincts of his race and the traditions of his city, the Byzantine sourly and insolently refused the request, saying that "the learning which had illustrated the Roman name should never be imparted to a barbarian."

From the Hindus the Arabs learned arithmetic, especially that valuable invention termed by us the Arabic numerals, but honourably ascribed by them to its proper source, under the designation of "Indian numerals." They also entitled their treatises on the subject "systems of Indian arithmetic." This admirable notation by nine digits and cipher occasioned a complete revolution in arithmetical computations. As in the case of so many other things, the Arab impress is upon it: our word cipher, and its derivatives, ciphering, etc., recall the Arabic word tsaphara or ciphra, the name for the 0, and meaning that which is blank or void. Mohammed Ben Musa, said to be the earliest of the Saracen authors on algebra, and who made the great improvement of substituting sines for chords in trigonometry, wrote also on this Indian system. He lived at the end of the ninth century; before the end of the tenth it was in common use among the African and Spanish mathematicians. Ebn Junis, A.D. 1008, used it in his astronomical works. From Spain it passed into Italy, its singular advantage in commercial computation causing it to be eagerly adopted in the great trading cities. We still use the word algorithm in reference to calculations. The study of algebra was intently cultivated among the Arabs, who gave it the name it bears. Ben Musa, just referred to, was the inventor of the common method of solving quadratic equations. In the application of mathematics to astronomy and physics they had been long distinguished. Almaimon had determined with considerable accuracy the obliquity of the ecliptic. His result, with those of some other Saracen astronomers, is as follows:—

*Their great improvements in arithmetic.*

*Their astronomical discoveries.*

| A.D. | | |
|---|---|---|
| 830. Almaimon | ............ | 23° 35' 52" |
| 879. Albategnius, at Aracte | ............ | 23° 35' 00 |
| 987. Aboul Wefa, at Bagdad | ............ | 23° 35' 00 |
| 995. Aboul Rihan, with a quadrant of 25 feet radius... | | 23° 35' 00 |
| 1080. Arzachael | ............ | 23° 34' 00 |

Almaimon had also ascertained the size of the earth from the measurement of a degree on the shore of the Red Sea,—an operation implying true ideas of its form, and in singular contrast with the doctrine of Constantinople and Rome. While the latter was asserting, in all its absurdity, the flatness of the earth, the Spanish Moors were teaching geography in their common schools from globes. In Africa, there was still preserved, with almost religious reverence, in the library at Cairo, one of brass, reputed to have belonged to the great astronomer Ptolemy. Al Idrisi made one of silver for Roger II., of Sicily; and Gerbert used one which he had brought from Cordova in the school he established at Rheims. It cost a struggle of several centuries, illustrated by some martyrdoms, before the dictum of Lactantius and Augustine could be overthrown. Among problems of interest that were solved may be mentioned the determination of the length of the year by Albategnius and Thebit Ben Corrah; and increased accuracy was given to the correction of astronomical observations by Albasen's great discovery of atmospheric refraction. Among the astronomers, some composed tables; some wrote on the measure of time; some on the improvement of clocks, for which purpose they were the first to apply the pendulum; some on instruments, as the astrolabe. The introduction of astronomy into Christian Europe has been attributed to the translation of the works of Mohammed Forgani. In Europe also, the Arabs were the first to build observatories; the Giralda, or tower of Seville, was erected under the superintendence of Geber, the mathematician, A.D. 1196, for that purpose. Its fate was not a little characteristic. After the expulsion of the Moors it was turned into a belfry, the Spaniards not knowing what else to do with it.

*Europe tries to hide its obligations to them.*

I have to deplore the systematic manner in which the literature of Europe has contrived to put out of sight our scientific obligations to the Mohammedans. Surely they cannot be much longer hidden. Injustice founded on religious rancour and national conceit cannot be perpetuated for ever. What should the modern astronomer say when, remembering the contemporary barbarism of Europe, he finds the Arab Abul Hassan speaking of tubes, to the extremities of which ocular and object diopters, perhaps sights, were attached, as used at Meragha?—what when he reads of the attempts of Abderrahman Sufi at improving the photometry of the stars? Are the astronomical tables of Ebn Junis (A.D. 1008), called the Hakemite tables, or the Ilkanic tables of Nasser Eddin Tasi, constructed at the great observatory just mentioned, Meragha, near Tauris, A.D. 1259, or the measurement of time by pendulum oscillations, and the methods of correcting astronomical tables by systematic observations,—are such things worthless indications of the mental state? The Arab has left his intellectual impress on Europe, as, before long, Christendom will have to confess; he has indelibly written it on the heavens, as any one may see who reads the names of the stars on a common celestial globe.

Our obligations to the Spanish Moors in the arts of life are even more marked than in the higher branches of science, perhaps only because our ancestors were better prepared to take advantage of things connected with daily affairs. They set an example of skilful agriculture, the practice of which was regulated by a code of laws. Not only did they attend to the cultivation of plants, introducing very many new ones; they likewise paid great attention to the breeding of cattle, especially sheep and the horse. To them we owe the introduction of the great products, rice, sugar, cotton, and also, as we have previously observed, nearly all the fine garden and orchard fruits, together with many less important plants, as spinach and saffron. To them Spain owes the culture of silk; they gave to Xeres and Malaga their celebrity for making wine. They introduced the Egyptian system of irrigation by floodgates, wheels, and pumps. They also promoted many important branches of industry; improved the manufacture of textile fabrics, earthenware, iron, steel; the Toledo sword-blades were everywhere prized for their temper. The Arabs, on their expulsion from Spain, carried the manufacture of a kind of leather, in which they were acknowledged to excel, to Morocco, from which country the leather itself has now taken its name. They also introduced inventions of a more ominous kind—gunpowder and artillery. The cannon they used appeared to have

*Improvements in the arts of life.*

been made of wrought iron. But perhaps they more than compensated for these evil contrivances by the introduction of the mariner's compass.

*Their commerce.*

The mention of the mariner's compass might lead us correctly to infer that the Spanish Arabs were interested in commercial pursuits, a conclusion to which we should also come when we consider the revenues of some of their khalifs. That of Abderrahman III. is stated at five and a half millions sterling—a vast sum if considered by its modern equivalent, and far more than could be possibly raised by taxes on the produce of the soil. It probably exceeded the entire revenue of all the sovereigns of Christendom taken together. From Barcelona and other ports an immense trade with the Levant was maintained, but it was mainly in the hands of the Jews, who, from the first invasion of Spain by Musa, had ever been the firm allies and collaborators of the Arabs. Together they had participated in the dangers of the invasion; together they had shared its boundless success; together they had held in irreverent derision, nay, even in contempt, the woman-worshippers and polytheistic savages beyond the Pyrenees,—as they mirthfully called those whose long-delayed vengeance they were in the end to feel; together they were expelled. Against such Jews as lingered behind, the hideous persecutions of the Inquisition were directed. But in the days of their prosperity they maintained a merchant marine of more than a thousand ships. They had factories and consuls on the Tanais. With Constantinople alone they maintained a great trade; it ramified from the Black Sea and East Mediterranean into the interior of Asia; it reached the ports of India and China, and extended along the African coast as far as Madagascar. Even in these commercial affairs the singular genius of the Jew and Arab shines forth. In the midst of the tenth century, when Europe was about in the same condition that Caffraria is now, enlightened Moors, like Abul Cassem, were writing treatises on the principles of trade and commerce. As on so many other occasions, on these affairs they have left their traces. The smallest weight they used in trade was the grain of barley, four of which were equal to one sweet pea, called in Arabic 'carat.' We still use the grain as our unit of weight, and still speak of gold as being so many carats fine.

Such were the Khalifs of the West; such their splendour, their luxury, their knowledge; such some of the obligations we are under to them,—obligations which Christian Europe, with singular insincerity, has ever been fain to hide. The cry against the misbeliever has long outlived the Crusades. Considering the enchanting country over which they ruled, it was not without reason that they caused to be engraven on the public seal, "The servant of the Merciful rests contented in the decrees of God." What more, indeed, could Paradise give them? But, considering also the evil end of all this happiness and pomp, this learning, liberality, and wealth, we may well appreciate the solemn truth which these monarchs, in their day of pride and power, grandly wrote in the beautiful mosaics on their palace walls, an ever-recurring warning to him who owes dominion to the sword, "There is no conqueror but God." *Obligations to the Khalif life of the West.*

The value of a philosophical or political system may be determined by its fruits. On this principle I examined in Chapter XII. the Italian system, estimating its religious merit from the biographies of the Popes, which afford the proper criterion. In like manner, the intellectual state of the Mohammedan nations at successive epochs may be ascertained from what is its proper criterion, the contemporaneous scientific manifestation. *Examination of Mohammedan science.*

At the time when the Moorish influences in Spain began to exert a pressure on the Italian system, there were several scientific writers, fragments of whose works have descended to us. As an architect may judge of the skill of the ancient Egyptians in his art from a study of the Pyramids, so from these relics of Saracenic learning we may demonstrate the intellectual state of the Mohammedan people, though much of their work has been lost and more has been purposely destroyed.

Among such writers is Alhazen; his date was about A.D. 1100. It appears that he resided both in Spain and Egypt, but the details of his biography are very confused. Through his optical works, which have been translated into Latin, he is *Review of the works of Alhazen.*

*He corrects the theory of vision.* best known to Europe. He was the first to correct the Greek misconception as to the nature of vision, showing that the rays of light come from external objects to the eye, and do not issue forth from the eye and impinge on external things, as, up to his time, had been supposed. His explanation does not depend upon mere hypothesis or supposition, but is plainly based upon anatomical investigation as well as on geometrical discussion.

*Determines the function of the retina.* He determines that the retina is the seat of vision, and that impressions made by light upon it are conveyed along the optic nerve to the brain. Though it might not be convenient, at the time when Alhazen lived, to make such an acknowledgment, no one could come to these conclusions, nor, indeed, know anything about these facts, unless he had been engaged in the forbidden practice of dissection.

*Explains single vision.* With felicity he explains that we see single when we use both eyes, because of the formation of the visual images on symmetrical portions of the two retinas. To the modern physiologist the mere mention of such things is as significant as the occurrence of an arch in the interior of the pyramid is to the architect. But Alhazen shows that our sense of sight is by no means a reliable guide, and that there are illusions arising from the course which the rays of light may take when they suffer refraction or reflection. It is in the discussion of one of these physical problems that his scientific greatness truly shines forth.

*Traces the course of a ray of light through the air.* He is perfectly aware that the atmosphere decreases in density with increase of height; and from that consideration he shows that a ray of light, entering it obliquely, follows a curvilinear path which is concave toward the earth; and that, since the mind refers the position of an object to the direction in which the ray of light from it enters the eye, the result must be an illusion as respects the starry bodies; they appear to us, to use the Arabic term, nearer to the *zenith* than they actually are, and not in their true place. We see them in the direction of the tangent to the curve of refraction as it reaches the eye.

*Astronomical refraction.* Hence also he shows that we actually see the stars and the sun and the moon before they have risen and after they have set,—a wonderful illusion. He shows that in its passage through the air the curvature of a ray increases with the in-

creasing density, and that its path does not depend on vapours
that chance to be present, but on the variation of density in
the medium. To this refraction he truly refers the shortening, *The hori-*
in their vertical diameter, of the horizontal sun and moon; to *and moon.*
its variations he imputes the twinkling of the fixed stars.
The apparent increase of size of the former bodies when they
are in the horizon he refers to a mental deception, arising from
the presence of intervening terrestrial objects. He shows that
the effect of refraction is to shorten the duration of night and
darkness by prolonging the visibility of the sun, and considering the reflecting action of the air, he deduces that beautiful
explanation of the nature of twilight—the light that we per- *Explains*
ceive before the rising and after the setting of the sun— *the twi-*
*light.*
which we accept at the present time as true. With extraordi- *Determines*
nary acuteness, he applies the principles with which he is *the height*
*of the at-*
dealing to the determination of the height of the atmosphere, *mosphere.*
deciding that its limit is nearly $58\frac{1}{2}$ miles.

All this is very grand. Shall we compare it with the contemporaneous monk miracles and monkish philosophy of Europe? It would make a profound impression if communicated
for the first time to a scientific society in our own age. Nor
perhaps does his merit end here. If the Book of the Balance
of Wisdom, for a translation of which we are indebted to M.
Khanikoff, the Russian consul-general at Tabriz, be the production of Alhazen, of which there seems to be internal proof,
it offers us evidence of a singular clearness in mechanical conception for which we should scarcely have been prepared, and,
if it be not his, at all events it indisputably shows the scientific acquirements of his age. In that book is plainly set forth *The weight*
the connection between the weight of the atmosphere and its *of the air.*
increasing density. The weight of the atmosphere was therefore understood before Torricelli. He shows that a body will
weigh differently in a rare and in a dense atmosphere; that
its loss of weight will be greater in proportion as the air is
more dense. He considers the force with which plunged *Principles*
bodies will rise through heavier media in which they are im- *of hydro-*
*statics.*
mersed, and discusses the submergence of floating bodies, as
ships upon the sea. He understands the doctrine of the cen-

*Theory of the balance.*

tre of gravity. He applies it to the investigation of balances and steelyards, showing the relations between the centre of gravity and the centre of suspension—when those instruments will set and when they will vibrate. He recognizes gravity as a force; asserts that it diminishes with the distance; but falls into the mistake that the diminution is as the distance, and not as its square. He considers gravity as terrestrial, and fails to perceive that it is universal,—that was reserved for Newton. He knows correctly the relation between the velocities, spaces, and times of falling bodies, and has very distinct ideas of capillary attraction. He improves the construction of that old Alexandrian invention, the hydrometer,—the instrument which, in a letter to his fair but pagan friend Hypatia, the good Bishop of Ptolemais, Synesius, six hundred years before, requests her to have made for him in Alexandria, as he wishes to try the wines he is using, his health being a little delicate. The determinations of the densities of bodies, as given by Alhazen, approach very closely to our own; in the case of mercury they are even more exact than some of those of the last century. I join, as, doubtless, all natural philosophers will do, in the pious prayer of Alhazen, that, in the day of judgment, the All-Merciful will take pity on the soul of Abur-Raihân, because he was the first of the race of men to construct a table of specific gravities; and I will add Alhazen's name thereto, for he was the first to trace the curvilinear path of a ray of light through the air. Though more than seven centuries part him from our times, the physiologists of this age may accept him as their compeer, since he received and defended the doctrine, now forcing its way, of the progressive developement of animal forms. He upheld the affirmation of those who said that man, in his progress, passes through a definite succession of states; not, however, "that he was once a bull, and was then changed to an ass, and afterward into a horse, and after that into an ape, and finally became a man." This, he says, is only a misrepresentation by "common people" of what is really meant. The "common people" who withstood Alhazen have representatives among us, themselves tho only example in the Fauna of the world of that non-develope-

*Gravity; capillary attraction; the hydrometer.*

*Tables of specific gravities.*

*The theory of developement of organisms.*

ment which they so loudly affirm. At the best they are only passing through some of the earlier forms of that series of transmutations to which the devout Mohammedan in the above quotation alludes.

The Arabians, with all this physical knowledge, do not appear to have been in possession of the thermometer, though they knew the great importance of temperature measures, employing the areometer for that purpose. They had detected the variation in density of liquids by heat, but not the variation in volume. In their measures of time they were more successful; they had several kinds of clepsydras. A balance clepsydra is described in the work from which I am quoting. But it was their great astronomer, Ebn Junis, who accomplished the most valuable of all chronometric improvements. He first applied the pendulum to the measure of time. La- *The pendulum clock.* place, in the fifth note to his 'Système du Monde,' avails himself of the observations of this philosopher, with those of Albategnius and other Arabians, as incontestable proof of the diminution of the eccentricity of the earth's orbit. He states, more- *Astronomical works of* over, that the observation of Ebn Junis of the obliquity of the *Ebn Junis.* ecliptic, properly corrected for parallax and refraction, gives for the year A.D. 1000 a result closely approaching to the theoretical. He also mentions another observation of Ebn Junis, October 31, A.D. 1007, as of much importance in reference to the great inequalities of Jupiter and Saturn. I have already *The Arabic* remarked that, in the writings of this great Arabian, the Ara- *numerals.* bic numerals and our common arithmetical processes are currently used. From Africa and Spain they passed into Italy, finding ready acceptance among commercial men, who recognized at once their value, and, as William of Malmesbury says, being a wonderful relief to the "sweating calculators;" an epithet of which the correctness will soon appear to any one who will try to do a common problem in multiplication or division by the aid of the old Roman numerals. It is said that Gerbert—Pope Sylvester—was the first to introduce a knowledge of them into Europe; he had learned them at the Mohammedan university of Cordova. It is in allusion to the cipher, which, placed after any of the other digits, increases by tenfold their value, that in a letter to his patron, the Emperor Otho III., with humility he playfully but truly says, "I am like the last of all the numbers."

*Arabian philosophy.*

The disuse of the Roman by the introduction of the Arabic numerals foreshadowed the result of a far more important—a political—contest between those rival names. But, before showing how the Arabian intellect pressed upon Rome, and the convulsive struggles of desperation which Rome made to resist it, I must for a moment consider the former under another point of view, and speak of Saracen philosophy. And here Algazzali shall be my guide. He was born A.D. 1058.

*The writings of Algazzali.*

Let us hear him speak for himself. He is relating his attempt to detach himself from the opinions which he had imbibed in his childhood: "I said to myself, 'My aim is simply to know the truth of things; consequently, it is indispensable for me to ascertain what is knowledge.' Now it was evident to me that certain knowledge must be that which explains the object to be known in such a manner that no doubt can remain, so that in future all error and conjecture respecting it must be impossible. Not only would the understanding then need no efforts to be convinced of certitude, but security against error is in such close connection with knowledge, that, even were an apparent proof of falsehood to be brought forward, it would cause no doubt, because no suspicion of error would be possible. Thus, when I have acknowledged ten to be more than three, if any one were to say, 'On the contrary, three is more than ten, and, to prove the truth of my assertion, I will change this rod into a serpent,' and if he were to change it, my conviction of his error would remain unshaken. His manœuvre would only produce in me admiration for his ability. I should not doubt my own knowledge.

*The certitude of knowledge.*

"Then was I convinced that knowledge which I did not possess in this manner, and respecting which I had not this certainty, could inspire me with neither confidence nor assurance; and no knowledge without assurance deserves the name of knowledge.

*Unreliability of the senses.*

"Having examined the state of my own knowledge, I found it divested of all that could be said to have these qualities, unless perceptions of the senses and irrefragable principles were to be considered such. I then said to myself, 'Now, having fallen into this despair, the only hope of acquiring incontestable convictions is by the perceptions of the senses and by necessary truths.' Their evidence seemed to me to be indubitable. I began however to examine the objects of sensation and speculation, to see if they possibly could admit of doubt. Then doubts crowded upon me in such numbers that my incertitude became complete. Whence results the confidence I have in sensible things? The strongest of all our senses is sight; and yet, looking at a shadow, and perceiving it to be fixed and immovable, we judge it to be deprived of movement; nevertheless, experience teaches us that, when we return to the same place an hour after, the shadow is displaced, for it does not vanish suddenly, but gradually, little by little, so as never to be at rest. If we look at the stars, they seem to be as small as money-pieces; but mathematical proofs convince us that they are larger than the earth. These and other things are judged by the senses, but rejected by reason as false. I abandoned the senses, therefore, having seen all my confidence in their truth shaken.

"'Perhaps,' said I, 'there is no assurance but in the notions of reason, that is to say, first principles, as that ten is more than three; the same thing cannot have been created and yet have existed from all eternity; to exist and not to exist at the same time is impossible.'

"Upon this the senses replied, 'What assurance have you that your confidence in reason is not of the same nature as your confidence in us? When you relied on us, reason stepped in and gave us the lie; had not reason been there, you would have continued to rely on us. Well, may there not exist some other judge superior to reason, who, if he appeared, would refute the judgments of reason in the same way that reason refuted us? The non-appearance of such a judge is no proof of his non-existence.' *Unreliability of reason.*

"I strove in vain to answer the objection, and my difficulties *The nature* increased when I came to reflect on sleep. I said to myself, *of dreams.* 'During sleep, you give to visions a reality and consistence, and you have no suspicion of their untruth. On awakening, you are made aware that they are nothing but visions. What assurance have you that all you feel and know when you are awake does actually exist? It is all true as respects your condition at that moment; but it is nevertheless possible that another condition should present itself which should be to your awakened state that which to your awakened state is now to you sleep; so that, as respects this higher condition, your waking is but sleep.'"

It would not be possible to find in any European work a clearer statement of the scepticism to which philosophy leads us than what is thus given by this Arabian. Indeed, it is not possible to put the argument in a more effective way. His perspicuity is in singular contrast with the obscurity of many metaphysical writers.

*Intellectual despair.*

"Reflecting on my situation, I found myself bound to this world by a thousand ties, temptations assailing me on all sides. I then examined my actions. The best were those relating to instruction and education, and even there I saw myself given up to unimportant sciences, all useless in another world. Reflecting on the aim of my teaching, I found it was not pure in the sight of the Lord. I saw that all my efforts were directed toward the acquisition of glory to myself. Having, therefore, distributed my wealth, I left Bagdad and retired into Syria, where I remained for two years in solitary struggle with my soul, combating my passions, and exercising myself in the purification of my heart and in preparation for the other world."

This is a very beautiful picture of the mental struggles and the actions of a truthful and earnest man. In all this the Christian philosopher can sympathize with the devout Mohammedan. After all, they are not very far apart. Algazzali is not the only one to whom such thoughts have occurred, but he has found words to tell his experience better than any other man. And what is the conclusion at which he arrives? The life of man, he says, is marked by three stages: "the first, or infantile stage, is that of pure sensation; the second, which begins at the age of seven, is that of understanding; the third is that of reason, by means of which the intellect perceives the

*Algazzali's ages of man.*

necessary, the possible, the absolute, and all those higher objects which transcend the understanding. But after this there is a fourth stage, when another eye is opened, by which man perceives things hidden from others,—perceives all that will be,—perceives the things that escape the perceptions of reason, as the objects of reason escape the understanding, and as the objects of the understanding escape the sensitive faculty. This is propheticism." Algazzali thus finds a philosophical basis for the rule of life, and reconciles religion and philosophy.

And now I have to turn from Arabian civilized life, its science, its philosophy, to another, a repulsive state of things. With reluctance I come back to the Italian system, defiling the holy name of religion with its intrigues, its bloodshed, its oppression of human thought, its hatred of intellectual advancement. Especially I have now to direct attention to two countries, the scenes of important events,—countries in which the Mohammedan influences began to take effect and to press upon Rome. These are the South of France and Sicily.

*Renewal of the operatives of Mohammedan influences.*

Innocent III. had been elected Pope at the early age of thirty-seven years, A.D. 1198. The Papal power had reached its culminating point. The weapons of the Church had attained their utmost force. In Italy, in Germany, in France and England, interdicts and excommunications vindicated the pontifical authority, as in the cases of the Duke of Ravenna, the Emperor Otho, Philip Augustus of France, King John of England. In each of these cases it was not for the sake of sustaining great moral principles or the rights of humanity that the thunder was launched,—it was in behalf of temporary political interests; interests that, in Germany, were sustained at the cost of a long war, and cemented by assassination; in France, strengthened by the well-tried device of an intervention in a matrimonial broil—the domestic quarrel of the king and queen about Agnes of Meran. "Ah, happy Saladin!" said the insulted Philip, when his kingdom was put under interdict, "he has no Pope above him. I too will turn Mohammedan."

*Interference of Innocent III. in France.*

So likewise in Spain, Innocent interfered in the matrimonial life of the King of Leon. The remorseless venality of the Papal government was in every direction felt. Portugal had already been advanced to the dignity of a kingdom on payment of an annual tribute to Rome. The King of Arragon held his kingdom as feudatory to the Pope.

In England, Innocent's interference assumed a different aspect. He attempted to assert his control over the Church in spite of the king, and put the nation under interdict because John would not permit Stephen Langton to be Archbishop of Canterbury. It was utterly impossible that affairs could go on with such an empire within an empire. For his contumacy John was excommunicated; but, base as he was, he defied his punishment for four years. Hereupon his subjects were released from their allegiance, and his kingdom offered to any one who would conquer it. In his extremity, the King of England is said to have sent a messenger to the Emir Al Moucnim, offering to become a Mohammedan. The religious sentiment was then no higher in him than it was, under a like provocation, in the King of France, whose thoughts turned in the same direction. But, pressed irresistibly by Innocent, John was compelled to surrender his realm, agreeing to pay to the Pope, in addition to Peter's pence, 1000 marks a year as a token of vassalage. When the prelates whom he had refused or exiled returned, he was compelled to receive them on his knees, —humiliations which aroused the indignation of the stout English barons, and gave strength to those movements which ended in extorting Magna Charta. Never, however, was Innocent more mistaken than in the character of Stephen Langton. John had, a second time, formally surrendered his realm to the Pope, and done homage to the legate for it; but Stephen Langton was the first—at a meeting of the chiefs of the revolt against the king, held in London, August 25th, 1213—to suggest that they should demand a renewal of the charter of Henry I. From this suggestion Magna Charta originated. Among the miracles of the age, he was the greatest miracle of all; his patriotism was stronger than his profession. The wrath of the pontiff knew no bounds when he learned that the Great Charter had been concealed. In his bull, he denounced

it as base and ignominious; he anathematized the king if he
observed it; he declared it null and void. It was not the policy
of the Roman court to permit so much as the beginnings of
such freedom. The appointment of Simon Langton to the
archbishopric of York was annulled. One De Gray was substituted for him. It illustrated the simony into which the Papal
government had fallen, that De Gray had become, in these
transactions, indebted to Rome £10,000. In fact, through the
operation of the Crusades, all Europe was tributary to the Pope.
He had his fiscal agents in every metropolis; his travelling
ones wandering in all directions, in every country, raising
revenue by the sale of dispensations for all kinds of offences,
real and fictitious—money for the sale of appointments, high
and low,—a steady drain of money from every realm. Fifty
years after the time of which we are speaking, Robert Grostête,
the Bishop of Lincoln and friend of Roger Bacon, caused to
be ascertained the amount received by foreign ecclesiastics in
England. He found it to be thrice the income of the king
himself. This was on the occasion of Innocent IV. demanding provision to be made for three hundred additional Italian
clergy by the Church of England, and that one of his nephews
—a mere boy—should have a stall in Lincoln cathedral.

*The drain of money from that country.*

While thus Innocent III. was interfering and intriguing with
every court, and laying every people under tribute, he did not
for a moment permit his attention to be diverted from the Crusades, the singular advantages of which to the Papacy had now
been fully discovered. They had given to the Pope a suzerainty in Europe, the control of its military as well as its monetary resources. Not that a man like Innocent could permit
himself to be deluded by any hopes of eventual success. The
Crusades must inevitably prove, so far as their avowed object
was concerned, a failure. The Christian inhabitants of Palestine were degraded and demoralized beyond description. Their
ranks were thinned by apostasy to Mohammedanism. In Europe, not only had the laity begun to discover that the money
provided for the wars in the Holy Land was diverted from its
purpose, and, in some inexplicable manner, found its way into
Italy,—even the clergy could not conceal their suspicions that

*Goading of Europe into a new crusade.*

the proclamation of a crusade was merely the preparation for a swindle. Nevertheless Innocent pressed forward his schemes, goading on Christendom by throwing into its face the taunts of the Saracens. "Where," they say, "is your God, who cannot deliver you out of our hands? Behold! we have defiled your sanctuaries; we have stretched forth our arm; we have taken at the first assault, we hold in despite of you, those your desirable places, where your superstition had its beginning. Where is your God? Let him arise and protect you and himself." "If thou be the Son of God, save thyself if thou canst; redeem the land of thy birth from our hands. Restore thy cross, that we have taken, to the worshippers of the Cross." With great difficulty, however, Innocent succeeded in preparing the fourth Crusade, A.D. 1202. The Venetians consented to furnish a fleet of transports. But the expedition was quickly diverted from its true purpose; the Venetians employing the Crusaders for the capture of Zara from the King of Hungary.

*The Crusade is used for the seizure of Constantinople.*

Still worse, and shameful to be said, partly from the lust of plunder and partly through ecclesiastical machinations it again turned aside for an attack upon Constantinople, and took that city by storm, A.D. 1204, thereby establishing Latin Christianity in the Eastern metropolis, but, alas! with bloodshed, rape, and fire. On the night of the assault more houses were burned than could be found in any three of the largest cities in France. Even Christian historians compare with shame the storming of Constantinople by the Catholics with the capture of Jerusalem by Saladin. Pope Innocent himself was compelled to protest against enormities that had outrun his intentions. He says: "They practised fornications, incests, adulteries in the sight of men. They abandoned matrons and virgins, consecrated to God, to the lewdness of grooms. They lifted their hands against the treasures of the churches,—what is more heinous, the very consecrated vessels,—tearing the tablets of silver from the very altars, breaking in pieces the most sacred things, carrying off crosses and relics." In St. Sophia, the silver was stripped from the pulpit; an exquisite and highly-prized table of oblation was broken in pieces; the sacred chalices were turned into drinking-cups; the gold fringe was

*Sack of the city by the Catholics.*

ripped off the veil of the sanctuary. Asses and horses were led into the churches to carry off the spoil. A prostitute mounted the patriarch's throne, and sang, with indecent gestures, a ribald song. The tombs of the emperors were rifled; and the Byzantines saw, at once with amazement and anguish, the corpse of Justinian—which even decay and putrefaction had for six centuries spared in his tomb—exposed to the violation of a mob. It had been understood among those who instigated these atrocious proceedings that the relics were to be brought into a common stock and equitably divided among the conquerors; but each ecclesiastic seized and secreted whatever he could. The idolatrous state of the Eastern Church is illustrated by some of these relics. Thus the Abbot Martin obtained for his monastery in Alsace the following inestimable articles:—1. A spot of the blood of our Saviour; 2. A piece of the true cross; 3. The arm of the Apostle James; 4. Part of the skeleton of John the Baptist; 5.—I hesitate to write such blasphemy—"A bottle of the milk of the Mother of God!" In contrast with the treasures thus acquired may be set relics of a very different kind, the remains of ancient art which they destroyed:—1. The bronze charioteers from the Hippodrome; 2. The she-wolf suckling Romulus and Remus; 3. A group of a sphinx, river-horse, and crocodile; 4. An eagle tearing a serpent; 5. An ass and his driver, originally cast by Augustus in memory of the victory of Actium; 6. A Bellerophon and Pegasus; 7. A bronze obelisk; 8. Paris presenting the apple to Venus; 9. An exquisite statue of Helen; 10. The Hercules of Lysippus; 11. A Juno, formerly taken from the temple at Samos. The bronzes were melted into coin, and thousands of manuscripts and parchments were burned. From that time the works of many ancient authors disappeared altogether.

With well-dissembled regret, Innocent took the new order of things in the city of Constantinople under his protection. The Bishop of Rome at last appointed the Bishop of Constantinople. The acknowledgment of Papal supremacy was complete. Rome and Venice divided between them the ill-gotten gains of their undertaking. If anything had been wanting to open the eyes of Europe, surely what had thus occurred should have been enough. The Pope and the Doge—the trader in human credulity and the trader of the Adriatic—had shared the spoils of a crusade meant by religious men for the relief of the Holy Land. The bronze horses, once brought by Augustus from Alexandria after his victory over Antony, and transferred from Rome to Constantinople by its founder, were set before the Church of St. Mark. They were the outward and visible sign of a less obvious event that was taking place. For to Venice was brought a residue of the literary treasures that had escaped the fire and the destroyer; and while her comrades in the outrage were satisfied, in their ignorance, with fictitious relics, she took possession of the poor remnant of the glorious works of art, of letters, and of science. Through these was hastened the intellectual progress of the West.

*The Pope and the Doge divide the spoil.*

*Works of art carried to Venice.*

So fell Constantinople, and fell by the parricidal hands of Christians. The days of retribution for the curse she had inflicted on Western civilization were now approaching. In these events she received a first instalment of her punishment. Three hundred years before, the historian Luitprand, who was sent by the Emperor Otho I. to the court of Nicephorus Phocas, says of her, speaking as an eye-witness, "That city, once so wealthy, so flourishing, is now famished, lying, perjured, deceitful, rapacious, greedy, niggardly, vainglorious;" and since Luitprand's time she had been pursuing a downward career.

*The punishment of Constantinople.*

It might have been expected that the concentration of all the literary and scientific treasures of the Roman empire in Constantinople should have given rise to great mental vigour—that to Europe she would have been a brilliant focus of light. But when the works on jurisprudence by Tribonian, under Justinian, have been mentioned, what is there that remains? There is Stephanus, the grammarian, who wrote a dictionary, and Procopius, the historian, who was secretary to Belisarius in his campaigns. There is then a long interval almost without a literary name, to Theophylact Simocatta, and to the 'Ladder of Paradise' of John Climacus. The mental excitement of the iconoclastic dispute presents us with John of Damascus; and the ninth century, the 'Myriobiblion' and 'Nomocanon' of Pho-

*The literary worthlessness of that city.*

tius. Then follows Constantine Porphyrogenitus, vainly and voluminously composing; and Basil II. doubtless truly expresses the opinion of the time, as he certainly does the verdict of posterity as regards the works of his country, when he says that learning is useless and unprofitable lumber. The 'Alexiad' of Anna Comnena, and the history of Byzantine affairs by Nicephorus Bryennius, hardly redeem their age. This barrenness and worthlessness was the effect of the system introduced by Constantine the Great. The long line of emperors had been consistent in one policy—the repression or expulsion of philosophy; and yet it is the uniform testimony of those ages that the Eastern convents were full of secret Platonism,—that, in stealth, the doctrines of Plato were treasured up in the cells of Asiatic monks. The Byzantines had possessed in art and letters all the best models in the world, yet in a thousand years they never produced one original. Millions of Greeks never advanced one step in philosophy or science,— never made a single practical discovery, composed no poem, no tragedy worth perusal. The spirit of their superficial literature—if literature it can be called—is well shadowed forth in the story of the patriarch Photius, who composed at Bagdad, at a distance from his library, an analysis of 280 works he had formerly read. The final age of the city was signalized by the Barlaamite controversy respecting the mysterious light of Mount Tabor,—the possibility of producing a beatific vision, and of demonstrating, by an unceasing inspection of the navel for days and nights together, the existence of two external principles, a visible and an invisible God! *The absurdity of its intellectual pursuits.*

What was it that produced this barrenness, this intellectual degradation in Constantinople? The tyranny of Theology over Thought. *Cause of all this.*

But with the capture of Constantinople by the Latins other important events were occurring. Everywhere an intolerance of Papal power was being engendered. The monasteries became infected, and even from the holy lips of monks words of ominous import might be heard. In the south of France the intellectual insurrection first took form. There the influence of the Mohammedans and Jews beyond the Pyrenees began to *Heresy follows literature. Spread of gay literature from Spain.*

58 *The Troubadours of Languedoc.*

manifest itself. The songs of gallantry; tensons, or poetical contests of minstrels; satires of gay defiance; rivalry in praise of the ladies; lays, serenades, pastourelles, rondoes, such as had already drawn forth the condemnation of the sedate Mussulmans of Cordova, had gradually spread through Spain and found a congenial welcome in France. The Troubadours were singing in the langue d'Oc in the south, and the Trouvères in the langue d'Oil in the north. Thence the merry epidemic spread to Sicily and Italy. Men felt that a relief from the grim ecclesiastic was coming. Kings, dukes, counts, knights, prided themselves on their gentle prowess. The humbler minstrels found patronage among ladies and at courts; sly satires against the priests, and amorous ditties, secured them a welcome among the populace. When the poet was deficient in voice, a jongleur went with him to sing: and often there was added the pleasant accompaniment of a musical instrument. The Provençal, or langue d'Oc, was thus widely diffused; it served the purposes of those unacquainted with Latin, and gave the Italians a model for thought and versification, to Europe the germs of many of its future melodies. While the young were singing, the old were thinking; while the gay were carried away with romance, the grave were falling into heresy. But, true to her instincts and traditions, the Church had shown her determination to deal rigorously with all such movements. Already, A.D. 1134, Peter de Bruéys had been burned in Languedoc for denying infant baptism, the worship of the cross, and transubstantiation. Already Henry the Deacon, the disciple of Peter, had been disposed of by St. Bernard. Already the valleys of Piedmont were full of Waldenses. Already the Poor Men of Lyons were proclaiming the portentous doctrine that the sanctity of a priest lay not in his office, but in the manner of his life. They denounced the wealth of the Church, and the intermingling of bishops in bloodshed and war; they denied transubstantiation, invocation of saints, purgatory, and especially directed their hatred against the sale of indulgences for sin. The rich cities of Languedoc were full of misbelievers. They were given up to poetry, music, dancing. Their people, numbers of whom had been in the Crusades

*The Troubadours and Trouvères.*

*Commencing resistance of Rome.*

or in Spain, had seen the Saracens. Admiration had taken
the place of detestation. Amid shouts of laughter, the Troubadours went through the land, wagging their heads, and
slyly winking their eyes, and singing derisive songs about the
amours of the priests, and amply earning denunciations as lewd
blasphemers and atheists. Here was a state of things demanding the attention of Innocent. The methods he took for its *Innocent
correction have handed his name down to the maledictions* *III. alarm-
of posterity. He dispatched a missive to the Count of Tou-* *ed at the
louse—who already lay under excommunication for alleged in-* *spread of
termeddling with the rights of the clergy,—charging him with* *heresy.*
harbouring heretics and giving offices of emolument to Jews.
The count was a man of gay life, having, in emulation of some
of his neighbours across the Pyrenees, not less than three
wives. His offences of that kind were, however, eclipsed by
those with which he was now formally charged. It chanced
that, in the ensuing disputes, the Pope's legate was murdered.
There is no reason to believe that Raymond was concerned in
the crime. But the indignant Pope held him responsible; in- *He pro-
stantly ordered to be published in all directions his excommu-* *claims a
nication, and called upon Western Christendom to engage in* *crusade
a crusade against him, offering, to whoever chose to take them,* *against the
the wealth and possessions of the offender. So thoroughly was* *Count of
he seconded by the preaching of the monks, that half a million* *Toulouse,*
of men, it is affirmed, took up arms.

For the count there remained nothing but to submit. He *And disci-
surrendered up his strong places, was compelled to acknow-* *plines him.*
ledge the crimes alleged against him, and the justice of his
punishment. He swore that he would no longer protect heretics. Stripped naked to his middle, with a rope round his
neck, he was led to the altar, and there scourged. But the
immense army that had assembled was not to be satisfied by
these inflictions on an individual, though the Pope might be.
They had come for blood and plunder, and blood and plunder
they must have. Then followed such scenes of horror as the *Atrocities
sun had never looked on before. The army was officered by* *of the Cru-
Roman and French prelates; bishops were its generals, an* *saders in
archdeacon its engineer. It was the Abbot Arnold, the legate* *the South
of France.*

of the Pope, who, at the capture of Beziers, was inquired of by a soldier, more merciful or more weary of murder than himself, how he should distinguish and save the Catholic from the heretic. "Kill them all," he exclaimed; "God will know his own." At the church of St. Mary Magdalene 7000 persons were massacred, the infuriated Crusaders being excited to madness by the wicked assertion that these wretches had been guilty of the blasphemy of saying, in their merriment, "S. Mariam Magdalenam fuisse concubinam Christi." It was of no use for them to protest their innocence. In the town twenty thousand were slaughtered, and the place then fired, to be left a monument of Papal vengeance. At the massacre of Lavaur 400 people were burned in one pile; it is remarked that "they made a wonderful blaze, and went to burn everlastingly in hell." Language has no powers to express the atrocities that took place at the capture of the different towns. Ecclesiastical vengeance rioted in luxury. The soil was steeped in the blood of men, the air polluted by their burning. From the reek of murdered women, mutilated children, and blasted cities, the Inquisition, that infernal institution, arose. Its projectors intended it not only to put an end to public teaching, but even to private thought. In the midst of these awful events, Innocent was called to another tribunal, to render his account. He died A.D. 1216.

*Institution of the Inquisition.*

It was during the pontificate of this great criminal that the mendicant orders were established. The course of ages had brought an unintelligibility into public worship. The old dialects had become obsolete; new languages were forming. Among those classes, daily increasing in number, whose minds were awakening, an earnest desire for instruction was arising. Multitudes were crowding to hear philosophical discourses in the universities, and heresy was spreading very fast. But it was far from being confined to the intelligent. The lower orders furnished heretics and fanatics too. To antagonize the labours of these zealots,—who, if they had been permitted to go on unchecked, would quickly have disseminated their doctrines through all classes of society,—the Dominican and Franciscan orders were founded. They were well adapted to their

*Establishment of mendicant orders*

duty. It was their business to move among the people, preaching to them, in their own tongue, wherever an audience could be collected. The scandal under which the Church was labouring because of her wealth could not apply to these, who lived by begging alms. Their function was not to secure their own salvation, but that of other men.

St. Dominic was born A.D. 1170. His birth and life were adorned with the customary prodigies. Miracles and wonders were necessary for anything to make a sensation in the West. If his was not an immaculate conception, he was free from original sin. He was regarded as the adopted son of the Virgin; some were even disposed to assign him a higher dignity than that. He began his operations in Languedoc; but, as the prospect opened out before him, he removed from that unpromising region to Rome, the necessary centre of all such undertakings as his. Here he perfected his organization; instituted his friars, nuns, and tertiaries; and consolidated his pretensions by the working of many miracles. He exorcized three matrons, from whom Satan issued forth under the form of a great black cat, which ran up a bell-rope and vanished. A beautiful nun resolved to leave her convent. Happening to blow her nose, it dropped off into her handkerchief; but, at the fervent prayer of St. Dominic, it was replaced, and in gratitude, tempered by fear, she remained. St. Dominic could also raise the dead. Nevertheless, he died A.D. 1221, having worthily obtained the title of the burner and slayer of heretics. To him has been attributed the glory or the crime of being the inventor of "the Holy Inquisition." In a very few years his order boasted of nearly five hundred monasteries, scattered over Europe, Asia, Africa.

St. Francis, the compeer of St. Dominic, was born A.D. 1182. His followers delighted to point out, as it would seem not without irreverence, a resemblance to the incidents that occurred at the birth of our Lord. A prophetess foretold it; he was born in a stable; angels sang forth peace and goodwill in the air; one, under the form of Simeon, bore him to baptism. In early life he saw visions and became ecstatic. His father, Peter Bernardini, a respectable tradesman, endeavoured to restrain his eccentricities, at first by persuasion, but eventually more forcibly, appealing for assistance to the bishop, to prevent the young enthusiast from squandering his means in alms to the poor. On that functionary's gently remonstrating, and pointing out to Francis his filial obligations, he stripped himself naked before the people, exclaiming, " Peter Bernardini was my father; I have now but one father, He that is in heaven." At this affecting renunciation of all earthly possessions and earthly ties, those present burst into tears, and the good bishop threw his own mantle over him. When a man has come to this pass, there is nothing he cannot accomplish.

*Authorization of these Orders.*
It is related that, when application was first made to Innocent to authorize the order, he refused; but, very soon recognizing the advantages that would accrue, he gave it his hearty patronage. So rapid was the increase, that in A.D. 1219 it numbered not fewer than five thousand brethren. It was founded on the principles of chastity, poverty, obedience. They were to live on alms, but never to receive money. After a life of devotion to the Church, St. Francis attained his reward, A.D. 1226. Two years previously to his death, by a miraculous intervention there were impressed on his person marks answering to the wounds on our Saviour. These were the celebrated stigmata. A black growth, like nails, issued forth from the palms of his hands and his feet; a wound from which blood and water distilled opened in his side. It is not to be wondered at that these prodigies met with general belief. This was the generation which received as inestimable relics, through Andrew of Hungary, the heads of St. Stephen and St. Margaret, the hands of St. Bartholomew and St. Thomas, a slip of the rod of Aaron, and one of the water-pots of the marriage at Cana in Galilee.

*Influence derived from these Orders.*
The Papal Government quickly found the prodigious advantage arising from the institution of these mendicant orders. Vowed to poverty, living on alms, the hosts of friars, begging and barefoot, pervaded all Europe, coming in contact, under the most favourable circumstances, with the lowest grades of society. They lived and moved among the populace, and yet were held sacred. The accusations of dissipation and luxury so

forcibly urged against the regular clergy were altogether inapplicable to these rope-bound, starving fanatics. Through them the Italian government had possession of the ear of Europe. The pomp of worship in an unknown tongue, the gorgeous solemnities of the Church, were far more than compensated by the preaching of these missionaries, who held forth in the vernacular wherever an audience could be had. Among the early ones, some had been accustomed to a wandering life. Brother Pacificus, a disciple of St. Francis, had been a celebrated Trouvère. In truth, they not only warded off the present pressing danger, but through them the Church retained her hold upon the labouring classes for several subsequent centuries. The Pope might truly boast that the Poor Men of the Church were more than a match for the Poor Men of Lyons. Their influence began to diminish only when they abandoned their essential principles, joined in the common race for plunder, and became immensely rich.

Not only did Innocent III. thus provide himself with an ecclesiastical militia suited to meet the obviously impending insurrection, he increased his power greatly but insidiously by the formal introduction of auricular confession. It was by the fourth Lateran Council that the necessity of auricular confession was first formally established. Its aim was that no heretic should escape, and that the absent priest should be paramount even in the domestic circle. In none but a most degraded and superstitious society can such an infamous institution be tolerated. It invades the sacred privacy of life,—makes a man's wife, children, and servants his spies and accusers. When any religious system stands in need of such a social immorality, we may be sure that it is irrecoverably diseased, and hastening to its end. *Introduction of auricular confession.*

Auricular confession led to an increasing necessity for casuistry, though that science was not fully developed until the time of the Jesuits, when it gave rise to an extensive literature, with a lax system and a false morality, guiding the penitent rather with a view to his usefulness to the Church than to his own reformation, and not hesitating at singular indecencies in its portion having reference to married life. *Development of casuistry.*

*Attitude of Innocent III.*

Great historical events often find illustrations in representative men. Such is the case in the epoch we are now considering. On one side stands Innocent, true to the instincts of his party, interfering with all the European nations; launching forth his interdicts and excommunications; steeped in the blood of French heretics; hesitating at no atrocity, even the outrage and murder of women and children, the ruin of flourishing cities, to compass his plans; in all directions, under a thousand pretences, draining Europe of its money; calling to his aid hosts of begging friars; putting forth imposture miracles; organizing the Inquisition, and invading the privacy of life by the contrivance of auricular confession.

*Attitude of Frederick II.*

On the other side stands Frederick II., the Emperor of Germany. His early life, as has been already mentioned (p. 25 of this volume), was spent in Sicily, in familiar intercourse with Jews and Arabs, and Sicily to the last was the favoured portion of his dominions. To his many other accomplishments he added the speaking of Arabic as fluently as a Saracen. He delighted in the society of Mohammedan ladies, who thronged his court. His enemies asserted that his chastity was not improved by his associations with these miscreant beauties.

*His Mohammedan tendencies.*

The Jewish and Mohammedan physicians and philosophers taught him to sneer at the pretensions of the Church. From such ridicule it is but a short step to the shaking off of authority. At this time the Spanish Mohammedans had become widely infected with irreligion; their greatest philosophers were infidel in their own infidelity. The two sons of Averrhoes of Cordova were residents at Frederick's court. Their father was one of the ablest men their nation ever produced: an experienced astronomer, he had translated the Almagest, and, it is affirmed, was the first who actually saw a transit of Mercury across the sun; a voluminous commentator on the works of Plato and Aristotle, but a disbeliever in all revelation. Even of Mohammedanism he said, alluding to the prohibition which the Prophet had enjoined on the use of the flesh of swine, "That form of religion is destitute of everything that can commend it to the approval of any understanding, unless it be that of a hog." In the Sicilian court, surrounded by such unholy influences, the character of the young emperor was formed. Italian poetry, destined for such a brilliant future, here first found a voice in the sweet Sicilian dialect. The emperor and his chancellor were cultivators of the gay science, and in the composition of sonnets were rivals. A love of amatory poetry had spread from the south of France.

With a view to the recovery of the Holy Land, Honorius III. had made Frederick marry Yolinda de Lusignan, the heiress of the kingdom of Jerusalem. It was not, therefore, to be wondered at that Frederick's frivolities soon drew upon him the indignation of the gloomy Pope Gregory IX., the very first act of whose pontificate was to summon a new crusade. To the exhortations and commands of the aged Pope the Emperor lent a most reluctant ear, postponing from time to time the period of his departure, and dabbling in doubtful negotiations, through his Mohammedan friends, with the Sultan of Egypt. He embarked at last, but in three days returned. The octogenarian Pope was not to be trifled with, and pronounced his excommunication. Frederick treated it with ostensible contempt, but appealed to Christendom, accusing Rome of avaricious intentions. Her officials, he said, were travelling in all directions, not to preach the Word of God, but to extort money. "The primitive Church, founded on poverty and simplicity, brought forth numberless saints. The Romans are now rolling in wealth. What wonder that the walls of the Church are undermined to the base, and threaten utter ruin." For saying this he underwent a more tremendous excommunication; but his partisans in Rome, raising an insurrection, expelled the Pope. And now Frederick set sail, of his own accord, on his crusading expedition. On reaching the Holy Land, he was received with joy by the knights and pilgrims; but the clergy held aloof from him as an excommunicated person. The pontiff had dispatched a swift-sailing ship to forbid their holding intercourse with him. His private negotiations with the Sultan of Egypt now came to maturity. The Christian camp was thronged with infidel delegates: some came to discuss philosophical subjects, some were the bearers of presents. Elephants and a bevy of dancing-girls were courteously sent by the Sultan to his friend, who, it is said, was not insensible to the witcheries of the Oriental beauties. He wore a Saracen dress. In his privacy he did not hesitate to say, "I came not here to deliver the Holy City, but to maintain my estimation among the Franks." To the Sultan he appealed, "Out of your goodness, surrender to me Jerusalem as it is, that I may be able to lift up my head among the kings of Christendom." Accordingly, the city was surrendered to him. The object of his expedition was accomplished. But the Pope was not to be deceived by such collusions. He repudiated the transactions altogether, and actually took measures to lay Jerusalem and the Saviour's sepulchre under interdict, and this in the face of the Mohammedans. While the Emperor proclaimed his successes to Europe, the Pope denounced them as coming from the union of Christ and Belial; alleging four accusations against Frederick:—1. That he had given the sword which he had received from the altar of St. Peter for the defence of the faith, as a present to the Sultan of Babylon; 2. That he had permitted the preaching of the Koran in the Holy Temple itself; 3. That he had excluded the Christians of Antioch from his treaty; 4. That he had bound himself, if a Christian army should attempt to cleanse the Temple and city from Mohammedan defilements, to join the Saracens.

*Who gives up Jerusalem to him.*

*The Pope denounces him.*

Frederick crowned himself at Jerusalem, unable to find any ecclesiastic who dared to perform the ceremony, and departed from the Holy Land. It was time, for Rome was intriguing against him at home, a false report of his death having been industriously circulated. He forthwith prepared to enter on his conflict with the pontiff. His Saracen colonies at Nocera and Luceria, in Italy, could supply him with 30,000 Mussulman soldiers, with whom it was impossible for his enemies to tamper. He managed to draw over the general sentiment of Europe to his side, and publicly offered to convict the Pope himself of negotiations with the infidels; but his antagonist, conveniently impressed with a sudden horror of shedding blood, gave way, and peace between the parties was made. It lasted nearly nine years.

*Frederick establishes Saracen posts in Italy.*

In this period, the intellectual greatness of Frederick, and the tendencies of the influences by which he was enveloped, were strikingly manifest. In advance of his age, he devoted himself to the political improvement of Sicily. He instituted representative parliaments; enacted a system of wise laws; asserted the principle of equal rights and equal burdens, and the supremacy of the law over all, even the nobles and the Church. He provided for the toleration of all professions, Jew and Mohammedan, as well as Christian; emancipated all the serfs of his domains; instituted cheap justice for the poor; forbade private war; regulated commerce—prophetically laying down some of those great principles, which only in our own time have been finally received as true; established markets and fairs; collected large libraries; caused to be translated such works as those of Aristotle and Ptolemy; built menageries for natural history; founded in Naples a great university; patronized the medical college at Salernum; made provisions for the education of promising but indigent youths. All over the land splendid architectural triumphs were created. Under him the Italian language first rose above a patois. Sculpture, painting, and music were patronized. His chancellor is said to have been the author of the oldest sonnet.

In the eye of Rome all this was an abomination. Were human laws to take the precedence of the law of God? Were the clergy to be degraded to a level with the laity? Were the Jew and the Mohammedan to be permitted their infamous rites? Was this new-born product of the insolence of human intellect—this so-called science—to be brought into competition with theology, the heaven-descended? Frederick and his parliaments, his laws and universities, his libraries, his statues, his pictures and sonnets, were denounced. Through all, the ever-watchful eye of the Church discerned the Jew and the Saracen, and held them up to the abhorrence of Europe. But Gregory was not unwilling to show what could be done by himself in the same direction. He caused a compilation of the Decretals to be issued, entrusting the work to one Raymond de Pennaforte, who had attained to celebrity as a literary opponent of the Saracens. It is amusing to remark that even this simple work of labour could not be promulgated without the customary embellishments. It was given out that an angel watched over his shoulder all the time he was writing.

*Outbreak of his quarrel with the Pope.*

Meantime an increasing vigilance was maintained against the dangerous results that would necessarily ensue from Frederick's movements. In Rome, many heretics were burned; many condemned to imprisonment for life. The quarrel between the Pope and the Emperor was again resumed; the latter being once more excommunicated, and his body delivered over to Satan for the good of his soul. Again Frederick appealed to all the sovereigns of Christendom. He denounced the pontiff as an unworthy vicar of Christ, "who sits in his court like a merchant, weighing out dispensations for gold,—himself writing and signing the bulls, perhaps counting the money. He has but one cause of enmity against me, that I refused to marry to his niece my natural son Enzio, now King of Sardinia." "In the midst of the Church sits a frantic prophet, a man of falsehood, a polluted priest." To this Gregory replied. The tenor of his answer may be gathered from its commencement: "Out of the sea a beast is arisen, whose name is written all over 'Blasphemy.'" "He falsely asserts that I am enraged at his refusing his consent to the marriage of my niece with his natural son. He lies more impudently when he says that I have pledged my faith to the Lombards." "In truth, this pestilent king maintains, to use his own words, that the world has been deceived by three impostors—Jesus Christ, Moses, and Mohammed; that of these, two died in honour, and the third was hanged on a tree. Even now, he has asserted, distinctly and loudly, that those are fools who aver that God, the Omnipotent Creator of the world, was born of a woman." This was in allusion to the celebrated and mysterious book, 'De Tribus Impostoribus,' in the authorship of which Frederick was accused of having been concerned.

*Who rouses Christendom against him.*

The pontiff had touched the right chord. The begging friars, in all directions, added to the accusations. "He has spoken of the Host as a mummery; he has asked how many gods might be made out of a cornfield; he has affirmed that, if the princes of the world would stand by him, he would easily make for mankind a better faith and a better rule of life; he has laid down the infidel maxim that 'God expects not a man to believe anything that cannot be demonstrated by reason.'" The opinion of Christendom rose against Frederick; its sentiment of piety was shocked. The pontiff proceeded to depose him, and offered his crown to Robert of France. But the Musulman troops of the Emperor were too much for the begging friars of the Pope. His Saracens were marching across Italy in all directions. The pontiff himself would have inevitably fallen into the hands of his mortal enemy had he not found a deliverance in death, A.D. 1241. Frederick had declared that he would not respect his sacred person, but, if victorious, would teach him the absolute supremacy of the temporal power. It was plain that he had no intention of respecting a religion which he had not hesitated to denounce as "a mere absurdity."

*Frederick uses his Saracen troops.*

Whatever may have been the intention of Innocent IV.—who, after the short pontificate of Celestine IV. and an interval, succeeded—he was borne into the same policy by the irresistible force of circumstances. The deadly quarrel with the Emperor was renewed. To escape his wrath, Innocent fled to France, and there in safety called the Council of Lyons. In a sermon, he renewed all the old accusations—the heresy and sacrilege—the peopling of Italian cities with Saracens, for the purpose of overturning the Vicar of Christ with those infidels—the friendship with the Sultan of Egypt—the African courtesans—the perjuries and blasphemies. Then was proclaimed the sentence of excommunication and deposition. The Pope and the bishops inverted the torches they held in their hands until they went out, uttering the malediction, "So may he be extinguished!" Again the Emperor appealed to Europe, but this time in vain. Europe would not forgive him his blasphemy. Misfortunes crowded upon him; his friends forsook him; his favourite son, Enzio, was taken prisoner; and he never smiled again after detecting his intimate, Pietro de Vinea, whom he had raised from beggary, in promising the

*Excommunication of Frederick.*

monks that he would poison him. The day had been carried by a resort to all means, justifiable and unjustifiable, good and evil. For thirty years Frederick had combated the Church and the Guelph party, but he sank in the conflict at last. When Innocent heard of the death of his foe, he might doubtless well think that what he had once asserted had at last become true: "We are no mere mortal man; we have the place of God upon earth." In his address to the clergy of Sicily he exclaimed, "Let the heavens rejoice, and let the earth be glad; for the lightning and tempest wherewith God Almighty has so long menaced your heads have been changed by the death of this man into refreshing zephyrs and fertilizing dews." This is that superhuman vengeance which hesitates not to strike the corpse of a man. Rome never forgives him who has told her of her impostures face to face; she never forgives him who has touched her goods.

*The triumph at his death.*

The Saracenic influences had thus found an expression in the South of France and in Sicily, involving many classes of society, from the Poor Men of Lyons to the Emperor of Germany; but in both places they were overcome by the admirable organization and unscrupulous rigour of the Church. She handled her weapons with singular dexterity, and contrived to extract victory out of humiliation and defeat. As ever since the days of Constantine, she had partisans in every city, in every village, in every family. And now it might have appeared that the blow she had thus delivered was final, and that the world, in contentment, must submit to her will. She had again succeeded in putting her iron heel on the neck of knowledge, and had stamped upon it amid the hatred of Christendom, reviling it as the monstrous but legitimate issue of the detested Mohammedanism.

*Power of the Church at this moment.*

But the fate of men is by no means an indication of the fate of principles. The fall of the Emperor Frederick was not followed by the destruction of the influences he represented. These not only survived him, but were destined, in the end, to overcome the power which had transiently overthrown them. We are now entering on the history of a period which offers to us not only external opposition to the current doctrines, but,

*Vitality of Frederick's principles.*

what is more ominous, internal mutiny. Notwithstanding the awful persecutions in the South of France,—notwithstanding the establishment of auricular confession as a detective means, and the Inquisition as a weapon of punishment,—notwithstanding the influence of the French king, St. Louis, canonized by the grateful Church,—heresy, instead of being extirpated, extended itself among the laity, and even spread among the ecclesiastical ranks. St. Louis, the representative of the hierarchical party, gathers influence only from the circumstance of his relations with the Church, of whose interests he was a fanatical supporter. So far as the affairs of his people were concerned, he can hardly be looked upon as anything better than a simpleton. His reliance for checking the threatened spread of heresy was a resort to violence—the faggot and the sword. In his opinion, " a man ought never to dispute with a misbeliever except with his sword, which he ought to drive into the heretic's entrails as far as he could." It was the signal glory of his reign that he secured for France that inestimable relic, the crown of thorns. This peerless memento of our Saviour's passion he purchased in Constantinople for an immense sum. But France was doubly and enviably enriched; for the Abbey of St. Denis was in possession of another, known to be equally authentic. Besides the crown, he also secured the sponge that was dipped in vinegar; the lance of the Roman soldier; also the swaddling-clothes in which the Saviour had first lain in the manger; the rod of Moses; and part of the skull of John the Baptist. These treasures he deposited in the " Holy Chapel" of Paris.

St. Louis.

His superstition,

Under the Papal auspices, St. Louis determined on a crusade; and nothing, except what we have already mentioned, can better show his mental imbecility than his disregard of all suitable arrangements for it. He thought that, provided the troops could be made to lead a religious life, all would go well; that the Lord would fight his own battles, and that no provisions of a military or worldly kind were needed. In such a pious reliance on the support of God, he reached Egypt with his expedition in June, A.D. 1249. The ever-conspicuous valour of the French troops could maintain itself in the battle-field, but not

And crusade.

His total failure.

against pestilence and famine. In March of the following year, as might have been foreseen, King Louis was the prisoner of the Sultan, and was only spared the indignity of being carried about as a public spectacle in the Mohammedan towns by a ransom, at first fixed at a million of Byzantines, but by the merciful Sultan voluntarily reduced one-fifth. Still, for a time, Louis lingered in the East, apparently stupefied by considering how God could in this manner have abandoned a man who had come to his help. Never was there a crusade with a more shameful end.

*The Inquisition attempts to arrest the intellectual revolt.*

Notwithstanding the support of St. Louis in his own dominions, the intellectual revolt spread in every direction, and that not only in France, but throughout all Catholic Europe. In vain the Inquisition exerted all its terrors: and what could be more terrible than its form of procedure? It sat in secret; no witness, no advocate was present; the accused was simply informed that he was charged with heresy, it was not said by whom. He was made to swear that he would tell the truth as regarded himself, and also respecting other persons, whether parents, children, friends, strangers. If he resisted he was committed to a solitary dungeon, dark and poisonous; his food was diminished; everything was done to drive him into insanity. Then the familiars of the Holy Office, or others in its interests, were by degrees to work upon him to extort confession as to himself or accusations against others. But this fearful tribunal did not fail to draw upon itself the indignation of men. Its victims, condemned for heresy, were perishing in all directions. The usual apparatus of death, the stake and faggots, had become unsuited to its wholesale and remorseless vengeance. The convicts were so numerous as to require pens made of stakes and filled with straw. It was thus that, before the Bishop of Rheims and seventeen other prelates, one hundred and eighty-three heretics, together with their pastor, were burned alive. Such outrages against humanity cannot be perpetrated without bringing in the end a retribution. In other countries the rising indignation was exasperated by local causes; in England, for instance, by the continual intrusion of Italian ecclesiastics into the richest benefices. Some of them were mere boys; many

*Burnings of heretics.*

were non-residents; some had not so much as seen the country from which they drew their ample wealth. The Archbishop of York was excommunicated, with torches and bells, because he would not bestow the abundant revenues of his Church on persons from beyond the Alps; but for all this, "he was blessed by the people." The archbishopric of Canterbury was held, A.D. 1241, by Boniface of Savoy, to whom had been granted by the Pope the first-fruits of all the benefices in his province. His rapacity was boundless. From all the ecclesiastics and ecclesiastical establishments under his control he extorted enormous sums. Some, who, like the Dean of St. Paul's, resisted him, were excommunicated; some, like the aged Subprior of St. Bartholomew's, were knocked down by his own hand. Of a military turn—he often wore a cuirass under his robes—he joined his brother, the Archbishop of Lyons, who was besieging Turin, and wasted the revenues of his see in England in intrigues and petty military enterprises against his enemies in Italy.

Not among the laity alone was there indignation against such a state of things. Mutiny broke out in the ranks of the Church. It was not that among the humbler classes the sentiment of piety had become diminished. The Shepherds, under the leadership of the Master of Hungary, passed by tens of thousands through France to excite the clergy to arouse for the rescue of good King Louis, in bondage to the Mussulmans. They asserted that they were commissioned by the Virgin, and were fed miraculously by the Master. Originating in Italy, the Flagellants also passed, two by two, through every city, scourging themselves for thirty-three days, in memory of the years of the Lord. These dismal enthusiasts emulated each other, and were rivals of the mendicant friars in their hatred of the clergy. The mendicants were beginning to justify that hesitation which Innocent displayed when he was first importuned to authorize them. The Papacy had reaped from these orders much good; it was now to gather a fearful evil. They had come to be learned men instead of ferocious bigots. They were now indeed among the most learned men of their times. They had taken possession of many of the seats of learning.

*Mutiny arising in the Church.*

*The Shepherds and Flagellants.*

In the University of Paris, out of twelve chairs of theology, three only were occupied by the regular clergy. The mendicant friars had entered into the dangerous paths of heresy. They became involved in that fermenting leaven that had come from Spain, and among them revolt broke out.

*The mendicant friars are affected.*

With an unerring instinct, Rome traced the insurrection to its true source. We have only to look at the measures taken by the Popes to understand their opinion. Thus Innocent III., A.D. 1215, regulated, by his legate, the schools of Paris, permitting the study of the Dialectics of Aristotle, but forbidding his physical and metaphysical works and their commentaries. These had come through an Arabic channel. A rescript of Gregory XI., A.D. 1231, interdicts those on natural philosophy until they had been purified by the theologians of the Church. These regulations were confirmed by Clement IV., A.D. 1265.

*Rome prohibits the study of science.*

## CHAPTER XVII.

### THE AGE OF FAITH IN THE WEST—(Continued).

#### OVERTHROW OF THE ITALIAN SYSTEM BY THE COMBINED INTELLECTUAL AND MORAL ATTACK.

ABOUT the close of the twelfth century appeared among the mendicant friars that ominous work, which, under the title of 'The Everlasting Gospel,' struck terror into the Latin hierarchy. It was affirmed that an angel had brought it from heaven, engraven on copper-plates, and had given it to a priest called Cyril, who delivered it to the Abbot Joachim. The abbot had been dead about fifty years, when there was put forth, A.D. 1250, a true exposition of the tendency of his book, under the form of an introduction, by John of Parma, the General of the Franciscans, as was universally suspected or alleged. Notwithstanding its heresy, the work displayed an enlarged and masterly conception of the historical progress of humanity. In this introduction, John of Parma pointed out that the Abbot Joachim, who had not only performed a pilgrimage to the Holy Land, but had been reverenced as a prophet, received as of unimpeachable orthodoxy, and canonized, had accepted as his fundamental position that Roman Christianity had done its work, and had now come to its inevitable termination. He proceeded to show that there are epochs or ages in the Divine government of the world; that, during the Jewish dispensation, it had been under the immediate influence of God the Father; during the Christian dispensation, it had been under that of God the Son; and that the time had now arrived when it would be under the influence of God the Holy Ghost;

*'The Everlasting Gospel.'*

*Introduction to it by the General of the Franciscans.*

that, in the coming ages, there would be no longer any need of faith, but all things would be according to wisdom and reason: it was the ushering-in of a new time. So spake, with needful obscurity, the Abbot Joachim, and so, more plainly, the General of the Franciscans in his Introduction. 'The Everlasting Gospel' was declared by its adherents to have supplanted the New Testament, as that had supplanted the Old—these three books constituting a threefold revelation, answering to the Trinity of the Godhead. At once there was a cry from the whole hierarchy. The Pope, Alexander IV., without delay, took measures for the destruction of the book. Whoever kept or concealed a copy was excommunicate. But among the lower mendicants—the Spiritualists, as they were termed—the work was held in the most devout repute. With them it had taken the place of the Holy Scriptures. So far from being suppressed, it was followed, in about forty years, A.D. 1297, by the Comment on the Apocalypse, by John Peter Oliva, who, in Sicily, had accepted the three epochs or ages, and divided the middle one—the Christian—into seven stages: the age of the Apostles; that of the Martyrs; that of Heresies; that of Hermits; that of the Monastic System; that of the overthrow of Anti-Christ, and that of the coming Millennium. He agreed with his predecessors in the impending abolition of Roman Christianity, stigmatized that Church as the purple harlot, and with them affirmed that the Pope and all his hierarchy had become superfluous and obsolete—" their work was done, their doom sealed." His zealous followers declared that the sacraments of the Church were now all useless, those administering them having no longer any jurisdiction. The burning of thousands of these "Fratricelli" by the Inquisition was altogether inadequate to suppress them. Eventually, when the Reformation occurred, they mingled among the followers of Luther.

To the internal and doctrinal troubles thus befalling the Church, material and foreign ones of the most vital importance were soon added. The true reason of the difficulties into which the Papacy was falling was now coming conspicuously into light. It was absolutely necessary that money should be drawn to Rome, and the sovereigns of the Western kingdoms,

France and England, from which it had hitherto been largely obtained, were determined that it should be so no longer. They themselves had equally urgent need of all that could be extorted. In France, even by St. Louis, it was enacted that the Papal power in the election of the clergy should be restrained; and, complaining of the drain of money from the kingdom to Rome, he applied the effectual remedy of prohibiting any such assessments or taxations for the future.

We have now reached the pontificate of Boniface VIII., an epoch in the intellectual history of Europe. Under the title of Celestine V. a visionary hermit had been raised to the Papacy,—visionary, for Peter Morrone (such was his name) had long been indulged in apparitions of angels and the sounds of phantom bells in the air. Peter was escorted from his cell to his supreme position by admiring crowds; but it very soon became apparent that the life of an anchoret is not a preparation for the duties of a Pope. The conclave of Cardinals had elected him, not from any impression of his suitableness, but because they were evenly balanced in two parties, neither of which would give way. They were therefore driven to a temporary and available election. But scarcely had this been done when his incapacity became conspicuous and his removal imperative. It is said that the friends of Benedetto Gaetani, the ablest of the Cardinals, through a hole perforated in the Pope's chamber wall, at midnight, in a hollow voice, warned him that he retained his dignity at the peril of his soul, and in the name of God commanded him to abdicate. And so, in spite of all importunity, he did. His abdication was considered by many pious men as striking a death-blow at Papal infallibility.

It was during his pontificate that the miracle of Loretto occurred. The house inhabited by the Virgin immediately after her conception had been converted, on the death of the Holy Family, into a chapel, and St. Luke had presented to it an image, carved by his own hands, still known as our Lady of Loretto. Some angels, chancing to be at Nazareth when the Saracen conquerors approached, fearing that the sacred relic might fall into their possession, took the house bodily in their hands, and, carrying it through the air, after several halts, finally deposited it at Loretto in Italy.

*[margin: Peter Morrone is Pope.]*

*[margin: Celestine V. terrified into abdication.]*

*[margin: The miracle of Loretto.]*

## Pope Boniface VIII.

**Boniface VIII.**

So Benedetto Gaetani, whether by such wily procurements or not, became Pope Boniface VIII., A.D. 1294. His election was probably due to King Charles, who held twelve electoral votes, the bitter personal animosity of the Colonnas having been either neutralized or overcome. The first care of Boniface was to consolidate his power and relieve himself of a rival. In the opinion of many it was not possible for a Pope to abdicate. Confinement in prison soon (A.D. 1296) determined that question.

**Ascent of Pope Celestine to heaven.**

The soul of Celestine was seen by a monk ascending the skies, which opened to receive it into heaven; and a splendid funeral informed his enemies that they must now acknowledge Boniface as the unquestioned Pope.

**Quarrel of Boniface and the Colonnas.**

But the princely Colonnas, the leaders of the Ghibelline faction in Rome, who had resisted the abdication of Celestine to the last, and were therefore mortal enemies of Boniface, revolted. He published a bull against them; he excommunicated them. With an ominous anticipation of the future,—for they were familiar with the Papal power, and knew where to touch it to the quick,—they appealed to a "General Council." Since supernatural weapons did not seem to avail, Boniface proclaimed a crusade against them. The issue answered his expectation. Palestrina, one of their strongholds, which in a moment of weakness they had surrendered, was utterly devastated and sown with salt. The Colonnas fled, some of them to France. There, in King Philip the Fair, they found a friend, who was destined to avenge their wrongs, and to inflict on the Papacy a blow from which it never recovered.

**Pecuniary necessities of Rome.**

This was the state of affairs at the commencement of the quarrel between Philip and Boniface. The Crusades had brought all Europe under taxation to Rome, and loud complaints were everywhere made against the drain of money into Italy. Things had at last come to such a condition that it was not possible to continue the Crusades without resorting to taxation of the clergy, and this was the true reason of the eventual lukewarmness, and even opposition to them. But the stream of money that had thus been passing into Italy had engendered habits of luxury and extravagance. Cost what it might, money must be had in Rome. The perennial necessity under

which the kings of England and France found themselves—
the necessity of revenue for the carrying out of their temporal
projects—could only be satisfied in the same way. The wealth
of those nations had insensibly glided into the hands of the
Church. In England, Edward I. compelled the taxation of *The King of England compels the clergy to pay taxes.*
the clergy. They resisted at first, but that sovereign found
an ingenious and effectual remedy. He directed his judges to
hear no cause in which an ecclesiastic was a complainant, but
to try every suit brought against them; asserting that those
who refused to share the burdens of the state had no right to
the protection of its laws. They forthwith submitted. In
the nature and efficacy of this remedy we for the first time
recognize the agency of a class of men soon to rise to power—
the lawyers.

In France, Philip the Fair made a similar attempt. It was *The King of France attempts it.*
not to be supposed that Rome would tolerate this trespassing
on what she considered her proper domain, and accordingly
Boniface issued the bull "*Clericis laicos,*" excommunicating
kings who should levy subsidies on ecclesiastics. Hereupon
Philip determined that, if the French clergy were not tributary to him, France should not be tributary to the Pope, and
issued an edict prohibiting the export of gold and silver from
France without his licence. But he did not resort to these
extreme measures until he had tried others which perhaps he
considered less troublesome. He had plundered the Jews, confiscated their property, and expelled them from his dominions.
The Church was fairly next in order; and, indeed, the mendi- *Is abetted by the mendicant friars,*
cant friars of the lower class, who, as we have seen, were disaffected by the publication of 'The Everlasting Gospel,' were
loud in their denunciations of her wealth, attributing the prevailing religious demoralization to it. They pointed to the
example of our Lord and his disciples; and when their antagonists replied that even He condescended to make use of money, the malignant fanatics maintained their doctrines, amid
the applause of a jeering populace, by answering that it was
not St. Peter, but Judas, who was entrusted with the purse,
and that the Pope stood in need of the bitter rebuke which
Jesus had of old administered to his prototype Peter, saying,

"Get thee behind me, Satan; for thou savourest not of the things that be of God, but of the things that be of men" (Mark viii. 33). Under that authority they affirmed that they might stigmatize the great culprit without guilt. So the king ventured to put forth his hand and touch what the Church had, and she cursed him to his face. At first a literary war ensued: the Pope published his bull, the king his reply. Already the policy which Philip was following, and the ability he was displaying, manifested that he had attached to himself that new power of which the King of England had taken advantage,—a power soon to become the mortal enemy of the ecclesiastic,— the lawyers. In the meantime, money must be had in Rome; when, by the singularly felicitous device of the proclamation of a year of jubilee, A.D. 1300, large sums were again brought into Italy.

*And ably sustained by the lawyers.*

*Device of the jubilee.*

Boniface had thus four antagonists on his hands—the King of France, the Colonnas, the lawyers, and the mendicants. By the latter, both high and low, he was cordially hated. Thus the higher English Franciscans were enraged against him because he refused to let them hold lands. They attempted to bribe him with 40,000 ducats; but he seized the money at the banker's, under the pretence that it had no owners, as the mendicants were vowed to poverty, and then denied the privilege. As to the lower Franciscans, heresy was fast spreading among them. They were not only infected with the doctrines of 'The Everlasting Gospel,' but had even descended into the abyss of irreligion one step more, by placing St. Francis in the stead of our Saviour. They were incessantly repeating in the ears of the laity that the Pope was Anti-Christ, "the Man of Sin." The quarrel between Philip and Boniface was every moment increasing in bitterness. The former seized and imprisoned a Papal nuncio, who had been selected because he was known to be personally offensive; the latter retaliated by the issue of bulls protesting against such an outrage, interfering between the king and his French clergy, and citing the latter to appear in Rome and take cognizance of their master's misdoings. The monarch was actually invited to be present and hear his own doom. In the lesser bull—if it be authentic—

*The four enemies of Boniface.*

*Collision between the French king and the Pope.*

and the king's rejoinder, both parties seem to have lost their
temper. This was followed by the celebrated bull *"Ausculta* — The bull
*Fili,"* at which the king's indignation knew no bounds. He *Fili."*
had it publicly burned in Paris at the sound of a trumpet;
assembled the States-General; and, under the advice of his
lawyers, skilfully brought the issue to this: Does the king
hold the realm of France of God or of the Pope? Without
difficulty it might be seen how the French clergy would be
compelled to act; since many of them held fiefs of the king,
all were in fear of the intrusion of Italian ecclesiastics into the
rich benefices. France, therefore, supported her monarch. On
his side, Boniface, in the bull *" Unam sanctam,"* asserted his — The bull
power by declaring that it is necessary to salvation to believe *sanctam."*
that "every human being is subject to the pontiff of Rome."
Philip, foreseeing the desperate nature of the approaching conflict, and aiming to attach his people firmly to him by putting himself forth as their protector against priestly tyranny,
again skilfully appealed to their sentiments by denouncing the
Inquisition as an atrocious barbarity, an outrage on human
rights, violating all law, resorting to new and unheard-of tortures, and doing deeds at which men's minds revolt with horror. In the South of France this language was thoroughly
understood. The lawyers, among whom William de Nogaret — William de
was conspicuous, ably assisted him; indeed, his whole move- Nogaret.
ment exhibited the extraordinary intelligence of his advisers.
It has been affirmed, and is perhaps not untrue, that De
Nogaret's father had been burned by the Inquisition. The
great lawyer was bent on revenge. The States-General, under — Action of
his suggestions, entertained four propositions:—1. That Boni- the States-General.
face was not the true Pope; 2. That he was a heretic; 3.
That he was a simoniac; 4. That he was a man weighed down
with crimes. De Nogaret, learning from the Colonnas how to
touch the Papacy in a vital point, demanded that the whole
subject should be referred to a "General Council," to be summoned by the king. A second meeting of the States-General
was held. William de Plaisian, the Lord of Vezenoble, ap- — Accusations
peared with charges against the Pope. Out of a long list, Pope.
many of which could not possibly be true, some may be men-

tioned:—that Boniface believed neither in the immortality nor incorruptibility of the soul, nor in a life to come, nor in the real presence in the Eucharist; that he did not observe the fasts of the Church—not even Lent; that he spoke of the cardinals, monks, and friars as hypocrites; that the Holy Land had been lost through his fault; that the subsidies for its relief had been embezzled by him; that his holy predecessor, Celestine, through his inhumanity had been brought to death; that he had said that fornication and other obscene practices were no sin; that he was a sodomite, and had caused clerks to be murdered in his presence; that he had enriched himself by simony; that his nephew's wife had borne him two illegitimate sons. These, with other still more revolting charges, were sworn to upon the Holy Gospels. The king appealed to a "General Council and to a legitimate Pope."

The quarrel had now become a mortal one. There was but one course for Boniface to take, and he took it. He excommunicated the king. He deprived him of his throne, and anathematized his posterity to the fourth generation. The bull was to be suspended in the porch of the Cathedral of Anagni on September 8; but William de Nogaret and one of the Colonnas had already passed into Italy. They hired a troop of banditti, and on September 7th attacked the pontiff in his palace at Anagni. The doors of a church which protected him were strong, but they yielded to fire. The brave old man, in his pontifical robes, with his crucifix in one hand and the keys of St. Peter in the other, sat down on his throne and confronted his assailants: his cardinals had fled through a sewer. So little reverence was there for God's vicar upon earth, that Sciarra Colonna raised his hand to kill him on the spot; but the blow was arrested by De Nogaret, who, with a bitter taunt, told him that here, in his own city, he owed his life to the mercy of a servant of the King of France—a servant whose father had been burned by the Inquisition. The pontiff was spared only to be placed on a miserable horse, with his face to the tail, and led off to prison. They meant to transport him to France to await the General Council. He was rescued, returned to Rome, was seized and imprisoned again. On the 11th of October he was dead.

*His seizure by De Nogaret, and his death.*

Thus, after a pontificate of nine eventful years, perished Boniface VIII. His history and his fate show to what a gulf Roman Christianity was approaching. His successor, Benedict XI., had but a brief enjoyment of power; long enough, however, to learn that the hatred of the King of France had not died with the death of Boniface, and that he was determined not only to pursue the departed pontiff's memory beyond the grave, but also to effect a radical change in the Papacy itself. A basket of figs was presented to Benedict by a veiled female. She had brought them, she said, from the Abbess of St. Petronilla. In an unguarded moment the pontiff ate of them without the customary precaution of having them previously tasted. Alas! what was the state of morals in Italy! A dysentery came on; in a few days he was dead. But the Colonnas had already taught the King of France how one should work who desires to touch the popedom; the event that had just occurred was the preparation for putting their advice into operation. The king came to an understanding with Bernard de Goth, the Archbishop of Bordeaux. Six conditions were arranged between them:—1. The reconciliation between the Church and the king; 2. The absolution of all persons engaged in the affair of Boniface; 3. Tenths from the clergy for five years; 4. The condemnation of the memory of Boniface; 5. The restoration of the Colonnas; 6. A secret article; what it was time soon showed. A swift messenger carried intelligence to the king's partisans in the College of Cardinals, and Bernard became Clement V. "It will be long before we see the face of another Pope in Rome!" exclaimed the Cardinal Matteo Orsini, with a prophetic instinct of what was coming when the conspiracy reached its developement. His prophecy was only too true. Now appeared what was that sixth, that secret article negotiated between King Philip and De Goth. Clement took up his residence at Avignon, in France. The tomb of the Apostles was abandoned. The Eternal City had ceased to be the metropolis of Christianity.

*Poisoning of Benedict XI.*

*Understanding between the king and the Archbishop of Bordeaux.*

*Removal of the Papacy to Avignon.*

But a French prelate had not bargained with a French king for the most eminent dignity to which a European can aspire without having given an equivalent. In as good faith as he could to his contract, in as good faith as he could to his present pre-eminent position, Clement V. proceeded to discharge his share of the obligation. To a certain extent King Philip was animated by an undying vengeance against his enemy, whom he considered as having escaped out of his grasp, but he was also actuated by a sincere desire of accomplishing a reform in the Church through a radical change in its constitution. He was resolved that the pontiffs should be accountable to the kings of France, or that France should more directly influence their conduct. To reconcile men to this, it was for him to show, with the semblance of pious reluctance, what was the state to which morals and faith had come in Rome. The trial of the dead Boniface was therefore entered upon, A.D. 1310. The Consistory was opened at Avignon, March 18. The proceedings occupied many months; many witnesses were examined. The main points attempted to be established by their evidence seem to have been these:—" That Boniface had declared his belief that there was no such thing as divine law—what was reputed to be such was merely the invention of men to keep the vulgar in awe by the terrors of eternal punishment; that it was a falsehood to assert the Trinity, and fatuous to believe it; that it was falsehood to say that a virgin had brought forth, for it was an impossibility; that it was falsehood to assert that bread is transubstantiated into the body of Christ; that Christianity is false, because it asserts a future life, of which there is no evidence save that of visionary people." It was in evidence that the Pope had said, " God may do the worst with me that he pleases in the future life; I believe as every educated man does, the vulgar believe otherwise. We have to speak as they do, but we must believe and think with the few." It was sworn to by those who had heard him disputing with some Parisians that he had maintained " that neither the body nor the soul rose again." Others testified that " he neither believed in the resurrection nor in the sacraments of the Church, and had denied that carnal gratifications are sins." The Primicerio of St. John's at Naples deposed that, when a cardinal, Boniface had said in his presence, " So that God gives me the good things of this life, I

care not a bean for that to come. A man has no more a soul
than a beast. Did you ever see any one who had arisen from
the dead?" He took delight in deriding the blessed Virgin;
"for," said he, "she was no more a virgin than my mother."
As to the presence of Christ in the Host, "it is nothing but
paste." Three knights of Lucca testified that when certain
venerable ambassadors, whose names they gave, were in the
presence of the Pope at the time of the jubilee, and a chaplain happened to invoke the mercy of Jesus on a person
recently dead, Boniface appalled all around by exclaiming,
"What a fool, to commend him to Christ! He could not
help himself, and how can he be expected to help others? He
was no Son of God, but a shrewd man and a great hypocrite."
It might seem impossible to exceed such blasphemy; and yet
the witnesses went on to testify to a conversation which he
held with the brave old Sicilian admiral, Roger Loria. This
devout sailor made the remark, in the Pope's presence, that if,
on a certain occasion, he had died, it was his trust that Christ
would have had mercy on him. To this Boniface replied,
"Christ! he was no Son of God; he was a man, eating and
drinking like ourselves; he never rose from the dead; no man
has ever risen. I am far mightier than he. I can bestow
kingdoms and humble kings." Other witnesses deposed to
having heard him affirm, "There is no harm in simony. There
is no more harm in adultery than in rubbing one's hands together." Some testified to such immoralities and lewdness in
his private life that the pages of a modern book cannot be
soiled with the recital.

In the meantime, Clement did all in his power to save the blackened memory of his predecessor. Every influence that could be brought to bear on the revengeful or politic king was resorted to, and at last with success. Perhaps Philip saw that he had fully accomplished his object. He had no design to destroy the Papacy; his aim was to revolutionize it,—to give to the kings of France a more thorough control over it; and, for the accomplishment of that purpose, to demonstrate to what a condition it had come through the present system. Whatever might be the decision, such evidence had been brought

*Philip con-
sents to ab-
stain from
the prose-
cution.*

forward as, notwithstanding its contradictions and apparent inconsistencies, had made a profound impression on every thinking man. It was the king's consummate policy to let the matter remain where it was. Accordingly, he abandoned all further action. The gratitude of Clement was expressed in a bull exalting Philip, attributing his action to piety, exempting him from all blame, annulling past bulls prejudicial to him, revoking all punishments of those who had been concerned against Boniface except fifteen persons, on whom a light and nominal penance was inflicted. In November, A.D. 1311, the Council of Vienne met. In the following year three Cardinals appeared before it to defend the orthodoxy and holy life of Pope Boniface. Two knights threw down their gauntlets to maintain his innocence by wager of battle. There was no accuser; no one took up the gage; and the council was at liberty quietly to dispose of the matter.

*The religious condition of Pope Boniface.*

How far the departed pontiff was guilty of the charges alleged against him was, therefore, never fairly ascertained. But it was a tremendous, an appalling fact, that charges of such a character could be even so much as brought forward, much more that a succeeding pontiff had to listen to them, and attribute intentions of piety to the accuser. The immoralities of which Boniface was accused were such as in Italy did not excite the same indignation as among the more moral people beyond the Alps; the heresies were those everywhere pervading the Church. We have already seen what a profound impression 'The Everlasting Gospel' had made, and how many followers and martyrs it had. What was alleged against Boniface was only that he had taken one step more in the downward course of irreligion. His fault lay in this, that in an evil hour he had given expression to thoughts which, considering his position, ought to have remained locked up in his inmost soul. As to the rest, if he was avaricious and accumulated enormous treasures, such as it was said the banditti of the Colonnas seized when they outraged his person, he was no worse than many other Popes. Clement V., his successor, died enormously rich; and, what was worse, did not hesitate to scandalize Europe by his prodigal munificence to the beautiful Brunisard, the Countess of Talleyrand, his lady.

The religious condition of Boniface, though not admitting of apology, is capable of explanation. By the Crusades all Europe had been wrought up to a fanatical expectation, doomed necessarily to disappointment. From them the Papacy had derived prodigious advantages both in money and power. It was now to experience fearful evils. It had largely promised rewards in this life, and also in the world to come, to those who would take up the Cross; it had deliberately pitted Christianity against Mohammedanism, and staked the authenticity of each on the issue of the conflict. In the face of the whole world it had put forth as the true criterion the possession of the holy places, hallowed by the life, the sufferings, the death, the resurrection of the Redeemer. Whatever the result might be, the circumstances under which this had been done were such that there was no concealing, no dissembling. In all Europe there was not a family which had not been pecuniarily involved in the Crusades, perhaps not one which had not furnished men. Was it at all to be wondered at that everywhere the people, accustomed to the logic of trial by battle, were terror-stricken when they saw the result? Was it to be wondered at that even still more dreadful heresies spontaneously suggested themselves? Was it at all extraordinary that, if there had been Popes sincerely accepting that criterion, the issue should be a Pope who was a sincere misbeliever? Was it extraordinary that there should be a loss of Papal prestige? It was the Papacy which had voluntarily, for its own ends, brought things into this evil channel, and the Papacy deserved a just retribution of discredit and ruin. It had wrought on the devout temper of religious Europe for its own sinister purposes; it had drained the Continent of its blood, and perhaps of what was more highly prized—its money; it had established a false issue, an unwarrantable criterion, and now came the time for it to reap consequences of a different kind —intellectual revolt among the people, heresy among the clergy. Nor was the Pope without eminent comrades in his sin. The Templars, whose duty it had been to protect pilgrims on the way to Jerusalem—who had therefore been long and thoroughly familiar with the state of events in Palestine—had been treading in the same path as the Pope. Dark rumours had begun to circulate throughout Europe that these, the very vanguard of Christianity, had not only proved traitors to their banner, but had actually become Mohammedanized. On their expulsion from the Holy Land, at the close of the Crusades, they spread all over Europe, to disseminate by stealth their fearful heresies, and to enjoy the riches they had acquired in the service they had betrayed. Men find a charm in having it mysteriously and secretly divulged to them that their long-cherished opinions are all a delusion. There was something fascinating in hearing privately, from those who could speak with authority, that, after all, Mohammed was not an impostor, but the author of a pure and noble Theism; that Saladin was not a treacherous assassin, a despicable liar, but a most valiant, courteous, and gentle knight. In his proceedings against the Templars, King Philip the Fair seems to have been animated by a pure intention of checking the disastrous spread of their opinions; yet William de Nogaret, who was his chief adviser on this matter as on that of Boniface, was not without reasons of personal hatred. It was said that he divided his wrath between the Templars and the Pope. They had had some connection with the burning of his father, and vengeance he was resolved to wreak upon them. Under colour of the charges against them, all the Templars in France were simultaneously arrested in the dawn of one day, October 13, A.D. 1807, so well devised were the measures. The Grand Master, Du Molay, was secured, not however without some perfidy. Now were openly brought forward the charges which struck Europe with consternation. Substantiation of them was offered by witnesses, but it was secured by submitting the accused to torture. The Grand Master, Du Molay, at first admitted their guilt of the accusations alleged. After some hesitation, the Pope issued a bull, commanding the King of England to do what the King of France had already done, to arrest the Templars and seize their property. His declaration, that one of the order, a man of high birth, had confessed to himself his criminality, seems to have made a profound im-

*They are arrested and tried.*

pression on the mind of the English king, and of many other persons until that time reluctant to believe. The Parliament and the University of Paris expressed themselves satisfied with the evidence. New examinations were held, and new convictions were made. The Pope issued a bull addressed to all Christendom, declaring how slowly, but, alas! how certainly, he had been compelled to believe in the apostasy of the order, and commanding that everywhere proceedings should be instituted against it. A Papal commission assembled in Paris, August 7, A.D. 1309. The Grand Master was had before it. He professed his belief in the Catholic faith, but now denied that the order was guilty of the charges alleged against it, as also did many of the other knights. Other witnesses were, however, brought forward, some of whom pretended to have abandoned the order on account of its foul acts. At the Porte St. Antoine, on many pleasant evenings in the following May, William de Nogaret revelled in the luxury of avenging the shade of his father. One hundred and thirteen Templars were, in slow succession, burned at stakes. The remorseless lawyer was repaying the Church in her own coin. Yet of this vast concourse of sufferers all died protesting their innocence; not one proved an apostate. Notwithstanding this most significant fact—for those who were ready to lay down their lives, and to meet with unshaken constancy the fire, were surely the bravest of the knights, and their dying declaration is worthy of our most reverent consideration—things were such, that no other course was possible than the abolition of the order, and this accordingly took place. The Pope himself seems to have been satisfied that the crimes had been perpetrated under the instigation or temptation of Satan; but men of more enlarged views appear to have concluded that, though the Templars were innocent of the moral abominations charged against them, a familiarity with other forms of belief in the East had undoubtedly sapped their faith. After a weary imprisonment of six years, embittered by many hardships, the Grand Master, Du Molay, was brought up for sentence. He had been found guilty. With his dying breath, " before heaven and earth, on the verge of death, when the least false-

*Found guilty and punished.*

*Burning of Du Molay.* hood bears like an intolerable weight on the soul," he declared the innocence of the order and of himself. The vesper-bell was sounding when Du Molay and a brother convict were led forth to their stakes, placed on an island in the Seine. King Philip himself was present. As the smoke and flames enveloped them, they continued to affirm their innocence. Some averred that forth from the fire Du Molay's voice sounded, "Clement! thou wicked and false judge, I summon thee to meet me within forty days at the bar of God." Some said that he also summoned the king. In the following year King Philip the Fair and Pope Clement the Fifth were both dead.

John XXII., elected after an interval of more than two years spent in rivalries and intrigues between the French and Italian Cardinals, continued the residence at Avignon. His movements took a practical turn in the commencement of a process for the recovery of the treasures of Clement from the Viscount de Lomenie. This was only a part of the wealth of the deceased Pope, but it amounted to a million and three quarters of florins of gold. The Inquisition was kept actively at work for the extermination of the believers in 'The Everlasting Gospel,' and the remnant of the Albigenses and Waldenses. But all this had no other result than that which eventually occurred—an examination of the authenticity and rightfulness of the Papal power. With an instinct as to the origin of the misbelief everywhere spreading, the Pope published bulls against the Jews, of whom a bloody persecution had arisen, and ordered that all their Talmuds and other blasphemous books should be burned. *Marsilio's work, 'The Defender of Peace.'* A physician, Marsilio of Padua, published a work, 'The Defender of Peace.' It was a philosophical examination of the principles of government, and of the nature and limits of the sacerdotal power. Its democratic tendency was displayed by its demonstration that the exposition of the law of Christianity rests not with the Pope nor any other priest, but with a general council; it rejected the Papal political pretensions; asserted that no one can be rightfully excommunicated by the Pope alone, and that he has no power of coercion over human thought; that the civil immunities of the clergy ought to be ended; that poverty and humility ought alone to be their characteristics; that society ought to provide them with a decent sustenance, but nothing more: their pomp, extravagance, luxury, and usurpations, especially that of tithes, should be abrogated; that neither Christ nor the Scriptures ever gave St. Peter a supremacy over the other Apostles; that, if history was to be consulted, St. Paul, and not St. Peter, was bishop of Rome—indeed, it was doubtful whether the latter was ever in that city, the Acts of the Apostles being silent on that subject. From these and many other such arguments he drew forty-one conclusions adverse to the political and ecclesiastical supremacy of the Pope.

It is not necessary to consider here the relations of John XXII. with Louis of Bavaria, nor of the antipope Nicholas; they belong merely to political history. But, as if to show how the intellectual movement was working its way, the Pontiff himself did not escape a charge of heresy. Though he had so much of temporal affairs upon his hands, John did not hesitate to raise the great question of the "beatific vision." In his opinion, the dead, even the saints, do not enjoy the beatific vision of God until after the judgment-day. At once there was a demand among the orthodox, "What! do not the Apostles, John, Peter, nay, even the blessed Virgin, stand yet in the presence of God?" The Pope directed the most learned theologians to examine the question, himself entering actively into the dispute. The University of Paris was involved. The King of France declared that his realm should not be polluted with such heretical doctrines. A single sentence explains the practical direction of the dogma, so far as the interests of the Church were concerned: "If the saints stand not in the presence of God, of what use is their intercession? What is the use of addressing prayers to them?" The folly of the Pontiff perhaps might be excused by his age. He was now nearly ninety years old. That he had not guided himself according to the prevailing sentiment of the lower religious orders, who thought that poverty was essential to salvation, appeared at his death, A.D. 1334. He left eighteen millions of gold florins in specie, and seven millions in plate and jewels.

His successor, Benedict XII., disposed of the question of the "beatific vision;" "It is only those saints who do not pass through Purgatory that immediately behold the Godhead." The pontificate of Benedict, which was not without many good features, hardly verified the expression with which he greeted the Cardinals when they elected him, "You have chosen an ass." His was a gay life. There is a tradition that to him is due the origin of the proverb, "As drunk as a Pope."

*Voluptuousness of Avignon.*

In the subsequent pontificate of Clement VI., A.D. 1342, the court at Avignon became the most voluptuous in Christendom. It was crowded with knights and ladies, painters and other artists. It exhibited a day-dream of equipages and banquets. The pontiff himself delighted in female society, but, in his weakness, permitted his lady, the Countess of Turenne, to extort enormous revenues by the sale of ecclesiastical promotions. Petrarch, who lived at Avignon at this time, speaks of it as a vast brothel. His own sister had been seduced by the holy father John XXII. During all these years the Romans had made repeated attempts to force back the Papal court to their city. With its departure all their profits had gone. But the fatal policy of electing Frenchmen into the College of Cardinals seemed to shut out every hope. The unscrupulous manner in which this was done is illustrated by the fact that Clement made one of his relatives, a lad of eighteen, a Cardinal.

*Rienzi.*

For a time the brief glories of Rienzi cast a flickering ray on Rome; but Rienzi was only a demagogue—an impostor. It was the deep impression made upon Europe that the residence at Avignon was an abandonment of the tomb of St. Peter, that compelled Urban V. to return to Rome. This determination was strengthened by a desire to escape out of the power of the kings of France, and to avoid the free companies, who had learned to extort bribes for sparing Avignon from plunder. He left Avignon, A.D. 1367, amid the reluctant grief of his Cardinals, torn from that gay and dissipated city, and in dread of the recollections and of the populace of Rome. And well it might be so; for not only in Rome, but all over Italy, piety was held in no respect, and the discipline of the Church in derision. When Urban sent to Barnabas Visconti, who was raising trouble in Tuscany, a bull of excommunication by the hands of two legates, Barnabas actually compelled them, in his presence, to eat the parchment on which the bull was written, together with the leaden seal and the silken string, and telling them that he hoped it would sit as lightly on their stomachs as it did on his, sent them back to their master! In a little time—it was but two years—absence from France became insupportable; the Pope returned to Avignon, and there died. It was reserved for his successor, Gregory XI., finally to end what was termed, from its seventy years' duration, the Babylonish captivity, and restore the Papacy to the Eternal City, A.D. 1376. *Irreverence of Barnabas Visconti. The Pope's return to Rome.*

But, though the Popes had thus returned to Rome, the effects of King Philip's policy still continued. On the death of Gregory XI., the conclave, meeting at Rome—for the conclave must meet where the Pope dies—elected Urban VI., under intimidation of the Roman populace, who were determined to retain the Papacy in their city; but, escaping away to Fondi, and repenting what they had thus done, they proclaimed his election void, and substituted Clement VII. for him. They were actually at one time on the point of choosing the King of France as Pope. Thus began the great schism. It was, in reality, a struggle between France and Italy for the control of the Papacy. The former had enjoyed it for seventy years; the latter was determined to recover it. The schism thus rested originally on political considerations, but these were doubtless exasperated by the conduct of Urban, whose course was overbearing, and even intolerable to his supporters. Nor did he amend as his position became more consolidated. In A.D. 1385, suspecting his Cardinals of an intention to seize him, declare him a heretic, and burn him, he submitted several of them to the torture in his own presence, while he recited his breviary. Escaping from Nocera, where he had been besieged, he caused the Bishop of Aquila to be killed on the roadside. Others he tied in sacks, and threw them into the sea at Genoa. It was supposed, not without reason, that he was insane. *Causes of the great schism.*

If there had been formerly pecuniary difficulty in support-

**Pecuniary necessities of the rival Popes.**

ing one Papal court, it of course became greater now that there were two. Such troubles, every day increasing, led at length to inauspicious political movements. There was an absolute necessity for drawing money to Rome, and also to Avignon. The device of a jubilee was too transitory and inadequate, even though, by an improvement in the theory of that festival, it was expedited by thirty-three years, answering to our Saviour's life. At Avignon, the difficulty of Clement, who was of amiable and polished manners, turned on the French Church being obliged to support him; and it is not to be wondered at that the French clergy looked with dislike on the pontifical establishment among them, since it was driven by its necessities to prey on all their best benefices. Under such circumstances, no other course was possible to the rival Popes and their successors than a thorough reorganization of the Papal financial system—the more complete developement of simony, indulgences, and other improper sources of emolument. In this matter Boniface IX. tripled the value of the annats upon the Papal books. Usurers or brokers, intervening between the purchasers of benefices and the Papal exchequer, were established; and it is said that, under the pressing difficulties of the case, benefices were known to have been sold, many times in succession, to different claimants in one week. Late applicants might obtain a preference for appointments on making a cash payment of twenty-five florins; an increased preference might be had for fifty. It became, at last, no unusual thing to write to kings and prelates for subsidies—a proof how greatly the Papacy had been weakened by the events of the times.

**Organisation of simony.**

**Indignation of religious Europe.**

But religious Europe could not bear with such increasing scandals. The rival Popes were incessantly accusing each other of falsehood and all manner of wickedness. At length the public sentiment found its expression in the Council of Pisa, called by the Cardinals on their own responsibility. This council summoned the two Popes—Benedict XIII. and Gregory XII.—before it, declared the crimes and excesses imputed to them to be true, and deposed them both, appointing in their stead Alexander V. There were now, therefore, three

Popes. But, besides thus rendering the position of things worse than it was before in this respect, the Council had taken the still more extraordinary step of overthrowing the autocracy of the Pope. It had been compelled by the force of circumstances to destroy the very foundation of Latin Christianity by assuming the position of superiority over the vicar of Christ. Now might be discerned by men of reflection the purely human nature of the Papacy. It had broken down. Out of the theological disputes of preceding years a political principle was obviously emerging; the democratic spirit was developing itself, and the hierarchy was in rebellion against its sovereign.

*Three Popes.*

Nor was this great movement limited to the clergy. In every direction the laity participated in it, pecuniary questions being in very many instances the incentive. Things had come to such a condition that it seemed to be of little moment what might be the personal character of the pontiff; the necessities of the position irresistibly drove him to replenish the treasury by shameful means. Thus, on Alexander's death, Balthazar Cossa, an evil but an able man, who succeeded as John XXIII., was not only compelled to extend the existing simoniacal practices of the ecclesiastical brokers' offices, but actually to derive revenue from the licensing of prostitutes, gambling-houses, and usurers. In England, for ages a mine of wealth to Rome, the tendency of things was shown by such facts as the remonstrance of the Commons with the Crown on the appointment of ecclesiastics to all the great offices; the allegations made by the "Good Parliament" as to the amount of money drawn by Rome from the kingdom. They asserted that it was five times as much as the taxes levied by the king, and that the Pope's revenue from England was greater than the revenue of any prince in Christendom. It was shown again by such facts as the passage of the statutes of Mortmain, Provisors, and Præmunire, and by the universal clamour against the mendicant orders. This dissatisfaction with the clergy was accompanied by a desire for knowledge. Thousands of persons crowded to the universities both on the Continent and in England. In a community thus well prepared, Wickliffe found no difficulty in disseminating his views. He had adopted

*Balthazar Cossa made Pope.*

*Dissatisfaction in England.*

*Wickliffe, the English reformer.*

in many particulars the doctrines of Berengar. He taught that the bread in the Eucharist is not the real body of Christ, but only its image; that the Roman Church has no true claim to headship over other churches; that its bishop has no more authority than any other bishop; that it is right to deprive a delinquent church of temporal possessions; that no bishop ought to have prisons for the punishment of those obnoxious to him; and that the Bible alone is a sufficient guide for a Christian man.

*He translates the Bible.*

His translation of the Bible into English was the practical carrying out of that assertion for the benefit of his own countrymen. All classes of society were becoming infected. The government for a season vacillated. It was said that every other man in England was a Lollard. The Lollards were Wickliffites. But the Church at last persuaded the government to let her try her hand, and the statute "de hæretico comburendo" was passed, A.D 1400. William Sautree,

*Burning of English heretics.*

a priest who had turned Wickliffite, was the first English martyr. John Badbee, a tailor, who denied transubstantiation— accused of having said that, if it were true, there were 20,000 gods in every corn-field in England—next suffered in like manner at the stake, in presence of the Prince of Wales. Lord Cobham, the head of the Lollards, who had denounced the Pope as Anti-Christ, the Son of Perdition, was imprisoned; but escaping, became involved in political movements, and suffered at length the double penalty for heresy and treason, being hung on a gallows with a fire blazing at his feet. It is interesting to remark the social rank of these three early martyrs. Heresy was pervading all classes, from the lowest to the highest.

*The Council of Constance depose the Pope.*

The Council of Constance met A.D. 1413. It had a threefold object:—1. The union of the Church under one Pope; 2. The reformation of the clergy; 3. The suppression of heresy. Its policy from the first was determined. It proclaimed itself supreme. It demanded the abdication of the Pope, John XXIII.; exhibited articles of accusation against him, some of them of such enormity as almost to pass belief, and justifying the epithet that he was "a devil incarnate." The suffrage of the council was changed. The plan of voting by nations, which reduced the Italians to a single vote, was introduced. These incidental facts may indicate to us that there were present men who understood thoroughly how to manage the machinery of such an assembly, and that the remark of Æneas Sylvius, afterward Pope Pius II., respecting the Council of Basle was equally true as to that of Constance, that it was not so much directed by the Holy Ghost as by the passions of men. The influence that lawyers were now exercising in social affairs—their habits of arrangement, of business, and intrigue—is strikingly manifested in the management of these assemblages; their arts had passed to the clergy, and even in part to the people. But how vast was the change that had occurred in the Papacy from the voluntary abdication of Celestine to the compulsory abdication of John!

To this council, also, came John Huss, under a safe-conduct from the Emperor Sigismund. Scarcely, however, had he arrived when he was imprisoned, this treachery being excused from the necessity of conceding it to the reforming party. On June 5th, A.D. 1410, Huss was brought in chains before the council. It was declared unlawful to keep faith with a heretic. His countrymen, the Bohemian lords present, protested against such perfidy, and loudly demanded his release. Articles of accusation, derived from his works, were presented. He avowed himself ready to defend his opinions. The uproar was so great that the council temporarily adjourned. Two days after, the trial was resumed. It was ushered in by an eclipse of the sun, said to have been total at Prague. No one of the bloodthirsty ecclesiastics laid to heart the solemn monition that, after his moment of greatest darkness was over, the sun shone forth with recovered effulgence again. The emperor was present, with all the fathers. The first accusation entered on related to transubstantiation. On this and on succeeding occasions the emperor took part in the discussions, among other things observing that, in his opinion, the prisoner was worthy of death. After a lengthy inquiry into his alleged errors, a form of recantation was prepared for Huss. With a modest firmness he declined it, concluding his noble answer with the words, " I appeal to Christ Jesus, the one all-powerful and all-just Judge.

*Arrest and murder of John Huss.*

*Noble conduct of Huss.*

To him I commend my cause, who will judge every man, not according to false witnesses and erring councils, but according to truth and man's desert." On July 1st the council met in full session. Thirty articles against Huss were read. Among other things, they alleged that he believed the material bread to be unchanged after the consecration. In his extremity the prisoner looked steadfastly at the traitor Sigismund, and solemnly exclaimed, "Freely came I here under the safe-conduct of the emperor." The conscience-stricken monarch blushed. Huss was then made to kneel down and receive his sentence. It condemned his writings and his body to the flames.

He was then degraded and despoiled of his orders. Some of the bishops mocked at him; some, more merciful, implored him to recant. They cut his hair in the form of a cross, and set upon his head a high paper crown on which devils were painted. "We devote thy soul to the devils in hell."—"And I commend my soul to the most merciful Lord Christ Jesus." He was then led forth. They passed by the bishop's palace, where Huss's books were burning. As they tied him with a piece of chain to his stake, the painted crown fell off, but the soldiers replaced it. "Let him and his devils be burned together." As the flames closed over him, he chanted psalms and prayed to the Redeemer. Can that be true which requires for its support the murder of a true man?

So acted, without a dissenting voice, the Council of Constance. It feared the spread of heresy, but it did not fear, perhaps did not consider, that higher tribunal to whose inexorable verdict councils and Popes and emperors must submit,—posterity. It asserted itself to be under the inspiration of the Holy Ghost. It took profit by a shameful perfidy. It was a conclave of murderers. It stifled the voice of an earnest man, solemnly protesting against a doctrine now derided by all Europe. The revolution it was compassing it inaugurated in blood, not alone that of John Huss, but also of Jerome of Prague. These martyrs were no common men. Poggio Bracciolini, an eye-witness, says, in a letter to Leonardo Aretino, speaking of the eloquence of Jerome, "When I consider what

*It murders, also, Jerome of Prague.*

his choice of words was, what his elocution, what his reasoning, what his countenance, his voice, his action, I must affirm, however much we may admire the ancients, that in such a cause no one could have approached nearer to the model of their eloquence."

*His singular eloquence.*

John XXIII. was compelled to abdicate. Gregory XII. died. Some time after, Benedict XIII. followed him. The council had elected Martin V., and in him found a master who soon put an end to its attempts. It had deposed one Pope and elected another; it had cemented the dominant creed with blood; it had authorized the dreadful doctrine that a difference in religious opinion justifies the breaking of plighted faith between man and man; it had attempted to perpetuate its own power by enacting that councils should be held every five years; but it had not accomplished its great object—ecclesiastical reform.

*What the council did.*

In a room attached to the Cathedral of Basle, with its roof of green and party-coloured tiles, the modern traveller reads on a piece of paper this inscription: "The room of the council where the famous Council of Basil was assembled. In this room Pope Eugene IV. was dethroned, and replaced by Felix V., Duke of Savoy and Cardinal of Repaile. The council began 1431, and lasted 1448." That chamber, with its floor of little red earthen flags and its oaken ceiling, witnessed great events.

*The Council of Basle.*

The democratic influence pervading the Church showed no symptoms of abatement. The fate of Huss had been avenged in blood and fire by the Bohemian sword. Eugenius IV., now pontiff, was afraid that negotiations would be entered upon with the Hussite chiefs. Such a treaty, he affirmed, would be blasphemy against God and an insult to the Pope. He was therefore bent on the prorogation of the council, and spared no means to accomplish his purpose. Its ostensible object was the reformation of the clergy; its real intent was to convert the Papal autocracy into a constitutional monarchy. To this end it cited the Pope, and, on his non-appearance, declared him and seventeen of the Cardinals in contumacy. He had denounced it as the Synagogue of Satan; on its part, it was assuming the functions of the Senate of Christendom. It had

*It declares the Pope in contumacy.*

prepared a great seal, and asserted that, in case of the death of the Pope, the election of his successor was vested in it. It was its firm purpose never again to leave that great event in the hands of a conclave of intriguing Italian Cardinals, but to entrust it to the representatives of united Christendom. After a due delay since he was declared in contumacy, the council suspended the Pope, and, slowly moving toward its object, elected Amadeus of Savoy, Felix V., his successor. It was necessary that its Pope should be a rich man, for the council had but slender means of offering him pecuniary support. Amadeus had that qualification. And perhaps it was far from being, in the eyes of many, an inopportune circumstance that he had been married and had children. We may discern, through the shifting scenes of the intrigues of the times, that the German hierarchy had come to the resolution that the election of the Pope should be taken from the Italians and given to Europe; that his power should be restricted; that he should no longer be the irresponsible vicar of God upon earth, but the accountable chief executive officer of Christendom; and that the right of marriage should be conceded to the clergy. These are significantly Teutonic ideas.

*Its real intentions.*

We have pursued the story of these events nearly as far as is necessary for the purpose of this book. We shall not, therefore, follow the details of the new schism. It fell almost without interest on Europe. Æneas Sylvius, the ablest man of the day, in three words gives us the true insight into the state of things: "Faith is dead." On the demise of Eugenius IV., Nicholas V. succeeded. An understanding was had with those in the interest of the council. It was dissolved. Felix V. abdicated. The morality of the times had improved. The Anti-Pope was neither blinded nor murdered. The schism was at an end.

*Cause and close of these troubles.*

Thus we have seen that the personal immoralities and heresy of the Popes brought on the interference of the King of France, who not only shook the Papal system to its basis, but destroyed its prestige by inflicting the most conspicuous indignity upon it. For seventy years Rome was disfranchised, and the rivalries of France and Italy produced the great schism, than which no-

*End of the intellectual influence of the Papacy.*

thing could be more prejudicial to the Papal power. We have seen that, aided by the pecuniary difficulties of the Papacy, the rising intellect of Europe made good its influence, and absolutely deposed the Pope. It was in vain to deny the authenticity of such a council; there stood the accomplished fact. At this moment there seemed no other prospect for the Italian system than utter ruin; yet wonderful to be said, a momentary deliverance came from a quarter whence no man would have expected. The Turks were the saviours of the Papacy.

At this point is the true end of the Italian system—that system which had pressed upon Europe like a nightmare. The great men of the times—the statesmen, the philosophers, the merchants, the lawyers, the governing classes,—they whose weight of opinion is recognized by the uneducated people at last, had shaken off the incubus and opened their eyes. A glimmering of the true state of things was breaking upon the clergy. No more with the vigour it once had possessed was the Papacy again to domineer over human thought and be the controlling agent of European affairs. Convulsive struggles it might make, but they were only death-throes. The sovereign pontiff must now descend from the autocracy he had for so many ages possessed, and become a small potentate, tolerated by kings in that subordinate position only because of the remnant of his influence on the uneducated multitude and those of feeble minds.

## CHAPTER XVIII.

### THE AGE OF FAITH IN THE WEST—*(Concluded).*

EFFECT OF THE EASTERN OR MILITARY ATTACK.—GENERAL REVIEW OF THE AGE OF FAITH.

The Eastern pressure.

FROM the West I have now to return to the East, and to describe the pressure made by Mohammedanism on that side. It is illustrated by many great events, but, above all, by the loss of Constantinople. The Greek Church, so long out of sight that it is perhaps almost forgotten by the reader, comes for a moment before us like a spectre from the dead.

Appearance of the Turks.

A wandering tribe of Turks had found its way into Asia Minor, and, under its leader Ertogrul and his son Othman, consolidated its power and commenced extending its influence by possessions taken from the Sultans of Iconium and the Byzantine empire. The third prince of the race instituted the Janissaries, a remarkable military force, and commenced driving the Greeks out of Asia Minor. His son Soliman crossed the Hellespont and captured Gallipoli, thus securing a foothold in Europe, A.D. 1358.

Extension of their power in Europe.

This accomplished, the Turkish influence began to extend rapidly. Thrace, Macedon, and Servia were subdued. Sigismund, the King of Hungary, was overthrown at the battle of Nicopolis by Bajazet. Southern Greece, the countries along the Danube, submitted, and Constantinople would have fallen had it not been for the unexpected irruption of Tamerlane, who defeated Bajazet and took him prisoner. The reign of Mohammed I., who succeeded, was occupied in the restoration of Turkish affairs. Under Amurath II., possession of the Euxine

shore was obtained, the fortifications across the Isthmus of
Corinth was stormed, and the Peloponnesus entered.

Mohammed II. became the Sultan of the Turks A.D. 1451. *The Byzantine sovereigns apply to the West.* From the moment of his accession, he turned all his power to the capture of Constantinople. Its sovereigns had long foreseen the inevitable event, and had made repeated attempts to secure military aid from the West. They were ready to surrender their religious belief. On this principle, the monk Barlaam was dispatched on an embassy to Benedict XII. to propose the reunion of the Greek and Latin churches, as it was delicately termed, and to obtain, as an equivalent for the concession, an army of Franks. As the danger became more urgent, John Palæologus I. sought an interview with Urban V., and, having been purified from his heresies respecting the supremacy of the Pope and the double procession of the Holy Ghost, was presented before the pontiff in the Church of St. Peter. The Greek monarch, after three genuflexions, was permitted to kiss the feet of the Holy Father and to lead by its bridle his mule. But, though they might have the will, the Popes had lost the power, and these great submissions were productive of no good. Thirty years subsequently, Manuel, the son and successor of Palæologus, took what might have seemed a more certain course. He travelled to Paris and to London to lay his distress before the kings of France and England, but he received only pity, not aid. At the Council of Constance Byzantine ambassadors appeared. It was, however, reserved for the synods of Ferrara and of Florence to mature, as far as might be, the negotiation. The second John Palæologus journeyed again into Italy, A.D. 1438; and while Eugenius was being deposed in the chamber at Basle, he was consummating the union of the East and the West in the Cathedral of Florence. In the pulpit of that edifice, on the sixth of July of that year, *The Greek Church yields to the Latin.* a Roman Cardinal and a Greek archbishop embraced each other before the people; Te Deum was chanted in Greek, mass was celebrated in Latin, and the Creed was read with the "Filioque." The successor of Constantine the Great had given up his religion, but he had received no equivalent—no aid. The state of the Church, its disorders and schisms, rendered any community of action in the West impossible.

*Mohammed II.*

The last, the inevitable hour at length struck. Mohammed II. is said to have been a learned man, able to express himself in five different languages; skilful in mathematics, especially in their practical application to engineering; an admirer of the fine arts; prodigal in his liberality to Italian painters. In Asia Minor, as in Spain, there was free-thinking among the disciples of the Prophet. It was affirmed that the Sultan, in his moments of relaxation, was often heard to deride the religion of his country as an imposture. His doubts in that particular were, however, compensated for by his determination to carry out the intention of his Mohammedan predecessors—the seizure of Constantinople.

*The siege of Constantinople.*

At this time the venerable city had so greatly declined that it contained only 100,000 inhabitants,—out of them only 4970 able or willing to bear arms. The besieging force was more than a quarter of a million of men. As Mohammed pressed on his works, the despairing emperor in vain looked for the long-promised effectual Western aid. In its extremity, the devoted metropolis was divided by religious feuds; and when a Latin priest officiated in St. Sophia, there were many who exclaimed that they would rather see the turban of the Sultan than the tiara of the Pope. In several particulars the siege of Constantinople marked out the end of old ages and the beginning of new. Its walls were shaken by the battering-rams of the past, and overthrown by cannon, just then coming into general use. Upon a plank road, shipping were passed through the open country, in the darkness of a single night, a distance of ten miles. The works were pushed forward toward the walls, on the top of which the pacing sentinel at length could hear the shouts of the Turks by their nocturnal fires. They were sounds such as Constantinople might well listen to. She had taught something different for many a long year. "God is God; there is but one God." In the streets an image of the Virgin was carried in solemn procession. Now or never she must come to the help of those who had done so much for her, who had made her a queen in heaven and a goddess upon earth. The cry of her worshippers was in vain.

On May 29th, 1453, the assault was delivered. Constan-

tine Palæologus, the last of the Roman emperors, putting off
his purple, that no man might recognize and insult his corpse
when the catastrophe was over, fell, as became a Roman emperor, in the breach. After his death resistance ceased, and
the victorious Turks poured into the town. To the church of
St. Sophia there rushed a promiscuous crowd of women and
children, priests, monks, religious virgins, and—men. Superstitions to the last, in this supreme moment they expected the
fulfilment of a prophecy that, when the Turks should have
forced their way to the square before that church, their progress would be arrested, for an angel with a sword in his
hand would descend from heaven and save the city of the Lord.
The Turks burst into the square, but the angel never came.

*Fall of the city.*

More than two-thirds of the inhabitants of Constantinople
were carried prisoners into the Turkish camp,—the men for
servitude, the women for a still more evil fate. The churches
were sacked. From the dome of St. Sophia its glories were
torn down. The divine images, for the sake of which Christendom had been sundered in former days, unresistingly submitted to the pious rage of the Mohammedans without working a single miracle, and, stripped of their gems and gold, were
brought to their proper value in the vile uses of kitchens and
stables. On that same day the muezzin ascended the loftiest turret of St. Sophia, and over the City of the Trinity proclaimed the Oneness of God. The Sultan performed his prayers
at the great altar, directing the edifice to be purified from its
idolatries and consecrated to the worship of God. Thence he
repaired to the palace, and reflecting on the instability of human prosperity, repeated, as he entered it, the Persian verse:
"The spider has woven his web in the imperial palace; the
owl hath sung her watch-song on the towers of Afrasiab."

This solemn event—the fall of Constantinople—accomplished, there was no need of any reconciliation of the Greek
and Latin Churches. The sword of Mohammed had settled
their dispute. Constantinople had submitted to the fate of
Antioch, Jerusalem, Alexandria, Carthage. Christendom was
struck with consternation. The advance of the Turks in Europe was now very rapid. Corinth and Athens fell, and the

*Terror of Christendom at the fall of Constantinople.*

reduction of Greece was completed. The confines of Italy were approached A.D. 1461. The Mohammedan flag confronted that peninsula along the Adriatic coast. In twenty years more Italy was invaded. Otranto was taken; its bishop killed at the door of his church. At this period, it was admitted that the Turkish infantry, cavalry, and artillery were the best in the world. Soliman the Magnificent took Belgrade A.D. 1520. Nine years afterward the Turks besieged Vienna, but were repulsed. Soliman now prepared for the subjugation of Italy, and was only diverted from it by an accident which turned him upon the Venetians. It was not until the battle of Lepanto that the Turkish advance was fairly checked. Even as it was, in the complicated policy and intrigues of Europe its different sovereigns could not trust one another; their common faith had ceased to be a common bond; in all it had been weakened, in some destroyed. Æneas Sylvius, speaking of Christendom, says, "It is a body without a head, a republic without laws or magistrates. The Pope or the emperor may shine as lofty titles, as splendid images; but they are unable to command, and no one is willing to obey." But, during this period of Turkish aggression, had not the religious dissensions of Christendom been decently composed, there was imminent danger that Europe would have been Mohammedanized. A bitter experience of past ages, as well as of the present, had taught it that the Roman Church was utterly powerless against such attacks. Safety was to be looked for, not in any celestial aid, but in physical knowledge and pecuniary resources, carried out in the organization of armies and fleets. Had her authority been derived from the source she pretended, she should have found an all-sufficient protection in prayer—indeed not even that should have been required. Men discovered at last that her litanies and her miracles were equally of no use, and that she must trust, like any other human tyranny, to cannon and the sword.

*Effect of the Turkish invasion.* The Turkish aggression led to the staying of the democratic outbreak in the bosom of the Church,—the abstaining for a season from any further sap of the Papal autocracy. It was necessary that ecclesiastical disputes, if they could not be ended, should at all events be kept for a time in abeyance; and so indeed they were, until the pent-up dissensions burst forth in "the Reformation." And thus, as we have related, by Mohammedan knowledge in the West Papal Christianity was well-nigh brought to ruin; thus, by a strange paradox, the Mohammedan sword in the East gave it for a little longer a renewed lease of political power, though never again of life.

To Nicholas V., a learned and able Pope, the catastrophe of Constantinople was the death-blow. He had been the intimate friend of Cosmo de' Medici, and from him had imbibed a taste for letters and art, but, like his patron, he had no love for liberty. It was through commerce that the Papacy first learned to turn to art. The ensuing developement of Europe was really based on the commerce of Upper Italy, and not upon the Church. The statesmen of Florence were the inventors of the balance of power. A lover of literature, Nicholas was the founder of the Vatican Library. He clearly perceived the only course in which the Roman system could be directed; that it was unfit for, and indeed incompatible with science, but might be brought in unison with art. Its influence upon the reason was gone, but the senses yet remained for it. In continuing his policy, the succeeding Popes acted with wisdom. They gratified the genius of their institutions, of their country, and their age. In the abundant leisure of monasteries, the monks had found occupation in the illumination of manuscripts. From the execution of miniatures they gradually rose to an undertaking of greater works. In that manner painting had originated in Italy in the twelfth century. Sculpture, at first merged in architecture, had extricated herself from that bondage in the fourteenth. The mendicant orders, acquiring wealth, became munificent patrons. From calligraphic illustrations to the grand works of Michael Angelo and Raffaele is a prodigious advance, yet it took but a short time to accomplish it.

*Nicholas V. a patron of art.*

*Gradual rise of the fine arts.*

I have now completed the history of the European Age of Faith as far as is necessary for the purposes of this book. It embraces a period of more than a thousand years, counting from the reign of Constantine. It remains to consider the intellectual peculiarity that marks the whole period—to review

*Review of the Age of Faith.*

briefly the agents that exerted an influence upon it and conducted it to its close.

*Philosophical peculiarities of the Age of Faith.*

Philosophically, the most remarkable peculiarity is the employment of a false logic, a total misconception of the nature of evidence. It is illustrated by miracle-proofs, trial by battle, ordeal tests, and a universal belief in supernatural agency even for objectless purposes. On the principles of this logic, if the authenticity of a thing or the proof of a statement be required, it is supposed to be furnished by an astounding illustration of something else. If the character of a princess is assailed, she offers a champion, he proves victorious, and therefore she was not frail. If a national assembly, after a long discussion, cannot decide "whether children should inherit the property of their father during the lifetime of their grandfather," an equal number of equal combatants is chosen for each side; they fight; the champions of the children prevail, and therefore the law is fixed in their favour. A relic of some martyr is bought at a great price; no one seeks to criticize the channel through which it has come, but every one asks, "Can it work a miracle?" A vast institution demands the implicit obedience of all men. It justifies its claim, not by the history of the past, but by promises and threats of the future. A decrepit crone is suspected of witchcraft. She is stripped naked and thrown into the nearest pond: if she sinks, she is innocent; if she swims, she is in commerce with the Devil. In all such cases the intrinsic peculiarity of the logic is obvious enough; it shows a complete misconception of the nature of evidence.

*The character of its logic.*

*Its adoption of supernaturalism.*

Yet this ratiocination governed Europe for a thousand years, giving birth to those marvellous and supernatural explanations of physical phenomena and events on which we now look back with unfeigned surprise, half disbelieving that it was possible for our ancestors to have credited such things. Against this preposterous logic the Mohammedans and Jews struck the first blows. We have already heard what Algazzali, the Arabian, says respecting the enchanter who would prove that three is greater than ten by changing a stick into a serpent. The circumstances under which the Jewish physicians acted we shall consider presently.

*The Jews and Saracens destroy supernaturalism.*

It will not be useless to devote a little space to this belief in the supernatural. It offers an opportunity of showing how false notions may become universal, embody themselves in law and practical life, and, wonderful to be said, how they may, without anything being done to destroy them, vanish from sight of themselves, like night-spectres before the day. At present we only encounter them among the lowest peasant grades, or those who have purposely been kept in the most abject state of ignorance. Less than a century ago the clergy of Spain wished to have the Opera prohibited, because that ungodly entertainment had given rise to a want of rain; but now, in a country so intellectually backward as that—a witch was burned there so lately as A.D. 1781—such an attempt would call up sly wit, and make the rabble of Madrid suspect that the archbishop was smarting under the rivalry of the prima donna, and that he was furbishing up the rusty ecclesiastical machinery to sustain his cause.

In the day of their power the ecclesiastical profession were the supporters of this delusion. They found it suitable to their interests, and, by dint of at first persuading others to believe, they at last, by habit, came to believe in it themselves. The Mohammedans and Jews were the first to assail it philosophically and by sarcasm, but its final ruin was brought about by the action of the two other professions, the legal and the medical. The lawyers, whose advent to power is seen in the history of Philip the Fair, and whose rise from that time was very rapid, were obliged to introduce the true methods of evidence; the physicians, from their pursuits, were perpetually led to the material explanation of natural phenomena in contradistinction to the mystical. It is to the honour of both these professions that they never sought for a perpetuation of power by schemes of vast organization, never attempted to delude mankind by stupendous impostures, never compelled them to desist from the expression of their thoughts, and even from thinking, by alliances with civil power. Far from being the determined antagonists of human knowledge, they uniformly fostered it, and, in its trials, defended it. The lawyers were hated because they replaced supernatural logic by philosophical logic; *Respective influences of the clergy, the lawyers, and physicians.*

the physicians, because they broke down the profitable but mendacious system of miracle-cures by relics and at shrines.

*Position of the Church.* Yet the Church is not without excuse. In all her varied history it was impossible to disentangle her from the principles which at the beginning had entered into her political organization. For good or evil, right or wrong, her necessity required that she should put herself forth as the possessor of all knowledge within the reach of human intellect—the infallible arbitress of every question that could arise among men. Doubtless it was a splendid imposture, capable for a time of yielding great results, but sooner or later certain to be unmasked. Early discovering the antagonism of science, which could not fail, in due season, to subject her pretensions to investigation, she lent herself to a systematic delusion of the illiterate, and thereby tried to put off that fatal day when creeds engendered in the darkness would have to be examined in the light, enforcing her attempt with an unsparing, often with a bloody hand. 

*She could not extricate herself from her false position.* It was for this reason that, when the inevitable time of trial came, no intellectual defence could be made in her behalf, and hence there only remained a recourse to physical and political compulsion. But such a compulsion, under such circumstances, is not only a testimony to the intrinsic weakness of that for which it is invoked, it is also a token that they who resort to it have lost all faith in any inherent power of the system they are supporting, and that, in truth, it is fast coming to an end.

*Successive order in supernatural ideas.* The reader will remark, from the incidents connected with supernatural delusions now to be related, that they follow a law of continuous variation, the particular embodiment they assumed changing with the condition of the human mind at each epoch under examination. For ages they are implicitly believed in by all classes; then to a few, but the number perpetually increasing, they become an idle story of barefaced imposture. At last humanity wakens from its delusion—its dream. The final rejection of the whole, in spite of the wonderful amount of testimony which for ages had accumulated, occurs spontaneously the moment that psychical developement has reached a certain point. There can be no more striking illustration of the definite advancement of the human mind. The boy who is terror-stricken in a dark room insensibly dismisses his idle fears as he grows up to be a man.

Clemens Romanus and Anastasius Sinaita, speaking of Simon Magus, say that he could make himself invisible; that he formed a man out of air; that he could pass bodily through mountains without being obstructed thereby; that he could fly and sit unharmed in flames; that he constructed animated statues and self-moving furniture, and not only changed his countenance into the similitude of many other men, but that his whole body could be transformed into the shape of a goat, a sheep, a snake; that, as he walked in the street, he cast many shadows in different directions; that he could make trees suddenly spring up in desert places; and, on one occasion, compelled an enchanted sickle to go into a field and reap twice as much in one day as if it had been used by a man. Of Apollonius of Tyana we are told that, after an unbroken silence of five years, he comprehended the languages of all animals and all men; that, under circumstances very picturesquely related, he detected the genius of a plague at Ephesus, and dragged him, self-convicted, before the people; that, at the wedding-dinner of Menippus, he caused all the dishes and viands to vanish, thereby compelling the bride to acknowledge that she was a vampire, intending to eat the flesh and lap the blood of her husband in the night; that he exhibited the prodigy of being in many places at the same time; raised a young woman from the dead; and, finally, weary of the world, ascended bodily into heaven.

*Oriental magicians—Simon Magus.*

*Greek thaumaturgists.*

As Arabian influence spread, ideas of an Oriental aspect appear. There are peris who live on perfumes, and divs who are poisoned by them; enchanted palaces; moving statues; veiled prophets, like Mokanna; brazen flying horses; charmed arrows; dervises who can project their soul into the body of a dead animal, giving it temporary life; enchanted rings, to make the wearer invisible, or give him two different bodies at the same time; ghouls who live in cemeteries, and at night eat the flesh of dead men. As the European counterpart of these Perso-Arabic ideas, there are fairies, and their dancing

*Introduction of an Arabian element.*

by moonlight, their tampering with children, and imposing changelings on horror-stricken mothers. Every one believes that wind and rain may be purchased of wizards, and that fair weather may be obtained and storms abated by prayer. Whoever attains to wealth or eminence does so by a compact with Satan, signed with blood. The head of the Church, Sylvester II., makes a brazen head, which speaks to him prophetically. He finds underground treasures in a subterraneous magic palace beneath a mountain. The protestator of the Greek emperor is accused of a conspiracy against his master's life by making invisible men. Robert Grostête, the Bishop of Lincoln, makes another speaking head. Nay, more, Albertus Magnus constructs a complete brazen man, so cunningly contrived as to serve him for a domestic. This was at the time that Thomas Aquinas was living with him. The household trouble arising from the excessive garrulity of this simulacrum grew so intolerable—for he was incessantly making mischief among the other inmates—that Thomas, unable to bear it any longer, took a hammer and broke the troublesome android to pieces. This reverend father, known among his contemporaries as the "seraphic doctor," was not without experience in the mysterious craft. Annoyed by the frequent passing of horses near his dwelling, he constructed a magical horse of brass, and buried it in the road. From that moment no animal could be made to pass his door. Among brazen heads of great celebrity is that of Friar Bacon and Friar Bungy. This oracle announced, "Time is; time was; time is past;" but perhaps it was some kind of clock. The alchemist Peter d'Apono had seven spirits in glass bottles. He had entrapped them by baiting with distilled dew, and imprisoned them safely by dexterously putting in the corks. He is the same who possessed a secret which it is greatly to be regretted that he did not divulge for the benefit of chemists who have come after him, that, whatever money he paid, within the space of one hour's time came back of itself again into his pocket. That was better than even the philosopher's stone.

These supernatural notions were at different times modified by two intrusive elements, the first being the Perso-Arabic just alluded to, the second derived from the North of Europe. This element was witchcraft; for, though long before, among Hebrews, Greeks, and Romans, decrepit women were known as witches,—as the Thessalian crone who raised a corpse from the dead for Sextus by lashing it with a snake,—it was not until a later period that this element was fairly developed. A bull of Pope Innocent VIII., published A.D. 1484, says, "It has come to our ears that numbers of both sexes do not avoid to have intercourse with the infernal fiends, and that by their sorceries they afflict both man and beast. They blight the marriage-bed; destroy the births of women and the increase of cattle; they blast the corn on the ground, the grapes in the vineyard, the fruits of the trees, and the grass and herbs of the field." At this time, therefore, the head of the Church had not relinquished a belief in these delusions. The consequences of the punishment he ordained were very dreadful. In the valleys of the Alps many hundred aged women were committed to the flames under an accusation of denying Christ, dishonouring the crucifix, and solemnizing a devil's sabbath in company with the fiend. Such persecutions, begun by Papal authority, continued among illiterate zealots till late times, and, as is well known, were practised even in America. Very masculine minds fell into these delusions. Thus Luther, in his work on the abuses attendant on private masses, says that he had conferences with the Devil on that subject, passing many bitter nights and much restless and wearisome repose; that once, in particular, Satan came to him in the dead of the night, when he was just awakened out of sleep. "The Devil," says Luther, "knows well enough how to construct his arguments, and to urge them with the skill of a master. He delivers himself with a grave and yet with a shrill voice. Nor does he use circumlocutions and beat about the bush, but excels in forcible statements and quick rejoinders. I no longer wonder that the persons whom he assails in this way are occasionally found dead in their beds. He is able to compress and throttle, and more than once he has so assaulted me and driven my soul into a corner, that I felt as if the next moment it must leave my body. I am of opinion that Gesner and

Œcolampadius came in that manner to their deaths. The Devil's manner of opening a debate is pleasant enough, but he soon urges things so peremptorily that the respondent in a short time knows not how to acquit himself."

*English wizards— Scotch witches.*

Social eminence is no preservative from social delusion. When it was affirmed that Agnes Sampson, with two hundred other Scotch witches, had sailed in sieves from Leith to North Berwick church to hold a banquet with the Devil, James I. had the torture applied to the wretched woman, and took pleasure in putting appropriate questions to her after the racking had been duly prolonged. It then came out that the two hundred crones had baptized and drowned a black cat, thereby raising a dreadful storm, in which the ship that carried the king narrowly escaped being wrecked. Upon this Agnes was condemned to the flames. She died protesting her innocence, and piteously calling on Jesus to have mercy on her, for Christian men would not. On the accession of James to the English throne he procured an Act of Parliament against any one convicted of witchcraft, sorcery, or enchantment, or having commerce with the Devil. Under this monstrous statute many persons suffered. At this time England was intellectually very backward. The statute remained until 1736

*French and English legal proceedings.*

unrepealed. The French preceded the English in putting a stop to these atrocities; for Louis XIV., A.D. 1672, by an order in council, forbade the tribunals from inflicting penalty in accusations of sorcery.

*The total disappearance of these delusions.*

Can the reader of the preceding paragraphs here pause without demanding of himself the value of human testimony? All these delusions, which occupied the minds of our forefathers, and from which not even the powerful and learned were free, have totally passed away. The moonlight has now no fairies; the solitude no genius; the darkness no ghost, no goblin. There is no necromancer who can raise the dead from their graves—no one who has sold his soul to the Devil and signed the contract with his blood—no augry apparition to rebuke the crone who has disquieted him. Divination, agromancy, pyromancy, hydromancy, cheiromancy, augury, interpreting of dreams, oracles, sorcery, astrology, have all gone. It is

350 years since the last sepulchral lamp was found, and that was near Rome. There are no gorgons, hydras, chimæras; no familiars; no incubus or succubus. The housewives of Holland no longer bring forth sooterkins by sitting over lighted chauffers. No longer do captains buy of Lapland witches favourable winds; no longer do our churches resound with prayers against the baleful influences of comets, though there still linger in some of our noble old rituals forms of supplication for dry weather and rain, useless but not unpleasing reminiscences of the past. The apothecary no longer says prayers over the mortar in which he is pounding, to impart a divine afflatus to his drugs. Who is there now that pays fees to a relic or goes to a saint-shrine to be cured? These delusions have vanished with the night to which they appertained, yet they were the delusions of fifteen hundred years. In their support might be produced a greater mass of human testimony than probably could be brought to bear on any other matter of belief in the entire history of man; and yet, in the nineteenth century, we have come to the conclusion that the whole, from the beginning to the end, was a deception! Let him, therefore, who is disposed to balance the testimony of past ages against the dictates of his own reason ponder on this strange history; let him who relies on the authority of human evidence in the guidance of his opinions now settle with himself what that evidence is worth.

*Value of human testimony.*

But, though in one sense this history is humiliating to the philosopher, in another it is full of interest. Supernaturalism, both in the individual and in society, appertains to a definite period of life. It is shaken off as men and nations approach maturity. The child and the youth people solitude and darkness with unrealities. The adult does not so much convince himself of their fictitious nature by reasoning on the results of his experience,—he grows out of them, as we see that society has done. Nevertheless, his emancipation is quickened if he is among those who instruct his curiosity and deride his fears. It was in this manner that the decline of supernaturalism in the West was very much accelerated by Jewish physicians. They, more than the lawyers, were concerned in the ending

*Supernaturalism appertains to a period of life.*

of these delusions. The apparitions, as is the nature of their kind, vanished away as soon as the crowing of the Æsculapian cock announced that the intellectual day of Europe was on the point of breaking. The Jews held in their hands much of the trade of the world; they were in perpetual movement and commercial intercommunication. Locomotion—for such is always its result—tended to make them intellectual. The persecutions under which they had long suffered bound their distant communities together. The Spanish Jews knew very well what was going on among their co-religionists beyond the Euphrates. As Cabanis says, "They were our factors and bankers before we knew how to read; they were also our first physicians." To this it may be added that they were, for centuries together, the only men in Europe who saw the course of human affairs from the most general point of view.

The Hellenizing Jewish physicians inoculated the Arabs with learning on their first meeting with them in Alexandria, obtaining a private and personal influence with many of the khalifs, and from that central point of power giving an intellectual character to the entire Saracenic movement. We have already seen that in this they were greatly favoured by the approximation of their unitarianism to that of the Mohammedans. The intellectual activity of the Asiatic and African Jews soon communicated an impulse to those of Europe. The Hebrew doctor was viewed by the vulgar with wonder, and fear, and hatred; no crime could be imputed to him too incredible. Thus Zedekias, the physician to Charles the Bald, was asserted to have devoured at one meal, in the presence of the court, a waggon-load of hay, together with its horses and driver. The titles of some of the works that appeared among them deserve mention, as displaying a strong contrast with the mystical designations in vogue. Thus Isaac Ben Soleiman, an Egyptian, wrote 'On Fevers,' 'On Medicine,' 'On Food and Remedies,' 'On the Pulse,' 'On Philosophy,' 'On Melancholy,' 'An Introduction to Logic.' The simplicity of these titles displays an intellectual clearness and precision of thought which have ever been shown by the Israelites. They are in themselves sufficient to convince us of the strong common sense which these men were silently infusing into the literature of Western Europe in ages of concealment and mystification. Roger Bacon, at a much later time, gave to one of his works the title of 'The Green Lion;' to another, 'The Treatise of Three Words.'

Since it was by the power and patronage of the Saracens that the Jewish physicians were acting, it is not surprising that the language used in many other compositions was Arabic. Translations were, however, commonly made into Hebrew, and, at a subsequent period, into Latin. Through the ninth century the Asiatic colleges maintained their previous celebrity in certain branches of knowledge. Thus the Jew Shabtai Donolo was obliged to go to Bagdad to complete his studies in astronomy. As, however, Arabian influence extended itself into Sicily and Italy, Jewish intelligence accompanied it, and schools were founded at Tarentum, Salerno, Bari, and other places. Here the Arab and Jew Orientalists first amalgamated with a truly European element—the Greek,—as is shown by the circumstance that in the college at Salerno instruction was given through the medium of all three languages. At one time, Pontus taught in Greek, Abdollah in Arabic, and Elisha in Hebrew. A similar influence of the Arab and Jew combined founded the University of Montpellier. *Foundation of colleges.*

After the foundation of medical colleges, the progress of medicine among the Jews was very rapid. Judged by our standard, in some respects it was peculiar. Thus they looked upon the practice of surgery as altogether mechanical, and therefore ignoble. A long list of eminent names might be extracted from the tenth and eleventh centuries. In it we should find Haroun of Cordova, Jehuda of Fez, Amram of Toledo. Already it was apparent that the Saracenic movement would aid in developing the intelligence of barbarian Western Europe through Hebrew physicians, in spite of the opposition encountered from theological ideas imported from Constantinople and Rome. Mohammedanism had all along been the patron of physical science; paganizing Christianity not only repudiated it, but exhibited toward it sentiments of contemptuous disdain and hatred. Hence physicians were *Medical studies among the Jews.*

*Imposture-medicine.*

viewed by the Church with dislike, and regarded as atheists by the people, who held firmly to the lessons they had been taught that cures must be wrought by relics of martyrs and bones of saints, by prayers and intercessions, and that each region of the body was under some spiritual charge, the first joint of the right thumb being in the care of God the Father, the second under that of the Blessed Virgin, and so on of other parts. For each disease there was a saint. A man with sore eyes must invoke St. Clara, but if it was an inflammation elsewhere he must turn to St. Anthony. An ague would demand the assistance of St. Pernel. For the propitiating of these celestial beings it was necessary that fees should be paid, and thus the practice of imposture-medicine became a great source of profit.

*The rabbis cultivate medicine.*

In all this there was no other intention than that of extracting money from the illiterate. With men of education and position it was different. Bishops, princes, kings, and Popes had each in private his Hebrew doctor, though all understood that he was a contraband luxury, in many countries pointedly and absolutely prohibited by the law. In the eleventh century nearly all the physicians in Europe were Jews. This was due to two different causes: the Church would tolerate no interference with her spiritual methods of treating disease, which formed one of her most productive sources of gain; and the study of medicine had been formally introduced into the rabbinical schools. The monk was prohibited a pursuit which gave to the rabbi an honourable emolument. From the older institutions offshoots in quick succession appeared, particularly in France. Thus the school of Narbonne was under the presidency of Doctor Rabbi Abou. There was also a flourishing school at Arles. In these institutions instruction was given through the medium of Hebrew and Arabic, the Greek element present at Salerno being here wanting. In the French schools, to the former languages Latin and Provençal were, in the course of time, added. The versatility of acquirement among the physicians, who were taking the lead in this intellectual movement, is illustrated both by the Spanish and French Jews. Some, like Djanah, a native of Cordova, acquired reputation in grammar, criticism, astronomy; others in poetry or theology.

If thus the social condition of the rabbis, who drew no income from their religious duties, induced them to combine the practice of medicine with their pursuits, great facilities had arisen for mental culture through the establishment of so many schools. Henceforth the Jewish physician is recognized as combining with his professional skill a profound knowledge of theology, mathematics, astronomy, philosophy, music, law. In a singular manner he stands aloof in the barbarian societies among whom he lives, looking down like a philosopher upon their idolatries, permitting, or even excusing them, like a statesman. Of those who thus adorned the eleventh century was Rabbi Solomon Ben Isaac, better known under the abbreviation Raschi—called by his countrymen the Prince of Commentators. He was equally at home in writing commentaries on the Talmud, or in giving instructions for great surgical operations, as the Cæsarean section. He was the greatest French physician of his age. Spain, during the same century, produced a worthy competitor to him, Ebn Zohr, physician to the court of Seville. His writings were in Hebrew, Arabic, Syriac, and both in prose and verse. He composed a treatise on the cure of diseases, and two on fevers. In singular contrast with the superstitious notions of the times, he possessed a correct view of the morbific nature of marsh miasm. He was followed by Ben Ezra, a Jew of Toledo, who was at once a physician, philosopher, mathematician, astronomer, critic, poet. He travelled all over Europe and Asia, being held in captivity for some time in India. Among his medical writings was a work on theoretical and practical medicine, entitled 'Book of Proofs.' Through the wars arising in Spain between the Mohammedans and Christians, many learned Jews were driven into France, imparting to that country, by their presence, a new intellectual impulse. Of such were Aben Tybbon, who gave to his own profession a pharmaceutical tendency by insisting on the study of botany and the art of preparing drugs. Ben Kimchi, a Narbonnese physician and grammarian, wrote commentaries on the Bible, sacred and moral poems, a Hebrew

*And other sciences.*

*Writings of the Spanish-Jewish physicians.*

grammar. Notwithstanding the opposition of the ecclesiastics, William, the Lord of Montpellier, passed an edict authorizing all persons, without exception, to profess medicine in the university of his city. This was especially meant for the relief of the Jews, though expressed in a general way. Spain, though she had thus lost many of her learned men, still continued to produce others of whom she had reason to be proud. Moussa Ben Maimon, known all over Europe as Maimonides, was recognized by his countrymen as "the Doctor, the Great Sage, the Glory of the West, the Light of the East, second only to Moses." He is often designated by the four initials R.M.B.M., that is, Rabbi Moses Ben Maimon, or briefly Rambam. His biography presents some points of interest. He was born at Cordova A.D. 1135, and, while yet young, wrote commentaries on the Talmuds both of Babylon and Jerusalem, and also a work on the Calendar; but, embracing Mohammedanism, he emigrated to Egypt, and there became physician to the celebrated Sultan Saladin. Among his works are medical aphorisms, derived from former Greek, Latin, Hebrew, and Arabic sources; an abridgment of Galen; and of his original treatises, which were very numerous, may be mentioned those 'On Hemorrhoids,' 'On Poisons and Antidotes,' 'On Asthma,' 'On the Preservation of Health'—the latter being written for the benefit of the son of Saladin—'On the Bites of Venomous Animals'—written by order of the Sultan—'On Natural History.' His 'Moreh Nevochim,' or 'Teacher of the Perplexed,' was an attempt to reconcile the doctrines of the Old Testament with reason. In addition to these, he had a book on Idolatry, and one on Christ. Besides Maimonides, the Sultan had another physician, Ebn Djani, the author of a work on the medical topography of the city of Alexandria. From the biographies of these learned men of the twelfth century it would seem that their religious creed hung lightly upon them. Not unfrequently they become converted to Mohammedanism.

It might be tedious if I should record the names and writings of the learned European Jews of the twelfth and thirteenth centuries, a period more prolific of these great men than even the preceding ages. But I cannot pass these later centuries

*Maimonides.*

*Later Jewish physicians.*

without mentioning the Alphonsine Tables, calculated for Alphonso, the king of Castile, by Mascha, his Hebrew physician. The irreligious tendency of the times is illustrated by the well-known sarcasm uttered by that Spanish monarch respecting the imperfect construction of the heavens, according to the Ptolemaic hypothesis. For long, however, the Jews had been dabbling in free-thinking speculations. Thus Aben Tybbon, above mentioned, anticipating that branch of science which has drawn upon itself, in later years, so much opprobrium, wrote a work containing a discussion of the causes which prevent the waters of the sea from encroaching on the land. Abba Mari, a Marseillese Jew, translated the 'Almagest' of Ptolemy and the Commentary of Averrhoes upon it. The school of Salerno was still sending forth its doctors. In Rome, Jewish physicians were very numerous, the Popes themselves employing them. Boniface VIII. had for his medical adviser Rabbi Isaac. At this period Spain and France were full of learned Jews; and perhaps partly by their exerting upon the higher classes with whom they came in contact too much influence, for the physician of a Christian prince was very often the rival of his confessor, and partly because the practice of medicine, as they pursued it, interfered with the gains of the Church, the clergy took the alarm, and caused to be re-enacted or enforced the ancient laws. The Council of Beziers, A.D. 1246, and the Council of Alby, A.D. 1254, prohibited all Christians from resorting to the services of an Israelitish physician. It would appear that these enactments had either fallen into desuetude or had failed to be enforced. The faculty of Paris, awakening at last to the danger of the case, caused, A.D. 1301, a decree to be published prohibiting either man or woman of the religion of Moses from practising medicine upon any person of the Catholic religion. A similar course was also taken in Spain. At this time the Jews were confessedly at the head of French medicine. It was the appointment of one of their persuasion, Profatius, as regent of the faculty of Montpellier, A.D. 1300, which drew down upon them the wrath of the faculty of Paris. This learned man was a skilful astronomer; he composed tables of the moon and of the longitudes of many Asiatic and African animosity between the Byzantine ecclesiastical system and all worldly wisdom was inextinguishable, though it was utterly foreign to Christianity. It was fastened by imperial violence on the nations, and made its appearance, with unabated force, at intervals of ages. The same evil instinct which tore Hypatia piecemeal in the church at Alexandria brought Galileo into the custody of the familiars of the Holy Office at Rome. The necessary consequence of this upholding ignorance by force was the emergence of ideas successively more and more depraved. Whoever will ingenuously compare the religious state of Italy in the fourteenth century with its state in the fourth—that is, the recent Italian with the old Roman—will find that among the illiterate classes nothing whatever had been accomplished. There were no elevated thoughts of holy things. From practical devotion God had altogether disappeared; the Saviour had been supplanted by the Blessed Virgin; and she herself—such was the increasing degradation—had been abandoned for the ignoble worship of apotheosized men, who, under the designation of saints, had engrossed all the votaries. There had been a rapid descent to the last degree of more than African abasement in bleeding statues and winking pictures. *Degraded state of Italy.*

In Europe there had been incorporated old forms of worship and old festivals with Christian ones without any scruple; the local gods and goddesses had been replaced by saints; for deification, canonization had been substituted. There had been produced a civilization, the character of which was its extraordinary intolerance. A man could not be suspected of doubting the popular belief without risk to his goods, his body, or his life. As a necessary consequence, there could be no great lawgivers, no philosophers, no poets. Society was pervaded by a systematic hypocrisy. This tyranny over others sometimes led to strange results. It caused the Jews to discover the art of making wealth invisible by means of bills of exchange and other such like means, so that money might be imperceptibly but instantaneously moved. *Rise of a new social system.*

Thus, after the dying out of Greek science, there followed, among the new population, an intellectual immobility, which soon became the centre of a vast number of growing interests *Influence of that new system.*

quickly and firmly crystallizing round it. For them it was essential that there should be no change—no advance. In the midst of jarrings and conflicts between those interests, that condition was steadfastly maintained, as if through instinct, by them all. It mattered not how antiquated were the forms insisted on, nor how far they outraged common sense. New life was given to decaying illusions, and in return, strength was gathered from them. Isis, with the moon between her feet, was planted, under a new name, on the Bosphorus and the Tiber. African theology, African ecclesiastical machinery, and African monasticism were made objects of reverence to unsuspecting Europe. Juvenal says that the Roman painters of his day lived on the goddess Isis. The Italian painters of a latter day lived on her modernized form.

*And degradation by African ideas.*

In such a condition of things the literary state could be no other than barren. Political combinations had not only prescribed an intellectual terminus, but had even laid down a rail upon which mental excursions were to be made, and from which there was no departing; or, if a turn-out was permitted, it was a tonsured man who stood at the switch. For centuries together, if we exclude theological writings, there was absolutely no literature worth the name. Life seems to have been spent in the pursuit of mere physical enjoyment, and that enjoyment of a very low kind. When in the south of France and Sicily literature began to dawn, it is not to be overlooked how much of it was of an amatory kind; and love is the strongest of the passions. The first aspect of Western literature was animal, not intellectual. A taste for learning excited, there reappeared in the schools the old treatises written a thousand years before, —the Elements of Euclid, the Geography of Ptolemy. Long after the Reformation there was an intellectual imbecility which might well excite our mirth, if it were not the index of a stage through which the human mind must pass. Often enough we see it interestingly in the interweaving of the old with the new ideas. If we take up a work on metallurgy, it commences with Tubal Cain; if on music, with Jubal. The history of each country is traced back to the sons of Noah, or at least to the fugitives from the siege of Troy. An admiration for classical

*No literature in the Age of Faith.*

*Its critical incorrectness.*

authors may perhaps be excused. It exhibited itself amusingly in the eccentricity of interlarding compositions of every kind with Greek and Latin quotations. It was an age of literary innocence, when no legend was too stupendous for credulity: when there was no one who had ever suspected that Tully, as they delighted to call him, was not a great philosopher, and Virgil not a great poet.

Of those ponderous, those massive folios on ecclesiastical affairs, at once the product and representatives of the time, but little needs here to be said. They boasted themselves as the supreme effort of human intellect; they laid claim to an enduring authority; to many they had a weight little less than the oracles of God. But if their intrinsic value is to be measured by their pretensions, and their pretensions judged of by their present use, what is it that must be said? Long ago their term was reached, long ago they became obsolete. They have no reader. Such must be the issue of any literature springing from an immovable and unexpanding basis, the offspring of thought that has been held in subjugation by political formulas, or of intellectual energies that have been cramped. Disuse of Patristic works.

The Roman ecclesiastical system, like the Byzantine, had been irrevocably committed in an opposition to intellectual developement. It professed to cultivate the morals, but it crushed the mind. Yet, in the course of events, this state of things was to come to an end through the working of other principles equally enduring and more powerful. They constitute what we may speak of under the title of the Arabian element. On preceding pages it has been shown that, on the passage of the Saracens through Egypt, they came under the influence of the Nestorians and Hellenizing Jews, acquiring from them a love of philosophy, which soon manifested itself in full energy from the banks of the Euphrates to those of the Guadalquivir. The hammer of Charles Martel might strike down the ranks of the Saracens on the field of Tours, but there was something intangible, something indestructible accompanying them, which the Frank chivalry could not confront. To the Church there was an evil omen. It has been well remarked that in the Provençal poetry there are noble bursts of crusa- Spread of science in France.

ding religious sentiment, but they are incorporated with a sovereign contempt for the clergy.

The biography of any of the physicians or alchemists of the thirteenth century would serve the purpose of illustrating the watchfulness of the Church, the unsound condition of the universities, the indirect patronage extended to heretics by eminent men, and the manner in which the rival powers, ecclesiasticism and philosophy, were preparing for their final conflict. As an example of the kind, I may present briefly that of Arnold de Villa Nova, born about A.D. 1250. He enjoyed a great reputation for his knowledge of medicine and alchemy. For some years he was physician to the King of Arragon. Under an accusation of defective orthodoxy he lost his position at Court, his punishment being rendered more effective by excommunication. Hoping to find in Paris more liberality than he had met with in Spain, he fled to that city, but was pursued by an adverse ecclesiastical influence with a charge of having sold his soul to the Devil, and of having changed a plate of copper into gold. In Montpellier, to which he was obliged to retire, he found a more congenial intellectual atmosphere, and was for long one of the regents of the faculty of medicine. In succession, he subsequently resided in Florence, Naples, Palermo, patronized and honoured by the Emperor Frederick II.,—at that time engaged in the attempt to unite Italy into one kingdom and give it a single language,—on account of his extraordinary reputation as a physician. Even the Pope, Clement V., notwithstanding the unfortunate attitude in which Arnold stood toward the Church, besought a visit from him, in hopes of relief from the stone. On his voyage for the purpose of performing the necessary operation, Arnold suffered shipwreck and was drowned. His body was interred at Genoa. The Pope issued an encyclic letter, entreating those who owed him obedience to reveal where Arnold's Treatise on the Practice of Medicine might be found, it having been lost or concealed. It appears that the chief offences committed by Arnold against the Church were that he had predicted the world would come to an end A.D. 1335; that he had said the bulls of the Pope were only the work of a man, and that the

*Marginal note: Illustration from the biography of Arnold.*

practice of charity is better than prayer, or even than the mass. If he was the author of the celebrated book 'De Tribus Impostoribus,' as was suspected by some, it is not remarkable that he was closely watched and disciplined. Like many of his contemporaries, he mingled a great deal of mysticism with his work, recommending, during his alchemical operations, the recitation of psalms, to give force to the agents used. Among other such things, he describes a seal, decorated with scriptural phrases, of excellent use in preserving one from sudden death. It appears, however, to have failed of its effect on the night when Arnold's ship was drifting on an Italian lee-shore, when he had most need of it.

The two antagonistic principles—ecclesiastical and intellectual—were thus brought in presence of each other. On other occasions they had been already in partial collision, as at the iconoclastic dispute which originated in the accusations of the Mohammedans and ended in the tearing asunder of Christendom. *Two impulses—intellectual and moral—in operation.*

Again there was a collision, a few centuries later, when the Spanish Moors and Jews began to influence the higher European classes. Among the bishops, sovereigns, and even Popes thus affected, there were many men of elevated views, who saw distinctly the position of Europe, and understood thoroughly the difficulties of the Church. It had already become obvious to them that it would be impossible to restrain the impulse arising from the vigorous movements of the Saracens, and that it was absolutely necessary so to order things that the condition of faith in Europe might be accommodated to, or even harmonized with, these philosophical conceptions, which it was quite clear would, soon or late, pervade the whole continent. This, as we have seen, is the explanation of the introduction of Scholasticism from the Arabian schools, and its accommodation to the Christian code, on which authority looked with so much favour at first. But hardly had this attempt been entered upon before it became manifest that the risks to be incurred through the remedy itself were as evil as the anticipated dangers. There was then no other course than for the Church to retrace her steps, ostensibly maintaining her consistency *Struggle of ecclesiasticism against the intellectual principle.*

by permitting scholastic literature, though declining scholastic theology. She thus allured the active intellect, arising in all directions in the universities, to fruitless and visionary pursuits. This policy, therefore, threw her back upon a system of oppression; it was the only course possible; yet there can be no doubt that it was entered upon with reluctance. We do injustice to the great men who guided ecclesiastical policy in those times when we represent them as recklessly committing themselves to measures at once violent and indefensible. They did make the attempt to institute an opposite policy; it proved not only a failure, but mischievous. They were then driven to check the spread of knowledge—driven by the necessities of their position. The fault was none of theirs; it dated back to the time of Constantine the Great; and the impossibility of either correcting or neutralizing it is only an example, as has been said, of the manner in which a general principle, once introduced, will overbear the best exertions of those attempting to struggle against it. We can appreciate the false position into which those statesmen were thrown when we compare their personal with their public relations. Often the most eminent persons lived in intimacy and friendship with Jewish physicians, who in the eye of the law, were enemies of society; often those who were foremost in the cultivation of knowledge—who, indeed, suffered excommunication for its sake—maintained amicable relations of a private kind with those who in public were the leaders of their persecutors. The systems were in antagonism, not the men. Arnold de Villa Nova, though excommunicated, was the physician of one Pope; Roger Bacon, though harshly imprisoned, was the friend and correspondent of another. These incidents are not at all to be mistaken for that compassion which the truly great are ever ready to show to erring genius. They are examples of what we often see in our own day, when men engaged in the movements of a great political party loyally carry out its declared principles to their consequences, though individually they might find in those consequences many things to which they could mentally object. Their private objection they thus yield for the sake of what appears to them, in a general way, a practical good.

*The difficulty was in the system, not in the men.*

Such was the state of affairs when the Arab element, having pervaded France and Italy, made its formal intellectual attack. It might almost have been foreseen in what manner that attack would be made, and the shape it would be likely to assume. Of the sciences, astronomy was the oldest and most advanced. Its beginning dates earlier than the historic period, and both in India and in Egypt it had long reached correctness, so far as its general principles were concerned. The Saracens had been assiduous cultivators of it in both its branches, observation and mathematical investigation. Upon one point, the figure and relations of the earth, it is evident that not the slightest doubt existed among them. Nay, it must be added that no learned European ecclesiastic or statesman could deny the demonstrated truths. Nevertheless, it so fell out that upon this very point the conflict commenced. In India the Brahmans had passed through this same trial—for different nations walk through similar paths—with a certain plausible success, by satisfying the popular clamour that there was, in reality, nothing inconsistent between the astronomical doctrine of the globular form and movement of the earth, and the mythological dogma that it rests upon a succession of animals, the lowest of which is a tortoise. But the strong common sense of Western Europe was not to be deluded in any such idle way. It is not difficult to see the point of contact, the point of pressure with the Church. The abstract question gave her no concern; it was the consequences that might possibly follow. The memorable battle was fought upon the question thus sharply defined: Is the earth a moving globe, a small body in the midst of blazing suns and countless myriads of worlds, or is it the central and greatest object in the universe, flat, and canopied over with a blue dome, motionless while all is in movement around it? The dispute thus definitely put, its issue was such as must always attend upon a controversy in which he who is defending is at once lukewarm and conscious of his own weakness. Never can moral interests, however pure, stand against intellect enforcing truth. On this ill-omened question the Church ventured her battle, and lost it.

Though this great conflict is embodied in the history of

Galileo, who has become its historical representative, the prime moving cause must not be misunderstood. From the Pyrenees had passed forth an influence which had infected all the learned men of Western Europe. Its tendency was altogether unfavourable to the Church. Moreover, the illiterate classes had been touched, but in a different way. To the first action the designation of the intellectual impulse may be given; to the latter, the moral. It is to be especially observed that in their directions these impulses conspired. We have seen how, through the Saracens and Jews conjointly, the intellectual impulse came into play. The moral impulse originated in a different manner, being due partly to the Crusades and partly to the state of things in Rome. On these causes it is therefore needful for us to reflect.

First, of the Crusades. There had been wrenched from Christendom its fairest and most glorious portions. Spain, the north of Africa, Egypt, Syria, Asia Minor, were gone. The Mohammedans had been repeatedly under the walls of Constantinople; its fall was only a question of time. They had been in the streets of Rome. They had marched across Italy in every direction. But perhaps the geographical losses, appalling as they were, did not appear so painful as the capture of the holy places: the birth-place of our Redeemer; the scene of his sufferings; the Mount of Olives; the Sea of Galilee; the Garden of Gethsemane; Calvary; the Sepulchre. Too often in their day of strength, while there were Roman legions at their back, had the bishops taunted Paganism with the weakness of its divinities, who could not defend themselves, their temples, or their sacred places. That logic was retaliated now. To many a sincere heart must many an ominous reflection have occurred. In Western Europe there was a strong common sense which quickly caught the true position of things—a common sense neither to be blinded nor hoodwinked. The astuteness of the Italian politicians was insufficient to conceal altogether the great fact, though it might succeed in dissembling its real significance for a time. The Europe of that day was very different from the Europe of ours. It was in its Age of Faith. Recently converted, as all recent converts do, it made its belief a living rule of action. In our times there is not upon that continent a nation which, in its practical relations with others, carries out to their consequences its ostensible, its avowed articles of belief. Catholics, Protestants, Mohammedans, they of the Greek communion, indiscriminately consort together under the expediencies of the passing hour. Statesmanship has long been dissevered from religion,—a fact most portentous for future times. But it was not so in the Middle Ages. Men then believed their form of faith with the same clearness, the same intensity with which they believed their own existence or the actual presence of things upon which they cast their eyes. The doctrines of the Church were to them no mere inconsequential affair, but an absolute, an actual reality, a living and a fearful thing. It would have passed their comprehension if they could have been assured that a day would come when Christian Europe, by a breath, could remove from the holy places the scandal of an infidel intruder, but, upon the whole, would consider it not worth her while to do so. How differently they acted! When, by the preaching of Peter the Hermit and his collaborators, who had received a signal from Rome, a knowledge had come to the ears of the reproach that had befallen Jerusalem and the sufferings of the pilgrims, their plain but straightforward common sense taught them at once what was the right remedy to apply, and forthwith they did apply it, and Christendom, precipitated headlong upon the Holy Land, was brought face to face with Mohammedanism. *Effect of the Crusades.* But what a scene awaited the zealous, the religious barbarians —for such they truly were—when Constantinople, with its matchless splendours, came in view! What a scene when they had passed into Asia Minor, that garden of the world, presenting city after city, with palaces and edifices, the pride of twenty centuries! How unexpected the character of those Saracens, whom they had been taught, by those who had incited them to their enterprise, to regard as no better than bloodthirsty fiends, but whom they found valiant, merciful, just! When Richard the Lion-hearted, King of England, lay in his tent consumed by a fever, there came into the camp camels laden with snow, sent by his enemy, the Sultan Saladin, to assuage his disease, the *Change of opinion in the Crusaders.*

## Immoralities of the Romans.

homage of one brave soldier to another. But when Richard was returning to England, it was by a Christian prince that he was treacherously seized and secretly confined. This was doubtless only one of many such incidents which had often before occurred. Even down to the meanest camp-follower, every one must have recognized the difference between what they had anticipated and what they had found. They had seen undaunted courage, chivalrous bearing, intellectual culture far higher than their own. They had been in lands filled with the prodigies of human skill. They did not melt down into the populations to whom they returned without imparting to them a profound impression, destined to make itself felt in the course of time.

*They discover the immoralities of Italy.*

But, secondly, as to the state of things in Rome. The movement into which all Europe had been thrown by these wars brought to light the true condition of things in Italy as respects morality. Locomotion in a population is followed by intellectual developement. The old stationary condition of things in Europe was closed by the Crusades. National movement gave rise to better observation, better information, and could not but be followed by national reflection. And though we are obliged to speak of the European population as being in one sense in a barbarous state, it was a moral population earnestly believing the truth of every doctrine it had been taught, and sincerely expecting that those doctrines would be carried to their practical application, and that religious profession must, as a matter of course, be illustrated by religious life. The Romans themselves were an exception to this. They had lived too long behind the scenes. Indeed, it may be said that all the Italian peninsula had emancipated itself from that delusion, as likewise certain classes in France, who had become familiar with the state of things during the residence of the Popes at Avignon. It has been the destiny of Southern France to pass, on a small scale, under the same influence, and to exhibit the same results as were appointed for all Europe at last.

And now, what was it that awakening Europe found to be the state of things in Italy? I avert my eyes from looking again at the biography of the Popes; it would be only to renew a scene of sin and shame. Nor can I, without injustice to truth, speak of the social condition of the inhabitants of that peninsula without relating facts which would compel my reader to turn over the page with a blush. I prefer to look at the maxims of political life which had been followed for many centuries, and which were first divulged by one of the greatest men that Italy has produced, in a work—A.D. 1513—truly characterized as a literary prodigy. Certainly nothing can surpass in atrocity the maxims therein laid down.

Machiavelli, in that work, tells us that there are three degrees of capacity among men:—that one understands things by his own natural powers; another, when they are explained to him; a third, not at all. In dealing with these different classes different methods are to be used. The last class, which is by far the most numerous, is so simple and weak that it is very easy to dupe those who belong to it. If they cease to believe of their own accord, they ought to be constrained by force, in the application of which, though there may be considerable difficulties at first, yet, these once overcome by a sufficient unscrupulousness, veneration, security, tranquillity, and happiness will follow. That, if a prince is constrained to make his choice, it is better for him to be feared than loved; he should remember that all men are ungrateful, fickle, timid, dissembling, and self-interested; that love depends on them, but fear depends on him, and hence it is best to prefer the latter, which is always in his own hands. That, as to governments, their form is of very little moment, though half-educated people think otherwise: the great aim of statesmanship should be permanence, which is worth everything else, being far more valuable than freedom. That, if a man wants to ruin a republic, his proper course is to set it on bold undertakings, which it is sure to mismanage; that men, being naturally wicked, incline to good only when they are compelled; they think a great deal more of the present than the past, and never seek change so long as they are made comfortable.

He recommends a ruler to bear in mind that, while the lower class of men may desert him, the superior will not only desert, but conspire. If such cannot with certainty be made reliable

*The principles of Italian statesmanship—Machiavelli.*

friends, it is very clearly necessary to put it out of their power to be enemies. Thus it may be observed that the frequent insurrections in Spain, Gaul, and Greece against the Romans were entirely due to the petty chiefs inhabiting those countries; but that, after they had once been put to death, everything went on very well. Up to a certain point, it should be the grand maxim of a wise government to render the people contented and to manage the nobles; but that, since hatred is just as easily incurred by good actions as by bad ones, there will occasionally arise the necessity of being wicked in order to maintain power, and, in such a case, there should be no hesitation; for, though it is useful to persevere in the path of rectitude while there is no inconvenience, we should deviate from it at once if circumstances indicate. A prudent prince ought not to keep his word to his own injury; he ought to bear in mind that one who always endeavours to act as duty dictates necessarily ensures his own destruction; that new obligations never extinguish the memory of former injuries in the minds of the superior order of men; that liberality, in the end, generally ensures more enemies than friends; that it is the nature of mankind to become as much attached to one by the benefits they render as by the favours they receive; that, where the question is as to the taking of life or the confiscation of property, it is useful to recollect that men forget the death of their relatives, but not the loss of their patrimony; that if cruelties should become expedient, they should be committed thoroughly and but once—it is very impolitic to resort to them a second time; that there are three ways of deciding any contest—by fraud, by force, or by law, and a wise man will make the most suitable choice; that there are also three ways of maintaining control in newly-conquered states that have once been free—by ruining them, by inhabiting them, or by permitting them to keep their own laws and to pay tribute. Of these the first will often be found the best, as we may see from the history of the Romans, who were experienced judges of such cases. That as respects the family of a rival but conquered sovereign, the greatest pains should be taken to extinguish it completely; for history proves, what many fabulous traditions relate, that dangerous political consequences have originated in the escape of some obscure or insignificant member; that men of the highest order, who are therefore of sound judgment,—who seek for actual social truths for their guidance rather than visionary models which never existed,—will conform to the decisions of reason and never be influenced by feelings of sentiment, unless it is apparent that some collateral advantage will arise from the temporary exhibition thereof; and that they will put a just estimate on the delusions in which the vulgar indulge, casting aside the so-called interventions of Divine Providence, which are, in reality, nothing more than the concatenation of certain circumstances following the ordinary law of cause and effect, but which, by interfering with the action of each other, have assumed a direction which the judgment of the wisest could not have foreseen.

Europe has visited with its maledictions the great political writer by whom these atrocious maxims have been recommended, forgetting that his offence consists, not in inventing, but in divulging them. His works thus offer the purest example we possess of physical statesmanship. They are altogether impassive. He views the management of a state precisely as he might do the construction of a machine, recommending that such a wheel or such a lever should be introduced, his only inquiry being whether it will accomplish his intention. As to any happiness or misery it may work, he gives himself no concern, unless, indeed, they evidently ought to enter into the calculation. He had suffered the rack himself under a charge of conspiracy, and borne it without flinching. But, before Machiavelli wrote, his principles had all been carried into practice; indeed, it would not be difficult to give abundant examples in proof of the assertion that they had been for ages regarded in Italy as rules of conduct.

Such was the morality which Europe detected as existing in Italy, carried out with inconceivable wickedness in public and private life; and thus the two causes we have been considering—contact with the Saracens in Syria and a knowledge of the real state of things in Rome—conspired together to produce what may be designated as the moral impulse, which,

*Conjoined effect of the intellectual and moral impulses.*

in its turn, conspired with the intellectual. Their association
foreboded evil to ecclesiastical authority, thus taken at great
disadvantage. Though, from its very birthday, that authority
had been in absolute opposition to the intellectual movement,
it might, doubtless, for a much longer time have successfully
maintained its conflict therewith, had the conditions remained
unchanged. Up to this time its chief strength reposed upon
its moral relations. It could point, and did point the attention of those whose mental culture enabled them to understand
the true position of affairs, to Europe, brought out of barbarism, and beginning a course of glorious civilization. That
achievement was claimed by the Church. If it was true that
she had thus brought it to pass, it had been altogether wrought
by the agency of her moral power, intellectual influence in
no manner aiding therein, but being uniformly, from the time
of Constantine the Great to that of the Reformation, instinctively repulsed. When, now, the moral power suffered so great
a shock, and was not only ready to go over to, but had actually allied itself with, the intellectual, there was great danger
to ecclesiastical authority. And hence we need not be surprised that an impression began to prevail among the clear-thinking men of the time that the real functions of that authority were completed in producing the partially-civilized
condition to which Europe had attained, the course of events
tending evidently to an elimination of that authority as an
active element in the approaching European system. To such
the Church might emphatically address herself, pointing out
the signal and brilliant results to which she had given rise, and
displaying the manifest evils which must inevitably ensue if
her relations, as then existing, should be touched. For it must
have been plain that the first effect arising from the coalition
of the intellectual with the moral element would be an assertion of the right of private judgment in the individual,—a
condition utterly inconsistent with the dominating influence of
authority. It was actually upon that very principle that the
battle of the Reformation was eventually fought. She might
point out—for it needed no prophetic inspiration—that, if once
this principle was yielded, there could be no other issue in

Christendom than a total decomposition; that though, for a little while, the separation might be limited to a few great confessions, these, under the very influence of the principle that had brought themselves into existence, must, in their turn, undergo disintegration, and the end of it be a complete anarchy of sects. In one sense it may be said that it was in wisdom that the Church took her stand upon this point, determining to make it her base of resistance; unwisely in another, for it was evident that she had already lost the initiative of action, and that her very resistance would constitute the first stage in the process of decomposition.

Europe had made a vast step during its Age of Faith. Spontaneously it had grown through its youth; and the Italians, who had furnished it with many of its ideas, had furnished it also many of its forms of life. In that respect justice has still to be done them. When Rome broke away from her connections with Constantinople, a cloud of more than Cimmerian darkness overshadowed Europe. It was occupied by wandering savages. Six hundred years organized it into families, neighbourhoods, cities. Those centuries found it full of bondmen; they left it without a slave. They found it a scene of violence, rapine, lust; they left it the abode of God-fearing men. Where there had been trackless forests, there were innumerable steeples glittering in the sun; where there had been bloody chieftains, drinking out of their enemies' skulls, there were grave ecclesiastics, fathoming the depths of free-will, predestination, election. Investing the clergy with a mysterious superiority, the Church asserted the equality of the laity before God, from the king to the beggar. It disregarded wealth and birth, and opened a career for all. Its influence over the family and domestic relations was felt through all classes. It ascertained a father by a previous ceremony; it enforced the rule that a wife passes into the family of her husband, and hence it followed that legitimate children belong to the father, illegitimate to the mother. It compelled women to domestic life, shut them out from the priesthood, and tried to exclude them from government. In a worldly sense, the mistake that Rome committed was this: she at-

*Contemporaneous changes in Europe.*

tempted to maintain an intellectual immobility in the midst of an advancing social state. She saw not that society could no more be stopped in its career, through her mere assertion that it could not and should not move, than that the earth could be checked in its revolution merely because she protested that it was at rest. She tried, first by persuasion and then by force, to arrest the onward movement; but she was overborne, notwithstanding her frantic resistance, by the impetuous current. Very different would it have been had the Italian statesmen boldly put themselves in the van of progress, and, instead of asserting an immutability and infallibility, changed their dogmas and maxims as the progress of events required. Europe need not to have waited for Arabs and Jews.

*Loss of power in Church organizations.*

In describing these various facts, I have endeavoured to point out impressively how the Church, so full of vigour at first, contained within itself the seeds of inevitable decay. From the period when it came into collision with the intellectual and moral elements, the origin of which we have traced, and which conspired together for its overthrow, it exhibited a gradual decline; first losing its influence upon nations, and ceasing to be in them a principle of public action; next, witnessing the alienation of the higher and educated classes, the process descending downward through the social scale, therein retracing the steps of its advance. When ecclesiasticism became so weak as to be unable to regulate international affairs, and was supplanted by diplomacy, in the castle the physician was more than a rival for the confessor, in the town the mayor was a greater man than the abbot. There remained a lingering influence over individuals, who had not yet risen above a belief that it could control their state after death. This decline of its ancient influence should be a cause of rejoicing to all intelligent men, for an ecclesiastical organization allying itself to political power can never now be a source of any good.

*Return of things to the ancient Christian times.*

In America we have seen the bond that held the Church and State together abruptly snapped. It is therefore well that, since the close of the Age of Faith, things have been coming back, with an accelerated pace, to the state in which they were in the early Christian times, before the founder of Constantinople beguiled the devotional spirit to his personal and family benefit,—to the state in which they were before ambitious men sought political advancement and wealth by organizing hypocrisy—when maxims of morality, charity, benevolence, were rules of life for individual man—when the monitions of conscience were obeyed without the suggestions of an outward, often an interested and artful prompter—when the individual lived not under the sleepless gaze, the crushing hand of a great overwhelming hierarchical organization, surrounding him on all sides, doing his thinking for him, directing him in his acts, making him a mere automaton, but in simplicity, humility, and truthfulness guiding himself according to the light given him, and discharging the duties of this troublesome and transitory life "as ever in his great Taskmaster's eye."

For the progressive degradations exhibited by the Roman Church during the Age of Faith, something may be offered as at once an explanation and an excuse. Machiavelli relates, in his 'History of Florence,'—a work which, if inferior in philosophical penetration to his 'Prince,' is of the most singular merit as a literary composition,—that Osporco, a Roman, having become Pope, exchanged his unseemly name for the more classical one Sergius, and that his successors have ever since observed the practice of assuming a new name. This incident profoundly illustrates the psychical progress of that Church. During the fifteen centuries that we have had under consideration—counting from a little before the Christian era—the population of Italy had been constantly changing. The old Roman ethnical element had become eliminated, partly through the republican and imperial wars, and partly through the slave system. The degenerated half-breeds, of whom the Peninsula was full through repeated northern immigrations, degenerated, as time went on, still more and more. After that blood-admixture had for the most part ceased, it took a long time for the base ethnical element which was its product to come into physiological correspondence with the country, for the adaptation of man to a new climate is a slow, a secular change.

But blood-degeneration implies thought-degeneration. It

*Connection of religious ideas in Italy with its ethnical state.*

is nothing more than might be expected that, in this mongrel race, customs and language, and even names should change—that rivers, and towns, and men should receive new appellations. As the great statesman to whom I have referred observes, Cæsar and Pompey had disappeared; John, Matthew, and Peter had come in their stead. Barbarized names are the outward and visible signs of barbarized ideas. Those early bishops of Rome, whose dignified acts have commanded our respect, were men of Roman blood, and animated with sentiments that were truly Latin; but the succeeding pontiffs, whose lives were so infamous and thoughts so base, were engendered of half-breeds. Nor was it until the Italian population had re-established itself in a physiological relation with the country—not until it had passed through the earlier stages of national life—that manly thoughts and true conceptions could be regained.

<small>Successive steps in the religious decline.</small> Ideas and dogmas that would not have been tolerated for an instant in the old, pure, homogeneous Roman race, found acceptance in this adulterated, festering mass. This was the true cause of the increasing debasement of Latin Christianity. He who takes the trouble to construct a chart of the religious conceptions as they successively struggled into light, will see how close was their connection with the physiological state of the Italian ethnical element at the moment. It is a sad and humiliating succession. Mariolatry; the invocation of saints; the supreme value of virginity; the working of miracles by relics; the satisfaction of moral crimes by gifts of money or goods to the clergy; the worship of images; Purgatory; the sale of benefices; transubstantiation, or the making of God by the priest; the materialization of God—that he has eyes, feet, hands, toes; the virtue of pilgrimages; vicarious religion, the sinner paying the priest to pray for him; the corporeality of spirits; the forbidding of the Bible to the laity; the descent to shrine-worship and fetichism; the doctrine that man can do more than his duty, and hence have a claim upon God; the sale by the priest of indulgences in sin for money.

But there is another, a very different aspect under which we must regard this Church. Enveloped as it was with the many evils of the times, the truly Christian principle which was at its basis perpetually vindicated its power, giving rise to numberless blessings in spite of the degradation and wickedness of man. As I have elsewhere ('Physiology,' page 626) remarked, "The civil law exerted an exterior power in human relations; Christianity produced an interior and moral change. The idea of an ultimate accountability for personal deeds, of which the old Europeans had an indistinct perception, became intense and precise. The sentiment of universal charity was exemplified not only in individual acts, the remembrance of which soon passes away, but in the more permanent institution of establishments for the relief of affliction, the spread of knowledge, the propagation of truth. Of the great ecclesiastics, many had risen from the humblest ranks of society, and these men, true to their democratic instincts, were often found to be the inflexible supporters of right against might. Eventually coming to be the depositaries of the knowledge that then existed, they opposed intellect to brute force, in many instances successfully; and by the example of the organization of the Church, which was essentially republican, they showed how representative systems may be introduced into the state. Nor was it over communities and nations that the Church displayed her chief power. Never in the world before was there such a system. From her central seat at Rome, her all-seeing eye, like that of Providence itself, could equally take in a hemisphere at a glance, or examine the private life of any individual. Her boundless influences enveloped kings in their palaces, and relieved the beggar at the monastery gate. In all Europe there was not a man too obscure, too insignificant, or too desolate for her. Surrounded by her solemnities, every one received his name at her altar; her bells chimed at his marriage, her knell tolled at his funeral. She extorted from him the secrets of his life at her confessionals, and punished his faults by her penances. In his hour of sickness and trouble her servants sought him out, teaching him, by her exquisite litanies and prayers, to place his reliance on God, or strengthening him for the trials of life by the example of the holy and just. Her prayers had an efficacy to give repose to the soul of his

*Statement of what the Church had actually done.*

dead. When, even to his friends, his lifeless body had become an offence, in the name of God she received it into her consecrated ground, and under her shadow he rested till the great reckoning-day. From little better than a slave she raised his wife to be his equal, and, forbidding him to have more than one, met her recompense for those noble deeds in a firm friend at every fireside. Discountenancing all impure love, she put round that fireside the children of one mother, and made that mother little less than sacred in their eyes. In ages of lawlessness and rapine, among people but a step above savages, she vindicated the inviolability of her precincts against the hand of power, and made her temples a refuge and sanctuary for the despairing and oppressed. Truly she was the shadow of a great rock in many a weary land!"

*Analysis of the career of the Church.* This being the point which I consider the end of the Italian system as a living force in European progress, its subsequent operation being directed to the senses and not to the understanding, it will not be amiss if for a moment we extend our view to later times and to circumstances beyond the strict compass of this book, endeavouring to ascertain therefrom the condition of the Church, especially as to many devout persons it may doubtless appear that she has lost none of her power.

*Four revolts against the Italian system.* On four occasions there have been revolts against the Italian Church system:—1st, in the thirteenth century, the Albigensian; 2nd, in the fourteenth, the Wickliffite; 3rd, in the sixteenth, the Reformation; 4th, in the eighteenth, at the French Revolution. On each of these occasions ecclesiastical authority has exerted whatever offensive or defensive power it possessed. Its action is a true indication of its condition at the time. Astronomers can determine the orbit of a comet or other celestial meteor by three observations of its position seen from the earth, and taken at intervals apart.

*The Albigensian revolt.* 1st. Of the Albigensian revolt. We have ascertained that the origin of this is distinctly traceable to the Mohammedan influences of Spain, through the schools of Cordova and Granada, pervading Languedoc and Provence. Had these agencies produced only the gay scenes of chivalry and courtesy as their material results, and, as their intellectual, war-ballads, satires, and amorous songs, they had been excused; but, along with such elegant frivolities, there was something of a more serious kind. A popular proverb will often betray national belief, and there was a proverb in Provence, "Viler than a priest." The offensive sectaries also quoted, for the edification of the monks, certain texts, to the effect "that, if a man will not work, neither let him eat." The event, in the hands of Simon de Montfort, taught them that there is such a thing as wresting Scripture to one's own destruction.

How did the Church deal with this Albigensian heresy? As those do who have an absolutely overwhelming power. She did not crush it—that would have been too indulgent; she absolutely annihilated it. Awake to what must necessarily ensue from the imperceptible spread of such opinions, she remorselessly consumed its birthplace with fire and sword; and, fearful that some fugitives might have escaped her vigilant eye, or that heresy might go wherever a bale of goods might be conveyed, she organized the Inquisition, with its troops of familiars and spies. Six hundred years have elapsed since these events, and the south of France has never recovered from the blow.

That was a persecution worthy of a sovereign—a persecution conducted on sound Italian principles of policy—to consider clearly the end to be attained, and adopt the means thereto without any kind of concern as to their nature. But it was a persecution that implied the possession of unlimited and irresponsible power.

2nd. Of the revolt of Wickliffe. We have also considered the state of affairs which aroused the resistance of Wickliffe. It is manifested by legal enactments early in the fourteenth century, such as that ecclesiastics shall not go armed, nor join themselves with thieves, nor frequent taverns nor chambers of strumpets, nor visit nuns, nor play at dice, nor keep concubines; by the Parliamentary bill of 1376, setting forth that the tax paid in England to the Pope for ecclesiastical dignities is fourfold as much as that coming to the king from the whole

*The revolt of Wickliffe.*

realm,—that alien clergy, who have never seen nor care to see their flocks, convey away the treasure of the country; by the homely preaching of John Ball, that all men are equal in the sight of God. Wickliffe's opposition was not only directed against corruptions of discipline in the Church, but equally against doctrinal errors. His dogma that "God bindeth not men to believe anything they cannot understand" is a distinct embodiment of the rights of reason, and the noble purpose he carried into execution of translating the Bible from the Vulgate shows in what direction he intended the application of that doctrine to be made. Through the influence of the queen of Richard the Second, who was a native of that country, his doctrines found an echo in Bohemia; Huss not only earnestly adopting his theological views, but also joining in his resistance to the despotism of the court of Rome and his exposures of the corruptions of the clergy. The political point of this revolt in England occurs in the refusal of Edward III., at the instigation of Wickliffe, to do homage to the Pope; the religious, in the translation of the Bible.

Though a bull was sent to London requiring the arch-heretic to be seized and put in irons, yet Wickliffe died in his bed, and his bones rested quietly in the grave for forty-four years. Ecclesiastical vengeance burned them at last and scattered them to the winds.

There was no remissness in the ecclesiastical authority, but there were victories won by the blind hero John Ziska. After the death of that great soldier—whose body was left by the road-side to the wolves and crows, and his skin dried and made into a drum—in vain was all that perfidy could suggest and all that brutality could execute resorted to; in vain the sword and fire were passed over Bohemia, and the last effort of impotent vengeance tried in England—the heretics could not be exterminated, nor the detested translation of the Bible destroyed.

*The revolt of Luther.*  3rd. Of the revolt of Luther. As we shall have, in a subsequent chapter, to consider the causes that led to the Reformation, it is not necessary to anticipate them in any detail here. The necessities of the Roman treasury, which suggested the doctrine of supererogation and the sale of indulgences as a ready means of relief, merely brought on a crisis which otherwise could not have been long postponed, the real point at issue being the right of interpretation of the Scriptures by private judgment.

The Church did not restrict her resistance to the use of ecclesiastical weapons,—those of a carnal kind she also employed. Yet we look in vain for the concentrated energy with which she annihilated the Albigenses, or the atrocious policy with which the Hussites were met. The times no longer permitted those things. But the struggle was maintained with unflinching constancy through the disasters and successes of one hundred and thirty years. Then came the peace of Westphalia, and the result of the contest was ascertained. The Church had lost the whole of northern Europe.

4th. Of the revolt of the philosophers. Besides the actual loss of the nations who openly fell away to Protestantism, a serious detriment was soon found to have befallen those still remaining nominally faithful to the Church. The fact of secession or adherence, depending, in a monarchy, on the personal caprice or policy of the sovereign, is by no means a true index of the opinions or relations of the subjects; and thus it happened that in several countries in which there was an outward appearance of agreement with the Church because of the attitude of the government, there was, in reality, a total disruption, so far as the educated and thinking classes were concerned. This was especially the case in France.

*The revolt of the philosophers.*

When the voyage of circumnavigation of the world by Magellan had for ever settled all such questions as those of the figure of the earth and the existence of the antipodes, the principles upon which the contest was composed between the conflicting parties are obvious from the most superficial perusal of the history of physics. Free thought was extorted for science, and, as its equivalent, an unmolested state for theology. It was an armed truce.

It was not through either of the parties to that conflict that new troubles arose, but through the action of a class fast rising into importance—literary men. From the beginning to the middle of the last century, these philosophers became more and more audacious in their attacks. Unlike the scientific, whose theological action was by implication rather than in a direct way, these boldly assaulted the intellectual basis of faith. The opportune occurrence of the American Revolution, by bringing forward, in a prominent manner, social evils and political methods for their cure, gave a practical application to the movement in Europe, and the Church was found unable to offer any kind of resistance.

*Movement of the Italian system.*
From these observations of the state of the Church at four different epochs of her career, we are able to determine her movement. There is a time of abounding strength, a time of feebleness, a time of ruinous loss, a time of utter exhaustion. What a difference between the eleventh and the eighteenth centuries! It is the noontide and the evening of a day of empire.

## CHAPTER XIX.

### APPROACH OF THE AGE OF REASON IN EUROPE.

#### IT IS PRECEDED BY MARITIME DISCOVERY.

I HAVE arrived at the last division of my work, the period in national life answering to maturity in individual. The objects to be considered differ altogether from those which have hitherto occupied our attention. We have now to find human authority promoting intellectual advancement, and accepting as its maxim that the lot of man will be ameliorated, and his power and dignity increased, in proportion as he is able to comprehend the mechanism of the world, the action of natural laws, and to apply physical forces to his use. *Peculiarities of the Age of Reason.*

The date at which this transition in European life was made will doubtless be differently given, according as the investigator changes his point of view. In truth, there is not in national life any real epoch, because there is nothing in reality abrupt. Events, however great or sudden, are consequences of preparations long ago made. In this there is a perfect parity between the course of national and that of individual life. In the individual, one state merges by imperceptible degrees into another, each in its beginning and end being altogether indistinct. No one can tell at what moment he ceased to be a child and became a boy—at what moment he ceased to be a youth and became a man. Each condition, examined at a suitable interval, exhibits characteristics perfectly distinctive, but, at their common point of contact, the two so overlap and blend, that, like the intermingling of shadow and light, the beginning of one and end of the other may be very variously estimated. *Natural periods merge into one another.*

148                 *The Epochs of Social Life.*

**Artificial epochs.**

In individual life, since no precise natural epoch exists, society has found it expedient to establish an artificial one, as, for example, the twenty-first year. The exigencies of history may be satisfied by similar fictions.

**Origin and end of the Age of Faith.**

A classical critic would probably be justified in selecting for his purpose the foundation of Constantinople as the epoch of the commencement of the Age of Faith, and its capture by the Turks as the close. It must be admitted that a very large number of historical events stand in harmony with that arrangement. A political writer would perhaps be disposed to postpone the date of the latter epoch to that of the treaty of Westphalia, for from that time theological elements ceased to have a recognized force, Protestant, Catholic, Mohammedan consorting promiscuously together in alliance or at war, according as temporary necessities might indicate. Besides these, other artificial epochs might be assigned, each doubtless having advantages to recommend it to our notice. But, after all, the chief peculiarity is obvious enough. It is the gradual decline of a system that had been in activity for many ages, and its gradual replacement by another.

**Prelude to the Age of Reason.**

As with the Age of Reason in Greece, so with the Age of Reason in Europe, there is a prelude marked by the gradual emergence of a sound philosophy; a true logic displaces the supernatural; experiment supersedes speculation. It is very interesting to trace the feeble beginnings of modern science in alchemy and natural magic in countries where no one could understand the writings of Alhazen or the Arabian philosophers. Out of many names that might be mentioned of those who took part in this movement, there are some that deserve recollection.

**Albertus Magnus, the Dominican.**

Albertus Magnus was born A.D. 1193. It was said of him that "he was great in magic, greater in philosophy, greatest in theology." By religious profession he was a Dominican. Declining the temptations of ecclesiastical preferment, he voluntarily resigned his bishopric, that he might lead in privacy a purer life. As was not uncommon in those days, he was accused of illicit commerce with Satan, and many idle stories were told of the miracles he wrought. At a great banquet, on a winter's day, he produced all the beauties of spring—trees in full foliage, flowers in perfume, meadows covered with grass; but, at a word, the phantom pageant was dissolved, and succeeded by appropriate wastes of snow. This was an exaggeration of an entertainment he gave, January 6th, 1259, in the hothouse of the convent garden. He interested himself in the functions of plants, was well acquainted with what is called the sleep of flowers, studied their opening and closing. He understood that the sap is diminished in volume by evaporation from the leaves. He was the first to use the word "affinity" in its modern acceptation. His chemical studies present us with some interesting details. He knew that the whitening of copper by arsenic is not a transmutation, but only the production of an alloy, since the arsenic can be expelled by heat. He speaks of potash as an alkali; describes several acetates; and alludes to the blackening of the skin with nitrate of silver.

Contemporary with him was Roger Bacon, born A.D. 1214. His native country has never yet done him justice, though his contemporaries truly spoke of him as "the Admirable Doctor." The great friar of the thirteenth century has been eclipsed by an unworthy namesake. His claims on posterity are enforced by his sufferings and ten years' imprisonment for the cause of truth.

*Roger Bacon, discoveries of.*

His history, so far as is known, may be briefly told. He was born at Ilchester, in Somersetshire, and studied at the University of Oxford. From thence he went to the University of Paris, where he took the degree of doctor of theology. He was familiar with Latin, Greek, Hebrew, and Arabic. Of mathematics he truly says, that "it is the first of all the sciences; indeed, it precedes all others, and disposes us to them." In advance of his age, he denied the authority of Aristotle, and tells us that we must substitute that of experiment for it. Of his astronomical acquirements we need no better proof than his recommendation to Pope Clement IV. to rectify the Calendar in the manner actually done subsequently. If to him be rightly attributed the invention of spectacles, the human race is his debtor. He described the true theory of telescopes and microscopes, saying that lenses may be ground and arranged in such a way as to render it possible to read at incredible distances the smallest letters, and to count grains of sand and dust, because of the magnitude of the angle under which we may perceive such objects. He foresaw the greatest of all inventions in practical astronomy—the application of optical means to instruments for the measurement of angles. He proposed the propulsion of ships through the water and of carriages upon roads with great velocity, without any animal power, by merely mechanical means, and speculated upon the possibility of making a flying machine. Admitting the truth of alchemy, he advised the experimenter to find out the method by which Nature makes metals, and then to imitate it. He knew that there are different kinds of air, and tells that there is one which will extinguish a flame. These are very clear views for an age which mistook the gases for leather-eared ghosts. He warned us to be cautious how we conclude that we have accomplished the transmutation of metals, quaintly observing that the distance between whitened copper and pure silver is very great. He showed that air is necessary for the support of fire, and was the author of the well-known experiment illustrating that point by putting a lighted lamp under a bell-jar and observing the extinction which takes place.

*Is persecuted and imprisoned.* There is no little significance in the expression of Friar Bacon that the ignorant mind cannot sustain the truth. He was accused of magical practices and of a commerce with Satan, though, during the life of Clement IV., who was his friend, he escaped without public penalties. This Pope had written to him a request that he would furnish him with an account of his various inventions. In compliance therewith, Bacon sent him the 'Opus Majus' and other works, together with several mathematical instruments which he had made, as Newton did, with his own hands. But, under the pontificate of Nicholas III., the accusation of magic, astrology, and selling himself to the Devil was again pressed; one point being that he had proposed to construct astronomical tables for the purpose of predicting future events. Apprehending the worst, he tried to defend himself by his composition 'De Nullitate Magiæ.' "Because these things are beyond your comprehension, you call them the works of the Devil; your theologians and canonists abhor them as the productions of magic, regarding them as unworthy of a Christian." But it was in vain. His writings were condemned as containing dangerous and suspected novelties, and himself committed to prison. There he remained for ten years, until, broken in health, he was released from his punishment by the intercession of some powerful and commiserating personages. He died at the age of seventy-eight years. On his death-bed, he uttered the melancholy complaint, "I repent now that I have given myself so much trouble for the love of science." If there be found in his works sentiments that are more agreeable to the age in which he lived than to ours, let us recollect what he says in his third letter to Pope Clement: "It is on account of the ignorance of those with whom I have had to deal that I have not been able to accomplish more."

A number of less conspicuous though not unknown names succeed to Bacon. There is Raymond Lully, who was said to have been shut up in the Tower of London and compelled to make gold for Edward II.; Guidon de Montanor, the inventor of the philosopher's balm; Clopinel, the author of the Romance of the Rose; Richard the Englishman, who makes the sensible remark that he who does not join theory to practice is like an ass eating hay, and not reflecting on what he is doing; Master Ortholan, who describes very prettily the making of nitric acid, and approaches to the preparation of absolute alcohol under the title of the quintessence of wine; Bernard de Treves, who obtained much reputation for the love-philters he prepared for Charles V. of France, their efficacy having been ascertained by experiments made on servant-girls; Bartholomew, the Englishman who first described the method of crystallizing and purifying sugar; Eck de Sulzbach, who teaches how metallic crystallizations, such as the tree of Diana, a beautiful silvery vegetation, may be produced. He proved experimentally that metals, when they oxidize, increase in weight; and says that in the month of November, A.D. 1489, he found that six pounds of an amalgam of silver heated for eight days augmented in weight three pounds. His number is, of course, erroneous, but his explanation is very surprising. "This augmentation

*Minor alchemists of England, France, and Germany.*

of weight comes from this, that a spirit is united with the metal; and what proves it is, that this artificial cinnabar, submitted to distillation, disengages that spirit." He was within a hair's-breadth of anticipating Priestley and Lavoisier by three hundred years.

*Augurelli, the poetical alchemist.* The alchemists of the fifteenth century not only occupied themselves with experiment; some of them, as Augurelli, aspired to poetry. He undertook to describe in Latin verses the art of making gold. His book, entitled 'Chrysopœia,' was dedicated to Leo X.,—a fact which shows the existence of a greater public liberality of sentiment at the commencement of the sixteenth century than heretofore. It is said that the author expected the Holy Father to make him a handsome recompense; but the good-natured Pope merely sent him a large empty sack, saying that he who knew how to make gold so admirably, only needed a purse to put it in.

*Basil Valentine introduces antimony.* The celebrated work of Basil Valentine, entitled 'Currus Triumphalis Antimonii,' introduced the metal antimony into the practice of medicine. The attention of this author was first directed to the therapeutical relations of the metal by observing that some swine, to which a portion of it had been given, grew fat with surprising rapidity. There were certain monks in his vicinity, who, during the season of Lent, had reduced themselves to the last degree of attenuation by fasting and other corporeal mortifications. On these Basil was induced to try the powers of the metal. To his surprise, instead of recovering their flesh and fatness, they were all killed; hence the name popularly given to the metal, antimoine, because it does not agree with the constitution of a monk. Up to this time it had passed under the name of stibium. Attended with a result not very different was the application of antimony in the composition of printer's type-metal. Administered internally, or thus mechanically used, this metal proved equally noxious to ecclesiastics.

*The new epoch.* It is scarcely necessary to continue the relation of these scientific trifles. Enough has been said to illustrate the quickly-spreading taste for experimental inquiry. I now hasten to the description of more important things.

In the limited space of this book I must treat these subjects, not as they should be dealt with philosophically, but in the manner that circumstances permit. Even with this imperfection, their description spontaneously assumes an almost dramatic form, the facts offering themselves to all reflecting men with an air of surpassing dignity. On one hand it is connected with topics the most sublime, on the other it descends to incidents the most familiar and useful; on one hand it elevates our minds to the relations of suns and myriads of worlds, on the other it falls to the every-day acts of our domestic and individual life; on one hand it turns our thoughts to a vista of ages so infinite that the vanishing point is in eternity, on the other it magnifies into importance the transitory occupation of a passing hour. Knowing how great are the requirements for the right treatment of such topics, I might shrink from this portion of my book with a conviction of incapacity. I enter upon it with hesitation, trusting rather to the considerate indulgence of the reader than to any worthiness in the execution of the work.

*Difficulty of treating it scientifically.*

In the history of the philosophical life of Greece, we have seen (Chapter II.) how important were the influences of maritime discovery and the rise of criticism. Conjointly they closed the Greek Age of Faith. In the life of Europe, at the point we have now reached, they came into action again. As on this occasion the circumstances connected with them are numerous and important, I shall consider them separately in this and the following chapter. And, first, of maritime enterprise, which was the harbinger of the Age of Reason in Europe. It gave rise to three great voyages—the discovery of America, the doubling of the Cape, and the circumnavigation of the earth.

*Approach of the Age of Reason.*

At the time of which we are speaking, the commerce of the Mediterranean was chiefly in two directions. The ports of the Black Sea furnished suitable depôts for produce brought down the Tanais and other rivers, and for a large portion of the India trade that had come across the Caspian. The seat of this commerce was Genoa.

*State of Mediterranean trade.*

The other direction was the south-east. The shortest course to India was along the Euphrates and the Persian Gulf, but the Red and Arabian Seas offered a cheaper and safer route. In the ports of Syria and Egypt were therefore found the larger part of the commodities of India. This trade centred in Venice. A vast developement had been given to it through the Crusades, the Venetians probably finding in the transport service of the Holy Wars as great a source of profit as in the India trade.

*Rivalry of Genoa and Venice.* Toward the latter part of the fourteenth century it became apparent that the commercial rivalry between Venice and Genoa would terminate to the disadvantage of the latter. The irruption of the Tartars and invasion of the Turks had completely dislocated her Asiatic lines of trade. In the wars between the two republics Genoa had suffered severely. Partly for this reason, and partly through the advantageous treaties that Venice had made with the sultans, giving her the privilege of consulates at Alexandria and Damascus, this republic had at last attained a supremacy over all competitors. The Genoese establishments on the Black Sea had become worthless.

*Attempt to reach India by the West.* With ruin before them, and unwilling to yield their Eastern connections, the merchants of Genoa had tried to retrieve their affairs by war; her practical sailors saw that she might be re-established in another way. There were among them some who were well acquainted with the globular form of the earth, and with what had been done by the Mohammedan astronomers for determining its circumference by the measurement of a degree on the shore of the Red Sea. These men originated the attempt to reach India by sailing to the west.

*Opposition to this scheme.* By two parties, the merchants and the clergy, their suggestions were received with little favour. The former gave no encouragement, perhaps because such schemes were unsuited to their existing arrangements; the latter disliked them because of their suspected irreligious nature. The globular form had been condemned by such fathers as Lactantius and Augustine. In the Patristic geography the earth is a flat surface, bordered by the waters of the sea, on the yielding support of which rests the crystalline dome of the sky. These doctrines were for the most part supported by passages from the Holy Scriptures, perversely wrested from their proper meaning. Thus Cosmas Indicopleustes, whose Patristic geography had been an authority for nearly eight hundred years, unanswerably disposed of the sphericity of the earth by demanding of its advocates how, in the day of judgment, men on the other side of a globe could see the Lord descending through the air!

Among the Genoese sailors seeking the welfare of their city was one destined for immortality—Christopher Columbus.

His father was a wool-comber, yet not a man of the common sort, for he procured for his son a knowledge of arithmetic, drawing, painting; and Columbus is said to have written a singularly beautiful hand. For a short time he was at the University of Pavia, but he went to sea at fourteen. After being engaged in the Syrian trade for many years, he had made several voyages to Guinea, occupying his time when not at sea in the construction of charts for sale, thereby supporting not only himself, but also his aged father, and finding means for the education of his brothers. Under these circumstances he had obtained a competent knowledge of geography, and, though the state of public opinion at the time did not permit such doctrines to be openly avowed, he believed that the sea is everywhere navigable, that the earth is round and not flat, that there are antipodes, that the torrid zone is habitable, and that there is a proportionable distribution of land in the northern and southern hemispheres. Adopting the Patristic logic when it suited his purpose, he reasoned that since the earth is made for man, it is not likely that its surface is too largely covered with water, and that, if there are lands, they must be inhabited, since the command was renewed at the flood that man should replenish the earth. He asked, "Is it likely that the sun shines upon nothing, and that the nightly watches of the stars are wasted on trackless seas and desert lands?" But to this reasoning he added facts that were more substantial. One Martin Vincent, who had sailed many miles to the west of the Azores, related to him that he had found, floating on the sea, a piece of timber carved evidently without iron. Another sailor, Pedro Correa, his brother-in-law, had met with

*Columbus, early life of.*

*His argument for lands to the west.*

enormous canes. On the coast of Flores the sea had cast up two dead men with large faces, of a strange aspect. Columbus appears to have formed his theory that the East Indies could be reached by sailing to the west about A.D. 1474. He was at that time in correspondence with Toscanelli, the Florentine astronomer, who held the same doctrine, and who sent him a map or chart constructed on the travels of Marco Polo. He offered his services first to his native city, then to Portugal, then to Spain, and, through his brother, to England; his chief inducement in each instance being that the riches of India might be thus secured. In Lisbon he had married. While he lay sick near Delem an unknown voice whispered to him in a dream, "God will cause thy name to be wonderfully resounded through the earth, and will give thee the keys of the gates of the ocean, which are closed with strong chains." The death of his wife appears to have broken the last link which held him to Portugal, where he had been since 1470. One evening, in the autumn of 1485, a man of majestic presence, pale, care-worn, and, though in the meridian of life, with silver hair, leading a little boy by the hand, asked alms at the gate of the Franciscan convent near Palos—not for himself, but only a little bread and water for his child. This was that Columbus destined to give to Europe a new world.

*Is confuted by the Council of Salamanca.*  In extreme poverty, he was making his way to the Spanish Court. After many wearisome delays his suit was referred to a council at Salamanca, before whom, however, his doctrines were confuted from the Pentateuch, the Psalms, the Prophecies, the Gospels, the Epistles, and the writings of the Fathers—St. Chrysostom, St. Augustine, St. Jerome, St. Gregory, St. Basil, St. Ambrose. Moreover, they were demonstrably inconsistent with reason; since, if even he should depart from Spain, "the rotundity of the earth would present a kind of mountain up which it was impossible for him to sail, even with the fairest wind;" and so he could never get back. The Grand Cardinal of Spain had also indicated their irreligious nature, and Columbus began to fear that, instead of receiving aid as a discoverer, he should fall into trouble as a heretic. However, after many years of mortification and procrastination, he at length prevailed with Queen Isabella; and on April 17, 1492, in the field before Granada, then just wrenched from the Mohammedans by the arms of Ferdinand and Isabella, he received his commission. With a nobleness of purpose, he desired no reward unless he should succeed; but, in that case, stipulated that he should have the title of Admiral and Viceroy, and that his perquisite should be one-tenth of all he should discover—conditions which show what manner of man this great sailor was. He had bound himself to contribute one-eighth to the expenses of the expedition: this he accomplished through the Pinzons of Palos, an old and wealthy seafaring family. These arrangements once ratified, he lost not a moment in completing the preparations for his expedition. The royal authority enabled him to take—forcibly, if necessary—both ships and men. But even with that advantage he would hardly have succeeded if the Pinzons had not joined heartily with him, personally sharing in the dangers of the voyage.

*Queen Isabella adopts his views.*

*The expedition prepared.*

The sun, by journeying to the west, rises on India at last. On Friday, August 3, 1492, the weary struggles and heart-sickness of eighteen years of supplication were over, and, as the day was breaking, Columbus sailed with three little ships from Palos, carrying with him charts constructed on the basis of that which Toscanelli had formerly sent, and also a letter to the Grand Khan of Tartary. On the 9th he saw the Canaries, being detained among them three weeks by the provisioning and repairing of his ships. He left them September 6th, escaping the pursuit of some caravels sent out by the Portuguese government to intercept him. He now steered due west. Nothing of interest occurred until nightfall on September 13th, when he remarked with surprise that the needle, which the day before had pointed due north, was varying half a point to the west, the effect becoming more and more marked as the expedition advanced. He was now beyond the track of any former navigator, and with no sure guide but the stars; the heaven was everywhere, and everywhere the sea. On Sunday, 16th, he encountered many floating weeds, and picked up what was mistaken for a live grasshopper. For some days the weeds increased in quantity, and retarded the sailing of the ships.

*The voyage across the Atlantic.*

On the 19th two pelicans flew on board. Thus far he had had an easterly wind; but on September 20th it changed to southwest, and many little birds, such as those that sing in orchards, were seen. His men now became mutinous, and reproached the king and queen for trusting to "this bold Italian, who wanted to make a great lord of himself at the price of their lives."

On September 25th Pinzon reported to him that he thought he saw land; but it proved to be only clouds. With great difficulty he kept down his mutinous crew. On October 2nd he observed the seaweeds drifting from east to west. Pinzon having seen in the Pinta a flight of parrots going to the southwest, the course was altered on October 7th, and he steered after them west-south-west; he had hitherto been on the parallel 26° N. On the evening of October 11th the signs of land had become so unmistakable that, after vesper hymn to the Virgin, he made an address of congratulation to his crew, and commended watchfulness to them. His course was now due west. A little before midnight, Columbus, on the forecastle of his ship, saw a moving light at a distance, and two hours after a signal-gun was fired from the Pinta. A sailor, Rodrigo de Triana, had descried land. The ships were laid to. As soon as day dawned, they made it out to be a verdant island. There were naked Indians upon the beach watching their movements. At sunrise, October 12th, 1492, the boats were manned and armed, and Columbus was the first European to set foot on the new tropical world.

*Discovery of America.*

*Events of the voyage.*

The chief events of the voyage of Columbus were—1st. The discovery of the line of no magnetic variation, which, as we shall see, eventually led to the circumnavigation of the earth. 2nd. The navigability of the sea to the remote west, the weeds not offering any insuperable obstruction. When the ships left Palos, it was universally believed that the final border or verge of the earth is where the western sky rests upon the sea, and the air and clouds, fogs and water are commingled. Indeed, that boundary could not actually be attained; for, long before it was possible to reach it, the sea was confused with inextricable weeds, through which a ship could not pass. This legend was perhaps derived from the stories of adventurous sailors, who had been driven by stress of weather toward the Sargasso Sea, and seen an island of weeds many hundreds of square miles in extent—green meadows floating in the ocean. 3rd. As to the new continent, Columbus never knew the nature of his own discovery. He died in the belief that it was actually some part of Asia, and Americus Vespucius entertained the same misconception. Their immediate successors supposed that Mexico was the Quinsay, in China, of Marco Polo. For this reason I do not think that the severe remark that the "name of America is a monument of human injustice," is altogether merited. Had the true state of things been known, doubtless the event would have been different. The name of America first occurs in an edition of Ptolemy's Geography, on a map by Hylacomylus.

Two other incidents of no little interest followed this successful voyage: the first was the destruction of Patristic geography; the second was the consequence of the flight of Pinzon's parrots. Though, as we now know, the conclusion that India had been reached was not warranted by the facts, it was on all sides admitted that the old doctrine was overthrown, and that the admiral had reached Asia by sailing to the west. This necessarily implied the globular form of the earth. As to the second, never was an augury more momentous than that flight of parrots. It has been well said that this event determined the distribution of Latin and German Christianity in the New World. *End of Patristic Geography.*

The discovery of America by Leif, the son of Eric the Red, A.D. 1000, cannot diminish the claims of Columbus. The wandering Scandinavians had reached the shores of America first in the vicinity of Nantucket, and had given the name of Vinland to the region extending from beyond Boston to the south of New York. But the memory of these voyages seems totally to have passed away, or the lands were confounded with Greenland, to which Nicholas V. had appointed a bishop A.D. 1448. Had these traditions been known to or respected by Columbus, he would undoubtedly have steered his ships more to the north. *Previous Scandinavian discovery.*

## Awful Results

**The Papal grant to Spain.**

Immediately on the return of Columbus, March 15, 1493, the King and Queen of Spain dispatched an ambassador to Pope Alexander VI. for the purpose of ensuring their rights to the new territories, on the same principle that Martin V. had already given to the King of Portugal possession of all lands he might discover between Cape Bojador and the East Indies, with plenary indulgence for the souls of those who perished in the conquest. The pontifical action was essentially based on the principle that pagans and infidels have no lawful property in their lands and goods, but that the children of God may rightfully take them away. The bull that was issued bears date May, 1493. Its principle is, that all countries under the sun are subject of right to Papal disposal. It gives to Spain, in the fulness of apostolic power, all lands west and south of a line drawn from the Arctic to the Antarctic pole, one hundred leagues west of the Azores. The donation includes, by the authority of Almighty God, whatever there is toward India, but saves the existing rights of any Christian princes. It forbids, under pain of excommunication, any one trading in that direction, threatening the indignation of Almighty God and his holy apostles Peter and Paul. It directs the barbarous nations to be subdued, and no pains to be spared for reducing the Indians to Christianity.

**The magnetic line of no variation.**

This suggestion of the line of no magnetic variation was due to Columbus, who fell into the error of supposing it to be immovable. The infallibility of the pontiff not extending to matters of science, he committed the same mistake. In a few years it was discovered that the line of no variation was slowly moving to the east. It coincided with the meridian of London in 1662.

**Patristic ethnical ideas.**

The obstacles that Patristic geography had thrown in the way of maritime adventure were thus finally removed, but Patristic ethnology led to a fearful tragedy. With a critical innocence that seems to have overlooked physical impossibilities and social difficulties, it had been the practice to refer the peopling of nations to legendary heroes or to the patriarchs of Scripture. The French were descended from Franeus, the son of Hector; the Britons from Brutus, the son of Æneas; the genealogy of the Saxon kings could be given, up to Adam; but it may excite our mirthful surprise that the conscientious Spanish chronicles could rise no higher than to Tubal, the grandson of Noah. The divisions of the Old World—Asia, Africa, and Europe—were assigned to the three sons of Noah, Shem, Ham, and Japheth; and the parentage of those continents was given to those patriarchs respectively. In this manner all mankind were brought into a family relationship, all equally the descendants of Adam, equally participators in his sin and fall. As long as it was supposed that the lands of Columbus were a part of Asia, there was no difficulty; but when the true position and relations of the American continent were discovered, that it was separated from Asia by an impassable waste of waters of many thousand miles, how did the matter stand with the new-comers thus suddenly obtruded on the scene? The voice of the Fathers was altogether against the possibility of their Adamic descent. St. Augustine had denied the globular form and the existence of antipodes; for it was impossible that there should be people on what was thus vainly asserted to be the other side of the earth, since none such are mentioned in the Scriptures. The lust of gold was only too ready to find its justification in the obvious conclusion; and the Spaniards, with an appalling atrocity, proceeded to act toward these unfortunates as though they did not belong to the human race. Already their lands and goods had been taken from them by apostolic authority. Their persons were next seized, under the text that the heathen are given as an inheritance, and the uttermost parts of the earth for a possession. It was one unspeakable outrage, one unutterable ruin, without discrimination of age or sex. They who died not under the lash in a tropical sun, died in the darkness of the mine. From sequestered sandbanks, where the red flamingo fishes in the grey of the morning; from fever-stricken mangrove thickets, and the gloom of impenetrable forests; from hiding-places in the clefts of the rocks, and the solitude of invisible caves; from the eternal snows of the Andes, where there was no witness but the all-seeing sun, there went up to God a cry of human despair. By millions upon millions, whole races and nations

*Denial that the Indians are men.*

*The American tragedy.*

were remorselessly cut off. The Bishop of Chiapa affirms that more than fifteen millions were exterminated in his time! From Mexico and Peru a civilization that might have instructed Europe was crushed out. Is it for nothing that Spain has been made a hideous skeleton among living nations, a warning spectacle to the world? Had not her punishment overtaken her, men would have surely said, "There is no retribution; there is no God!" It has been her evil destiny to ruin two civilizations, Oriental and Occidental, and to be ruined thereby herself. With circumstances of dreadful barbarity she expelled the Moors, who had become children of her soil by as long a residence as the Normans have had in England from William the Conqueror to our time. In America she destroyed races more civilized than herself. Expulsion and emigration have deprived her of her best blood, her great cities have sunk into insignificance, and towns that once had more than a million of inhabitants can now only show a few scanty thousands.

<small>The crime of Spain.</small>

The discovery of America agitated Europe to its deepest foundations. All classes of men were affected. The populace went wild at once with a lust of gold and a love of adventure. Well might Pomponius Lætus, under process for his philosophical opinions in Rome, shed tears of joy when tidings of the great event reached him; well might Leo X., a few years later, sit up till far in the night reading to his sister and his cardinals the 'Oceanica' of Anghiera.

If Columbus failed in his attempt to reach India by sailing to the west, Vasco de Gama succeeded by sailing to the south. He doubled the Cape of Good Hope, and retraced the track of the ships of Pharaoh Necho, which had accomplished the same undertaking two thousand years previously. The Portuguese had been for long engaged in an examination of the coast of Africa under the bull of Martin V., which recognized the possibility of reaching India by passing round that continent. It is an amusing instance of making scientific discoveries by contract, that King Alphonso made a bargain with Ferdinand Gomez, of Lisbon, for the exploration of the African coast; the

<small>Vasco de Gama. African coasting-voyages.</small>

stipulation being that he should discover not less than three hundred miles every year, and that the starting-point should be Sierra Leone.

We have seen that a belief in the immobility of the line of no magnetic variation had led Pope Alexander VI. to establish a perpetual boundary between the Spanish and Portuguese possessions and fields of adventure. That line be considered to be the natural boundary between the eastern and western hemispheres. An accurate determination of longitude was therefore a national as well as a nautical question. Columbus had relied on astronomical methods; Gilbert, at a subsequent period, proposed to determine it by magnetical observations. The variation itself could not be accounted for on the doctrine vulgarly received, that magnetism is an effluvium issuing forth from the root of the tail of the Little Bear, but was scientifically, though erroneously, explained by Gilbert's hypothesis that earthy substance is attractive—that a needle approaching a continent will incline toward it; and hence, that in the midst of the Atlantic, being equally disturbed by Europe and America, it will point evenly between both. *Papal confines of Spain and Portugal.*

Pedro de Covilho had sent word to King John II., from Cairo, by two Jews, Rabbi Abraham and Rabbi Joseph, that there was a south cape of Africa which could be doubled. They brought with them an Arabic map of the African coast. This was about the time that Bartholomew Diaz had reached the Cape in two little pinnaces, of fifty tons apiece. He sailed in August, 1486, and returned in December, 1487, with an account of his discovery. Covilho had learned from the Arabian mariners, who were perfectly familiar with the east coast, that they had frequently been at the south of Africa, and that there was no difficulty in passing round the continent that way. *News that Africa might be doubled.*

A voyage to the south is even more full of portents than one to the west. The accustomed heavens seem to sink away, and new stars are nightly approached. Vasco de Gama set sail July 9, 1497, with three ships and one hundred and sixty men, having with him the Arab map. King John had employed his Jewish physicians, Roderigo and Joseph, to devise *De Gama's successful voyage.*

what help they could from the stars. They applied the astrolabe to marine use, and constructed tables. These were the same doctors who had told him that Columbus would certainly succeed in reaching India, and advised him to send out a secret expedition in anticipation, which was actually done, though it failed through want of resolution in its captain. Encountering the usual difficulties, tempestuous weather and a mutinous crew, who conspired to put him to death, De Gama succeeded, November 20, in doubling the Cape. On March 1 he met seven small Arab vessels, and was surprised to find that they used the compass, quadrants, sea-charts, and "had divers maritime mysteries not short of the Portugals." With joy he soon after recovered sight of the northern stars, for so long unseen. He now bore away to the north-east, and on May 19, 1498, reached Calicut, on the Malabar coast.

*He reaches India.*

The consequences of this voyage were to the last degree important. The commercial arrangements of Europe were completely dislocated; Venice was deprived of her mercantile supremacy; the hatred of Genoa was gratified; prosperity left the Italian towns; Egypt, hitherto supposed to possess a pre-eminent advantage as offering the best avenue to India, suddenly lost her position; the commercial monopolies so long in the hands of the European Jews were broken down. The discovery of America and passage of the Cape were the first steps of that prodigious maritime developement soon exhibited by Western Europe. And since commercial prosperity is forthwith followed by the production of men and concentration of wealth, and moreover implies an energetic intellectual condition, it appeared before long that the three centres of population, of wealth, of intellect, were shifting westwardly. The front of Europe was suddenly changed; the British islands, hitherto in a sequestered and eccentric position, were all at once put in the van of the new movement.

*A commercial revolution the result.*

Commercial rivalry had thus passed from Venice and Genoa to Spain and Portugal. The circumnavigation of the earth originated in a dispute between these kingdoms respecting the Molucca Islands, from which nutmegs, cloves, and mace were obtained. Ferdinand Magellan had been in the service of the King of Portugal; but an application he had made for an increase of half a ducat a month in his stipend having been refused, he passed into the service of the King of Spain, along with one Ruy Falero, a friend of his, who, among the vulgar, bore the reputation of a conjuror or magician, but who really possessed considerable astronomical attainments, devoting himself to the discovery of improved means for finding the place of a ship at sea. Magellan persuaded the Spanish government that the Spice Islands could be reached by sailing to the west, the Portuguese having previously reached them by sailing to the east; and, if this were accomplished, Spain would have as good a title to them, under the bull of Alexander VI., as Portugal. Five ships, carrying 237 men, were accordingly equipped, and on August 10, 1519, Magellan sailed from Seville. The Trinitie was the admiral's ship, but the San Vittoria was destined for immortality. He struck boldly for the south-west, not crossing the trough of the Atlantic as Columbus had done, but passing down the length of it, his aim being to find some cleft or passage in the American continent through which he might sail into the Great South Sea. For seventy days he was becalmed under the line. He then lost sight of the north star, but courageously held on toward the "pole antartike." He nearly foundered in a storm, "which did not abate till the three fires called St. Helen, St. Nicholas, and St. Clare appeared playing in the rigging of the ships." In a new land, to which he gave the name of Patagoni, he found giants "of good corporature" clad in skins; one of them, a very pleasant and tractable giant, was terrified at his own visage in a looking-glass. Among the sailors, alarmed at the distance they had come, mutiny broke out, requiring the most unflinching resolution in the commander for its suppression. In spite of his watchfulness, one ship deserted him and stole back to Spain. His perseverance and resolution were at last rewarded by the discovery of the strait named by him San Vittoria in affectionate honour of his ship, but which, with a worthy sentiment, other sailors soon changed to "the Strait of Magellan." On November 28, 1520, after a year and a quarter of struggling,

he issued forth from its western portals and entered the Great
South Sea, shedding tears of joy, as Pigafetti, an eye-witness,
relates, when he recognized its infinite expanse—tears of stern
joy that it had pleased God to bring him at length where he
might grapple with its unknown dangers. Admiring its illimitable but placid surface, and exulting in the meditation of
its secret perils soon to be tried, he courteously imposed on it
the name it is for ever to bear, "the Pacific Ocean." While
baffling for an entry into it, he observed with surprise that in
the month of October the nights are only four hours long, and
"considered, in this his navigation, that the pole antartike
hath no notable star like the pole artike, but that there be
two cloudes of little stars somewhat dark in the middest, also
a cross of fiue clear stars, but that here the needle becomes so
sluggish that it needs must be moved with a bit of loadstone
before it will rightly point."

*The Pacific Ocean crossed.*
And now the great sailor, having burst through the barrier
of the American continent, steered for the north-west, attempting to regain the equator. For three months and twenty days
he sailed on the Pacific, and never saw inhabited land. He
was compelled by famine to strip off the pieces of skin and
leather wherewith his rigging was here and there bound, to
soak them in the sea, and then soften them with warm water,
so as to make a wretched food; to eat the sweepings of the
ship and other loathsome matter; to drink water turned putrid by keeping; and yet he resolutely held on his course,
though his men were dying daily. As is quaintly observed,
their gums grew over their teeth, and so they could not eat.
He estimated that he sailed over this unfathomable sea not
less than 12,000 miles.

In the whole history of human undertakings there is nothing
that exceeds, if indeed there is anything that equals, this voyage of Magellan. That of Columbus dwindles away in comparison. It is a display of superhuman courage, superhuman
perseverance,—a display of resolution not to be diverted from
its purpose by any motive or any suffering, but inflexibly persisting to its end. Well might his despairing sailors come to
the conclusion that they had entered on a trackless waste of

waters, endless before them and hopeless in a return. "But, though the Church hath evermore from Holy Writ affirmed that the earth should be a wide-spread plain bordered by the waters, yet he comforted himself when he considered that in the eclipses of the moon the shadow cast of the earth is round; and as is the shadow, such in like manner is the substance." It was a stout heart—a heart of triple brass—which could thus, against such authority, extract unyielding faith from a shadow.

This unparalleled resolution met its reward at last. Magellan reached a group of islands north of the equator—the Ladrones. In a few days more he became aware that his labours had been successful; he met with adventurers from Sumatra. But, though he had thus grandly accomplished his object, it was not given to him to complete the circumnavigation of the globe. At an island called Zebu, or Mutan, he was killed, either, as has been variously related, in a mutiny of his men, or—as they declared—in a conflict with the savages, or insidiously by poison. "The General," they said, "was a very brave man, and received his death-wound in his front; nor would the savages yield up his body for any ransom." Through treason and revenge it is not unlikely that he fell, for he was a stern man; none but a very stern man could have accomplished so daring a deed. Hardly was he gone when his crew learned that they were actually in the vicinity of the Moluccas, and that the object of their voyage was fulfilled. On the morning of November 8, 1521, having been at sea two years and three months, as the sun was rising they entered Tidore, the chief port of the Spice Islands. The King of Tidore swore upon the Koran alliance to the King of Spain.

I need not allude to the wonderful objects—destined soon to become common to voyagers in the Indian Archipelago—that greeted their eyes: elephants in trappings; vases and vessels of porcelain; birds of Paradise, "that fly not, but be blown by the wind;" exhaustless stores of the coveted spices, nutmegs, mace, cloves. And now they prepared to bring the news of their success back to Spain. Magellan's lieutenant, Sebastian de Elcano, directed his course for the Cape of Good

Hope, again encountering the most fearful hardships. Out of his slender crew he lost twenty-one men. He doubled the Cape at last; and on September 7, 1522, in the port of St. Lucar, near Seville, under his orders, the good ship San Vittoria came safely to an anchor. She had accomplished the greatest achievement in the history of the human race,—she had circumnavigated the earth.

Magellan thus lost his life in his enterprise, and yet he made an enviable exchange. Doubly immortal, and thrice happy! for he impressed his name indelibly on the earth and the sky, on the strait that connects the two great oceans, and on those clouds of starry worlds seen in the southern heavens. He also imposed a designation on the largest portion of the surface of the globe. His lieutenant, Sebastian de Elcano, received such honours as kings can give. Of all armorial bearings ever granted for the accomplishment of a great and daring deed, his were the proudest and noblest—the globe of the world, belted with the inscription, " Primus circumdedisti me!"

*Elcano, the lieutenant of Magellan.*

*Results of the circumnavigation.*

If the circumnavigation of the earth by Magellan did not lead to such splendid material results as the discovery of America and the doubling of the Cape, its moral effects were far more important. Columbus had been opposed in obtaining means for his expedition because it was suspected to be of an irreligious nature. Unfortunately, the Church, satisfying instincts impressed upon her as far back as the time of Constantine, had asserted herself to be the final arbitress in all philosophical questions, and especially in this of the figure of the earth had committed herself against its being globular. Infallibility can never correct itself—indeed, it can never be wrong. Rome never retracts anything; and, no matter what the consequences, never recedes. It was thus that a theological dogma—infallibility—came to be mixed up with a geographical problem, and that problem liable at any moment to receive a decisive solution. So long as it rested in a speculative position, or could be hedged round with mystification, the real state of the case might be concealed from all except the more intelligent class of men; but after the circumnavigation had actually been accomplished, and was known to every one, there was, of course, nothing more to be said. It had now become altogether useless to bring forward the authority of Lactantius, of St. Augustine, or of other Fathers, that the globular form is impious and heretical. Henceforth the fact was strong enough to overpower all authority, an exercise of which could have no other result than to injure itself. It remained only to permit the dispute to pass into oblivion; but even this could not occur without those who were observant being impressed with the fact that physical science was beginning to display a fearful advantage over Patristicism, and presenting unmistakable tokens that ere long she would destroy her ancient antagonist.

In the midst of these immortal works it is hardly worth speaking of minor things. Two centuries had wrought a mighty change in the geographical ideas of Western Europe. The travels of Marco Polo, about A.D. 1295, had first given some glimmering of the remote East, the interest in which was doubtless enhanced by the irruption of the Moguls. Sir John Mandeville had spent many years in the interior of Asia before the middle of the next century. Conti had travelled in Persia and India between 1419 and 1444. Cadamosto, a Venetian, in 1455 had explored the west coast of Africa. Sebastian Cabot had rediscovered Newfoundland, and, persisting in the attempt to find a north-west passage to China, had forced his way into the ice to 67° 30′ N. By 1525 the American coast-line had been determined, from Tierra del Fuego to Labrador. New Guinea and part of Australia had been discovered. The fleet of Cabral, attempting to double the Cape of Good Hope in 1500, was driven to Brazil. A ship was sent back to Portugal with the news. Hence, had not Columbus sailed when he did, the discovery of America could not have been long postponed. Balboa saw the Great South Sea September 25th, 1513. Wading up to his knees in the water with his sword in one hand and the Spanish flag in the other, he claimed that vast ocean for Castile. Nothing could now prevent the geography of the world from being completed.

I cannot close these descriptions of maritime adventure

*Minor voyages and travels.*

without observing that they are given from the European point of view. The Western nations have complacently supposed that whatever was unknown to them was therefore altogether unknown. We have seen that the Arabs were practically and perfectly familiar with the fact that Africa might be circumnavigated; the East Indian geography was thoroughly understood by the Buddhist priesthood, who had, on an extensive scale, carried forward their propagandism for twenty-five hundred years in those regions. But doubtless the most perfect geographical knowledge existed among the Jews, those cosmopolite traders who conducted mercantile transactions from the Azores to the interior of China, from the Baltic to the coast of Mozambique. It was actually through them that the existence of the Cape of Good Hope was first made known in Europe. Five hundred years before Columbus, the Scandinavian adventurers had discovered America, but so low was the state of intelligence in Europe that the very memory of those voyages had been altogether lost. The circumnavigation of the earth is, however, strictly the achievement of the West. I have been led to make the remarks in this paragraph, since they apply again on another occasion—the introduction of what is called the Baconian philosophy, the principles of which were not only understood, but carried into practice in the East eighteen hundred years before Bacon was born.

*Participation of other nations in these events.*

It is scarcely necessary that I should offer any excuse for devoting a few pages to a digression on the state of affairs in Mexico and Peru. Few things illustrate more strikingly the doctrine which it is the object of this book to teach.

*Progress of man in the New World the same as in the Old.*

The social condition of America at its discovery demonstrates that similar ideas and similar usages make their appearance spontaneously in the progress of civilization of different countries, showing how little they depend on accident, how closely they are connected with the organization, and therefore with the necessities, of man. From important ideas and great institutions down to the most trifling incidents of domestic life, so striking is the parallel between the American aborigines and Europeans that with difficulty do we divest ourselves of the impression that there must have been some intercommunication. Each was, however, pursuing an isolated and spontaneous progress; and yet how closely does the picture of life in the New World answer to that in the Old! The monarch of Mexico lived in barbaric pomp; wore a golden crown resplendent with gems; was aided in his duties by a privy council; the great lords held their lands of him by the obligation of military service. In him resided the legislative power, yet he was subject to the laws of the realm. The judges held their office independently of him, and were not liable to removal by him. The laws were reduced to writing, which, though only a system of hieroglyphics, served its purpose so well that the Spaniards were obliged to admit its validity in their courts, and to found a professorship for perpetuating a knowledge of it. Marriage was regarded as an important social engagement. Divorces were granted with difficulty. Slavery was recognized in the case of prisoners of war, debtors, and criminals; but no man could be born a slave in Mexico. No distinction of castes was permitted. The government mandates and public intelligence were transmitted by a well-organized postal service of couriers, able to make two hundred miles a day. The profession of arms was the recognised avocation of the nobility; the military establishments, whether in active service in the field, or as garrisons in large towns, being supported by taxation on produce or manufactures. The armies were divided into corps of 10,000, and these again into regiments of 400. Standards and banners were used; the troops executed their evolutions to military music, and were provided with hospitals, army surgeons, and a medical staff. In the human hives of Europe, Asia, and America, the bees were marshalled in the same way, and were instinctively building their combs alike. *Mexico; its political system.*

The religious state is a reflection of that of Europe and Asia. Their worship was an imposing ceremonial. The common people had a mythology of many gods, but the higher classes were strictly Unitarian, acknowledging one almighty, invisible Creator. Of the popular deities, the god of war was the chief. He was born of a virgin, and conceived by immaculate con- *Its religion, priesthood, and ceremonies.*

ception of a ball of bright-coloured feathers floating on the air. The priest administered a rite of baptism to infants for the purpose of washing away their sins, and taught that there are rewards and punishments in a life to come,—a paradise for the good, a hell of darkness for the wicked. The hierarchy descended by due degrees from the chief priests, who were almost equal to the sovereign in authority, down to the humble ecclesiastical servitors. Marriage was permitted to the clergy. They had monastic institutions, the inmates praying thrice a day and once at night. They practised ablutions, vigils, penance by flagellation or pricking with aloe thorns. They compelled the people to auricular confession, required of them penance, gave absolution. Their ecclesiastical system had reached a strength which was never attained in Europe, since absolution by the priests for civil offences was an acquittal in the eye of the law. It was the received doctrine that men do not sin of their own free will, but because they are impelled thereto by planetary influences. With sedulous zeal, the clergy engrossed the duty of public education, thereby keeping society in their grasp. Their writing was on cotton cloth or skins, or on papyrus made of the aloe. At the conquest, immense collections of this kind of literature were in existence; but the first Archbishop of Mexico burnt, as was affirmed, a mountain of such manuscripts in the market-place, stigmatizing them as magic scrolls. About the same time, and under similar circumstances, Cardinal Ximenes burnt a vast number of Arabic manuscripts in Granada.

*Its literary condition.*

The condition of astronomy in Mexico is illustrated as it is in Egypt, by the calendar. The year was of eighteen months, each month of twenty days, five complementary ones being added to make up the three hundred and sixty-five. The month had four weeks, the week five days; the last day, instead of being for religious purposes, was market-day. To provide for the six additional hours of the year, they intercalated twelve days and a half every fifty-two years. At the conquest, the Mexican calendar was in a better condition than the Spanish. As in some other countries, the clergy had for ecclesiastical purposes a lunar division of time. The day had sixteen hours,

*Divisions of time— the week, month, year.*

### Agriculture, and Mechanical Arts.

commencing at sunrise. They had sun-dials for determining the hour, and also instruments for the solstices and equinoxes. They had ascertained the globular form of the earth and the obliquity of the ecliptic. The close of the fifty-second year was celebrated with grand religious ceremonials; all the fires were suffered to go out, and new ones kindled by the friction of sticks. Their agriculture was superior to that of Europe; there was nothing in the Old World to compare with the menageries and botanical gardens of Huaxtepec, Chapultepec, Istapalapan, and Tezcuco. They practised with no inconsiderable skill the more delicate mechanical arts, such as those of the jeweller and enameller. From the aloe they obtained pins and needles, thread, cord, paper, food, and an intoxicating drink. They made earthenware, knew how to lacquer wood, employed cochineal as a scarlet dye. They were skilful weavers of fine cloth, and excelled in the production of feather-work, their gorgeous humming-birds furnishing material for that purpose. In metallurgy they were behind the Old World, not having the use of iron; but, as the Old World had formerly done, they employed bronze in its stead. They knew how to move immense masses of rock; their great calendar stone, of porphyry, weighed more that fifty tons, and was brought a distance of many miles. Their trade was carried on, not in shops, but by markets or fairs held on the fifth day. They employed a currency of gold dust, pieces of tin, and bags of cacao. In their domestic economy, though polygamy was permitted, it was in practice confined to the wealthy. The women did not work abroad, but occupied themselves in spinning, embroidering, feather-work, music. Ablution was resorted to both before and after meals; perfumes were used at the toilet. The Mexicans gave to Europe tobacco, snuff, the turkey, chocolate, cochineal. Like us, they had in their entertainments solid dishes, with suitable condiments, gravies, sauces, and desserts of pastries, confections, fruits, both fresh and preserved. They had chafing-dishes of silver or gold. Like us, they knew the use of intoxicating drinks; like us, they not unfrequently took them to excess; like us, they heightened their festivities with dancing and music. They had theatrical and pantomimic

*Private life, mechanical arts, trade.*

*Luxury of the higher classes.*

shows. At Tezcuco there was a council of music, which moreover exercised a censorship on philosophical works, as those of astronomy and history. In that city North American civilization reached its height. The king's palace was a wonderful work of art. It was said that 200,000 men were employed in its construction. Its harem was adorned with magnificent tapestries of featherwork; in its garden were fountains, cascades, baths, statues, alabasters, cedar groves, forests, and a wilderness of flowers. In conspicuous retirement in one part of the city was a temple, with a dome of polished black marble, studded with stars of gold, in imitation of the sky. It was dedicated to the omnipotent, invisible God. In this no sacrifices were offered, but only sweet-scented flowers and gums. The prevailing religious feeling is expressed by the sentiments of one of the kings, many of whom had prided themselves in their poetical skill: "Let us," he says, "aspire to that heaven where all is eternal, and where corruption never comes." He taught his children not to confide in idols, but only to conform to the outward worship of them in deference to public opinion.

*Their monotheism and philosophical sentiments.*

To the preceding description of the social condition of Mexico I shall add a similar brief account of that of Peru, for the conclusions to be drawn from a comparison of the spontaneous process of civilization in these two countries with the process in Europe is of importance to the attainment of a just idea of the developement of mankind. The most competent authorities declare that the Mexicans and Peruvians were ignorant of each other's existence.

*Peru—unknown to Mexico.*

In one particular especially is the position of Peru interesting. It presents an analogy to Upper Egypt, that cradle of the civilization of the Old World, in this, that its sandy coast is a rainless district. This sandy coast region is about sixty miles in width, hemmed in on the east by grand mountain-ranges, which diminish in size on approaching the Isthmus of Panama, the entire length of the Peruvian empire having been nearly 2400 miles; it reached from the north of the equator to what is now known as Chili. In breadth it varied at different points. The east wind, which has crossed the Atlantic, and is therefore

*Its geographical peculiarities. A rainless country like Egypt.*

charged with humidity, being forced by the elevation of the
South American continent, and especially by the range of the
Andes, upward, is compelled to surrender most of its moisture,
which finds its way back to the Atlantic in those prodigious
rivers that make the country east of the Andes the best-watered
region of the world; but as soon as that wind has crossed the
mountain ridge and descends on the western slope, it becomes
a dry and rainless wind, and hence the district intervening to
the Pacific has but a few insignificant streams. The sides of this *Its system of agriculture.*
great mountain-range might seem altogether unadapted to the
pursuit of agriculture, but the state of Peruvian civilization
is at once demonstrated when it is said that those mountain
slopes had become a garden, immense terraces having been
constructed wherever required, and irrigation on a grander
scale than that of Egypt carried on by gigantic canals and
aqueducts. Advantage was taken of the different mean annual
temperatures at different altitudes to pursue the cultivation
of various products, for difference in height topographically
answers to difference in latitude geographically; and thus, in a
narrow space, the Peruvians had every variety of temperature,
from that corresponding to the hottest portions of Southern
Europe to that of Lapland. In the mountains of Peru, as has
been graphically said, man sees "all the stars of the heavens
and all the families of plants." On plateaus at a great elevation
above the sea there were villages and even cities. Thus
the plain upon which Quito stands, under the equator, is nearly
ten thousand feet high. So great was their industry that the
Peruvians had gardens and orchards above the clouds; and on
ranges still higher, flocks of lamas, in regions bordering on the
limit of perpetual snow.

Through the entire length of the empire two great military *Its great roads and engineering.*
roads were built; one on the plateau, the other on the shore.
The former, for nearly 2000 miles, crossed sierras covered with
snow, was thrown over ravines, or went through tunnels in the
rocks; it scaled the more difficult precipices by means of stairways.
Where it was possible, it was carried over the mountain
clefts by filling them with masonry, or, where that could
not be done, suspension bridges were used, the cables being

made of osiers or maguey fibres. Some of these cables are said to have been as thick as a man, and two hundred feet long. Where such bridges could not be thrown across, and a stream flowed in the bottom of the mountain valley, the passage was made by ferry-boats or rafts. As to the road itself, it was about twenty feet in breadth, faced with flags covered with bitumen, and had mile-stones. Our admiration at this splendid engineering is enhanced when we remember that it was accomplished without iron and gunpowder. The shore-road was built on an embankment, with a clay parapet and shade-trees on each side; where circumstances called for it, piles were used. Every five miles there was a post-house. The public couriers, as in Mexico, could make, if necessary, two hundred miles a day. Of these roads, Humboldt says that they were among the most useful and most stupendous ever executed by the hand of man. The reader need scarcely be told that there were no such triumphs of skill in Spain. From the circumstance that there were no swift animals as the horse or dromedary, the width of these roads was sufficient, since they were necessarily used for foot-passage alone.

*And express by couriers.*

In Cuzco, the metropolis, was the imperial residence of the Inca and the Temple of the Sun. It contained edifices which excited the amazement of the Spanish filibusters themselves,—streets, squares, bridges, fortresses surrounded by turreted walls, subterranean galleries by which the garrison could reach important parts of the town. Indeed, the great roads we have spoken of might be regarded as portions of an immense system of military works spread all over the country, and having their centre at Cuzco.

*Cuzco—the military centre.*

The imperial dignity was hereditary, descending from father to son. As in Egypt, the monarch not unfrequently had his sisters for wives. His diadem consisted of a scarlet tasselled fringe round his brow, adorned with two feathers. He wore earrings of great weight. His dress of lama-wool was dyed scarlet, inwoven with gold and studded with gems. Whoever approached him bore a light burden on the shoulder as a badge of servitude, and was barefoot. The Inca was not only the representative of the temporal, but also of the spiritual

*The Inca—the Lord of the Empire.*

power. He was more than supreme pontiff, for he was a descendant of the Sun, the god of the nation. He made laws, imposed taxes, raised armies, appointed or removed judges at his pleasure. He travelled in a sedan ornamented with gold and emeralds; the roads were swept before him, strewn with flowers, and perfumed. His palace at Yucay was described by the Spaniards as a fairy scene. It was filled with works of Indian art; images of animals and plants decorated the niches of its wall; it had an endless labyrinth of gorgeous chambers, and here and there shady crypts for quiet retirement. Its baths were great golden bowls. It was embosomed in artificial forests. The imperial ladies and concubines spent their time in beautifully furnished chambers, or in gardens, with cascades and fountains, grottoes and bowers. It was in what few countries can boast of, a temperate region in the torrid zone. *The national palace.*

The Peruvian religion ostensibly consisted of a worship of the Sun, but the higher classes had already become emancipated from such a material association, and recognised the existence of one almighty, invisible God. They expected the resurrection of the body and the continuance of the soul in a future life. It was their belief that in the world to come our occupations will resemble those we have followed here. Like the Egyptians, who had arrived at similar ideas, the Peruvians practised embalming, the mummies of their Incas being placed in the Temple of the Sun at Cuzco, the kings on the right, the queens on the left, clad in their robes of state, and with their hands crossed on their bosoms, seated in golden chairs, waiting for the day when the soul will return to reanimate the body. The mummies of distinguished personages were buried in a sitting posture under tumuli of earth. To the Supreme Being but one temple was dedicated. It was in a sacred valley, to which pilgrimages were made. In the Peruvian mythology, heaven was above the sky, hell in the interior of the earth— it was the realm of an evil spirit called Cupay. The general resemblance of these to Egyptian doctrines may forcibly impress upon us that they are ideas with which the human mind necessarily occupies itself in its process of intellectual development. As in all other countries, the educated classes were *Religion of Peru, its establishments and ceremonial.*

greatly in advance of the common people, who were only just emerging from fetichism, and engrossed in the follies of idolatry and man-worship. Nevertheless, the government found it expedient to countenance the vulgar delusion; indeed, the political system was actually founded upon it. But the Peruvians were in advance of the Europeans in this respect, that they practised no persecutions upon those who had become mentally emancipated. Besides the sun, the visible god, other celestial bodies were worshipped in a subordinate way. It was supposed that there were spirits in the wind, lightning, thunder; genii in the mountains, rivers, springs, and grottoes. In the great Temple of the Sun at Cuzco an image of that deity was placed so as to receive the rays of the luminary at his rising; a like artifice had been practised in the Serapion at Alexandria. There was also a sanctuary dedicated to the Sun in the island of Titicaca, and, it is said, between three and four hundred temples of a subordinate kind in Cuzco. To the great temple were attached not fewer than four thousand priests and fifteen hundred vestal virgins, the latter being entrusted with the care of the sacred fire, and from them the most beautiful were chosen to pass into the Inca's seraglio. The popular faith had a ritual and a splendid ceremonial, the great national festival being at the summer solstice. The rays of the sun were then collected by a concave mirror, and a fire rekindled thereby, or by the friction of wood.

*Social system—the nobility, the people.*

As to their social system, polygamy was permitted, but practically it was confined to the higher classes. Social subordination was thoroughly understood. The Inca Tupac Yupanqui says, "Knowledge was never intended for the people, but only for those of generous blood." The nobility were of two orders—the polygamic descendants of the Incas, who were the main support of the state, and the adopted nobles of nations that had been conquered. As to the people, nowhere else in the whole world was such an extraordinary policy of supervision practised. They were divided into groups of ten, fifty, one hundred, five hundred, one thousand, ten thousand, and over the last an Inca noble was placed. Through this system a rigid centralization was ensured, the Inca being the pivot upon which all the national affairs turned. It was an absolutism worthy of the admiration of many existing European nations. The entire territory was divided into three parts: one belonged to the Sun, one to the Inca, one to the people. As a matter of form, the subdivision was annually made; in practice, however, as perhaps must always be the result of such agrarianism, the allotments were continually renewed. All the land was cultivated by the people, and in the following order:—first, that of the Sun, then that of the destitute and infirm, then that of the people, and lastly that of the Inca. The Sun and the Inca owned all the sheep, which were shared, and their wool distributed to the people, or cotton furnished in its stead. The Inca's officers saw that it was all woven, and that no one was idle. An annual survey of the country, its farming and mineral products, was made, the inventory being transmitted to the government. A register was kept of births and deaths; periodically, a general census was taken. The Inca, at once emperor and pope, was enabled, in that double capacity, to exert a rigorous patriarchal rule over his people, who were treated like mere children,—not suffered to be oppressed, but compelled to be occupied; for, with a worldly wisdom which no other nation presents, labour was here acknowledged not only as a means, but also as an end. In Peru a man could not improve his social state; by these refinements of legislation he was brought into an absolutely stationary condition. He could become neither richer nor poorer; but it was the boast of the system that every one lived exempt from social suffering,—that all enjoyed competence. Organization of labour.

The army consisted of 200,000 men. Their weapons were bows, lances, slings, battle-axes, swords; their means of defence, shields, bucklers, helmets, and coats of quilted cotton. Each regiment had its own banner, but the imperial standard, the national emblem, was a rainbow, the offspring of the Sun. The swords and many of the domestic implements were of bronze; the arrows were tipped with quartz or bone, or points of gold and silver. A strict discipline was maintained on marching, granaries and depôts being established at suitable distances on the roads. With a policy inflexibly persisted in, the gods Military system; warlike resources.

of conquered countries were transported to Cuzco, and the vanquished compelled to worship the Sun; their children were obliged to learn the Peruvian language, the government providing them teachers for that purpose. As an incitement, this knowledge was absolutely required as a condition for public office. To amalgamate the conquered districts thoroughly, their inhabitants were taken away by ten thousand, transported to distant parts of the empire—not, as in the Old World, to be worked to death as slaves, but to be made into Peruvians; an equal number of natives were sent in their stead, to whom, as a recompense for their removal, extraordinary privileges were given. It was an immemorial policy of the empire to maintain a profound tranquillity in the interior, and perpetual war on the frontiers.

*Peruvian literature— the quipus.* The philosophical advancement of the Peruvians was much retarded by their imperfect method of writing,—a method greatly inferior to that of Egypt. A cord of coloured threads, called quipus, was only indifferently suited to the purposes of enumeration, and by no means equal to hieroglyphics as a method of expressing general facts. But it was their only system. Notwithstanding this drawback, they had a literature consisting of poetry, dramatic compositions, and the like. Their scientific attainments were inferior to the Mexican. Their year was divided into months, their months into weeks. They had gnomons to indicate the solstices. One in the form of an obelisk, in the centre of a circle, on which was marked an east and west line, indicated the equinox. These gnomons were destroyed by the Spaniards, in the belief that they were for idolatrous purposes; for, on the national festivals, it was customary to decorate them with leaves and flowers. As the national religion consisted in the worship of the Sun, it was not without reason that Quito was regarded as a holy place, from its position upon the equator.

*Agriculture carried to perfection.* In their extraordinary provisions for agriculture, the national pursuit, the skill of the Peruvians is well seen. A rapid elevation from the sea-level to the heights of the mountains gave them, in a small compass, every variety of climate, and they availed themselves of it. They terraced the mountain-sides, filling the terraces with rich earth. They excavated pits in the sand, surrounded them with adobe walls, and filled them with manured soil. On the low level they cultivated bananas and cassava; on the terraces above, maize and quinoa; still higher, tobacco; and above that, the potato. From a comparatively limited surface, they raised great crops by judiciously using manures, employing for that purpose fish, and especially guano. Their example has led to the use of the latter substance for a like purpose in our own times in Europe. The whole civilized world has followed them in the cultivation of the potato. The Peruvian bark is one of the most invaluable remedies. Large tracts of North America would be almost uninhabitable without the use of its active alkaloid, quinine, which actually, in no insignificant manner, reduces the percentage mortality throughout the United States.

Indispensably necessary to their agricultural system were their great water-works. In Spain there was nothing worthy of being compared with them. The aqueduct of Condesuya was nearly five hundred miles long. Its engineers had overcome difficulties in a manner that might well strike modern times with admiration. Its water was distributed as prescribed by law; there were officers to see to its proper use. From these great water-works, and from their roads, it may be judged that the architectural skill of the Peruvians was far from insignificant. They constructed edifices of porphyry, granite, brick; but their buildings were for the most part low, and suitable to an earthquake country. *The great aqueduct of Condesuya.*

I have dwelt at some length on the domestic history of Mexico and Peru because it is intimately connected with one of the philosophical principles which it is the object of this book to teach, viz. that human progress takes place under an unvarying law, and therefore in a definite way. The trivial incidents mentioned in the preceding paragraphs may perhaps have seemed insignificant or wearisome, but it is their very commonness, their very familiarity, that gives them, when rightly considered, a surprising interest. There is nothing in these minute details but what we find to be perfectly natural from the European point of view. They might be, for that *The stages of human development are always the same.*

matter, instead of reminiscences of the spontaneous evolution of a people shut out from the rest of the world by impassable oceans, a relation of the progress of some European or Asiatic nation. The man of America proceeded forward in his course of civilization as did the man of the Old World, devising the same institutions, guided by the same intentions, constrained by the same desires. From the great features of his social system down to the little details of his domestic life, there is a sameness with what was done in Asia, Africa, Europe. But similar results imply a similar cause. What, then, is there possessed in common by the Chinese, the Hindoo, the Egyptian, the European, the American? Surely not climate, nor equal necessities, nor equal opportunity. Simply nothing but this—corporeal organization! As automatons constructed in the same way will do the same things, so, in organic forms, samenesses of structure will give rise to identity of function and similarity of acts. The same common sense guides men all over the world. Common sense is a function of common organization. All natural history is full of illustrations. It may be offensive to our pride, but it is none the less true, that, in his social progress, the free-will of which man so boasts himself in his individual capacity disappears as an active influence, and the domination of general and inflexible laws becomes manifest. The free-will of the individual is supplanted by instinct and automatism in the race. To each individual bee the career is open; he may taste of this flower, and avoid that; he may be industrious in the garden, or idle away his time in the air; but the history of one hive is the history of another hive; there will be a predestined organization—the queen, the drones, the workers. In the midst of a thousand unforeseen, uncalculated, variable acts, a definite result, with unerring certainty, emerges; the combs are built in a preordained way, and filled with honey at last. From bees, and wasps, and ants, and birds—from all that low animal life on which he looks with such supercilious contempt, man is destined one day to learn what in truth he really is.

*Analogy between societies of men and societies of animals.*

*The crime of Spain in America.*

For a second reason also I have dwelt on these details. The enormous crime of Spain in destroying this civilization has never yet been appreciated in Europe. After an attentive consideration of the facts of the case, I agree in the conclusion of Carli, that at the time of the conquest the moral man in Peru was superior to the European, and, I will add, the intellectual man also. In Spain, or even in all Europe, was there to be found a political system carried out into the practical details of actual life, and expressed in great public works as its outward, visible, and enduring sign, which could at all compare with that of Peru? Its only competitor was the Italian system, but that for long had been actively used to repress the intellectual advancement of man. In vain the Spaniards excuse their atrocities on the plea that a nation like the Mexican, which permitted cannibalism, should not be regarded as having emerged from the barbarous state; and that one which, like Peru, sacrificed human hecatombs at the funeral solemnities of great men, must have been savage. Let it be remembered that there is no civilized nation whose popular practices do not lag behind its intelligence; let it be remembered that in this respect Spain herself also was guilty. In America, human sacrifice was part of a religious solemnity, unstained by passion. The auto da fé of Europe was a dreadful cruelty; not an offering to heaven, but a gratification of spite, hatred, fear, vengeance—the most malignant passions of earth. There was no spectacle on the American continent at which a just man might so deeply blush for his race as that presented in Western Europe when the heretic, from whom confession had been wrung by torture, passed to his stake in a sleeveless garment, with flames of fire and effigies of an abominable import depicted upon it. Let it be remembered that by the Inquisition, from 1481 to 1808, 340,000 persons had been punished, and of these nearly 32,000 burnt. Let what was done in the south of France be remembered. Let it be also remembered that, considering the worthlessness of the body of man, and that, at the best, it is at last food for the worm,—considering the infinite value of his immortal soul, for the redemption of which the agony and death of the Son of God were not too great a price to pay, indignities offered to the body are less wicked than indignities offered to the soul. It would be well for him

*The Spaniard and the American.*

*European and American human sacrifices.*

who comes forward as an accuser of Mexico and Peru in their sin, to dispose of the fact that at that period the entire authority of Europe was directed to the perversion, and even total repression of thought,—to an enslaving of the mind, and making that noblest creation of Heaven a worthless machine. To taste of human flesh is less criminal in the eye of God than to stifle human thought.

*Antiquity of American civilisation.*

Lastly, there is another point, to which I will with brevity allude. It has been widely asserted that Mexican and Peruvian civilization was altogether a recent affair, dating at most only two or three centuries before the conquest. It would be just as well to say that there was no civilization in India before the time of the Macedonian invasion because there exist no historic documents in that country anterior to that event. The Mexicans and Peruvians were not heroes of a romance, to whom wonderful events were of common occurrence, whose lives were regulated by laws not applying to the rest of the human race, who could produce results in a day for which elsewhere a thousand years are required. They were men and women like ourselves, slowly and painfully, and with many failures, working out their civilization. The summary manner in which they have been disposed of reminds us of the amusing way in which the popular chronology deals with the hoary annals of Egypt and China. Putting aside the imperfect methods of recording events practised by the autochthons of the Western world, he who estimates rightly the slowness with which man passes forward in his process of civilization, and collates therewith the prodigious works of art left by those two nations—an enduring evidence of the point to which they had attained—will find himself constrained to cast aside such idle assertions as altogether unworthy of confutation, or even of attention.

# CHAPTER XX.

### APPROACH OF THE AGE OF REASON IN EUROPE.

#### IT IS PRECEDED BY THE RISE OF CRITICISM.

IN estimating the influences of literature on the approach of the Age of Reason in Europe, the chief incidents to be considered are the disuse of Latin as a learned language, the formation of modern tongues from the vulgar dialects, the invention of printing, the decline of the power of the pulpit, and its displacement by that of the press. These, joined to the moral and intellectual influences at that time predominating, led to the great movement known as the Reformation. *The rise of criticism.*

As if to mark out to the world the real cause of its intellectual degradation, the regeneration of Italy commenced with the exile of the Popes to Avignon. During their absence, so rapid was the progress that it had become altogether impossible to make any successful resistance, or to restore the old condition of things on their return to Rome. The moment that the leaden cloud which they had kept suspended over the country was withdrawn, the light from heaven shot in, and the ready peninsula became instinct with life. *Epoch of the intellectual movement.*

The unity of the Church, and therefore its power, required the use of Latin as a sacred language. Through this Rome had stood in an attitude strictly European, and was enabled to maintain a general international relation. It gave her far more power than her asserted celestial authority, and, much as she claims to have done, she is open to condemnation that, with such a signal advantage in her hands, never again to be enjoyed by any successor, she did not accomplish much more. *Use of Latin as a sacred language.*

Had not the sovereign pontiffs been so completely occupied with maintaining their temporalities in Italy, they might have made the whole Continent advance like one man. Their officials could pass without difficulty into every nation, and communicate without embarrassment with each other, from Ireland to Bohemia, from Italy to Scotland. The possession of a common tongue gave them the administration of international affairs, with intelligent allies speaking the same language in all directions.

*Causes of the dislike of Rome to the Greek.*

Not, therefore, without cause was the hatred manifested by Rome to the restoration of Greek and introduction of Hebrew, and the alarm with which she perceived the modern languages forming out of the aboriginal and vulgar dialects. The prevalence of Latin was the condition of her power, its deterioration the measure of her decay, its disuse the signal of her limitation to a little principality in Italy. In fact, the developement of European languages was the instrument of her overthrow. Besides their forming an effectual communication between the low, dissatisfied ecclesiastics and the illiterate populace, there was not one of them that did not display in its earliest productions a sovereign contempt for her. We have seen how it was with the poetry of Languedoc.

*And danger from modern languages.*

The rise of the many-tongued European literature was therefore coincident with the decline of Papal Christianity. European literature was impossible under the Catholic rule. A grand, and solemn, and imposing religious unity enforced the literary unity which is implied in the use of a single language. No more can a living thought be embodied in a dead language than activity be imparted to a corpse. That principle of stability which Italy hoped to give to Europe essentially rested on the compulsory use of a dead tongue. The first token of intellectual emancipation was the movement of the great Italian poets, led by Dante, who often, not without irreverence, broke the spell. Unity in religion implies unity through a sacred language, and hence the non-existence of particular national literatures.

*Public disadvantages of a sacred tongue.*

*Effect of modern languages.*

Even after Rome had suffered her great discomfiture on the scientific question respecting the motion of the earth, the conquering party was not unwilling to veil its thoughts in the Latin tongue, partly because it thereby ensured a more numerous class of intelligent readers, and partly because ecclesiastical authority was now disposed to overlook what must otherwise be treated as offensive, since to write in Latin was obviously a pledge of abstaining from an appeal to the vulgar. The effect of the introduction of modern languages was to diminish intercommunication among the learned.

The movement of human affairs, for so many years silent and imperceptible, was at length coming to a crisis. An appeal to the emotions and moral sentiments at the basis of the system, the history of which has occupied us so long, had been fully made, and found ineffectual. It was now the time for a like appeal to the understanding. Each age of life has its own logic. The logic of the senses is in due season succeeded by that of the intellect. Of faith there are two kinds, one of acquiescence, one of conviction; and a time inevitably arrives when emotional faith is supplanted by intellectual. *Approach of a crisis in Europe.*

As if to prove that the impending crisis was not the offspring of human intentions, and not occasioned by any one man, though that man might be the sovereign pontiff, Nicholas V. found in his patronage of letters and art a rival and friend in Cosmo de' Medici. An instructive incident shows how great a change had taken place in the sentiments of the higher classes. Cosmo, the richest of Italians, who had lavished his wealth on palaces, churches, hospitals, libraries, was comforted on his death-bed, not, as in former days would have been the case, by ministers of religion, but by Marsilius Ficinus, the Platonist, who set before him the arguments for a future life, and consoled his passing spirit with the examples and precepts of Greek philosophy, teaching him thereby to exchange faith for hope, forgetting that too often hopes are only the day-dreams of men, not less unsubstantial and vain than their kindred of the night. Ficinus had perhaps come to the conviction that philosophy is only a higher stage of theology, the philosopher a very enlightened theologian. He was the representative of Platonism, which for so many centuries had been hidden from the sight of men in Eastern monasteries since its *Cosmo de' Medici, Florence.* *Reappearance of Platonism in Italy.*

overthrow in Alexandria, and which was now emerging into existence in the favouring atmosphere of Italy. His school looked back with delight, and even with devotion, to the illustrious Pagan times, commemorating by a symposium, on November 13th, the birthday of Plato. The Academy of Athens was revived again in the Medicean gardens of Florence. Not that Ficinus is to be regarded as a servile follower of the great philosopher. He alloyed the doctrines of Plato with others derived from a more sinister source—the theory of the Mohammedan Averrhoes, of which it was an essential condition that there is a soul of humanity, through their relations with which individual souls are capable of forming universal ideas, for such, Averrhoes asserted, is the necessary consequence of the emanation theory.

*Doctrines of Marsilius Ficinus.*

Under such auspices, and at this critical moment, occurred the revival of Greek literature in Italy. It had been neglected for more than seven hundred years. In the solitary instances of individuals to whom here and there a knowledge of that language was imputed, there seem satisfactory reasons for supposing that their acquirements amounted to little more than the ability of translating some "petty patristic treatise." The first glimmerings of this revival appear in the thirteenth century; they are somewhat more distinct in the fourteenth. The capture of Constantinople by the Latin Crusaders had done little more than diffuse a few manuscripts and works of art, along with the more highly-prized monkish relics, in the West. It was the Turkish pressure, which all reflecting Greeks foresaw could have no other result than the fall of the Byzantine power, that induced some persons of literary tastes to seek a livelihood and safety in Italy.

*Revival of Greek learning in Italy.*

In the time of Petrarch, 1304-1374, the improvement did not amount to much. That illustrious poet says that there were not more than ten persons in Italy who could appreciate Homer. Both Petrarch and Boccaccio spared no pains to acquaint themselves with the lost tongue. The latter had succeeded in obtaining for Leontius Pilatus, the Calabrian, a Greek professorship at Florence. He describes this Greek teacher as clad in the mantle of a philosopher, his countenance

*Gradual progress of the Restoration.*

hideous, his face overshadowed with black hair, his beard long and uncombed, his deportment rustic, his temper gloomy and inconstant, but his mind was stored with the treasures of learning. Leoutius left Italy in disgust, but returning again, was struck dead by lightning in a storm while tied to the mast of the ship. The author from whom I am quoting significantly adds that Petrarch laments his fate, but nervously asks whether "some copy of Euripides or Sophocles might not be recovered from the mariners."

The restoration of Greek to Italy may be dated A.D. 1395, at which time Chrysoloras commenced teaching it. A few years after Aurispa brought into Italy two hundred and thirty-eight Greek manuscripts; among them were Plato and Pindar. The first endeavour was to translate such manuscripts into Latin. To a considerable extent, the religious scruples against Greek literature were giving away; the study found a patron in the Pope himself, Eugenius IV. As the intention of the Turks to seize Constantinople became more obvious, the emigration of learned Greeks into Italy became more frequent. And yet, with the exception of Petrarch, and he was scarcely an exception, not one of the Italian scholars was an ecclesiastic.

Lorenzo de' Medici, the grandson of Cosmo, used every exertion to increase the rising taste, generously permitting his manuscripts to be copied. Nor was it alone to literature that he extended his patronage. In his beautiful villa at Fiesole the philosophy of the old times was revived; his botanic garden at Careggi was filled with Oriental exotics. From 1470 to 1492, the year of his death, his happy influence continued. He lived to witness the ancient Platonism overcoming the Platonism of Alexandria, and the pure doctrine of Aristotle expelling the base Aristotelian doctrine of the schools.

*Lorenzo de' Medici, his villas, gardens, and philosophy.*

The latter half of the fifteenth century revealed to Western Europe two worlds, a new one and an old; the former by the voyage of Columbus, the latter by the capture of Constantinople: one destined to revolutionize the industrial, the other the religious condition. Greek literature, forced into Italy by the Turkish arms, worked wonders; for Latin Europe found

*Effects instantly produced by the Greek language.*

with amazement that the ancient half of Christendom knew nothing whatever of the doctrine or of the saints of the West. Now was divulged the secret reason of that bitter hatred displayed by the Catholic clergy to Grecian learning. It had sometimes been supposed that the ill-concealed dislike they had so often shown to the writings of Aristotle was because of the Arab dress in which his Saracen commentators had presented him; now it appeared that there was something more important, more profound. It was a terror of the Greek itself. Very soon the direction toward which things must inevitably tend became manifest; the modern languages, fast developing, were making Latin an obsolete tongue, and political events were giving it a rival—Greek—capable of asserting over it a supremacy; and not a solitary rival, for to Greek it was clear that Hebrew would soon be added, bringing with it the charms of a hoary antiquity and the sinister learning of the Jew. With a quick, a jealous suspicion, the ecclesiastic soon learned to detect a heretic from his knowledge of Greek and Hebrew, just as is done in our day from a knowledge of physical science. The authority of the Vulgate, that cornerstone of the Italian system, was, in the expectation of Rome, inevitably certain to be depreciated; and, in truth, judging from the honours of which that great translation was soon despoiled by the incoming of Greek and Hebrew, it was declared, not with more emphasis than truth, yet not perhaps without irreverence, that there was a second crucifixion between two thieves. Long after the times of which we are speaking, the University of Paris resisted the introduction of Greek into its course of studies, not because of any dislike to letters, but because of its anticipated obnoxious bearing on Latin theology.

*Causes of the prevailing dislike of Greek.*

We can scarcely look in any direction without observing instances of the wonderful change taking place in the opinions of men. To that disposition to lean on a privileged mediating order, once the striking characteristic of all classes of the laity in Europe, there had succeeded a sentiment of self-reliance. Of this perhaps no better proof can be furnished than the popularity of the work reputed to have been written by Thomas

*Tendency of 'The Imitation of Christ.'*

à Kempis, and entitled 'The Imitation of Christ.' It is said to have had probably more readers than any other book except the Bible. Its quick celebrity is a proof how profoundly ecclesiastical influence had been affected, for its essential intention was to enable the pious to cultivate their devotional feeling without the intervention of the clergy. Such a work, if written in the present day, would have found an apt and popular title in 'Every Man his own Priest.' There is no reason for supposing that the condition to which men had at that time been brought, as the general result of Italian Christianity, was one of intense selfishness, as has been asserted; the celebrity of this book was rather dependent on a profound distrust everywhere felt in the clergy, both as regards morals and intellect. And why should we be surprised that such should be the case with the laity, when in all directions the clergy themselves were giving proof that they could not trust their own strength? They could not conceal their dread at the incoming of the Greek; they could not speak without horror of the influence of the Hebrew; they were loud in their protestations against the study of Pagan philosophy, and held up to the derision and condemnation of the world science denounced by them as profane. They foresaw that that fictitious unity of which they had boasted was drawing to an end; that men would become acquainted with the existence and history of churches more ancient, and therefore more venerable than the Roman, and, like it, asserting an authenticity upon unimpeachable proofs. But once let sects with such an impressive prestige be introduced to the knowledge of the West, once let the appearance of inviolate unity be taken from the Latin Church, and nothing could prevent a spontaneous decomposition forthwith occurring in it. It must break up into sects, which, in their turn, must break up, in process of time, into smaller and smaller divisions, and, through this means, the European must emerge at last into individual liberty of thought. The compelling hand of ecclesiastical tyranny must be removed, and universal toleration ensue. Nor were such anticipations mere idle suspicions, for such was the course that events actually took. Scarcely had the

*Danger to the unity of the Church.*

Reformation occurred when sectarian subdivisions made their appearance, and in modern times we see that an anarchy of sects is the inevitable harbinger of individual liberty of thought.

As we have just said, it was impossible to look in any direction on the latter half of the fifteenth century without recognizing the wonderful change. It had become obviously useless any longer to assert an immobility of humanity when men were standing face to face with the new forms into which it had been transposed. New ideas had driven out old ones. Natural phenomena could not again be likened to human acts, nor the necessities of man regarded as determining the movements of the universe. A better appreciation of the nature of evidence was arising, perhaps in part through the influence of the lawyers, but in part through a commencing taste for criticism. We see it in such facts as the denial that a miracle can be taken as the proof of anything else than the special circumstances with which it is connected; we see it in the assertion that the martyrdom of men in support of a dogma, so far from proving its truth, proves rather its doubtfulness, no geometer having ever thought it worth his while to die in order to establish any mathematical proposition, truth needing no such sacrifices, which are actually unserviceable and useless to it, since it is able spontaneously to force its own way. In Italy, where the popular pecuniary interests were obviously identical with those of the Church, a dismal disbelief was silently engendering.

*Higher requirements in evidence.*

*Disbelief arising in Italy.*

And now occurred an event the results of which it is impossible to exaggerate.

*Invention of printing; its early history.*

About A.D. 1440 the art of printing seems to have been invented in Europe. It is not material to our purpose to inquire into the particulars of its history, whether we should attribute it to Coster of Haarlem or Gutenberg of Mentz, or whether, in reality, it was introduced by the Venetians from China, where it had been practised for nearly two thousand years. In Venice a decree was issued in 1441 in relation to printing, which would seem to imply that it had been known there for some years. Coster is supposed to have printed the

'Speculum Humanæ Salvationis' about 1440, and Gutenberg and Faust the Mentz Bible, without date, 1455. The art reached perfection at once; their Bible is still admired for its beautiful typography. Among the earliest specimens of printing extant is an exhortation to take up arms against the Turks, 1454; there are also two letters of indulgence of Nicholas V. of the same date. In the beginning each page was engraved on a block of wood, but soon movable types were introduced. Impressions of the former kind pass under the name of block books; at first they were sold as manuscripts. Two of Faust's workmen commenced printing in Italy, but not until 1465; they there published an edition of 'Lactantius,' one of 'Cicero de Officiis,' and one of 'Augustine de Civitate Dei.' The art was carried to France 1469, and in a few years was generally practised in all the large European towns. The printers were their own booksellers; the number of copies in each edition usually about three hundred. Folios were succeeded by quartos, and in 1501 duodecimos were introduced. Very soon the price of books was reduced by four-fifths, and existing interests required regulations not only respecting the cost, but also respecting the contents. Thus the University of Paris established a tariff for their sale, and also exercised a supervision in behalf of the Church and the State. From the outset it was clear that printing would inevitably influence the intellectual movement synchronously occurring. *Early books and booksellers.*

Some authors have endeavoured to estimate the intellectual condition of different countries in Europe at the close of the fifteenth century by the literary activity they displayed in the preparation and printing of editions of books. Though it is plain that such estimates can hardly be rigorously correct, since to print a book not only implies literary capacity, but also the connections of business and trade, and hence works are more likely to be issued in places where there is a mercantile activity, yet such estimates are perhaps the most exact that we can now obtain; they also lead us to some very interesting and unexpected results of singular value in their connection with that important epoch. Thus it appears that in all Europe, between 1470 and 1500, more than ten thousand editions of books and *Measure of the contemporaneous mental state of nations.*

pamphlets were printed, and of them a majority in Italy, demonstrating that Italy was in the van of the intellectual movement. Out of this large number, in Venice there had been printed 2835; Milan, 625; Bologna, 298; Rome, 925; fifty other Italian cities had presses; Paris, 751; Cologne, 530; Nuremberg, 382; Leipsic, 351; Basle, 320; Strasburg, 520; Augsburg, 256; Louvain, 116; Mentz, 134; Deventer, 169; London, 130; Oxford, 7; St. Alban's, 4.

*Italy compared with the rest of Europe.*

Venice, therefore, took the lead. England was in a very backward state. This conclusion is confirmed by many other circumstances, which justify the statement that Italy was as far advanced intellectually in 1400 as England in 1600. Paris exhibits a superiority sixfold over London, and in the next ten years the disproportion becomes even more remarkable, for in Paris four hundred and thirty editions were printed, in London only twenty-six. The light of learning became enfeebled by distance from its Italian focus. As late as 1550, a complete century after the establishment of the art, but seven works had been printed in Scotland, and among them not a single classic. It is an amusing proof how local tastes were consulted in the character of the books thus put forth, that the first work issued in Spain, 1474, was on the 'Conception of the Virgin.'

*Effect of printing on literature and the Church. Cheapening of books.*

The invention of printing operated in two modes altogether distinct: first, in the multiplying and cheapening of books, and, second, in substituting reading for pulpit instruction.

First, as to the multiplication and cheapening of books, there is no reason to suppose that the supply had ever been inadequate. As, under the Ptolemies, book-manufacture was carried forward in the museum at Alexandria to an extent which fully satisfied demands, so in all the great abbeys there was an apartment—the Scriptorium—for the copying and making of books. Such a sedentary occupation could not but be agreeable to persons of a contemplative or quiet habit of life. But Greece, Rome, Egypt—indeed, all the ancient governments except that of China, were founded upon elements among which did not appear that all-important one of modern times, a reading class. Information passed from mouth to mouth, not from eye to eye. With a limited demand, the compensation to the copier was sufficient, and the cost to the purchaser moderate. It is altogether a mistake to suppose that the methods and advantages of printing were unknown. Modifications of that art were used wherever occasion called for them. We do not need the Roman stamps to satisfy us of that fact; every Babylonian brick and signet-ring is an illustration. Printing processes of various kinds were well enough known. The real difficulty was the want of paper. That substance was first made in Europe by the Spanish Moors from the fine flax of Valencia and Mercia. Cotton-paper, sold as "charta Damascena," had been previously made at Damascus, and several different varieties had long been manufactured in China. The want of paper. Damascus paper.

Had there been more readers, paper would have been more abundantly produced, and there would have been more copiers —nay, even there would have been printers. An increased demand would have been answered by an increased supply. As soon as such a demand arose in Europe the press was introduced, as it had been thousands of years before in China.

So far as the public is concerned, printing has been an unmixed advantage; not so, however, in its bearing on authors. The longevity of books is greatly impaired, a melancholy conclusion to an ambitious intellect. The duration of many ancient books which have escaped the chances of time is to be hoped for no more. In this shortening of their term the excessive multiplication of works greatly assists. A rapid succession soon makes those of distinction obsolete, and then consigns them to oblivion. No author can now expect immortality. His utmost hope is only this, that his book may live a little longer than himself. Longevity of books curtailed.

But it was with printing as with other affairs of the market, an increased demand gave origin to an increased supply, which, in its turn reacting, increased the demand. Cheap books bred readers. When the monks, abandoning their useless and lazy life of saying their prayers a dozen times a day, turned to the copying and illustrating of manuscripts, a mental elevation of the whole order was the result; there were more monks who Multiplication of books.

o 2

could read. And so, on the greater scale, as books through the press became more abundant, there were more to whom they became a necessity.

*The mode of communicating knowledge changes.*

But, secondly, as to the change which ensued in the mode of communicating information—a change felt instantly in the ecclesiastical, and, at a later period, in the political world. The whole system of public worship was founded on the condition of a non-reading people; hence the reading of prayers and the sermon. Whoever will attentively compare the thirteenth with the nineteenth century cannot fail to see how essential oral instruction was to the former, how subordinate to the latter. The invention of the printing-press gave an instant, a formidable rival to the pulpit. It made possible that which had been impossible before in Christian Europe—direct communication between the government and the people without any religious intermedium, and was the first step in that important change subsequently carried out in America, the separation of Church and State. Though in this particular the effect was desirable, in another its advantages are doubtful, for the Church adhered to her ancient method when it had lost very much of its real force, and this even at the risk of falling into a lifeless and impassive condition.

*Injury to pulpit instruction.*

*Influence of church services on the people.*

And yet we must not undervalue the power once exercised on a non-reading community by oral and scenic teachings. What could better instruct it than a formal congregating of neighbourhoods together each Sabbath-day to listen in silence and without questioning? In those great churches, the architectural grandeur of which is still the admiration of our material age, nothing was wanting to impress the worshipper. The vast pile, with its turrets or spire pointing to heaven; its steep inclining roof; its walls, with niches and statues; its echoing belfry; its windows of exquisite hues and of every form, lancet, or wheel, or rose, through which stole in the many-coloured light; its chapels, with their pictured walls; its rows of slender, clustering columns, and arches tier upon tier; its many tapering pendants; the priest emerging from his scenic retreat; his chalice and forbidden wine; the covering paten, the cibory, and the pix. Amid clouds of incense from smoking censers, the blaze of lamps, and tapers, and branching candlesticks, the tinkling of silver bells, the play of jewelled vessels and gorgeous dresses of violet, green, and gold, banners and crosses were borne aloft through lines of kneeling worshippers in processional services along the aisles. The chanting of litanies and psalms gave a foretaste of the melodies of heaven, and the voices of the choristers and sounds of the organ now thundered forth glory to God in the highest, now whispered peace to the broken in spirit.

If such were the influences in the cathedral, not less were those that gathered round the little village church. To the peasant it was endeared by the most touching incidents of his life. At its font his parents had given him his name; at its altar he had plighted his matrimonial vows; beneath the little grass mounds in its yard there awaited the resurrection those who had been untimely taken away. Connected thus with the profoundest and holiest sentiments of humanity, the pulpit was for instruction a sole and sufficient means. Nothing like it had existed in paganism. The irregular, ill-timed, occasional eloquence of the Greek republican orators cannot for an instant be set in comparison with such a steady and enduring systematic institution. In a temporal as well as in a spiritual sense, the public authorities appreciated its power. Queen Elizabeth was not the only sovereign who knew how to thunder through a thousand pulpits.

*Influence of village churches.*

For a length of time, as might have been expected, considering its power and favouring adventitious circumstances, the pulpit maintained itself successfully against the press. Nevertheless, its eventual subordination was none the less sure. If there are disadvantages in the method of acquiring knowledge by reading, there are also signal advantages; for, though upon the printed page the silent letters are mute and unsustained by any scenic help, yet often—a wonderful contradiction—they pour forth emphatic eloquence, that can make the heart leap with emotion, or kindle on the cheek the blush of shame. The might of persuasiveness does not always lie in articulate speech. The strong are often the silent. God never speaks.

*The pulpit yields to the press.*

There is another condition which gives to reading a great advantage over listening. In the affairs of life, how wide is the difference between having a thing done for us and doing it ourselves! In the latter case, how great is the interest awakened, how much more thorough the examination, how much more perfect the acquaintance! To listen implies merely a passive frame of mind; to read, an active. But the latter is more noble.

*Listening and reading.*

From these and other such considerations, it might have been foreseen that the printing-press would at last deprive the pulpit of its supremacy, making it become ineffective, or reducing it to an ancillary aid. It must have been clear that the time would arrive when, though adorned by the eloquence of great and good men, the sermon would lose its power for moving popular masses or directing public thought.

*Decline of pulpit influence.*

Upon temporal as well as ecclesiastical authority, the influence of this great change was also felt. During the Turkish war of 1563 newspapers first made their appearance in Venice. They were in manuscript. The 'Gazette de France' commenced in 1631. There seems to be doubt as to the authenticity of the early English papers reputed to have been published during the excitement of the Spanish Armada, and of which copies remain in the British Museum. It was not until the civil wars that, under the names of Mercuries, Intelligences, etc., newspapers fairly established themselves in England.

*Newspapers; their origin.*

What I have said respecting the influence of the press upon religious life applies substantially to civil life also. Oratory has sunk into a secondary position, being every day more and more thoroughly supplanted by journalism. No matter how excellent it may be in its sphere of action, it is essentially limited, and altogether incompetent to the influencing of masses of men in the manner which our modern social system requires. Without a newspaper, what would be the worth of the most eloquent parliamentary attempts? It is that which really makes them instruments of power, and gives to them political force, which takes them out of a little circle of cultivated auditors, and throws them broadcast over nations.

*Decline of power in parliamentary eloquence.*

Such was the literary condition of Western Europe, such

the new power that had been found in the press. These were but initiatory to the great drama now commencing. We have already seen that synchronously with this intellectual there was a moral impulse coming into play. The two were in harmony. At the time now occupying our attention there was a possibility for the moral impulse to act under several different forms. The special mode in which it came into effect was determined by the pecuniary necessities of Italy. It very soon, however, assumed larger proportions, and became what is known to us as the Reformation. The movement against Rome, that had been abandoned for a century, was now recommenced. *(Dawn of the Reformation.)*

The variation of human thought proceeds in a continuous manner, new ideas springing out of old ones either as corrections or developements, but never spontaneously originating. With them as with organic forms, each requires a germ, a seed. The intellectual phase of humanity observed at any moment is therefore an embodiment of many different things. It is connected with the past, is in unison with the present, and contains the embryo of the future. *(Variation of human thought.)*

Human opinions must hence, of absolute necessity, undergo transformation. What has been received by one generation as undoubted, to a subsequent one becomes so conspicuously fallacious as to excite the wonder of those who do not distinctly appreciate the law of psychical advance that it could ever have been received as true. These phases of transformation are not only related in a chronological way, so as to be obvious when we examine the ideas of society at epochs of a few years or of centuries apart—they exist also contemporaneously in different nations or in different social grades of the same nation, according as the class of persons considered has made a greater or less intellectual progress.

Notwithstanding the assertion of Rome, the essential ideas of the Italian system had undergone unavoidable modifications. An illiterate people, easily imposed upon, had accepted as true the asseveration that there had been no change even from the apostolic times. But the time had now come when that fiction could no longer be maintained, the divergence no longer concealed. In the new state of things, it was impossible that *(Variations in Italian ideas.)*

dogmas in absolute opposition to reason, such as that of transubstantiation, could any longer hold their ground. The scholastic theology and scholastic philosophy, though supported by the universities, had become obsolete. With the revival of pure Latinity and the introduction of Greek, the foundations of a more correct criticism were laid. An age of erudition was unavoidable, in which whatever could not establish its claims against a searching examination must necessarily be overthrown.

*The Reformation; its history.* We are thus brought to the great movement known as the Reformation. The term is usually applied in reference to the Protestant nations, and therefore is not sufficiently comprehensive, for all Europe was in truth involved. A clear understanding of its origin, its process, its effects, is perhaps best obtained by an examination of the condition of the northern and southern nations, and the issue of the event in each respectively.

*The preparatory state of Germany, France, England.* Germany had always been sincere, and therefore always devout. Of her disposition she had given many proofs from the time when the Emperor Otho descended into Italy, his expedition having been, as was said, an armed procession of ecclesiastics resolved to abate the scandals of the Church. The Councils of Constance and Basle may be looked upon as an embodiment of the same sentiment. The resolution to limit the Papal authority, and to put a superior over the Pope, arose from a profound conviction of the necessity of such a measure. Those councils were precursors of the coming Reformation. In other countries events had long been tending in the same direction: in Sicily and Italy by the acts of Frederick II.; in France through those of Philip the Fair. The educated had been estranged by the Saracens and Jews; the enthusiastic, by such works as the 'Everlasting Gospel;' the devout had been shocked by the tale of the Templars and the detected immoralities in Rome; the patriotic had been alienated by the assumptions of the Papal court and its incessant intermeddling in political affairs; the inferior, unreflecting orders were in all directions exasperated by its importunate, unceasing exactions of money. In England, for instance, though less advanced intellectually than the southern nations, the commencement of the Reformation is perhaps justly referred as far back as the reign of Edward III., who, under the suggestion of Wickliffe, refused to do homage to the Pope; but a series of weaker princes succeeding, it was not until Henry VII. that the movement could be continued. In that country the immediately exciting causes were no doubt of a material kind, such as the alleged avarice and impurity of the clergy, the immense amount of money taken from the realm, the intrusion of foreign ecclesiastics. In the south of France and in Italy, where the intellectual condition was much more advanced, the movement was correspondingly of a more intellectual kind. To this difference between the north and south must be referred, not only the striking geographical distribution of belief which was soon apparent, but also the speedy and abrupt limitation of the Reformation, restrictedly so called.

In recent ages, under her financial pressure, Rome had asserted that the infinite merits of our Saviour, together with the good works of supererogation of many holy men, constituted, as it were, a fund, from which might be discharged penalties of sins of every kind, for the dead as well as the living, and therefore available for those who had passed into Purgatory, as well as for us who remain. This fund, committed to the care of St. Peter and his successors, may be disbursed, under the form of indulgences, by sale for money. A traffic in indulgences was thus carried on to a great extent through the medium of the monks, who received a commission upon the profits. Of course, it is plain that the religious conception of such a transaction is liable to adverse criticism—the bartering for money so holy a thing as the merit of our Redeemer. This was, however, only the ostensible explanation, which it was judged necessary to present to sincerely pious communities; behind it there lay the real reason, which was essentially of a political kind. It was absolutely necessary that Papal Rome should control a revenue far beyond that arising in a strictly legitimate way. As all the world had been drained of money by the senate and Cæsars for the support of republican or imperial power, so too there was a need of a like supply for the use of the pontiffs. The collec-

tion of funds had often given rise to contentions between the
ecclesiastical and temporal authorities, and in some of the
more sturdy countries had been resolutely resisted. To collect a direct tax is often a troublesome affair; but such is human nature, a man from whom it might be difficult to extort
the payment of an impost lawfully laid, will often cheerfully
find means to purchase for himself indulgence for sin. In
such a semi-barbarian but yet religious population as that with
which the Church was dealing, it was quite clear that this
manner of presenting things possessed singular advantages, an
obvious equivalent being given for the money received. The
indulgence implied not only a release from celestial, but also,
in many cases, from civil penalties. It was an absolute gua-
rantee from hell.

*Martin Luther.*

It is said that the attention of Martin Luther, formerly an
Augustinian monk, was first attracted to this subject by the
traffic having been conferred on the Dominicans instead of
upon his own order, at the time when Leo X. was raising funds
by this means for building St. Peter's at Rome, A.D. 1517.
That was probably only an insinuation of Luther's adversa-
ries, and is very far from being borne out by his subsequent
conduct. His first public movement was the putting forth of
ninety-five theses against the practice. He posted them on
the door of the cathedral of Wittenberg, and enforced them
in his sermons, though at this time he professed obedience to
the Papal authority. With a rapidity probably unexpected by
him, his acts excited public attention so strongly, that, though
the Pope was at first disposed to regard the whole affair as a
mere monkish squabble for gains, it soon became obvious, from
the manner in which the commotion was spreading, that something must be done to check it. The Pope therefore summoned Luther to Rome to answer for himself; but, through
the influence of certain great personages, and receiving a submissive letter from the accused, he, on reconsideration, referred
the matter to Cardinal Cajetan, his legate in Germany. The
Cardinal, on looking into the affair, ordered Luther to retract;
and now came into prominence the mental qualities of this
great man. Luther, with respectful firmness, refused; but

remembering John Huss, and fearing that the imperial safe-conduct which had been given to him would be insufficient for his protection, he secretly returned to Wittenberg, having first however solemnly appealed from the Pope, ill-informed at the time, to the Pope when he should have been better instructed. Thereupon he was condemned as a heretic. Undismayed, he continued to defend his opinions; but finding himself in imminent danger, he fell upon the suggestion which, since the days of Philip the Fair, had been recognized as the true method of dealing with the Papacy, and appealed to a general council as the true representative of the Church, and therefore superior to the Pope, who is not infallible any more than St. Peter himself had been. To this denial of Papal authority he soon added a dissent from the doctrines of purgatory, auricular confession, absolution. It was now that the grand idea, which had hitherto silently lain at the bottom of the whole movement, emerged into prominence—the right of individual judgment—under the dogma that it is not Papal authority which should be the guide of life, but the Bible, and that the Bible is to be interpreted by private judgment. Thus far it had been received that the Bible derives its authenticity and authority from the Church; now it was asserted that the Church derives her authenticity and authority from the Bible. At this moment there was but one course for the Italian court to take with the audacious offender, for this new doctrine of the right of exercising private judgment in matters of faith was dangerous to the last extreme, and not to be tolerated for a moment. Luther was therefore ordered to recant, and to burn his own works, under penalty, if disobedient, of being excommunicated, and delivered over unto Satan. The bull thus issued directed all secular princes to seize his person and punish his crimes. *The right of individual judgment asserted. Excommunication of Luther.*

But Luther was not to be intimidated; nay more, he retaliated. He denounced the Pope, as Frederick and the Fraticelli had formerly done, as the Man of Sin, the Anti-Christ. He called upon all Christian princes to shake off his tyranny. In the presence of a great concourse of applauding spectators, he committed the volumes of the canon law and the bull of excommunication to the flames. The Pope now issued another *He resists, and publicly burns the Bull.*

bull, expelling him from the Church. This was in January,
1521. This separation opened to Luther an unrestrained
career. He forthwith proceeded to an examination of the
Italian system of theology and policy, in which he was joined
by many talented men who participated in his views. The
Emperor Charles V. found it necessary to use all his influence
to check the spreading Reformation. But it was already too
late, for Luther had obtained the firm support of many personages of influence, and his doctrines were finding defenders
among some of the ablest men in Europe.

An imperial diet was therefore held at Worms, before which
Luther, being summoned, appeared. But nothing could induce
him to retract his opinions. An edict was published, putting
him under the ban of the empire; but the Elector of Saxony
concealed him in the castle of Wartburg. While he was in
this retirement his doctrines were rapidly extending, the Au-
gustinians of Wittenberg not hesitating to change the usages
of the Church, abolishing private masses, and giving the cup
as well as the bread to the laity.

*And the revolt spreads.*

While Germany was agitated to her centre, a like revolt
against Italian supremacy broke out in Switzerland. It too
commenced on the question of indulgences, and found a leader
in Zuinglius.

*The Swiss Reformation. Zuinglius.*

Even at this early period the inevitable course of events was
beginning to be plainly displayed in sectarian decomposition;
for, while the German and Swiss Reformers agreed in their relation toward the Papal authority, they differed widely from
each other on some important doctrinal points, more especially
as to the nature of the Eucharist. The Germans supposed
that the body and blood of Christ are actually present in the
bread and wine in some mysterious way; the Swiss believed
that those substances are only emblems or symbols. Both
totally rejected the Italian doctrine of transubstantiation. The
old ideas of Berengar were therefore again fermenting among
men. An attempt was made, under the auspices of the Land-
grave of Hesse, to compose the dissension in a conference at
Marburg; but it was found, after a long disputation, that
neither party would give up its views, and they therefore sepa-

rated, as it was said, in Christian charity, but not in brotherhood.

At the first Diet of Spires, held in 1526, it was tried to procure the execution of the sentence passed upon Luther; but the party of the Reformation proved to be too strong for the Catholics. At a second diet, held at the same place three years subsequently, it was resolved that no change should be made in the established religion before the action of a general council, which had been recommended by both diets, should be known. On this occasion the Catholic interest preponderated sufficiently to procure a revocation of the power which had been conceded to the princes of the empire, of managing for a time the ecclesiastical matters of their own dominions. Against this action several of the princes and cities *protested*, this being the origin of the designation Protestants subsequently given to the Reformers. At a diet held the following year at Augsburg, a statement, composed by Luther and Melanchthon, of the doctrines of the Reformers, was presented; it also treated to some extent of the errors and superstitions of the Catholics. This is what is known as the Confession of Augsburg. But the diet not only rejected it, but condemned most of its doctrines. The Protestants, therefore, in an assembly at Smalcalde, contracted a treaty for their common defence, and this may be looked upon as the epoch of organization of the Reformation. This league did not, however, include the Reformers of Switzerland, who could not conscientiously adopt the Confession of Augsburg, which was its essential basis. The Sacramentarians, as they were called, became thus politically divided from the Lutherans. Moreover, in Switzerland the process of decomposition went on, Calvin establishing a new sect, characterized by the manner in which it insisted on the Augustinian doctrines of predestination and election, by the abolition of all festivals, and the discontinuance of Church ceremonies. At a later period the followers of Zuinglius and Calvin coalesced.

The political combinations which had thus occurred as Protestantism rapidly acquired temporal power, gave rise, as might have been anticipated, to wars. The peace of Augsburg, 1555, furnished the Reformers the substantial advantages they sought

—freedom from Italian ecclesiastical authority, the right of all Germans to judge for themselves in matters of religion, equality in civil privileges for them and the Catholics. A second time, sixty-four years subsequently, war broke out—the Thirty Years' War—and finally the dispute was composed by the treaty of Westphalia. This may be regarded as the culmination of the Reformation. Peace was made in spite of all the intrigues and opposition of Rome.

*Extent of the movement.* The doctrines of the Reformation were adopted with singular avidity throughout the north of Europe, and established themselves for a time in France and in Italy. Even as early as 1558 a report of the Venetian ambassador estimates the Catholics of the German empire at only one-tenth of the population. For twenty years not a student of the University of Vienna had become a priest.

*The revolt in Italy.* Such was the Reformation among the German nations. It is not possible, however, to comprehend correctly that great movement without understanding the course of events in Italy, for that peninsula was involved, though in a very different way. In its intellectual condition it was far in advance of the rest of Europe, as is proved by such facts as those to which we have alluded respecting the printing of books. Between it and the nations of which we have been speaking there was also a wide difference in material interests. What was extorted from them was enjoyed by it. The mental and material condition of Italy soon set a limit to the progress of the Reformation.

*Position of the Italians.* The Italians had long looked upon the transalpine nations with contempt. On the principle that the intellectually strong may lawfully prey on the intellectually weak, they had systematically drained them of their wealth. As we exchange with savages beads, and looking-glasses, and nails, for gold, they had driven a profitable barter with the valiant but illiterate barbarians, exchanging possessions in heaven for the wealth of the earth, and selling for money immunities or indulgences for sin. But in another respect they had looked upon them with dread—they had felt the edge of the French and German sword. The educated classes, though seeking the widest liberty of thought for themselves, were not disposed to more than a very select propagandism of opinions, which plainly could only be detrimental to the pecuniary interests of their country. Their faith had long ago ceased to be that of conviction; it had become a mere outward patriotic acquiescence. Even those who were willing enough to indulge themselves in the utmost latitude of personal free-thinking, never made an objection when some indiscreet zealot of their own kind was compelled by ecclesiastical pressure to flee beyond the Alps. No part of Europe was so full of irreligion as Italy. It amounted to a philosophical infidelity among the higher classes; to Arianism among the middle and less instructed; to an utter carelessness, not even giving itself the trouble of disbelief, among the low. The universities and learned academics were hotbeds of heresy; thus the University of Padua was accused of having been for long a focus of atheism, and again and again learned academies, as those of Modena and Venice, had been suppressed for heresy. The device of the Academy of the Lyncei indicated only too plainly the spirit of these institutions; it was a lynx, with its eyes turned upward to heaven, tearing the triple-headed Cerberus with its claws. Nor was this alarming condition restricted to Italy; France had long participated in it. From the University of Paris, that watch-tower of the Church, the alarm had often been sounded—now it was against men; now against books. Once, under its suggestions, the reading of the physics and metaphysics of Aristotle had been prohibited, and works of philosophy interdicted, until they should have been corrected by the theologians of the Church. The physical heresies of Galileo, the pantheism of Cæsalpinus, had friendly counterparts in France. Even the head of the Church, Leo X., at the beginning of the Reformation, could not escape obloquy, and stories were circulated touching his elevation to the pontificate at once prejudicial to his morals and to his belief. In such an ominous condition, the necessity of carrying out the policy to which Italy had so long been committed perpetually forced the Papal government to acts against which the instructed judgment of its own officials revolted. It was a continual struggle between their duty and their disposition. Why should they have

*State of their universities.*

*State of the learned academies.*

*False position of the Papacy.*

thought it expedient to suppress the Koran when it was printed in Venice, 1530? Why, when Paul IV., 1559, promulgated the Index Expurgatorius of prohibited books, was it found necessary that not less than forty-eight editions of the Bible should be included in it, sixty-one printers put under the ban, and all their publications forbidden—at first the interdict being against all prohibited books, and, on this being found insufficient, even those that had not been permitted being prohibited? Why was it that Galileo was dealt with so considerately and yet so malignantly? It was plain that toleration, either of men or books, was altogether irreconcilable with the principles of the Holy See, and that under its stern exigencies the former must be disposed of, and the latter suppressed or burnt, no matter what personal inclinations or favouring sentiments might be in the way. If any faltering took place in the carrying out of this determination, the control of Rome over the human mind would be put into the most imminent jeopardy.

*Check of the Reformation in Italy.*

So stood affairs in Italy at the beginning and during the active period of the Reformation, the ancient system inexorably pressing upon the leading men, and impelling them to acts against which their better judgment revolted. They were bound down to the interests of their country, those interests being interwoven with conditions which they could no longer intellectually accept. For men of this class the German and Swiss reformations did not go far enough. They affirmed that things were left just as inconsistent with reason, just as indefensible as before. Doubtless they considered that the paring away of the worship of saints, of absolution for money, penances, indulgences, freedom from Papal taxation, the repudiation of intrusive foreign ecclesiastics, was all to the detriment of the pecuniary interests of Italy. They affirmed that the doctrines put forth by the Reformers made good their ground, not through the force of reason, but through appeals to the ignorant, and even to women; not through an improved and sounder criticism, but, as it was declared, through the inward light of the Spirit; that nothing had been done to alleviate the ancient intolerant dogmatism, the forcible suppression of freedom of thought. Leo X., it is well known, at first altogether mistook the nature of the Reformation. He was a man of refined tastes and pleasure, delighting in sumptuous feasts, and too often scandalizing the devout by his indecent conversation and licentious conduct. He gloried in being the patron of the learned, devoting all his attention to the progress of literature and the fine arts, a connoisseur in antiques. The amenities of the life of an accomplished gentleman were not to be disturbed. He little dreamt that in the coarse German monk there was an antagonist worthy of the Papacy. The gay Italians looked upon Luther with ineffable contempt, as introducing ideas even more absurd than those he was trying to displace, and, what was perhaps a still greater offence, upholding his bad doctrines in worse Latin. They affected to believe that they discerned a taint of insanity in the Reformer's account of his conflicts with the Devil, yet were willing to concede that there was a method in his madness, since he was bent on having a wife. In their opinion, the result of the German movement must be exceedingly detrimental to learning, and necessarily lead to the production of very vulgar results, exciting among the common people a revolutionary and destructive spirit. Nor was this personal distaste for Luther altogether undeserved. The caricatures which that great man permitted himself to put forth were too indelicate to be described to a modern reader. They would be worthy of our disgust and indignation did we not find some palliation in the coarseness of the communities and times in which he lived. Leo awoke to his blunder when it was too late, and found that he had been superciliously sneering at what he should have combated with all his might. *Leo X.; his character.*

It is now more than three centuries since the Reformation commenced, and we are able, with some degree of accuracy, to ascertain its influence. Founded, as it was, on the right of private interpretation of the Scriptures, it introduced a better rule of life, and made a great advance toward intellectual liberty. It compelled men to be more moral, and permitted them to be more learned. For the traditions of superstition it substituted the dictates of common sense; it put an end to the disgraceful miracles that for so many ages had been the *Check of the Reformation in Europe.*

scandal of Europe. The assertion of the Italians that it was a great injury to letters is untrue. Though not to be regarded in any respect as a learned man, Luther approved of the study of Greek and Hebrew, recognized by all parties to be dangerous to the Latin system. And even if the accusation be admitted that he approved of their cultivation, not from any love to them, but from hatred to it, the world was equally a gainer. Toward the close of his life it seemed as if there was no other prospect for Papal power than total ruin; yet at this day, out of three hundred millions of Christians, more than half own allegiance to Rome. Almost as if by enchantment the Reformation suddenly ceased to advance. Rome was not only able to check its spread, but even to gain back a portion of what she had lost. The cause of this, which may seem at first an extraordinary result, is not to be attributed to any supernatural influence, as some have supposed. When natural causes suffice, it is needless to look for supernatural.

*Its causes were not supernatural.*

Though there might be sovereigns who, like Henry VIII., had personal reasons for discontent with the Italian court; though there were some who sought to usurp the power and prerogatives of the Popes; though there might be nobles who, as the Prince of Wales's tutor wrote to Sir W. Paget, were "importunate wolves, as are able to devour chantries, cathedral churches, universities, and a thousand times as much;" some who desired the plunder of establishments endowed by the piety of ages, and who therefore lent all their influence in behalf of this great revolution; there was among such, and above such, that small but all-important body of men who see human affairs from the most general point of view. To these, whatever might be the nation to which they happened to belong, it was perfectly evident that the decomposition of faith which had set in, if permitted to go on unchecked, could not possibly end in any other way than in producing an anarchy of sects. In their opinion the German Reformation did not go far enough. It still practically left untouched the dependency of the Church upon the State. In the southern nations of the Continent it had merely irritated the great European ulcer, whereas what was required was the complete amputa-

*Influence of statesmen and philosophers.*

tion of the rotten mass. In their judgment, it was better to leave things as they were, until a thorough eradication could be accomplished; and this, at the time, was obviously impossible. Not understanding, perhaps, how much human affairs are developed according to law, and how little by the volition of individuals, they liberally conceded that Catholicism had been the civilizing agency of Europe, and had become inwoven with the social fabric for good or for evil. It could not now be withdrawn without pulling the whole texture to pieces. Moreover, the curtain of Papal authority, which at one time enveloped all Europe in its ample folds, had, in the course of these late events, been contracted and stretched across the Continent, dividing the northern and southern nations from each other. The people of the south saw on its embroidered surface nothing but forms of usefulness and beauty; they on the north a confusion of meaningless threads. But the few who considered it as a whole, and understood the relations of both sides, knew well enough that the one is the necessary incident of the other, and that it is quite as useless to seek for explanations as to justify appearances. To them it was perfectly clear that the tranquillity and happiness of Christendom were best subserved by giving no encouragement to opinions which had already occasioned so much trouble, and which seemed to contain in their very constitution principles of social disorganization.

A second reason for the sudden loss of expansive force in the Reformation is found in its own intrinsic nature. The principle of decomposition which it represented, and with which it was inextricably entangled, necessarily implied oppugnancy. For a short season the attention of Protestantism was altogether directed to the Papal authority, from which it had so recently separated itself; but, with its growing strength and ascertained independence, that object ceased to occupy it, becoming, as it were, more distant and more obscure. Upon the subordinate divisions which were springing from it, or which were of collateral descent from the original Catholic stock, the whole view of each denomination was concentrated. The bitterness once directed against the Papacy lost none of its

*Influence of the nature of the Reformation.*

**Effect of sectarian disputes.**

intensity when pointed at rivals or enemies nearer home. Nor was it alone dissensions among the greater sects, oppositions such as those between the Church of England and the Church of Scotland, whose discords were founded on points admitted by all to be great and essential; the same principle ran down through all the modes of sectarian combination as they emerged into life, producing among those of equal power struggles, and in the strong toward the weak persecution. Very soon the process of decomposition had advanced to such an extent that minor sects came into existence on very unessential points. Yet even among these little bodies there was just as much acrimony, just as much hatred, as among the great. These differences were carried into the affairs of civil life, each sect forming a society within itself, and abstaining, as far as might be, from association with its rivals. Of such a state of things the necessary result was weakness, and, had there been no other reason, this in itself would have been quite sufficient in the end to deprive Protestantism of its aggressive power. An army divided against itself is in no condition to make warfare against a watchful and vigorous enemy.

**Want of concentrated power.**

But this was not all. It was in the nature of Protestantism from its outset that it was not constructive. Unlike its great antagonist, it contained no fundamental principle that could combine distant communities and foreign countries together. It originated in dissent, and was embodied by separation. It could not possess a concentrated power, nor recognize one apostolic man who might compress its disputes, harmonize its powers, wield it as a mass. For the attainment of his aims the Protestant had only wishes, the Catholic had a will. The Church of England, of Scotland, or of any other Protestant nation, undoubtedly did discharge its duty excellently well for the community in which it was placed; but, at the most, it was only a purely local institution, altogether insignificant in comparison with that great old Church, hoary and venerable with age, which had seen every government and every institution in Europe come into existence, many of them at its bidding, which had extirpated Paganism from the Roman empire, com-

pelled the Cæsars to obey its mandates, precipitated the whole
white race upon the Holy Land; that great old Church, once
the more than imperial sovereign of Christendom, and of
which the most respectable national Church was only a fragment of a fragment.

Very different was it with Catholicism. It possessed an organization which concentrated in the hand of one man irresistible power, and included all the southern countries of Europe not Mohammedan. It could enforce its policy by the armies and fleets of obedient kings. It is not surprising, when this state of things is considered, that the spread of the Reformation was limited to its first fervour,—that the men who saw its origin saw also its culmination. It is not to be wondered at that, with the political weakening arising from a tendency to subdivision and disintegration on one side, and the preparing of a complete and effective organization against the danger that was threatening on the other, the issue should have turned out as it did.
<sub>Condition of Catholicism.</sub>

Rome, awaking at last to her danger, met the Reformation with four weapons—a counter-reformation, an increased vigour in the Inquisition, the institution of the Jesuits, and a greater embellishment of worship. The disposition of the northern nations was to a simplification of worship, that of the south to adorn it with whatever could captivate the senses. Ranke asserts that the composition of the mass of Marcellus by Palestrina, 1500, had a wonderful effect in the revival of religion; there can be no doubt that it constituted an epoch in devotion. But of all these, the first and best was a moral change which she instantly imposed upon herself. Henceforth it was her intention that in the chair of St. Peter should never again be seen atheists, poisoners, thieves, murderers, blasphemers, adulterers, but men who, if they were sometimes found, as must be the case considering the infirmities of humanity, incompetent to deal with the great trials which often befell them, were yet of such personal purity, holiness of life, and uprightness of intention, as to command profound respect. Those scandals that hitherto had everywhere disgraced her began to disappear, a true reformation, but not a schism, occurring
<sub>The means of resistance resorted to by Rome.</sub>
<sub>A counter-reformation.</sub>

through all ecclesiastical grades. Had Protestantism produced no other result than this, it would have been an unspeakable blessing to the world.

*The Inquisition brought into activity.*

By another very different means the Italian power sought to ensure its domination—by an increased activity of the Inquisition. It is difficult to understand how men of capacity could have justified this iniquitous institution. Certainly it could not have been upon any principles of Christian morality, nor even upon those of high statesmanship. For the Inquisition to accomplish its purpose, it must needs be as all-seeing as Providence, as inexorable as the grave; not inflicting punishments which the sufferer could remember, but remorselessly killing outright; not troubling itself to ascertain the merits of a case and giving the accused the benefits of a doubt, but regarding suspicion and certainty as the same thing. If worked with the unscrupulous, impassive resolution of Machiavellism, this great engine for the coercion of the human mind could be made to accomplish its purpose. It thoroughly extinguished Protestantism in Spain and Italy, and in those countries maintained a barrier against the progressive reason of man.

*The Jesuits are established.*

But the most effective weapon to which the Papacy resorted was the institution of the order of the Jesuits. It was established by a bull of Paul III., 1540, the rules being that the general chosen for life should be obeyed as God; that they should vow poverty, chastity, obedience, and go wherever they were commanded; their obedience was to the Pope, not to the Church,—a most politic distinction, for thereby an unmistakable responsibility was secured. They had no regular hours of prayer; their duties were preaching, the direction of consciences, education. By the Jesuits, Rome penetrated into the remotest corners of the earth, established links of communication with her children who remained true to her in the heart of Protestant countries, and, with a far-seeing policy for the future, silently engrossed the education of the young. At the confessional she extorted from women the hidden secrets of their lives and those of their families, took the lead in devotion wherever there were pious men, and was equally foremost in the world of fashion and dissipation. There was no

*Their influence all over the world.*

guise under which the Jesuit might not be found;—a barefoot beggar, clothed in rags; a learned professor, lecturing gratuitously to scientific audiences; a man of the world, living in profusion and princely extravagance; there have been Jesuits the wearers of crowns. There were no places into which they did not find their way: a visitor to one of the loyal old families of England could never be sure but that there was a Jesuit hidden in the garret or secreted behind the wainscot of the bedroom. They were the advisers of the leading men of the age, sat in the cabinets of kings, and were their confessors. They boasted that they were the link between religious opinion and literature. With implicit and unquestioning obedience to his superior, like a good soldier, it was the paramount duty of the Jesuit to obey his orders, whatever those orders might be. It was for him to go, at the summons of a moment, with his life in his hand, to the very centre of Pagan or of reformed and revolted countries, where his presence was death by law, and execute the mission entrusted to him. If he succeeded, it was well; if he should fall, it was also well. To him all things were proper for the sake of the Church. It was his business to consider how the affair he had in hand was to be most surely accomplished,—to resort to justifiable means if they should appear sufficient, if not, to unjustifiable; to the spiritual weapon, but also to be prepared with the carnal; to sacrifice candour if the occasion should require, if necessary even truth, remembering that the end justifies the means, if that end is the good of the Church.

While some religious orders were founded on retirement, and aimed at personal improvement by solitude, the Jesuits were instructed to mix in the affairs of men, and gather experience in the ways of worldly wisdom. And since it is the infirmity of humanity, whatever may be the vigour of its first intentions, too often to weary in well-doing, provision was made to reinforce the zeal of those becoming lukewarm, to admonish the delinquent, by making each a spy on all the others, under oath to reveal everything to his superior. In that manner a control was exercised over the brotherhood in all parts of the world. In Europe they had, in a very short time, stealthily but largely

engrossed public education; had mixed themselves up with
every public affair; were at the bottom of every intrigue,
making their power felt though the control they exerted over
sovereigns, ministers of state, and great court ladies, influencing the last through the spiritual means of the confessional, or
by the more natural, but equally effectual entanglements of re-
quited love.  Already they had recognized the agency of commerce in promoting and diffusing religious belief, and hence
simultaneously became great missionaries and great merchants.
With the Indies, East and West, they carried forward extensive commercial undertakings, and had depôts in various parts
of Europe.  In these operations they were necessarily absolved from their vows of poverty, and became immensely rich.
In South America they obtained a footing in Paraguay, and
commenced their noble attempt at the civilization of the Indians, bringing them into communities, teaching them social
usages, agricultural arts, and the benefits arising to themselves
and the community from labour.  They gave them a military
organization, subdivided, according to the European system,
into the customary arms—infantry, cavalry, artillery;  they
supplied them with munitions of war.  It was their hope that
from this basis they should be able to spread the rule of the
Church over America, as had been done in preceding ages over
Europe.

*Causes of their sup-pression.*
An intolerable apprehension of their invisible presence and
unscrupulous agency made all Europe put them down at last.
The amenities of exquisite courteousness, the artifices of infinite dissimulation, cannot for ever deceive.  Men found, by
bitter experience, that under the silken glove there was an iron
hand.  From their general in Rome, who was absolute commander of their persons, and unchallengeable administrator
of their prodigious wealth, down to the humblest missionary
who was wearing away his life among the Andes, or on the
banks of the Hoang-ho, or in the solitary prairies of Missouri,
or under the blazing sun of Abyssinia; whether he was con-
fessing the butterfly ladies of Paris, whispering devilish suggestions into the ear of the King of Spain, consoling the dying
peasant in an Irish cabin, arguing with mandarins in the palace

of the Emperor of China, stealing away the hearts of the rising generation in the lower schools and academies, extorting the admiration of learned societies by the profundity of his philosophy and the brilliancy of his scientific discoveries; whether he was to be seen in the exchanges and marts of the great capitals, supervising commercial operations on a scale which up to that time had been attempted by none but the Jews; whether he was held in an English jail as a suspected vagabond, or sitting on the throne of France; whether he appeared as a great landed proprietor, the owner of countless leagues in the remote parts of India or South America; whether he was mixing with crowds in the streets of London, and insinuating in Protestant ears the rights of subjects to oppose, and even depose, their monarchs, or in the villages of Castile and Leon, preaching before Catholic peasants the paramount duty of a good Christian implicitly to obey the mandates of his king; wherever the Jesuit was, or whatever he was doing, men universally felt that the thing he had in hand was only auxiliary to some higher, some hidden design. The stealth, and silence, and power became at last so intolerable that they were banished from France, Spain, Portugal, and other Catholic countries. But such was their vitality, that, though the order was abolished by a Papal bull in 1773, they have been again restored.

Though it is sometimes said that Rome, in this manner, by her admirable combinations and irresistible movement, succeeded at last in checking the Reformation, a full consideration of the state of affairs would lead us to receive that assertion with very considerable restriction. She came out of the conflict much less powerful than she had entered it. If we attribute to her policy all that it can justly claim, we must also attribute to causes over which she had no kind of control their rightful influence. The Reformation had been, to no small extent, due to the rise of criticism, which still continued its developement, and was still fruitful of results. Latin had fallen from its high estate; the modern languages were in all directions expanding and improving; the printing-press was not only giving Greek learning to the world, but countless translations and commentaries. The doctrine successfully established by Luther and

*Effects of change of opinion among the learned.*

his colleagues, the right of private interpretation and judgment, was the practical carrying out of the organic law of criticism to the highest affairs with which man can be concerned —affairs of religion. The Reformation itself, philosophically considered, really meant the casting off of authority, the installation of individual inquiry and personal opinion. If criticism, thus standing upon the basis of the Holy Scriptures, had not hesitated to apply itself to an examination of public faith, and, as the consequence thereof, had laid down new rules for morality and the guidance of life, it was not to be expected that it would hesitate to deal with minor things,—that it would spare the philosophy, the policy, the literature of antiquity. And so, indeed, it went on, comparing classical authors with classical authors, the Fathers with the Fathers, often the same writer with himself. Contradictions were pointed out, errors exposed, weakness detected, and new views offered of almost everything within the range of literature.

*Effects of criticism on religion and literature.*

From this burning ordeal one book alone came out unscathed. It was the Bible. It spontaneously vindicated for itself what Wickliffe in the former times, and Luther more lately, had claimed for it. And not only did it hold its ground, but it truly became incalculably more powerful than ever it had been before. The press multiplied it in every language without end, until there was scarcely a cottage in reformed Europe that did not possess a copy.

*The Bible.*

But if criticism was thus the stimulating principle that had given life to the Reformation, it had no little to do with its pause; and this is the influence over which Rome had no kind of control, and to which I have made allusion. The phases through which the Reformation passed were dependent on the coincident advances of learning. First it relied on the Scriptures, which were to the last its surest support; then it included the Fathers. But, from a more intimate study of the latter, many erudite Protestants were gradually brought back to the ancient fold. Among such may be mentioned Erasmus, who by degrees became alienated from the Reformers, and subsequently Grotius, the publication of whose treatise, 'De Jure Belli et Pacis,' 1625, really constituted an epoch in the

*Decline of the value of patristic learning.*

political system of Europe. This great man had gradually become averse to the Reformation, believing that, all things considered, it had done more harm than good; he had concluded that it was better to throw differences into oblivion for the sake of peace, and to enforce silence on one's own opinions, rather than to expect that the Church should be compelled to accommodate herself to them. If such men as Erasmus, Casaubon, and Grotius had been brought to this dilemma by their profound philosophical meditations, their conclusion was confirmed among the less reflecting by the unhappy intolerance of the new as well as the old Church. Men asked what was the difference between the vindictiveness with which Rome dealt with Antonio de Dominis, at once an ecclesiastic and a natural philosopher, who, having gone over to Protestantism and then seceded, imprudently visited Rome, was there arrested, and, dying, his body was dug up and burnt, and the rigour of Calvin, who seized Servetus, the author of the 'Christianismi Restitutio,' and in part the discoverer of the circulation of the blood, when he happened to pass through Geneva, and committed him to the flames. *Moral effects of persecutions.*

Criticism had thus, in its earlier stage, produced well-marked results. As it developed it lost none of its power. It had enthroned patristic theology; now it wrenched from its hand the sceptre. In the works of Daillé it showed that the Fathers are of no kind of use—they are too contradictory of one another; even Jeremy Taylor speaks of their authority and reputation as clean gone for ever. In a few years they had sunk into desuetude, a neglect shared by many classical authors, whose opinions were now only quoted with a respectful smile. The admiration for antiquity was diminishing under the effect of searching examination. Books were beginning to appear, turning the old historians into ridicule for their credulity. The death of Servetus was not without advantage to the world. There was not a pious or thoughtful man in all reformed Europe who was not shocked when the circumstances under which that unhappy physician had been brought to the stake at Geneva by John Calvin were made known. For two hours he was roasted in the flames of a slow *End of patristicism.* *The burning of Servetus by Calvin.*

fire, begging for the love of God that they would put on more wood, or do something to end his torture. Men asked, with amazement and indignation, if the atrocities of the Inquisition were again to be revived. On all sides they began to inquire how far it is lawful to inflict the punishment of death for difference of opinion. It opened their eyes to the fact that, after all they had done, the state of civilization in which they were living was still characterized by its intolerance. In 1546 the Venetian ambassador at the court of Charles V. reported to his government that in Holland and Friesland more than thirty thousand persons had suffered death at the hands of justice for Anabaptist errors. From such an unpromising state of things toleration could only emerge with difficulty. It was the offspring, not of a philosophical charity, but of the checked animosities of ever-multiplying sects, and their detected impossibility of coercing one another.

*The Reformation continued in America.* The history of the Reformation does not close where many European authors have imagined, in a balanced and final distribution of the north and south between the Protestant and the Catholic. The pred stined issue of sectarian differences and dissensions is individual liberty of thought. So long as there was one vast overshadowing, intolerant corporation, every man must bring his understanding to its measure, and think only as it instructed him to do. As soon as dissenting confessions gathered sufficient military power to maintain their right of existence—as soon as from them, in turn, incessant offshoots were put forth, toleration became not only possible, but inevitable, and that is perhaps as far as the movement has at this time advanced in Europe. But Macaulay and others who have treated of the Reformation have taken too limited a view of it, *Separation of Church and State.* supposing that this was its point of arrest. It made another enormous stride when, at the American revolution, the State and the Church were solemnly and openly dissevered from one another. Now might the vaticinations of the prophets of evil expect to find credit; a great people had irrevocably broken off its politics from its theology, and it might surely have been expected that the unbridled interests, and instincts, and passions of men would have dragged everything into the abyss of anarchy. Yet what do we, who are living nearly a century *Emergence of liberty of thought.* after that time, find the event to be? Sectarian decomposition, passing forward to its last extreme, is the process by which individual mental liberty is engendered and maintained. A grand and imposing religious unity implies tyranny to the individual; the increasing emergence of sects gives him increasing latitude of thought—with their utmost multiplication he gains his utmost liberty. In this respect, unity and liberty are in opposition; as the one diminishes, the other increases. The Reformation broke down unity; it gave liberty to masses of men grouped together in sufficient numbers to ensure their position; it is now invisibly but irresistibly making steps, never to be stayed until there is an absolute mental emancipation for man.

Great revolutions are not often accomplished without much suffering and many crimes. It might have been supposed before the event, perhaps it is supposed by many who are not privileged to live among the last results, that this decomposition of religious faith must be to the detriment of personal and practical piety. Yet America, in which, of all countries, the *The American clergy.* Reformation at the present moment has furthest advanced, should offer to thoughtful men much encouragement. Its cities are filled with churches built by voluntary gifts; its clergy are voluntarily sustained, and are, in all directions, engaged in enterprises of piety, education, mercy. What a difference between their private life and that of ecclesiastics before the Reformation! Not, as in the old times, does the layman look upon them as the cormorants and curse of society; they are his faithful advisers, his honoured friends, under whose suggestion and supervision are instituted educational establishments, colleges, hospitals, whatever can be of benefit to men in this life, or secure for them happiness in the life to come.

# CHAPTER XXI.

## DIGRESSION ON THE CONDITION OF ENGLAND AT THE END OF THE AGE OF FAITH.

### RESULTS PRODUCED BY THE AGE OF FAITH.

*Results of the Age of Faith.*

ARRIVED at the commencement of the Age of Reason, we might profitably examine the social condition of those countries destined to become conspicuous in the new order of things. I have not space to present such an examination as extensively as it deserves, and must limit my remarks to that nation which, of all others, is most interesting to the reader — that England, which we picture to ourselves as foremost in civilization, her universities dating back for many centuries; her charters and laws, on which individual, and therefore social liberty rests, spoken of as the ancient privileges of the realm; her people a clear-headed race, lovers and stout defenders of freedom. During by far the greater part of the past period she had been Catholic, but she had also been reformed — ever, as she will always be, religious. A correct estimate of her national and individual life will point out to us all that had been done in the Age of Faith. From her condition we may gather what is the progress made by man when guided by such theological ideas as those which had been her rule of life.

*The social condition produced in England.*

The following paragraphs convey an instructive lesson: they dissipate some romantic errors; they are a verdict on a political system from its practical results. What a contrast with the prodigious advancement within a few years when the Age of Reason had set in! How strikingly are we reminded of the inconsequential, the fruitless actions of youth, and the deliberate, the durable undertakings of manhood!

For many of the facts I have now to mention the reader will find authorities in the works of Lord Macaulay and Mr. Froude on English history. My own reading in other directions satisfies me that the picture here offered represents the actual condition of things.

At the time of the suppression of the monasteries in England, the influences which had been in operation for so many centuries had come to an end. Had they endured for a thousand years longer, they could have accomplished nothing more. The condition of human life shows what their uses and what their failures had been. There were forests extending over great districts; fens forty or fifty miles in length, reeking with miasm and fever, though round the walls of the abbeys there might be beautiful gardens, green lawns, shady walks, and many murmuring streams. In trackless woods, where men should have been, herds of deer were straying; the sandy hills were alive with conies, the downs with flocks of bustard. The peasant's cabin was made of reeds or sticks plastered over with mud. His fire was chimneyless—often it was made of peat. In the objects and manner of his existence he was but a step above the industrious beaver who was building his dam in the adjacent stream. There were highwaymen on the roads, pirates on the rivers, vermin in abundance in the clothing and beds. The common food was pease, vetches, fern-roots, and even the bark of trees. There was no commerce to put off famine. Man was altogether at the mercy of the seasons. The population, sparse as it was, was perpetually thinned by pestilence and want. Nor was the state of the townsman better than that of the rustic; his bed was a bag of straw, with a fair round log for his pillow. If he was in easy circumstances, his clothing was of leather; if poor, a wisp of straw wrapped round his limbs kept off the cold. It was a melancholy social condition when nothing intervened between reed cabins in the fen, the miserable wigwams of villages, and the conspicuous walls of the castle and monastery. Well might they who lived in those times bewail the lot of the ague-stricken peasant, and point, not without indignation, to the troops of pilgrims, mendicants, pardoners, and ecclesiastics of every grade who hung round the

*Condition at the suppression of the monasteries.*

Church, to the nightly wassail and rioting drunkenness in the castle-hall, secure in its moats, its battlements, and its warders. The local pivots round which society revolved were the red-handed baron, familiar with scenes of outrage and deeds of blood, and the abbot, indulging in the extreme of luxury, magnificent in dress, exulting in his ambling palfrey, his hawk, his hounds. Rural life had but little improved since the time of Cæsar; in its physical aspect it was altogether neglected. As to the mechanic, how was it possible that he could exist where there were no windows made of glass, no, not of oiled paper, no workshop warmed by a fire? For the poor there was no physician; for the dying, the monk and his crucifix. The aim was to smooth the sufferer's passage to the next world, not to save him for this. Sanitary provisions there were none, except the paternoster and the ave. In the cities the pestilence walked unstayed, its triumphs numbered by the sounds of the death-crier in the streets or the knell for the soul that was passing away.

Our estimate of the influence of the system under which men were thus living as a regulator of their passions may at this point derive much exactness from incidents such as those offered by the history of syphilis and the usages of war. For this purpose we may for a moment glance at the Continent.

*Moral state indicated by the spread of syphilis.* The attention of all Europe was suddenly arrested by a disease which broke out soon after the discovery of America. It raged with particular violence in the French army commanded by Charles VIII. at the siege of Naples, A.D. 1495, and spread almost like an epidemic. It was syphilis. Though there have been medical authors who supposed that it was only an exacerbation of a malady known from antiquity, that opinion cannot be maintained after the learned researches of Astrue. That it was something recognized at the time as altogether new seems to be demonstrated by the accusations of different nations against each other of having given origin to it. Very soon, however, the truth appeared. It had been brought by the sailors of Columbus from the West Indies. Its true character, and the conditions of its propagation, were fully established by Fernel.

## State of Morals.

Now, giving full weight to the fact that the virulence of a disease may be greatest at its first invasion, but remembering that there is nothing in the history of syphilis that would lead us to suppose it ever was, or indeed could be infectious, but only contagious, or communicated by direct contact from person to person; remembering also the special circumstances under which, in this disease, that contagion is imparted, the rapidity of its spread all over Europe is a significant illustration of the fearful immorality of the times. If contemporary authors are to be trusted, there was not a class, married or unmarried, clergy or laity, from the Holy Father, Leo X., to the beggar by the wayside, free from it. It swept over Europe, not as Asiatic cholera did, running along the great lines of trade, and leaving extensive tracts untouched, settling upon and devastating great cities here and there, while others had an immunity. The march of syphilis was equable, unbroken, universal, making good its ground from its point of appearance in the south-west, steadily and swiftly taking possession of the entire Continent, and offering an open manifestation and measure of the secret wickedness of society.

If thus the sins man practises in privacy became suddenly and accidentally exposed, that exposure showing how weak is the control that any system can exercise over human passions, we are brought to the same melancholy conclusion when we turn to those crimes that may be perpetrated in the face of day. The usages of war in the civil contests of the fifteenth century, *And by the usages of war.* or in the religious conflicts of the sixteenth and seventeenth, are perfectly appalling; the annals of those evil days are full of wanton and objectless barbarities, refusal of quarter, murder in cold blood, killing of peasants. Invading armies burnt and destroyed everything in their way; the taking of plunder and ransom of prisoners were recognized sources of wealth. Prosperous countries were made "a sea of fire;" the horrible atrocities of the Spaniards in America were rivalled by those practised in Europe; deliberate directions were given to make whole tracts "a desert." Attempts had been made to introduce some amelioration into warfare again and again, either by forbidding hostilities at certain times, as was the object of the "truces of God," repeatedly enforced by ecclesiastical authority, or by establishing between the combatants themselves those courtesies which are at once the chief grace and glory of chivalry; but, to judge by the result as offered, even so late as the eighteenth century, those attempts must be regarded as having proved altogether abortive.

*Backward condition of England.*  England, at the close of the Age of Faith, had for long been a chief pecuniary tributary to Italy, the source from which large revenues had been drawn, the fruitful field in which herds of Italian ecclesiastics had been pastured. A wonderful change was impending. At the beginning of the sixteenth century the island was far more backward intellectually and politically than is commonly supposed. Its population hardly reached five millions, and was stationary at that point, not so much because of the effects of civil and foreign war as merely through the operation of ordinary economical causes. There was no reason to call more men into existence. It was regarded as good statesmanship to maintain the population at a constant standard. The municipal policy corresponded to the national; it was not so much advanced as that contemporaneously existing in Peru. Swarms of idle ecclesiastics had set such a pernicious example that the indisposition among common people to work had become quite a formidable difficulty. In every village there were stocks for the punishment of " valiant beggars," as they were termed. By the act of 1531, vagrants "whole and mighty in body" caught begging for the first time might be whipped at the cart-tail; the second time their ears were to be slit; by the act of 1536, if caught the third time, they were to be put to death. In all directions large towns were falling into decay, a misfortune popularly attributed to the laziness of the lower orders, but in reality due to causes of a very different kind. Hitherto land had been the representative of authority and the source of power. Society had been organized upon that imperfect basis; a descending scale of landed proprietors had been established, and in that system every man had a place assigned to him, just as in Peru, though less perfectly. It was a system of organized labour, the possession of land being a trust, not a property. But now commerce

*Apparent decline of its prosperity.*

was beginning to disturb the foundations on which all these arrangements had been sustained, and to compel a new distribution of population; trading companies were being established; men were unsettled by the rumours or realities of immense fortunes rapidly gained in foreign adventure. Maritime enterprise was thus not only dislocating society, but even destroying its spirit, substituting self-interest for loyalty. A nation so illiterate that many of its peers in Parliament could neither read nor write, was hardly able to trace the troubles befalling it to their proper source; with one voice it imputed them to the bad example and shortcomings of the clergy. Long before Henry VIII., England was ready for the suppression of the monasteries. She regarded them as the very hotbeds of her evils. There were incessant complaints against the clergy for their scandalous lusts, for personal impurities such as in modern times we do not allude to, for their holding of livings in plurality, for their extortion of exorbitant profits, and neglect in the discharge of their duty. In the public opinion, to so great an extent had these immoralities gone, that it was openly asserted that there were one hundred thousand women in England made dissolute by the clergy. It was well known that brothels were kept in London for their use. It was affirmed that the confessional was shamefully abused, and, through it, advantage taken of females; that the vilest crime in an ecclesiastic might be commuted for money, six shillings and eightpence being sufficient in the case of mortal sin. Besides these general causes of complaint, there were some which, though of a minor, were not of a less irritating kind; such, for instance, as the mortuary, soul-shot, or corpse present, a claim for the last dress worn by persons brought to a priest for burial, or some exaggerated commutation thereof.

*It is imputed to the clergy.*

*Causes of irritation of the laity against the clergy.*

That such was the demoralized condition of the English Church, and such its iniquitous relations to the people, we have the most unimpeachable evidence, under circumstances of an imposing and solemn character. The House of Commons brought an accusation against the clergy before the king. When Parliament met A.D. 1529, that House, as its very first act, declared to the sovereign that sedition and heresy were

*Accusation against the clergy by the House of Commons.*

pervading the land, and that it had become absolutely necessary to apply a corrective. It affirmed that the troubles into which the realm had fallen were attributable to the clergy; that the chief foundation, occasion, and cause thereof was the parallel jurisdiction of the Church and State; that the incompatible legislative authority of Convocation lay at the bottom of the mischief. Among other specific points it alleged the following:—That the houses of convocation made laws without the royal assent, and without the consent or even the knowledge of the people; that such laws were never published in the English language, and that nevertheless men were daily punished under them without ever having had an opportunity to eschew the penalties; that the demoralization extended from the Archbishop of Canterbury down to the lowest priest, that dignitary having tampered with the dispatch of justice in his Court of Arches; that parsons, vicars, priests, and curates were in the habit of denying the administration of the sacraments save upon the payment of money; that poor men were harassed without any legal cause in the spiritual courts for the mere purpose of extortion, and exorbitant fees were exacted from them without cause; that the probate of wills was denied except on the gratification of the appetite of prelates and ordinaries for money; that the high ecclesiastics extorted large sums for the induction of persons into benefices, and that they did daily confer benefices on "young folk," their nephews and relatives, being minors, for the purpose of detaining the fruits and profits in their own hands; that the bishops illegally imprisoned, sometimes for a year or more, persons in their jails, without informing them of the cause of their imprisonment or the name of their accuser; that simple, unlearned men, and even "well-witted" ones, were entrapped by subtle questions into heresy in the ecclesiastical courts, and punishment procured against them.

These are serious charges; they imply that the Church had degenerated into a contrivance for the extortion of money. The House of Commons petitioned the king to make such laws as should furnish a remedy. The king submitted the petition to the bishops, and required of them an answer.

In that answer the ecclesiastical manner of thought is very striking. The bishops insist that the laws of the realm shall give way to the canon law, or, if incompatible, shall be altered so as to suit it; they identify attacks on themselves with those on the doctrine of the Church, a time-honoured and well-tried device; they affirm that they have no kind of enmity against the laymen, "their ghostly children," but only against the pestilent poison of heresy; that their authority for making laws is grounded on the Scriptures, to which the laws of the realm must be made to conform; that they cannot conscientiously permit the king's consent to the laws, since that would be to put him in the stead of God, under whose inspiration they are made; that, as to troubling poor men, it is the Holy Ghost who inspireth them to acts tending to the wealth of his elect folk, that, if any ecclesiastic hath offended in this respect, though "in multis offendimus omnes," as St. James hath it, let him bear his own fault, and let not the whole Church be blamed; that the Protestants, their antagonists, are lewd, idle fellows, who have embraced the abominable opinions recently sprung up in Germany; that there are many advantages in commuting Church penances and censures for money; that tithes are a divine institution, and that debts of money owing to God may be recovered after one hundred or seven hundred years of non-payment, since God can never lose his rights thereto; that, however, it is not well to collect a tithe twice over; that priests may lawfully engage in secular occupations of a certain kind; that the punishments inflicted on the laymen have been for the health of their souls, and that, generally, the saints may claim powers to which common men are not entitled.

A fierce struggle between the Commons and the bishops ensued; but the House was firm, and passed several bills, and among them the Clergy Discipline Act. The effect was to cut down ecclesiastical incomes, probate and legacy duties were defined, mortuaries were curtailed, extortionate fees for burial terminated, clergymen were forbidden to engage in farming, tanning, brewing, or to buy merchandise for the purpose of selling it again. It was made unlawful any longer to hold eight or nine benefices, or to purchase dispensations for not doing duty; they were compelled to reside in the parishes for the care of which they were paid, under penalty of £10 a month; and it was made a high penal offence to obtain dispensations from any of the provisions of this act from Rome.

*The Church is compelled to submit.* Nothing could be more significant of the position of the parties than the high-toned, the conservative moderation of these acts. The bishops did not yield, however, without a struggle. In all directions from the pulpits arose a cry of "atheism," "lack of faith," "heresy." But the House resolutely stood to its ground. Still more, it sent its speaker to the king with a complaint against the Bishop of Rochester, who had dared to stigmatize it as "infidel." The bishop was compelled to equivocate and apologize.

*The king is sustained by his people.* The English nation and their king were thus together in the suppression of the monasteries; they were together in the enforcing of ecclesiastical reforms. It was nothing but this harmony which so quickly brought the clergy to reason, and induced them, in 1532, to anticipate both Parliament and the people in actually offering to separate themselves from Rome. In the next year the king had destroyed the vast power which in so many centuries had gathered round ecclesiastical institutions, and had forced the clergy into a fitting subordination. Henceforth there was no prospect that they would monopolize all the influential and lucrative places in the realm; henceforth, year by year, with many vicissitudes and changes, their power continued to decline. Their special pursuit, theology, was separated more and more perfectly from politics. In the House of Lords, of which they had once constituted one-half, they became a mere shadow.

*Religious feeling of the nation changed.* Henry VIII. cannot, therefore, be properly considered as the author of the downfall of ecclesiasticism in England, though he was the instrument by which it was ostensibly accomplished. The derisive insinuation that the Gospel light had flashed upon him from Anna Boleyn's eyes was far from expressing all the truth. The nullity of Papal disciplines, excommunications, interdicts, penances, proved that the old tono of thought was utterly decayed. This oblivion of old emotions, this obsoleteness of old things, was by no means confined to England. On the Continent the attacks of Erasmus on the monks were everywhere received with applause. In 1527 one printer issued an edition of 24,000 copies of the 'Colloquies' of Erasmus, and actually sold them all. He understood the signs of the times.

From this digression on parties and policy in England, let us again return to special details, descending for that purpose to the close of the seventeenth century. For a long time London had been the most populous capital in Europe; yet it was dirty, ill built, without sanitary provisions. The deaths were one in twenty-three each year; now, in a much more crowded population, they are not one in forty. Much of the country was still heath, swamp, warren. Almost within sight of the city was a tract twenty-five miles round, nearly in a state of nature; there were but three houses in it. Wild animals roamed here and there, very much as they do in the Western territories of North America. It is incidentally mentioned that Queen Anne, on a journey to Portsmouth, saw a herd of five hundred red deer. With such small animals as the marten and badger, found everywhere, there was still seen occasionally the wild bull.

*State of England at the close of the seventeenth century.*

*Wild state of the country.*

Nothing more strikingly shows the social condition than the provisions for locomotion. In the rainy seasons the roads were all but impassable, justifying the epithet often applied to them of being in a horrible state. Through such gullies, half filled with mud, carriages were dragged, often by oxen, or, when horses were used, it was as much a matter of necessity as in the city a matter of display to drive half-a-dozen of them. If the country was open, the track of the road was easily mistaken. It was no uncommon thing for persons to lose their way, and have to spend the night out in the open air. Between places of considerable importance the roads were sometimes very little known, and such was the difficulty for wheeled carriages that a principal mode of transport was by pack-horses, of which passengers took advantage, stowing themselves away between the packs. We shall probably not dissent from their

*Locomotion: the roads and carriages.*

complaint that this method of travelling was hot in summer and cold in winter. The usual charge for freight was 1s. 3d. a ton per mile. Toward the close of the century what were termed "flying coaches" were established; they could move at the rate of from thirty to fifty miles in a day. Many persons thought the risk so great that it was a tempting of Providence to go in them. The mail-bag was carried on horseback at about five miles an hour. A penny-post had been established in the City, but with much difficulty, for many long-headed men, who knew very well what they were saying, had denounced it as an insidious "Popish contrivance."

*The mails: penny-post disliked.*

Only a few years before the period under consideration Parliament had resolved that "all pictures in the royal collection which contained representations of Jesus or the Virgin Mother should be burnt; Greek statues were delivered over to Puritan stonemasons to be made decent." A little earlier, Lewis Muggleton had given himself out as the last and greatest of the prophets, having power to save or damn whom he pleased. It had been revealed to him that God is only six feet high, and the sun only four miles off. The country beyond the Trent was still in a state of barbarism, and near the sources of the Tyne there were people scarcely less savage than American Indians, their "half-naked women chanting a wild measure, while the men, with brandished dirks, danced a war-dance."

*Lewis Muggleton; his doctrines.*

At the beginning of the eighteenth century there were thirty-four counties without a printer. The only press in England north of the Trent was at York. As to private libraries, there were none deserving the name. "An esquire passed for a great scholar if 'Hudibras,' Baker's 'Chronicle,' Tarleton's 'Jests,' and the 'Seven Champions of Christendom' lay in his hall-window." It might be expected that the women were ignorant enough when very few men knew how to write correctly or even intelligibly, and it had become unnecessary for clergymen to read the Scriptures in the original tongues.

*Printing-presses and private libraries.*

Social discipline was very far from being of that kind which we call moral. The master whipped his apprentice, the pedagogue his scholar, the husband his wife. Public punishments partook of the general brutality. It was a day for the rabble

*Social discipline; its barbarity.*

when some culprit was set in the pillory to be pelted with brickbats, rotten eggs, and dead cats; when women were fastened by the legs in the stocks at the market-place, or a pilferer flogged through the town at the cart-tail, a clamour not unfrequently arising unless the lash were laid on hard enough "to make him howl." In punishments of higher offenders these whippings were perfectly horrible; thus Titus Oates, after standing twice in the pillory, was whipped, and, after an interval of two days, whipped again. A virtuoso in these matters gives us the incredible information that he counted as many as seventeen hundred stripes administered. So far from the community being shocked at such an exhibition, they appeared to agree in the sentiment that, "since his face could not be made to blush, it was well enough to try what could be done with his back." Such a hardening of heart was in no little degree promoted by the atrocious punishments of state offenders: thus, after the decapitation of Montrose and Argyle, their heads decorated the top of the Tolbooth; and gentlemen, after the rising of Monmouth, were admonished to be careful of their ways, by hanging in chains to their park gate the corpse of a rebel to rot in the air.

To a debased public life private life corresponded. The houses of the rural population were huts covered with straw-thatch; their inmates, if able to procure fresh meat once a week, were considered to be in prosperous circumstances. One-half of the families in England could hardly do that. Children of six years old were not unfrequently set to labour. The lord of the manor spent his time in rustic pursuits; was not an unwilling associate of pedlars and drovers; knew how to ring a pig or shoe a horse; his wife and daughters "stitched and spun, brewed gooseberry wine, cured marigolds, and made the crust for the venison pasty." Hospitality was displayed in immoderate eating, and drinking of beer, the guest not being considered as having done justice to the occasion unless he had gone under the table. The dining-room was uncarpeted; but then it was tinted with a decoction of "soot and small beer." The chairs were rush-bottomed. In London the houses were mostly of wood and plaster, the streets filthy beyond

*Private life in different classes of society.*

expression. After nightfall a passenger went at his peril, for chamber windows were opened and slop-pails unceremoniously emptied down. There were no lamps in the streets until Master Heming established his public lanterns. As a necessary consequence, there were plenty of shoplifters, highwaymen, and burglars.

*General immorality and brutality.*

As to the moral condition, it is fearfully expressed in the statement that men not unfrequently were willing to sacrifice their country for their religion. Hardly any personage died who was not popularly suspected to have been made away with by poison, an indication of the morality generally supposed to prevail among the higher classes. If such was the state of society in its serious aspect, it was no better in its lighter. We can scarcely credit the impurity and immodesty of the theatrical exhibitions. What is said about them would be beyond belief if we did not remember that they were the amusements of a community whose ideas of female modesty and female sentiment were altogether different from ours. Indecent jests were put into the mouths of lively actresses, and the dancing was not altogether of a kind to meet our approval. The rural clergy could do but little to withstand this flood of immorality.

*Degraded condition of the lower clergy.*

Their social position for the last hundred years had been rapidly declining; for though the Church possessed among her dignitaries great writers and great preachers, her lower orders, partly through the political troubles that had befallen the state, but chiefly in consequence of sectarian bitterness, had been reduced to a truly menial condition. It was the business of the rich man's chaplain to add dignity to the dinner-table by saying grace "in full canonicals," but he was also intended to be a butt for the mirth of the company. "The young Levite," such was the phrase then in use, "might fill himself with the corned beef and the carrots, but as soon as the tarts and cheese-cakes made their appearance he quitted his seat, and stood aloof till he was summoned to return thanks for the repast," the daintiest part of which he had not tasted. If need arose, he could curry a horse, "carry a parcel ten miles," or "cast up the farrier's bill." The "wages" of a parish priest were at starvation-point. The social degradation of the ecclesiastic is well illustrated by an order of Queen Elizabeth, that no clergyman should presume to marry a servant-girl without the consent of her master or mistress.

The clergy, however, had not fallen into this condition without in a measure deserving it. Their time had been too much occupied in persecuting Puritans and other sectaries, with whom they would have gladly dealt in the same manner as they had dealt with the Jews, who, from the thirteenth century till Cromwell, were altogether interdicted from public worship. The University of Oxford had ordered the political works of Buchanan, Milton, and Baxter to be publicly burnt in the court of the schools. The immortal vagabond, Bunyan, had been committed to jail for preaching out of his head the way of salvation to the common people, and had remained there twelve years, the stout old man refusing to give his promise not to offend in that manner again. The great doctrine inculcated from the pulpit was submission to temporal power. Men were taught that rebellion is a sin not less deadly than witchcraft. On a community thirsting after the waters of life were still inflicted wearisome sermons respecting "the wearing of surplices, position at the Eucharist, or the sign of the cross at baptism," things that were a stench in the nostrils of the lank-haired Puritan, who with his hands clasped on his bosom, his face corrugated with religious astringency, the whites of his eyes turned up to heaven, rocking himself alternately on his heels and the tips of his toes, delivered, in a savoury prayer uttered through his nose, all such abominations of the Babylonish harlot to the Devil, whose affairs they were.

*Burning of books and persecution of preachers.*

*The Puritan's hatred of orthodoxy.*

In administering the law, whether in relation to political or religious offences, there was an incredible atrocity. In London, the crazy old bridge over the Thames was decorated with grinning and mouldering heads of criminals, under an idea that these ghastly spectacles would fortify the common people in their resolves to act according to law. The toleration of the times may be understood from a law enacted by the Scotch Parliament, May 8, 1685, that whoever preached or heard in a conventicle should be punished with death and the confiscation of his goods. That such an infamous spirit did not con-

*Brutal administration of the law.*

tent itself with mere dead-letter laws there is too much practical evidence to permit any one to doubt. A silly labouring man, who had taken it into his head that he could not conscientiously attend the Episcopal worship, was seized by a troop of soldiers, "rapidly examined, convicted of nonconformity, and sentenced to death in the presence of his wife, who led one little child by the hand, and it was easy to see was about to give birth to another. He was shot before her face, the widow crying out in her agony, 'Well, sirs, well, the day of reckoning will come.'" Shrieking Scotch Covenanters were submitted to torture by crushing their knees flat in the boot; women were tied to stakes on the sea-sands and drowned by the slowly advancing tide because they would not attend Episcopal worship, or branded on their cheeks and then shipped to America; gallant but wounded soldiers were hung in Scotland for fear they should die before they could be got to England. In the troubles connected with Monmouth's rising, in one county alone, Somersetshire, two hundred and thirty-three persons were hanged, drawn, and quartered, to say nothing of military executions, for the soldiers amused themselves by hanging a culprit for each toast they drank, and making the drums and fifes play, as they said, to his dancing. It is needless to recall such incidents as the ferocity of Kirk's lambs, for such was the name popularly given to the soldiers of that colonel, in allusion to the Paschal lamb they bore on their flag; or the story of Tom Boilman, so nicknamed from having been compelled by those veterans to seethe the remains of his quartered friends in melted pitch. Women, for such idle words as women are always using, were sentenced to be whipped at the cart's tail through every market town in Dorset; a lad named Tutching was condemned to be flogged once a fortnight for seven years. Eight hundred and forty-one human beings, judicially condemned to transportation to the West India islands, and suffering all the horrible pains of a slave-ship in the middle passage, "were never suffered to go on deck;" in the holds below, "all was darkness, stench, lamentation, disease, and death." One-fifth of them were thrown overboard to the sharks before they reached their destination, and the rest obliged to be fattened before they could be offered in the market to the Jamaica planters. The court ladies, and even the Queen of England herself, were so utterly forgetful of womanly mercy and common humanity as to join in this infernal traffic. That princess requested that a hundred of the convicts should be given to her. "The profit which she cleared on the cargo, after making a large allowance for those who died of hunger and fever during the passage, cannot be estimated at less than a thousand guineas."

It remains to add a few words respecting the state of literature. This, at the end of the seventeenth century, had become indescribably profligate, and, since the art of reading was by no means generally cultivated, the most ready method of literary communication was through theatrical representation. It was for that reason that play-writing was the best means of literary remuneration, if we except the profit derived from the practice, which, to some extent, survives, though its disgraceful motive has ceased, of dedicating books to rich men for the sake of the fee they would give. It is said that books have actually been printed in consideration of the profits of the dedication. Especially in the composition of plays was it judged expedient to minister to the depraved public taste by indecent expressions, or allusions broad and sly. The playwright was at the mercy of an audience who were critical on that point, and in a position, if he should not come up to the required standard, to damn him and his work in an instant. From these remarks must be excepted the writings of Milton, which are nowhere stained by such a blemish. And yet posterity will perhaps with truth assert that Paradise Lost has wrought more intellectual evil than even its base contemporaries, since it has familiarized educated minds with images which, though in one sense sublime, in another are most unworthy, and has taught the public a dreadful materialization of the great and invisible God. A Manichean composition in reality, it was mistaken for a Christian poem.

*Profligate condition of literature.*

*Milton's Paradise Lost.*

The progress of English literature not only offers striking proofs of the manner in which it was affected by theatrical representations, but also furnishes an interesting illustration of that

*The English theatre.*

necessary course through which intellectual developement must pass. It is difficult for us, who live in a reading community, to comprehend the influence once exercised by the pulpit and the stage in the instruction of a non-reading people. As late as the sixteenth century they were the only means of mental access to the public; and we should find, if we were to enter on a detailed examination of either one or the other, that they furnish a vivid reflection of the popular intellectual condition. Leaving to others such interesting researches into the comparative anatomy of the English pulpit, I may, for a moment, direct attention to theatrical exhibitions.

*Its successive phases.* There are three obvious phases through which the drama has passed, corresponding to as many phases in the process of intellectual developement. These are, respectively, the miracle play, corresponding to the stage of childhood; the moral, corresponding to that of youth; the real, corresponding to that of manhood. In them respectively the supernatural, the theological, the positive predominates. The first went out of fashion soon after the middle of the fifteenth century, the second continued for about one hundred and fifty years, the third still remains. By the miracle play is understood a representation of Scripture incidents, enacted, however, without any regard to the probabilities of time, place, or action; such subjects as the Creation, the Fall of man, the Deluge, being considered as suitable, and in these scenes, without any concern for chronology, other personages, as the Pope or Mohammed, being introduced, or the Virgin Mary wearing a French hood, or Virgil worshipping the Saviour. Our forefathers were not at all critical historians; they indulged without stint in a highly pleasing credulity. They found no difficulty in admitting that Mohammed was originally a cardinal, who turned heretic out of spite because he was not elected Pope; that, since the taking of the true cross by the Turks, all Christian children have twenty-two instead of thirty-two teeth, as was the case before that event; and that men have one rib less than women, answering to that taken from Adam. The moral play personifies virtues, vices, passions, goodness, courage, honesty, love. The real play introduces human actors, with a plot free from the supernatural, and probability is outraged as little as possible. Its excellence consists in the perfect manner in which it delineates human character and action.

The miracle play was originally introduced by the Church, the first dramas of the kind, it is said, having been composed by Gregory Nazianzen. They were brought from Constantinople by the Crusaders; the Byzantines were always infatuated with theatrical shows. The parts of these plays were often enacted by ecclesiastics, and not unfrequently the representations took place at the abbey gate. So highly did the Italian authorities prize the influence of these exhibitions on the vulgar, that the Pope granted a thousand days of pardon to any person who should submit to the pleasant penance of attending them. All the arguments that had been used in behalf of picture-worship were applicable to these plays; even the Passion, Resurrection, and Ascension were represented. Over illiterate minds a coarse but congenial influence was obtained; a recollection, though not an understanding, of sacred things. In the play of "the Fall of Lucifer," that personage was introduced, according to the vulgar acceptation, with horns, and tail, and cloven hoof; his beard, however, was red, our forefathers having apparently indulged in a singular antipathy against hair of that colour. There still remain accounts of the expenses incurred on some of these occasions, the coarse quaintness of which is not only amusing, but also shows the debased ideas of the times. For instance, in "Mysteries," enacted at Coventry, are such entries as "paid for a pair of gloves for God;" "paid for gilding God's coat;" "dyvers necessaries for the trimmynge of the Father of Heaven." In the play of the "Shepherds," there is provision for green cheese and Halton ale, a suitable recruitment after their long journey to the birthplace of our Saviour. "Payd to the players for rehearsal: imprimis, to to God, iis. viiid.; to Pilate his wife, iis.; item, for keeping fyer at hell's mouth, iiid." A strict attention to chronology is not exacted; Herod swears by Mohammed, and promised one of his councillors to make him Pope. Noah's wife, who, it appears, was a termagant, swears by the Virgin Mary that she will not go into the ark, and, indeed, is only constrained so to do by

*Miracle plays; their nature.*

a sound cudgelling administered by the patriarch, the rustic justice of the audience being particularly directed to the point that such a flogging should not be given with a stick thicker than her husband's thumb. The sentiment of modesty seems not to have been very exacting, since in the play of "the Fall of Man," Adam and Eve appear entirely naked; one of the chief incidents is the adjustment of the fig-leaves. Many such circumstances might be related, impressing us perhaps with an idea of the obscenity and profanity of the times. But this would scarcely be a just conclusion. As the social state improved, we begin to find objections raised by the more thoughtful ecclesiastics, who refused to lend the holy vestments for such purposes, and at last succeeded in excluding these exhibitions from consecrated places. After dwindling down by degrees, these plays lingered in the booths at fairs or on market-days, the Church having resigned them to the guilds of different trades, and these, in the end, giving them up to the mountebank. And so they died. Their history is the outward and visible sign of a popular intellectual condition in process of passing away.

*Moral plays; their nature.* The mystery and miracle plays were succeeded by the moral play. It has been thought by some, who have studied the history of the English theatre, that these plays were the result of the Reformation, with the activity of which movement their popularity was coincident. But perhaps the reader who is impressed with the principle of that definite order of social advancement so frequently referred to in this book will agree with me, that this relation of cause and effect can hardly be sustained, and that devotional exercises and popular recreations are in common affected by antecedent conditions. Of the moral play, a very characteristic example still remains, under the title of "Everyman." It often delineates personification and allegory with very considerable power. This short phase of our theatrical career deserves a far closer attention than it has hitherto obtained, for it has left an indelible impression on our literature. I think that it is to this, in its declining days, that we are indebted for much of the machinery of Bunyan's 'Pilgrim's Progress.' Whoever will compare that work with such plays as 'Everyman' and 'Lusty Juventus,' cannot fail to be struck with their resemblances. Such personages as "Good Counsel," "Abominable Living," "Hypocrasie," in the play, are of the same family as those in the 'Progress.' The stout Protestantism of both is at once edifying and amusing. An utter contempt for "holy stocks and holy stones, holy clouts and holy bones," as the play has it, animates them all. And it can hardly be doubted that the immortal tinker, in the carnal days when he played at tipcat and romped with the girls on the village green at Elstow, indulged himself in the edification of witnessing these dramatic representations.

As to the passage from this dramatic phase to the real, in which the character and actions of man are portrayed, to the exclusion of the supernatural, it is only necessary to allude with brevity—indeed, it is only necessary to recall one name, and that one name is Shakspeare. He stands, in his relations to English literature, in the same position that the Greek sculptors stood with respect to ancient art, embodying conceptions of humanity in its various attributes with indescribable skill, and with an exquisite agreement to nature.

*Real plays. Shakspeare.*

Not without significance is it that we find mystery in the pulpit and mystery on the stage. They appertain to social infancy. Such dramas as those I have alluded to, and many others that, if space had permitted, might have been quoted, were in unison with the times. The abbeys were boasting of such treasures as the French hood of the Virgin, "her smocke or shifte," the manger in which Christ was laid, the spear which pierced his side, the crown of thorns. The transition from this to the following stage is not without its political attendants, the prohibition of interludes containing anything against the Church of Rome, the royal proclamation against preaching out of one's own brain, the appearance of the Puritan upon the national stage, an increasing acerbity of habit and sanctimoniousness of demeanour.

*The pulpit and the stage.*

With peculiar facility we may, therefore, through an examination of the state of the drama, determine national mental condition. The same may be done by a like examination of the state of the pulpit. Whoever will take the trouble to compare the results together cannot fail to observe how remarkably they correspond.

Such was the state of the literature of amusement; as to political literature, even at the close of the period we are considering, it could not be expected to flourish after the judges had declared that no man could publish political news except he had been duly authorized by the Crown. Newspapers were, however, beginning to be periodically issued, and, if occasion called for it, broadsides, as they were termed, were added. In addition, news-letters were written by enterprising individuals in the metropolis, and sent to rich persons who subscribed for them; they then circulated from family to family, and doubtless enjoyed a privilege which has not descended to their printed contemporary, the newspaper, of never becoming stale. Their authors compiled them from materials picked up in the gossip of the coffee-houses. The coffee-houses, in a non-reading community, were quite an important political as well as social institution. They were of every kind, Prelatical, Popish, Puritan, Scientific, Literary, Whig, Tory. Whatever a man's notions might be, he could find in London, in a double sense, a coffee-house to his taste. In towns of considerable importance the literary demand was insignificant; thus it is said that the father of Dr. Johnson, the lexicographer, hawked books from town to town, and was accustomed to open a stall in Birmingham on market-days, and it is added that this supply of literature was equal to the demand.

*Newspapers and coffeehouses.*

The liberty of the press has been of slow growth. Scarcely had printing been invented, when it was found necessary everywhere to place it under some restraint, as was, for instance, done by Rome in her Index Expurgatorius of prohibited books, and the putting of printers who had offended under the ban; the action of the University of Paris, alluded to on page 193 of this volume, was essentially of the same kind. In England, at first, the press was subjected to the common law; the Crown judges themselves determined the offence, and could punish the offender with fine, imprisonment, or even death. Within the last century this power of determination has been taken from them, and a jury must decide, not only on the fact,

*Liberty of the press slowly secured.*

*Its present state.*

but also on the character of the publication, whether libellous, seditious, or otherwise offensive. The press thus came to be a reflector of public opinion, casting light back upon the public; yet, as with other reflectors, a portion of the illuminating power is lost. The restraints under which it is laid are due, not so much to the fear that liberty would degenerate into licence, for public opinion would soon correct that; they are rather connected with the necessities of the social state.

Whoever will examine the condition of England at successive periods during her passage through the Age of Faith will see how slow was her progress, and will perhaps be surprised to find at its close how small was her advance. The ideas that had served her for so many centuries as a guide had rather obstructed than facilitated her way. But whoever will consider what she has done since she fairly entered on her Age of Reason will remark a wonderful contrast. There has not been a progress in physical conditions only—a securing of better food, better clothing, better shelter, swifter locomotion, the procurement of individual happiness, an extension of the term of life. There has been a great moral advancement. Such atrocities as those mentioned in the foregoing paragraphs are now impossible, and so unlike our own manners that doubtless we read of them at first with incredulity, and with difficulty are brought to believe that these are the things our ancestors did. What a difference between the dilatoriness of the past, its objectless exertions, its unsatisfactory end, and the energy, the well-directed intentions of the present age, which have already yielded results like the prodigies of romance!

*Contrast between progress in the ages of Faith and Reason.*

## CHAPTER XXII.

### THE EUROPEAN AGE OF REASON.

REJECTION OF AUTHORITY AND TRADITION, AND ADOPTION OF SCIENTIFIC TRUTH.—DISCOVERY OF THE TRUE POSITION OF THE EARTH IN THE UNIVERSE.

THE Age of Reason in Europe was ushered in by an astronomical controversy.

*An astronomical problem.*

Is the earth the greatest and most noble body in the universe, round which, as an immovable centre, the sun, and the various planets, and stars revolve, ministering by their light and other qualities to the wants and pleasures of man, or is it an insignificant orb—a mere point—submissively revolving, among a crowd of compeers and superiors, around a central sun? The former of these views was authoritatively asserted by the Church; the latter, timidly suggested by a few thoughtful and religious men at first, in the end gathered strength and carried the day.

*Its important consequences.*

Behind this physical question—a mere scientific problem—lay something of the utmost importance—the position of man in the universe. The conflict broke out upon an ostensible issue, but every one saw what was the real point in the dispute.

*Treatment of the Age of Reason.*

In the history of the Age of Reason in Europe, which is to fill the remaining pages of this book, I am constrained to commence with this astronomical controversy, and have therefore been led by that circumstance to complete the survey of the entire period from the same, that is, the scientific point of view. Many different modes of treating it spontaneously present themselves; but so vast are the subjects to be brought under consideration, so numerous their connections, and so limited the space at my disposal, that I must give the preference to one which, with sufficient copiousness, offers also precision. Whoever will examine the progress of European intellectual advancement thus far manifested will find that it has concerned itself with three great questions:—1. The ascertainment of the position of the earth in the universe; 2. The history of the earth in time; 3. The position of man among living beings. Under this last is ranged all that he has done in scientific discovery, and all those inventions which are the characteristics of the present industrial age.

Where am I? What am I? we may imagine to have been the first exclamations of the first man awakening to conscious existence. Here, in our Age of Reason, we have been dealing with the same thoughts. They are the same which, as we have seen, occupied Greek intellectual life.

When Halley's comet appeared in 1456, it was described by those who saw it as an object of "unheard-of magnitude;" its tail, which shook down "diseases, pestilence, and war" upon earth, reached over a third part of the heavens. It was considered as connected with the progress of Mohammed II., who had just then taken Constantinople. It struck terror into all people. From his seat, invisible to it, in Italy, the sovereign pontiff, Calixtus III., issued his ecclesiastical fulminations; but the comet in the heavens, like the sultan on the earth, pursued its course undeterred. In vain were all the bells in Europe ordered to be rung to scare it away; in vain was it anathematized; in vain were prayers put up in all directions to stop it. True to its time, it punctually returns from the abysses of space, uninfluenced by anything save agencies of a material kind. A signal lesson for the meditations of every religious man.

*Roman astronomical ideas.*

Among the clergy there were, however, some who had more correct cosmic ideas than those of Calixtus. A century before Copernicus, Cardinal de Cusa had partially adopted the heliocentric theory, as taught in the old times by Philolaus, Pythagoras, and Archimedes. He ascribed to the earth a globular

*More correct ideas among some of the clergy.*

form, rotation on its axis, and a movement in space; he believed that it moves round the sun, and both together round the pole of the universe.

*The geocentric and heliocentric theories.*  By geocentric theory is meant that doctrine which asserts the earth to be the immovable centre of the universe; by heliocentric theory that which demonstrates the sun to be the centre of our planetary system, implying, as a necessary inference, that the earth is a very small and subordinate body revolving round the sun.

*The geocentric doctrine adopted by the Church.*  I have already, in sufficient detail, described how the Roman Church had been constrained by her position to uphold the geocentric doctrine. She had come to regard it as absolutely essential to her system, the intellectual basis of which she held would be sapped if this doctrine should be undermined. Hence it was that such an alarm was shown at the assertion of the globular form of the earth, and hence the surpassing importance of the successful voyage of Magellan's ship. That indisputable demonstration of the globular figure was ever a solid support to the scientific party in the portentous approaching conflict.

*Preparations for the heliocentric doctrine.*  Preparations had been silently making for a scientific revolution in various directions. The five memoirs of Cardinal Alliacus 'On the Concordance of Astronomy with Theology,' show the turn that thought was taking. His 'Imago Mundi' was published in 1460, and is said to have been a favourite work with Columbus. In the very Cathedral of Florence, Toscanelli had constructed his celebrated gnomon, 1468; a sun-ray, auspicious omen! being admitted through a plate of brass in the lantern of the cupola. John Müller, better known as Regiomontanus, had published an abridgment of Ptolemy's 'Almagest,' 1520. Euclid had been printed with diagrams on copper as long before as 1482, and again in Venice twenty-three years subsequently. The 'Optics' of Vitello had been published 1533. Fernel, physician to Henry II. of France, had even ventured so far, supported by Magellan's voyage, as to measure, 1527, the size of the earth, his method being to observe the height of the pole at Paris, then to proceed northward until its elevation was increased exactly one degree, and to ascertain the distance between the stations by the number of revolutions of his carriage wheel. He concluded that it is 24,480 Italian miles round the globe. The last attempt of the kind had been that of the Khalif Almaimon, seven hundred years previously on the shore of the Red Sea, and with nearly the same result. The mathematical sciences were undergoing rapid advancement. Rhæticus had published his trigonometrical tables; Cardan, Tartaglia, Scipio Ferreo, and Stofel were greatly improving algebra.

The first formal assertion of the heliocentric theory was made in a timid manner, strikingly illustrative of the expected opposition. It was by Copernicus, a Prussian, speaking of the revolutions of the heavenly bodies; the year was about 1536. In his preface, addressed to Pope Paul III., whether written by himself, or, as some have affirmed, for him by Andreas Osiander, he complains of the imperfections of the existing system, states that he has sought among ancient writers for a better way, and so had learned the heliocentric doctrine. "Then I too began to meditate on the motion of the earth, and, though it appeared an absurd opinion, yet, since I knew that in previous times others had been allowed the privilege of feigning what circles they chose in order to explain the phenomena, I conceived that I might take the liberty of trying whether, on the supposition of the earth's motion, it was possible to find better explanations than the ancient ones of the revolutions of the celestial orbs."

*Copernicus, the works of.*

"Having, then, assumed the motions of the earth, which are hereafter explained, by laborious and long observation I at length found that, if the motions of the other planets be compared with the revolution of the earth, not only their phenomena follow from the suppositions, but also that the several orbs and the whole system are so connected in order and magnitude that no one point can be transposed without disturbing the rest, and introducing confusion into the whole universe."

The apologetic air with which he thus introduces his doctrine is again remarked in his statement that he had kept his book for thirty-six years, and only now published it at the entreaty

*Introduction of his system.*

of Cardinal Schomberg. The Cardinal had begged of him a manuscript copy. "Though I know that the thoughts of a philosopher do not depend on the judgment of the many, his study being to seek out truth in all things as far as is permitted by God to human reason, yet, when I considered how absurd my doctrine would appear, I long hesitated whether I should publish my book, or whether it were not better to follow the example of the Pythagoreans and others, who delivered their doctrine only by tradition and to friends." He concludes:

*He fears being accused of heresy.*

"If there be vain babblers, who, knowing nothing of mathematics, yet assume the right of judging on account of some place of Scripture perversely wrested to their purpose, and who blame and attack my undertaking, I heed them not, and look upon their judgments as rash and contemptible."

Copernicus clearly recognized not only the relative position of the earth, but also her relative magnitude. He says the magnitude of the world is so great that the distance of the earth from the sun has no apparent magnitude when compared with the sphere of the fixed stars.

*Early correction of the Copernican theory.*

To the earth Copernicus attributed a triple motion—a daily rotation on her axis, an annual motion round the sun, a motion of declination of the axis. The latter seemed to be necessary to account for the constant direction of the pole; but as this was soon found to be a misconception, the theory was relieved of it. With this correction, the doctrine of Copernicus presents a clear and great advance, though in the state in which he offered it he was obliged to retain the mechanism of epicycles and eccentrics, because he considered the planetary motions to be circular. It was the notion that, since the circle is the most simple of all geometrical forms, it must therefore be the most natural, which led to this imperfection. His work was published in 1543. He died a few days after he had seen a copy.

Against the opposition it had to encounter, the heliocentric theory made its way slowly at first. Among those who did adopt it were some whose connection served rather to retard its progress, because of the ultraism of their views or the doubtfulness of their social position. Such was Bruno, who contributed largely to its introduction into England, and who *Giordano Bruno of Nola.* was the author of a work on the 'Plurality of Worlds,' and of the conception that every star is a sun, having opaque planets revolving round it,—a conception to which the Copernican system suggestively leads. Bruno was born seven years after the death of Copernicus. He became a Dominican, but, like so many other thoughtful men of the times, was led into heresy on the doctrine of transubstantiation. Not concealing his opinions, he was persecuted, fled, and led a vagabond life in foreign countries, testifying that wherever he went he found scepticism under the polish of hypocrisy, and that he sought not against the belief of men, but against their pretended belief. For teaching the rotation of the earth he had to flee to *He teaches the heliocentric theory.* Switzerland, and thence to England, where, at Oxford, he gave lectures on cosmology. Driven from England, France, and Germany in succession, he ventured in his extremity to return to Italy, and was arrested in Venice, where he was kept in prison in the Piombi for six years, without books, or paper, or friends. Meantime the Inquisition demanded him as having written heretical works. He was therefore surrendered to Rome, and, after a further imprisonment of two years, tried, excommunicated, and delivered over to the secular authorities, to be punished "as mercifully as possible, and without the shedding of his blood," the abominable formula for burning a man alive. He had collected all the observations that had been made respecting the new star in Cassiopeia, 1572; he had taught that space is infinite, and that it is filled with self-luminous and opaque worlds, many of them inhabited,—this being his capital offence. He believed that the world is animated by an intelligent soul, the cause of forms but not of matter; that it lives in all things, even such as seem not to live; that everything is ready to become organized; that matter is the mother of forms and then their grave; that matter and the soul of the world constitute God. His ideas were therefore pantheistic, "Est Deus in nobis." In his 'Cena de le Cenere' he insists that the Scripture was not intended to teach science, but morals only. The severity with which he was treated was provoked by his asseverations that he was struggling with an orthodoxy that had neither morality nor belief. This was the aim of his work entitled 'The Triumphant Beast.' He was burnt at Rome, Febuary 16, 1600. With both a present and prophetic truth, he nobly responded, when the atrocious sentence was passed upon him, "Perhaps it is with greater fear that ye pass this sentence upon me than I receive it." His tormentors jocosely observed, as the flames shut him out for ever from view, that he had gone to the imaginary worlds he had so wickedly feigned.

*And is burnt alive as a heretic.*

This vigorous but spasmodic determination of the Church to defend herself was not without effect. It enabled her to hold fast the timid, the time-servers, the superficial. Among such may be mentioned Lord Bacon, who never received the Copernican system. With the audacity of ignorance, he presumed to criticize what he did not understand, and, with a superb conceit, disparaged the great Copernicus. He says, "In the system of Copernicus there are many and grave difficulties; for the threefold motion with which he encumbers the earth is a serious inconvenience, and the separation of the sun from the planets, with which he has so many affections in common, is likewise a harsh step; and the introduction of so many immovable bodies in nature, as when he makes the sun and stars immovable, the bodies which are peculiarly lucid and radiant, and his making the moon adhere to the earth in a sort of epicycle, and some other things which he assumes, are proceedings which mark a man who thinks nothing of introducing fictions of any kind into nature, provided his calculations turn out well." The more closely we examine the writings of Lord Bacon, the more unworthy does he seem to have been of the great reputation which has been awarded to him. The popular delusion to which he owes so much originated at a time when the history of science was unknown. They who first brought him into notice knew nothing of the old school of Alexandria. This boasted founder of a new philosophy could not comprehend, and would not accept, the greatest of all scientific doctrines when it was plainly set before his eyes.

*Lord Bacon.*

*Rejects the Copernican doctrine.*

It has been represented that the invention of the true method of physical science was an amusement of Bacon's

bours of relaxation from the more laborious studies of law and
duties of a court. His chief admirers have been persons of a
literary turn, who have an idea that scientific discoveries are
accomplished by a mechanico-mental operation. Bacon never The practical uselessness of his philosophy.
produced any great practical result himself; no great physicist
has ever made any use of his method. He has had the same
to do with the developement of modern science that the inventor of the orrery has had to do with the discovery of the
mechanism of the world. Of all the important physical discoveries, there is not one which shows that its author made it
by the Baconian instrument. Newton never seems to have
been aware that he was under any obligation to Bacon. Archimedes, and the Alexandrians, and the Arabians, and Leonardo da Vinci did very well before he was born; the discovery
of America by Columbus and the circumnavigation by Magellan can hardly be attributed to him, yet they were the consequences of a truly philosophical reasoning. But the investigation of nature is an affair of genius, not of rules. No man
can invent an organon for writing tragedies and epic poems.
Bacon's system is, in its own terms, an idol of the theatre.
It would scarcely guide a man to a solution of the riddle of
Ælia Lælia Crispis, or to that of the charade of Sir Hilary.

Few scientific pretenders have made more mistakes than His scientific errors.
Lord Bacon. He rejected the Copernican system, and spoke
insolently of its great author; he undertook to criticize ad-
versely Gilbert's treatise 'De Magnete;' he was occupied in
the condemnation of any investigation of final causes, while
Harvey was deducing the circulation of the blood from Acquapendente's discovery of the valves in the veins; he was doubtful whether instruments were of any advantage, while Galileo
was investigating the heavens with the telescope. Ignorant
himself of every branch of mathematics, he presumed that
they were useless in science, but a few years before Newton
achieved by their aid his immortal discoveries. It is time that
the sacred name of philosophy should be severed from its long
connection with that of one who was a pretender in science, a
time-serving politician, an insidious lawyer, a corrupt judge,
a treacherous friend, a bad man.

But others were not so obtuse as Bacon. Gilbert, one of the best of the early English experimentalists, an excellent writer on magnetism, adopted the views of Copernicus. Milton, in 'Paradise Lost,' set forth in language such as he only could use the objections to the Ptolemaic, and the probabilities of the Copernican system. Some of the more liberal ecclesiastics gave their adhesion. Bishop Wilkins not only presented it in a very popular way, but also made some sensible suggestions explanatory of the supposed contradictions of the new theory to the Holy Scriptures. It was, however, among geometricians, as Napier, Briggs, Horrox, that it met with its best support. On the Continent the doctrine was daily making converts, and nightly gathering strength from the accordance of the tables of the motions of the heavenly bodies calculated upon its principles with actual observation.

It is by no means uninteresting to notice the different classes of men among whom this great theory was steadily winning its way. Experimental philosophers, Republican poets, Episcopal clergymen, Scotch lords, west of England schoolmasters, Italian physicists, Polish pedants, painstaking Germans, each from his own special point of view, was gradually receiving the light; and doubtless, from such varied influence, the doctrine would have vindicated its supremacy at last, though it might have taken a long time. On a sudden, however, there occurred a fortunate event, which led forthwith to that result by a new train of evidence, bringing the matter, under the most brilliant circumstances, clearly to the apprehension of every one. This great and fortunate event was the invention of the telescope.

It is needless for us to enter on any examination of the authorship of this invention. It is enough for our purpose to know that Lippershey, a Dutchman, had made one toward the close of 1608, and that Galileo, hearing of the circumstance, but without knowing the particulars of the construction, in April or May of the following year invented a form of it for himself. Not content with admiring how close and large it made terrestrial objects, he employed it for examining the heavens. On turning it to the moon, he found that she has

mountains casting shadows, and valleys like those of the earth.
The discovery of innumerable fixed stars—not fewer than forty *Telescopic astronomical discoveries.*
were counted by him in the well-known group of the Pleiades
—up to that time unseen by man, was felt at once to offer an
insuperable argument against the opinion that these bodies
were created only to illuminate the night; indeed, it may be
said that this was a death-blow to the time-honoured doctrine
of the human destiny of the universe. Already Galileo began
to encounter vulgar indignation, which accused him loudly of
impiety. On January 7th, 1610, he discovered three of Jupiter's satellites, and a few days later the fourth. To these he
gave the designation of the Medicean stars, and in his 'Sidereal Messenger' published an account of the facts he had thus
far observed. As it was perceived at once that this planet
offered a miniature representation of the ideas of Copernicus
respecting the solar system, this discovery was received by the
astronomical party with the liveliest pleasure, by the ecclesiastical with the most bitter opposition, some declaring that it
was a mere optical deception, some a purposed fraud, some that
it was sheer blasphemy, and some, fairly carrying out to its consequences the absurd philosophy of the day, asserted that, since
the pretended satellites were invisible to the naked eye, they
must be useless, and being useless, they could not exist. Continuing his observations, Galileo found that Saturn differs in
an extraordinary manner from other planets; but the telescope he used not being sufficient to demonstrate the ring, he
fell into the mistake that the body of the planet is triple. This
was soon followed by the discovery of the phases of Venus,
which indisputably established for her a motion round the sun,
and actually converted what had hitherto, on all hands, been
regarded as one of the weightiest objections against the Copernican theory, into a most solid support. "If the doctrine of
Copernicus be true, the planet Venus ought to show phases
like the moon, which is not the case;" so said the objectors.
Copernicus himself saw the difficulty, and tried to remove it
by suggesting that the planet might be transparent. The telescope of Galileo for ever settled the question by showing that
the expected phases do actually exist.

In the garden of Cardinal Bandini at Rome, A.D. 1611, *Commencing opposition to Galileo.* Galileo publicly exhibited the spots upon the sun. He had observed them the preceding year. Goaded on by the opposition his astronomical discoveries were bringing upon him, he addressed a letter in 1613 to the Abbé Castelli, for the purpose of showing that the Scriptures were not intended as a scientific authority. This was repeating Bruno's offence. Hereupon the Dominicans, taking the alarm, commenced to attack him from their pulpits. It shows how reluctantly, and with what misgivings the higher ecclesiastics entered upon the quarrel, that Maraffi, the general of the Dominicans, apologized to Galileo for what had taken place. The astronomer now published another letter reiterating his former opinions, asserting that the Scriptures were only intended for our salvation, and otherwise defending himself, and recalling the fact that Copernicus had dedicated his book to Pope Paul III.

*He is summoned to Rome.* Through the suggestion of the Dominicans, Galileo was now summoned to Rome to account for his conduct and opinions before the Inquisition. He was accused of having taught that the earth moves; that the sun is stationary; and of having attempted to reconcile these doctrines with the Scriptures. *Is condemned by the Inquisition,* The sentence was that he must renounce these heretical opinions, and pledge himself that he would neither publish nor defend them for the future. In the event of his refusal he was to be imprisoned. With the fate of Bruno in his recollection, he assented to the required recantation, and gave the promise demanded. The Inquisition then proceeded to deal with the Copernican system, condemning it as heretical; the letters of Galileo, which had given rise to the trouble, were prohibited; also Kepler's epitome of the Copernican theory, and also the work of Copernicus. *Which condemns the Copernican system.* In their decree prohibiting this work, 'De Revolutionibus,' the Congregation of the Index, March 5, 1616, denounced the new system of the universe as "that false Pythagorean doctrine utterly contrary to the Holy Scriptures."

Again it appears how reluctant the Roman authorities were to interfere, and how they were impelled rather by the necessity of their position than by their personal belief in the course they had been obliged to take. After all that had passed, the

Pope, Paul V., admitted Galileo to an audience, at which he  *The personal sentiments of the Pope.*
professed to him personally the kindest sentiments, and assured
him of safety. When Urban VIII. succeeded to the pontifical
chair, Galileo received the distinction of not less than six
audiences; the Pope conferred on him several presents, and
added the promise of a pension for his son. In a letter to the
Duke of Florence his Holiness used the most liberal language,
stated how dear to him Galileo was, that he had very lovingly
embraced him, and requested the duke to show him every favour.

Whether it was that, under these auspicious circumstances,  *Galileo publishes 'The System of the World.'*
Galileo believed he could with impunity break through the
engagement he had made, or whether an instinctive hatred of
that intellectual despotism and hypocrisy which was weighing
upon Europe became irrepressible in his breast, in 1632 he
ventured on the publication of his work, entitled 'The System
of the World,' its object being to establish the truth of the
Copernican doctrine. It is composed in the dialogue form,
three speakers being introduced, two of them true philosophers,
the third an objector. Whatever may have been the personal
opinion of the Pope, there can be no doubt that his duty rendered
it necessary for him to act. Galileo was therefore again
summoned before the Inquisition, the Tuscan ambassador expostulating
against the inhumanity of thus dealing with an old
man in ill-health. But no such considerations were listened
to, and Galileo was compelled to appear at Rome, February,
1633, and surrendered himself to the Holy Office. The Pope's
nephew did all in his power to meet the necessity of the Church
and yet to spare the dignity of science. He paid every attention
to the personal comfort of the accused. When the time
came for Galileo to be put into solitary confinement, he endeavoured
to render the imprisonment as light as possible;
but, finding it to prey upon the spirits of the aged philosopher,
he, on his own responsibility, liberated him, permitting him to
reside in the house of the Tuscan ambassador. The trial being  *Is again condemned by the Inquisition.*
completed, Galileo was directed to appear, on June 22, to hear
his sentence. Clothed in the penitential garment, he received
judgment. His heretical offences were specified, the pledges

he had violated recited; he was declared to have brought upon himself strong suspicions of heresy, and to be liable to the penalties thereof; but from these he might be absolved if, with a sincere heart, he would abjure and curse his heresies. However, that his offences might not altogether go unpunished, and that he might be a warning to others, he was condemned to imprisonment during the pleasure of the Inquisition, his 'Dialogues' were prohibited by public edict, and for three years he was directed to recite, once a week, the seven penitential Psalms.

*His degradation and punishment.*

In his garment of disgrace the aged philosopher was now made to fall upon his knees before the assembled Cardinals, and, with his hand on the Gospels, to make the required abjuration of the heliocentric doctrine, and to give the pledges demanded. He was then committed to the prison of the Inquisition; the persons who had been concerned in the printing of his book were punished; and the sentence and abjuration were formally promulgated, and ordered to be publicly read in the universities. In Florence, the adherents of Galileo were ordered to attend in the Church of Santa Croce to witness his disgrace. After a short imprisonment in the jail of the Inquisition, he was ordered to Arcetri, and confined in his own house. Here severe misfortunes awaited him; his favourite daughter died; he fell into a state of melancholy; an application that he might go to Florence for the sake of medical advice was refused. It became evident that there was an intention to treat him with inexorable severity. After five years of confinement, permission was reluctantly accorded to him to remove to Florence for his health; but still he was forbidden to leave his house, or receive his friends, or even to attend mass during Passion Week without a special order. The Grand-duke tried to abate this excessive severity, directing his ambassador at the court of Rome to plead the venerable age and ill-health of the immortal convict, and that it was desirable to permit him to communicate certain scientific discoveries he had made to some other person, such as Father Castelli. Not even that was accorded unless the interview took place in the presence of an official of the Inquisition. Soon after Galileo was remanded to Arcetri. He spent the weary hours in composing his work on Local Motion, his friends causing it to be surreptitiously published in Holland. His infirmities and misfortunes now increased. In 1637 he became totally blind. In a letter he plaintively says, referring to his calamity, "So it pleases God, it shall therefore please me also." The exquisite refinement of ecclesiastical vengeance pursued him remorselessly, and now gave him permission to see his friends when sight was no longer possible. It was at this period that an illustrious stranger, the author of 'Paradise Lost,' visited him. Shortly after he became totally deaf; but to the last he occupied himself with investigations respecting the force of percussion. He died, January, 1642, in the seventy-eighth year of his age, the prisoner of the Inquisition. True to its instincts, that infernal institution followed him beyond the grave, disputing his right to make a will, and denying him burial in consecrated ground. The Pope also prohibited his friends from raising to him a monument in the church of Santa Croce, in Florence. It was reserved for the nineteenth century to erect a suitable memorial in his honour.

The result of the discoveries of Copernicus and Galileo was thus to bring the earth to her real position of subordination and to give sublimer views of the universe. Mœstlin expresses correctly the state of the case when he says, "What is the earth and the ambient air with respect to the immensity of space? It is a point, a punctule, or something, if there be anything, less." It had been brought down to the condition of one of the members of a family—the solar system. And since it could be no longer regarded as holding all other bodies in submissive attendance upon it, dominating over their movements, there was reason to suppose that it would be found to maintain interconnections with them in the attitude of an equal or subordinate; in other words, the general relations would be discovered expressive of the manner in which all the planetary members of the solar system sustain their movements round the sun.

Among those whose minds were thoroughly occupied with this idea, Kepler stands pre-eminently conspicuous. It is not at all surprising, considering the mode of thought of those times, that he regarded his subject with a certain mysticism. They who condemn his manner of thus viewing things do not duly appreciate the mental condition of the generation in which he lived. Whatever may be said on that point, no one can deny him a marvellous patience, an almost superhuman painstaking disposition. Guess after guess, hypothesis after hypothesis, he submitted to computations of infinite labour, and doubtless he speaks the melancholy truth when he says, "I considered and reflected till I was almost mad." Yet, in the midst of repeated disappointment, he held, with a truly philosophical determination, firmly to the belief that there must be some physical interconnection among the parts of the solar system, and that it would certainly be displayed by the discovery of laws presiding over the distances, times, and velocities of the planets. In these speculations he was immersed before the publications of Galileo. In his 'Mysterium Cosmographicum' he says, "In the year 1595 I was brooding with the whole energy of my mind on the subject of the Copernican system."

*Discovery of Kepler's laws.* In 1609 he published his work entitled 'On the Motion of Mars.' This was the result of an attempt, upon which he had been engaged since the beginning of the century, to reconcile the motions of that planet to the hypothesis of eccentrics and epicycles. It ended in the abandonment of that hypothesis, and in the discovery of the two great laws now known as the first and second laws of Kepler. They are respectively that the orbits of the planets are elliptical, and that the areas described by a line drawn from the planet to the sun are proportional to the times.

In 1617 he was again rewarded by the discovery which passes under the designation of Kepler's third law; it expresses the relation of the mean distances of the planets from the sun with the times of their revolutions: "the squares of the periodic times are in the same proportion as the cubes of the distances." In his 'Epitome of the Copernican Astronomy,' published 1622, he showed that this law likewise holds good for the satellites of Jupiter as regards their primary.

Humboldt, referring to the movement of Jupiter's satellites, remarks:—"It was this which led Kepler, in his 'Harmonices Mundi,' to state, with the firm confidence and security of a German spirit of philosophical independence, to those whose opinions bore sway beyond the Alps, 'Eighty years have elapsed during which the doctrines of Copernicus regarding the movement of the earth and the immobility of the sun have been promulgated without hindrance, because it was deemed allowable to dispute concerning natural things and to elucidate the works of God, and, now that new testimony is discovered in proof of the truth of those doctrines—testimony which was not known to the spiritual judges,—ye would prohibit the promulgation of the true system of the structure of the universe.'" *His remonstrance with the Church.*

Thus we see that the heliocentric theory, as proposed by Copernicus, was undergoing rectification. The circular movements admitted into it, and which had burdened it with infinite perplexity, though they had hitherto been recommended by an illusive simplicity, were demonstrated to be incorrect. They were replaced by the real ones, the elliptical. Kepler, as was his custom, ingenuously related his trials and disappointments. Alluding on one occasion to this, he says: "My first error was that the path of a planet is a perfect circle,—an opinion which was a more mischievous thief of my time, in proportion as it was supported by the authority of all philosophers, and apparently agreeable to metaphysics." *Rectification of the Copernican theory.*

The philosophical significance of Kepler's discoveries was not recognized by the ecclesiastical party at first. It is chiefly this, that they constitute a most important step to the establishment of the doctrine of the government of the world by law. But it was impossible to receive these laws without seeking for their cause. The result to which that search eventually conducted not only explained their origin, but also showed that, as laws, they must, in the necessity of nature, exist. It may be truly said that the mathematical exposition of their origin constitutes the most splendid monument existing of the intellectual power of man. *The philosophical import of these laws.*

Before the heliocentric theory could be developed and made to furnish a clear exposition of the solar system, which is obviously the first step to just views of the universe, it was necessary that the science of mechanics should be greatly improved,—indeed, it might be said, created; for during those dreary ages following the establishment of Byzantine power, nothing had been done toward the acquisition of correct views either in statics or dynamics. It was impossible that Europe, in her lower states of life, could produce men capable of commencing where Archimedes left off. She had to wait for the approach of her Age of Reason for that.

The man of capacity at last came. Leonardo da Vinci was born A.D. 1452. The historian Hallam, enumerating some of his works, observes, "His knowledge was almost preternatural." Many of his writings still remain unpublished. Long before Bacon, he laid down the maxim that experience and observation must be the foundation of all reasoning in science; that experiment is the only interpreter of nature, and is essential to the ascertainment of laws. Unlike Bacon, who was ignorant of mathematics, and even disparaged them, he points out their supreme advantage. Seven years after the voyage of Columbus, this great man—great at once as an artist, mathematician, and engineer—gave a clear exposition of the theory of forces obliquely applied on a lever; a few years later he was well acquainted with the earth's annual motion. He knew the laws of friction subsequently demonstrated by Amontons, and the principle of virtual velocities; he described the camera obscura before Baptista Porta, understood aerial perspective, the nature of coloured shadows, the use of the iris, and the effects of the duration of visible impressions on the eye. He wrote well on fortification, anticipated Castelli on hydraulics, occupied himself with the fall of bodies on the hypothesis of the earth's rotation, treated of the times of descent along inclined planes and circular arcs, and of the nature of machines. He considered, with singular clearness, respiration and combustion, and foreshadowed one of the great hypotheses of geology, the elevation of continents.

This was the commencement of the movement in Natural Philosophy; it was followed up by the publication of a work on the principles of equilibrium by Stevinus, 1586. In this the author established the fundamental property of the inclined plane, and solved, in a general manner, the cases of forces acting obliquely. Six years later Galileo's treatise on Mechanics appeared, a fitting commencement of that career which, even had it not been adorned with such brilliant astronomical discoveries, would alone have conferred the most illustrious distinction upon him.

The dynamical branch of Mechanics is that which is under most obligation to Galileo. To him is due the establishment of the three laws of motion. They are to the following effect, as given by Newton:— *Discovery of the laws of motion.*

(1.) Every body perseveres in its state of rest or of uniform motion in a right line unless it is compelled to change that state by forces impressed thereon.

(2.) The alteration of motion is ever proportional to the motive force impressed, and is made in the direction of the right line in which that force is impressed.

(3.) To every action there is always opposed an equal reaction, or the mutual actions of two bodies upon each other are always equal, and directed to contrary parts.

Up to this time it was the general idea that motion can only be maintained by a perpetual application, impression, or expenditure of force. Galileo himself for many years entertained that error, but in 1638 he plainly states in his 'Dialogues on Mechanics' the true law of the uniformity and perpetuity of motion. Such a view necessarily implies a correct and clear appreciation of the nature of resistances. No experimental motion that man can establish is unrestrained. But a perception of the uniformity and perpetuity of motion lies at the very basis of physical astronomy. With difficulty the true idea was attained. The same may be said as respects rectilinear direction, for many supposed that uniform motion can only take place in a circle.

The establishment of the first law of motion was essential to the discovery of the laws of falling bodies, in which the descent is made under the influence of a continually acting force, the velocity increasing in consequence thereof. Galileo saw clearly that, whether a body is moving slowly or swiftly, *Establishment of the first law of motion;*

it will be equally affected by gravity. This principle was with difficulty admitted by some, who were disposed to believe that a swiftly moving body would not be as much affected by a constant force like gravity as one the motion of which is slower. With difficulty, also, was the old Aristotelian error eradicated that a heavy body falls more swiftly than a light one.

*And of the second;*
The second law of motion was also established and illustrated by Galileo. In his 'Dialogues' he shows that a body projected horizontally must have, from what has been said, a uniform horizontal motion, but that it will also have compounded therewith an accelerated motion downward. Here again we perceive it is necessary to retain a steady conception of this intermingling of forces without deterioration, and, though it may seem simple enough to us, there were some eminent men of those times who did not receive it as true. The special case offered by Galileo is theoretically connected with the paths of military projectiles, though in practice, since they move in a resisting medium, the air, their path is essentially different from the parabola. Curvilinear motions, which necessarily arise from the constant action of a central force, making a body depart from the rectilinear path it must otherwise take, are chiefly of interest, as we shall presently find, in the movements of the celestial bodies.

*And of the third.*
A thorough exposition of the third law of motion was left by Galileo to his successors, who had directed their attention especially to the determination of the laws of impact. Indeed, the whole subject was illustrated and the truth of the three laws being verified in many different cases by an examination of the phenomena of freely falling bodies, pendulums, projectiles, and the like. Among those who occupied themselves with such labours may be mentioned Torricelli, Castelli, Viviani, Borelli, Gassendi. Through the investigations of these, and other Italian, French, and English natural philosophers, the principles of Mechanics were solidly established, and a necessary preparation made for their application in astronomy. By this time every one had become ready to admit that the motion of the planetary bodies would find an explanation on these principles.

The steps thus far taken for an explanation of the movements of the planets in curvilinear paths therefore consisted in the removal of the old misconception that for a body to continue its motion forward in a straight line a continued application of force is necessary, the first law of motion disposing of that error. In the next place, it was necessary that clear and distinct ideas should be held of the combination or composition of forces, each continuing to exercise its influence without deterioration or diminution by the other. The time had now come for it to be shown that the perpetual movement of the planets is a consequence of the first law of motion; their elliptic paths, such as had been determined by Kepler, a consequence of the second. Several persons almost simultaneously had been brought nearly to this conclusion without being able to solve the problem completely. Thus Borelli, A.D. 1666, in treating of the motions of Jupiter's satellites, distinctly shows how a circular motion may arise under the influence of a central force; he even uses the illustration so frequently introduced of a stone whirled round in a sling. In the same year a paper was presented to the Royal Society by Mr. Hooke, "explicating the inflection of a direct motion into a circular by a supervening attractive principle." Huygens also, in his "Horologium Oscillatorium," had published some theorems on circular motions, but no one as yet had been able to show how elliptical orbits could, upon these principles, be accounted for, though very many had become satisfied that the solution of this problem would before long be given.

*Application of Mechanics to the celestial motions.*

In April, 1686, the 'Principia' of Newton was presented to the Royal Society. This immortal work not only laid the foundation of Physical Astronomy, it also carried the structure thereof very far toward its completion. It unfolded the mechanical theory of universal gravitation, upon the principle that all bodies tend to approach each other with forces directly as their masses, and inversely as the squares of their distances.

*Newton; publication of the 'Principia.'*

To the force producing this tendency of bodies to approach each other the designation of attraction of gravitation, or of gravity, is given. All heavy bodies fall to the earth in such a way that the direction of their movement is toward its centre.

*Propounds the theory of universal gravitation.*

Newton proved that this is the direction in which they must necessarily move under the influence of an attraction of every one of the particles of which the earth is composed, the attraction of a sphere taking effect as if all its particles were concentrated in its centre.

*Preparation for Newton.* — Galileo had already examined the manner in which gravity acts upon bodies as an accelerating force, and had determined the connection between the spaces of descent and the times. He illustrated such facts experimentally by the use of inclined planes, by the aid of which the velocity may be conveniently diminished without otherwise changing the nature of the result. He had also demonstrated that the earth's attraction acts equally on all bodies. This he proved by enclosing various substances in hollow spheres, and showing that, when they were suspended by strings of equal length and made to vibrate, the time of oscillation was the same for all. Upon the invention of the air-pump, a more popular demonstration of the same fact was given by the experiment proving that a gold coin and a feather fall equally swiftly in an exhausted receiver. Galileo had also proved, by experiments on the leaning tower of Pisa, that the velocity of falling bodies is independent of their weight. It was for these experiments that he was expelled from that city.

*Extension of attraction or gravity.* — Up to the time of Newton there were only very vague ideas that the earth's attraction extended to any considerable distance. Newton was led to his discovery by reflecting that at all altitudes accessible to man gravity appears to be undiminished, and that therefore it may possibly extend as far as the moon, and actually be the force which deflects her from a rectilinear path, and makes her revolve in an orbit round the earth. Admitting the truth of the law of the inverse square, it is easy to compute whether the moon falls from the tangent she would describe if the earth ceased to act upon her by a quantity proportional to that observed in the case of bodies falling near the surface. In the first calculations made by Newton, he found that the moon is deflected from the tangent thirteen feet every minute; but, if the hypothesis of gravitation was true, her deflection should be fifteen feet. It is no trifling evidence of the scrupulous science of this great philosopher that hereupon he put aside the subject for several years, without, however, abandoning it. At length, in 1682, learning the result of the measures of a degree which Picard had executed in France, and which affected the estimate of the magnitude of the earth which he had used, and therefore the distance of the moon, he repeated the calculations with these improved data. It is related that "he went home, took out his old papers, and resumed his calculations. As they drew to a close, he became so much agitated that he was obliged to desire a friend to finish them." The expected coincidence was verified. And thus it appeared that the moon is retained in her orbit and made to revolve round the earth by the force of terrestrial gravity.

These calculations were founded upon the hypothesis that the moon moves in a circular orbit with a uniform velocity. But in the 'Principia' it was demonstrated that when a body moves under the influence of an attractive force, varying as the inverse squares of the distances, it must describe a conic section, with a focus at the centre of force, and under the circumstances designated by Kepler's laws. Newton, therefore, did far more than furnish the expected solution of the problem of elliptical motion, and it was now apparent that the existence of those laws might have been foreseen, since they arise in the very necessities of the case. *The cause of Kepler's laws.*

This point gained, it is obvious that the evidence was becoming unquestionable, that as the moon is made to revolve round the earth through the influence of an attractive force exercised by the earth, so likewise each of the planets is compelled to move in an elliptical orbit round the sun by his attractive force. The heliocentric theory, at this stage, was presenting physical evidence of its truth. It was also becoming plain that the force we call gravitation must be imputed to the sun, and to all the planetary bodies as well as to the earth. Accordingly, this was what Newton asserted in respect to all material substance. *Resistless spread of the heliocentric theory.*

But it is a necessary consequence of this theory that many apparent irregularities and perturbations of the bodies of the *Perturbations accounted for.*

solar system must take place by reason of the attraction of each upon all the others. If there were but one planet revolving round the sun, its orbit might be a mathematically perfect ellipse; but the moment a second is introduced, perturbation takes place in a variable manner as the bodies change their positions or distances. An excessive complication must therefore be the consequence when the number of bodies is great. Indeed, so insurmountable would these difficulties be, that the mathematical solution of the general problem of the solar system would be hopeless were it not for the fact that the planetary bodies are at very great distances from one another, and their masses, compared with the mass of the sun, very small.

*Results of the theory of gravitation.* Taking the theory of gravitation in its universal acceptation, Newton, in a manner that looks as if he were divinely inspired, succeeded in demonstrating the chief inequalities of the moon and planetary bodies; in determining the figure of the earth—that it is not a perfect sphere, but an oblate spheroid; in explaining the precession of the equinoxes and the tides of the ocean. To such perfection have succeeding mathematicians brought the doctrine, that the most complicated movements and irregularities of the solar system have been satisfactorily accounted for and reduced to computation. Trusting to these principles, not only has it been found possible, knowing the mass of a given planet, to determine the perturbations it may produce in adjacent ones, but even the inverse problem has been successfully attacked, and from the perturbations the place and mass of a hitherto unknown planet determined. It was thus that, from the deviations of Uranus from his theoretical place, the necessary existence of an exterior disturbing planet was foreseen; and our times have witnessed the intellectual triumph of geometers directing where the telescope should point in order to find a new planet. The discovery of Neptune was thus accomplished.

It adds to our admiration of the wonderful intellectual powers of Newton to know that the mathematical instrument he used was the ancient geometry. Not until subsequently was the analytical method resorted to and cultivated. This method possesses the inestimable advantage of relieving us from the mental strain which would otherwise oppress us. It has been truly said that the symbols think for us. Dr. Whewell, looking at the thing from this point of view, observes: "No one for sixty years after the publication of the 'Principia,' and, with Newton's methods, no one up to the present day, has added anything of value to his deductions. We know that he calculated all the principal lunar inequalities; in many of the cases he has given us his processes, in others only his results. But who has presented in his beautiful geometry or deduced from his simple principles any of the inequalities which he left untouched? The ponderous instrument of synthesis, so effective in his hands, has never since been grasped by any one who could use it for such purposes; and we gaze at it with admiring curiosity, as on some gigantic implement of war which stands idle among the memorials of ancient days, and makes us wonder what manner of man he was who could wield as a weapon what we can hardly lift as a burden."

*The 'Principia': its incomparable merit.*

Such was the physical meaning of Newton's discoveries; their philosophical meaning was of even greater importance. The paramount truth was resistlessly coming into prominence—that the government of the solar system is under necessity, and that it is mathematically impossible for the laws presiding over it to be other than they are.

*Philosophical import of Newton's discoveries.*

Thus it appears that the law of gravitation holds good throughout our social system. But the heliocentric theory, in its most general acceptation, considers every fixed star as being, like the sun, a planetary centre. Hence, before it can be asserted that the theory of gravitation is truly universal, it must be shown that it holds good in the case of all other systems. The evidence offered in proof of this is altogether based upon the observations of the two Herschels on the motions of the double stars. Among the stars there are some in such close proximity to each other that Sir W. Herschel was led to suppose that it would be possible, from observations upon them, to ascertain the stellar parallax. While engaged in these inquiries, which occupied him for many years, he dis-

*Unity of idea in the construction of the universe.*

covered that many of these stars are not merely optically in proximity, as being accidentally in the same line of view, but are actually connected physically, revolving round each other in regular orbits. The motions of these double suns is, however, in many instances so slow as to require many years for a satisfactory determination. Sir John Herschel therefore continued the observations of his father, and, with other mathematicians, investigated the characteristics of these motions. The first instance in which the true elliptic elements of the orbit of a binary star were determined was given by M. Savary in the case of ξ Ursæ Majoris, indicating an elliptic orbit of 58¼ years. But the period of others, since determined, is very much longer; thus, in σ Coronæ, it is, according to Mr. Hind, more than 736 years. From the fact that the orbits in which these stars move round each other are elliptical, it necessarily follows that the law of gravitation, according to the inverse square, holds good in them. Considering the prodigious distances of these bodies, and the departure, as regards structure of the systems to which they belong, from the conditions obtaining in our unisolar system, we may perhaps assert the prevalence of the law of gravitation throughout the universe.

*Gravitation of double stars.*

If, in association with these double suns—sometimes, indeed, they are triple, and occasionally, as in the case of ε Lyræ, quadruple—there are opaque planetary globes, such solar systems differ from ours not only in having several suns instead of a single one, but since the light emitted is often of different tints, one star shining with a crimson, and another with a blue light, the colours not always complementary to one another, a wonderful variety of phenomena must be the result, especially in their organic creations; for organic forms, both vegetable and animal, primarily depend on the relations of coloured light. How varied the effects where there are double, triple, or even quadruple sunrises, and sunsets, and noons, and the hours marked off by red, or purple, or blue tints!

*Coloured light of double stars.*

It is impossible to look back on the history of the theory of gravitation without sentiments of admiration, and, indeed, of pride. How felicitous has been the manner in which have been explained the inequalities of a satellite like the moon

*Grandeur of Newton's discoveries.*

under the disturbing influence of the sun; the correspondence between the calculated and observed quantities of those inequalities; the extension of the doctrine to satellites of other planets, as those of Jupiter; the determination of the earth's figure; the causes of the tides; the different force of gravity in different latitudes, and a multitude of other phenomena. The theory asserted for itself that authority which belongs to intrinsic truth. It enabled mathematicians to point out facts not yet observed, and to foretell future events.

And yet how hard it is for truth to force its way when bigotry resists! In 1771, the University of Salamanca, being urged to teach physical science, refused, and this was its answer: "Newton teaches nothing that would make a good logician or metaphysician; and Gassendi and Descartes do not agree so well with revealed truth as Aristotle does."

Among the interesting results of Newton's theory may be mentioned its application to superior inequalities, such as the acceleration of the moon's mean motion, that satellite moving somewhat quicker now than she did ages ago. Laplace detected the cause of this phenomenon in the influence of the sun upon the moon, combined with the secular variation of the eccentricity of the earth's orbit. Moreover, he showed that this secular inequality of the motion of the moon is periodical, that it requires millions of years to re-establish itself, and that, after an almost inconceivable time, the acceleration becomes a retardation. In like manner, the same mathematician explained the observed acceleration in the mean motion of Jupiter, and retardation of that of Saturn, as arising from the mutual attraction of the two planets, and showed that this secular inequality has a period of 929½ years. With such slow movements may be mentioned the diminution of the obliquity of the ecliptic, which has been proceeding for ages, but which will reach a limit and then commence to increase. These secular motions ought not to be without interest to those who suffer themselves to adopt the patristic chronology of the world, who suppose that the earth is only six thousand years old, and that it will come to an end in about one thousand years more. They must accept, along with that prepos-

*The earth in time.*

terous delusion, its necessary consequences, that the universe has been so badly constructed, and is such a rickety machine, that it cannot hold together long enough for some of its wheels to begin to revolve. Astronomy offers us many illustrations of the scale upon which the world is constructed as to time, as well as that upon which it is constructed as to space.

*Dominion of law in the universe.*

From what has been said, the conclusion forces itself upon us that the general laws obtaining as respects the earth, hold good likewise for all other parts of the universe; a conclusion sustained not only by the mechanism of such motions as we have been considering, but also by all evidence of a physical kind accessible to us. The circumstances under which our sun emits light and heat, and thereby vivifies his attendant planets, are indisputably the same as those obtaining in the case of every fixed star, each of which is a self-luminous sun. There is thus an aspect of homogeneousness in the structure of all systems in the universe, which, though some have spoken of it as if it were the indication of a uniformity of plan, and therefore the evidence of a primordial idea, is rather to be looked upon as the proof of unchangeable and resistless law.

*Ruin of anthropocentric ideas.*

What, therefore, now becomes of the doctrine authoritatively put forth, and made to hold its sway for so many centuries, that the earth is not only the central body of the universe, but, in reality, the most noble body in it; that the sun and other stars are mere ministers or attendants for human use? In the place of these utterly erroneous and unworthy views, far different conceptions must be substituted. Man, when he looks upon the countless multitude of stars,—when he reflects that all he sees is only a little portion of those which exist, yet that each is a light- and life-giving sun to multitudes of opaque, and therefore invisible worlds,—when he considers the enormous size of these various bodies and their immeasurable distance from one another, may form an estimate of the scale of magnitude on which the world is constructed, and learn therefrom his own unspeakable insignificance.

In one beat of a pendulum a ray of light would pass eight

times round the circumference of the earth. Thus we may take the sunbeam as a carpenter does his measuring-rule; it serves as a gauge in our measurements of the universe. A sunbeam would require more than three years to reach us from α Centauri; nine and a quarter years from 61 Cygni; from α Lyræ twelve years. These are stars whose parallax has been determined, and which are therefore nearest to us.

*Aids for measurements in the universe.*

Of suns visible to the naked eye there are about 8000, but the telescope can discern in the Milky Way more than eighteen millions, the number increasing as more powerful instruments are used. Our cluster of stars is a disk divided into two branches at about one-third of its length. In the midst of innumerable compeers and superiors, the sun is not far from the place of bifurcation, and at about the middle of the thickness. Outside the plane of the Milky Way the appearance would be like a ring, and, still further off, a nebulous disk.

*Clusters of stars.*

From the contemplation of isolated suns and congregated clusters we are led to the stupendous problem of the distribution of matter and force in space, and to the interpretation of those apparent phantoms of self-luminous vapour, circular and elliptic disks, spiral wreaths, rings and fans whose edges fade doubtfully away, twins and triplets of phosphorescent haze connected together by threads of light and grotesque forms of indescribable complexity. Perhaps in some of these gleaming apparitions we see the genesis, in some the melting away of universes. There is nothing motionless in the sky. In every direction vast transformations are occurring, yet all things proclaim the eternity of matter and the undiminished perpetuity of force.

*Distribution of matter and force in space.*

The theory of gravitation, as delivered by Newton, thus leads us to a knowledge of the mathematical construction of the solar system, and inferentially likewise to that of other systems; but it leaves without explanation a large number of singular facts. It explains the existing conditions of equilibrium of the heavenly bodies, but its tells us nothing of their genesis; or, at the best, in that particular it falls back on the simple fiat of God.

*Limit of the theory of gravitation.*

The facts here referred to conduct us, however, to another

**Phenomena of the solar system.**

and far higher point of view. Some of them, as enumerated by Laplace, are the following:—1. All the planets and their satellites move in ellipses of such small eccentricity that they are nearly circles; 2. The movements of the planets are in the same direction and nearly in the same plane; 3. The movements of the satellites are in the same direction as those of the planets; 4. The movements of rotation of these various bodies and of the sun are in the same direction as their orbital motions, and in planes little different.

**The nebular hypothesis.**

The nebular hypothesis requires us to admit that all the ponderable material now constituting the various bodies of the solar system once extended, in a rarefied or nebulous and rotating condition, beyond the confines of the most distant planet. That postulate granted, the structure and present condition of the system may be mathematically deduced.

For, as the vast rotating spheroid lost its heat by radiation, it contracted, and its velocity of rotation was necessarily increased; and thus were left behind from its equatorial zone, by reason of the centrifugal force, rotating rings, the same result occurring periodically again and again. These rings must lie all in one plane. They might break, collapsing into one rotating spheroid, a planet; or into many, asteroids; or maintain the ring-like form. From the larger of these secondary rotating spheroids other rings might be thrown off, as from the parent mass; these, in their turn breaking and becoming spheroids, constitute satellites, whose movements correspond to those of their primaries.

We might, indeed, advance a step further, and show how, by the radiation of heat from a motionless nebula, a movement of rotation in a determinate direction could be engendered; and that upon these principles, the existence of a nebulous matter admitted, and the present laws and forces of nature regarded as having been unchanged, the manner of origin of the solar system might be deduced, and all those singular facts previously alluded to explained; and not only so, but there is spontaneously suggested the cause of many minor peculiarities not yet mentioned.

For it follows from the nebular hypothesis that the large

planets should rotate rapidly, and the small ones more slowly; that the outer planets and satellites should be larger than the inner ones. Of the satellites of Saturn, the largest is the outermost; of those of Jupiter, the largest is the outermost save one. Of the planets themselves, Jupiter is the largest, and outermost save three. These cannot be coincidences, but must be due to law. The number of satellites of each planet, with the doubtful exception of Venus, might be foreseen, the presence of satellites and their number being determined by the centrifugal force of their primary. The hypothesis also points out the time of revolution of the planets in their orbits, and of the satellites in theirs; it furnishes a reason for the genesis and existence of Saturn's rings, which are indeed its remaining witnesses—their position and movements answering to its requirements. It accounts for the physical state of the sun, and also for the physical state of the earth and moon as indicated by their geology. It is also not without furnishing reasons for the existence of comets as integral members of our system; for their singular physical state; for the eccentric, almost parabolic orbits of so many of them; for the fact that there are as many of them with a retrograde as with a direct motion; for their more frequent occurrence about the axis of the solar system than in its plane; and for their general antithetical relations to planets. *Facts accounted for by it.*

If these and very many other apparently disconnected facts follow as the mechanical necessities of the admission of a gravitating nebula—a very simple postulate—it becomes important to ascertain whether, by actual observation, the existence of such material forms may be demonstrated in any part of the universe. It was the actual telescopic observation of such objects that led Herschel to the nebular hypothesis. He concluded that there are two distinct kinds of nebulæ: one consisting of clusters of stars so remote that they could not be discerned individually, but that these may be discerned by sufficient telescopic power; the other being of a hazy nature, and incapable of resolution. Nebulæ do not occur at random in the heavens: the regions poorest in stars are richest in them; they are few in the plane of our sidereal system, but *Whether nebulæ actually exist.*

numerous about its poles, in that respect answering to the occurrence of comets in the solar system. The resolution of many of these hazy patches of light into stars by no means disproves the truly nebulous condition of many others.

*Opposition to the nebular hypothesis.*
Notwithstanding the great authority of the astronomers who introduced it, the nebular hypothesis has encountered much adverse criticism; not so much, however, from its obvious scientific defects, such as its inability to deal with the case of Uranus, as from moral and extraneous considerations. There is a line in Aristophanes which points out precisely the difficulty,—

'Ο Ζεὺς οὐκ ὢν, ἀλλ' ἀντ' αὐτοῦ Δῖνος νυνὶ βασιλεύων.

A reluctance to acknowledge the presidency of law in the existing constitution and movements of the solar system has been yielded, only to be succeeded by a reluctance to acknowledge the presidency of law in its genesis. And yet whoever will reflect on the subject will be drawn to the conclusion that the principle involved was really settled by Newton in his 'Principia,'—that is to say, when it became geometrically certain that Kepler's laws originate in a mathematical necessity.

As matters now stand, the nebular hypothesis may be regarded as the first superficial, and therefore imperfect, glimpse of a series of the grandest problems soon to present themselves for solution—the mathematical distribution of matter and force in space, and the variations of that distribution in time.

*The intellectual ruin of ecclesiasticism.*
Such is the history of the dispute respecting the position of the earth in the universe. Not without reason, therefore, have I assigned the pontificate of Nicholas V. as the true close of the intellectual dominion of the Church. From that period the sceptre had passed into another hand. In all directions Nature was investigated, in all directions new methods of examination were yielding unexpected and beautiful results. On the ruins of its ivy-grown cathedrals, Ecclesiasticism, surprised and blinded by the breaking day, sat solemnly blinking at the light and life about it, absorbed in the recollection of the night that had passed, dreaming of new phantoms and delusions in its wished-for return, and vindictively striking its talons at

*of the Age of Reason.* 275

any derisive assailant who incautiously approached too near. I have not space to describe the scientific activity displayed in all directions; to do it justice would demand volumes. Mathematics, physics, chemistry, anatomy, medicine, and all the many branches of human knowledge received an impulse. Simultaneously with the great events I have been relating, every one of these branches was advancing. Vieta made the capital improvement of using letters as general symbols in algebra, and applied that science to geometry. Tycho, emulating Hipparchus of old, made a new catalogue of the stars; he determined that comets are beyond the moon, and that they cut the crystalline firmament of theology in all directions. Gilbert wrote his admirable book on the magnet; Gesner led the way to zoology, taking it up at the point to which the Saracens had continued Aristotle, by the publication of his work on the history of animals; Belon at the same time, 1540, was occupied with fishes and birds. Fallopius and Eustachius, Arantius and Varolius, were immortalizing themselves by their dissections: the former reminding us of the times of Ptolemy Philadelphus, when he naïvely confesses "the Duke of Tuscany was obliging enough to send living criminals to us, whom we killed and then dissected." Piccolomini laid the foundations of general anatomy by his description of cellular tissue. Coiter created pathological anatomy; Prosper Alpinus, diagnosis; Plater, the classification of disease; and Ambrose Paré, modern surgery. Such were the occupations and prospect of science at the close of the sixteenth century.

*Wonderful development of scientific activity.*

Scarcely had the seventeenth opened when it became obvious that the movement, far from slackening, was only gathering force. It was the age of Galileo. Descartes introduced the theory of an ether and vortices; but, hearing of the troubles that had befallen Galileo, was on the point of burning his papers. Several years later, he was restrained from publishing his Cosmos "from a pious desire not to treat irreverently the decrees of the holy chair against the planetary movement of the earth." This was in 1633, when the report of the sentence of the Inquisition was made known. He also developed Vieta's idea of the application of algebra to geometry, and brought into pro-

*The movement becomes still more vigorous.*

T 2

minence the mechanical fact, destined to an important application in physical astronomy, that every curvilinear deflection is due to a controlling force. To him, among Europeans, also is to be attributed the true explanation of the rise of water in an exhausted space—"the weight of the water counterbalances that of the air." Napier perfected his great and useful invention of logarithms. Hydraulics was created by Castelli, hydrostatics by Torricelli, who also discovered barometric variations: both were pupils of Galileo. Fabricius ab Acquapendente discovered the valves in the veins, Servetus almost detected the course of the circulation. Harvey completed what Servetus had left unfinished, and described the entire course of the blood; Asellius discovered the lacteals; Van Helmont introduced the theory of vitality into medicine, and made the practice or art thereof consist in regulating by diet the archeus, whose seat he affirmed to be in the stomach. In strong contrast with this phantasy, Sanctorio laid the foundation of modern physiology by introducing the balance into its inquiries. Pascal, by a decisive experiment, established the doctrines of the weight and pressure of the air, and published some of the most philosophical treatises of the age: "his 'Provincial Letters' did more than anything to ruin the name of the Jesuits." The contagion spread to the lawyers: in 1672 appeared Puffendorf's work on the 'Law of Nature and Nations.' The phlogistic theory, introduced by Beecher and perfected by Stahl, created chemistry, in contradistinction to the Arabian alchemy. Otto Guericke invented the air-pump, Boyle improved it; Hooke, among many other discoveries, determined the essential conditions of combustion. Far above all contemporaries in mathematical learning and experimental skill, Newton was already turning his attention to the "reflections, refractions, inflections, and colours of light," and introducing the idea of attractions into physics. Ray led the way to comparative anatomy in his synopsis of quadrupeds; Swammerdam improved the art of dissection, applying it to the general history of insects; Lister published his synopsis of shells; Tournefort and Malpighi devoted themselves to botany; Grew discovered the sexes of plants, Brown the quinary arrangement of flowers.

Geology began to shake loose from the trammels of theology, and Burnet's 'Sacred Theory of the Earth' could not maintain its ground against more critical investigations. The Arabian doctrine of the movement of the crust of the earth began to find supporters. Lister ascertained the continuity of strata over great distances; Woodward improved mineralogy; the great mathematician, Leibnitz, the rival of Newton, propounded the doctrine of the gradual cooling of the globe, the descent of its strata by fracture, the deposit of sedimentary rocks, and their induration. Among physicians, Willis devoted himself to the study of the brain, traced the course of the nerves and classified them, and introduced the doctrine of the localization of functions in the brain. Malpighi and Leuwenhoeck applied the microscope as an aid to anatomy; the latter discovered spermatozoa. Graaf studied the function of the generative organs; Borelli attempted the application of mathematics to muscular movement; Duverney wrote on the sense of hearing, Mayow on respiration; Ruysch perfected the art of injection, and improved minute anatomy.

But it is in vain to go on. The rest of these pages would be consumed in an attempt to record the names of the cultivators of science, every year increasing in number, and to do justice to their works. From the darkness that had for so many ages enveloped it, the human mind at last emerged into light. The intellectual motes were dancing in the sunbeam, and making it visible in every direction.

Despairing thus to do justice to individual philosophers and individual discoveries, there is, however, one most important event to which I must prominently allude. It is the foundation of learned societies. Imitating the examples of the Academia Secretorum Naturæ, instituted at Naples, 1560, by Baptista Porta, and of the Lyncean Academy, founded 1603 by Prince Frederick Cesi at Rome for the promotion of natural philosophy, the Accademia del Cimento was established at Florence, 1637; the Royal Society of London, 1645; and the Royal Academy of Sciences in Paris, 1666.

*Institution of scientific societies.*

Arrived at the close of the description of this first great

*Review of anthropocentric philosophy.*

victory of scientific truth over authority and tradition, it is well for us to pause and look back on the progress of man from the erroneous inferences of his social infancy to the true conclusions of his maturity,—from anthropocentric ideas, which in all nations and parts of the world have ever been the same, to the discovery of his true position and insignificance in the universe.

*The sky; apparent nature of.*

We are placed in a world surrounded with illusions. The daily events of our life and the objects before us tend equally to deceive us. If we cast our eyes on the earth, it seems to be made only to minister to our pleasures or our wants. If we direct our attention to the sky, that blue and crystalline dome, the edges of which rest on the flat land or the sea—a glacial vault, which Empedocles thought was frozen air, and the Fathers of the Church the lowest of the seven concentric strata of heavens —we find a thousand reasons for believing that whatever it covers was intended by some Good Being for our use. Of the various living things placed with us beneath it, all are of an inferior grade when compared with ourselves, and all seem intended for us. The conclusions at which we thus arrive are strengthened by a principle of vanity implanted in our hearts, unceasingly suggesting to us that this pleasant abode must have been prepared for our reception, and furnished and ornamented expressly for our use.

*Anthropocentric ideas of God.*

But reflection teaches us that we came not hither of ourselves, and that doubtless the same Good Being who prepared this delightful abode brought us as tenants into it. From the fact of our own existence, we are insensibly and inevitably led to infer the existence of God; from the favourable circumstances in which our lot is cast, we gather evidences of His goodness; and in the energy which natural phenomena often display, we see the tokens of His power. What other explanation can we give of tempests in the sea or lightning in the heavens? Moreover, it is only during a part of our time— our waking hours—that we are brought in relation with these material things; for the rest, when we are asleep, a state in which we spend more than a third part of our life, we are introduced to other scenery, other beings, another world. From these we gather that there are agents of an intangible and more ethereal mould, perhaps of the nature of Him who brought us here, perhaps His subordinates and messengers. Whence do they issue and whither do they go? Is there not beyond the sky above us a region to which our imperfect vision cannot penetrate, but which may be accessible to them from the peaks of elevated mountains, or to be reached only with wings? And thus we picture to ourselves a heaven shut off from earth, with all its sins and cares, by the untroubled and impenetrable sky; a place of light and repose, its pavement illuminated by the sun and countless other shining bodies; a place of peace, but also a place of power. *Of the world and heaven.*

Still more, a thousand facts of our life teach us that we are exposed to influences of an evil nature as well as to those that are good. How often, in our dreams, does it happen that we are terror-stricken by the approach of hideous forms, faces of fearful appearance, from which we vainly struggle to escape. Is it not natural for us to attribute the evil we see in the world to these, as the good to those? and, since we cannot conceive of the existence of beings without assigning them a place, where shall we find for these malignant spirits a habitation? Is it not in the dark region beneath the ground, far away from the realms of light—a region from which, through the volcano, smoke and burning sulphur are cast into this upper world—a place of everlasting fire and darkness, whose portals are in caves and solitudes of unutterable gloom? *Of evil beings and hell.*

Placed thus on the boundary between such opposing powers, man is the sport of circumstances, sustained by beings who seek his happiness, and tempted by those who desire his destruction. Is it at all surprising that, guided by such obvious thoughts and simple reasonings, he becomes superstitious? that he sees in every shadow a spirit, and peoples every solitary place with invisibles? that he casts a longing look to the good beings who can protect him, seeking to invoke their aid by entreaties, and to propitiate their help by free-will sacrifices of things that are pleasant and valuable? Open to such influences himself, why should he not believe in the efficacy of prayer? His conscious superiority lends force to his suspicion that he *Of man, the supernatural.*

is a worthy object for the opposing powers to contend for, a conclusion verified by the inward strifes he feels, as well as by the trials of life to which he is exposed.

*His Immortality and future life.* But dreams at night, and sometimes visions by day, serve to enforce the conclusion that life is not limited to our transitory continuance here, but endures hereafter. How often at night do we see the well-known forms of those who have been dead a long time appearing before us with surprising vividness, and hear their almost forgotten voices? These are admonitions full of the most solemn suggestions, profoundly indicating to us that the dead still continue to exist, and that what has happened to them must also happen to us, and we too are destined for immortality. Perhaps involuntarily we associate these conclusions with others, expecting that in a future life good men will enjoy the society of good beings like themselves, the evil being dismissed to the realms of darkness and despair. And as human experience teaches us that a final allotment can only be made by some superior power, we expect that He who was our Creator shall also be our Judge; that there is an appointed time and a bar at which the final destination of all who have lived shall be ascertained, and eternal justice measure out its punishments and rewards.

*Inducements to morality.* From these considerations there arises an inducement for us to lead a virtuous life, abstaining from wickedness and wrong; to set apart a body of men who may mediate for us, and teach us, by precept and example, the course it is best for us to pursue; to consecrate places, such as groves or temples, to which we may resort, as the more immediate habitations of the Deity.

Such are the leading doctrines of Natural Theology of primitive man, both in the old and new continent. They arise from the operations of the human mind considering the fitness of things.

Just as we have in Comparative Anatomy the structure of different animals examined, and their identities and differences set forth, thereby establishing their true relations; just as we have in Comparative Physiology the functions of one organic being compared with those of another, to the end that we may therefrom deduce their proper connections, so, from the mythologies of various races of men, a Comparative Theology is to be constructed. Alone through such a science can correct conclusions be arrived at respecting this, the most important of the intellectual operations of man, the definite process of his religious opinions. But it must be borne in mind that Comparative Theology illustrates the result or effect of the phase of life, and is not its cause.

*Course of Comparative Theology.*

As man advances in knowledge, he discovers that of his primitive conclusions some are doubtless erroneous, and many require better evidence to establish their truth incontestably. A more prolonged and attentive examination gives him reason, in some of the most important particulars, to change his mind. He finds that the earth on which he lives is not a floor covered over with a starry dome, as he once supposed, but a globe self-balanced in space. The crystalline vault, or sky, is recognized as an optical deception. It rests upon the earth nowhere, and is no boundary at all; there is no kingdom of happiness above it, but a limitless space, adorned with planets and suns. Instead of a realm of darkness and woe in the depths on the other side of the earth, men like ourselves are found there, pursuing, in Australia and New Zealand, the innocent pleasures and encountering the ordinary labours of life. By the aid of such lights as knowledge gradually supplies, he comes at last to discover that this, our terrestrial habitation, instead of being a chosen, a sacred spot, is only one of similar myriads, more numerous than the sands of the sea, and prodigally scattered through space.

*Corrections of anthropomorphic ideas.*

Never, perhaps, was a more important truth discovered. All the visible evidence was in direct opposition to it. The earth, which had hitherto seemed to be the very emblem of immobility, was demonstrated to be carried with a double motion, with prodigious velocity, through the heavens; the rising and setting of the stars were proved to be an illusion; and, as respects the size of the globe, it was shown to be altogether insignificant when compared with multitudes of other neighbouring ones,—insignificant doubly by reason of its actual dimensions, and by the countless numbers of others like it in

*Consequence of discovering the form of the earth.*

*Detection of its insignificance.*

form, and doubtless, like it, the abodes of many orders of life.

And so it turns out that our earth is a globe of about twenty-five thousand miles in circumference. The voyager who circumnavigates it spends no inconsiderable portion of his life in accomplishing his task. It moves round the sun in a year, but at so great a distance from that luminary that, if seen from him, it would look like a little spark traversing the sky. It is thus recognised as one of the members of the solar system. Other similar bodies, some of which are of larger, some of smaller dimensions, perform similar revolutions round the sun in appropriate periods of time.

*Other solar systems.*

If the magnitude of the earth be too great for us to attach to it any definite conception, what shall we say of the compass of the solar system? There is a defect in the human intellect which incapacitates us for comprehending distances and periods that are either too colossal or too minute. We gain no clearer insight into the matter when we are told that a comet which does not pass beyond the bounds of the system may perhaps be absent on its journey for more than a thousand years. Distances and periods such as these are beyond our grasp. They prove to us how far human reason excels imagination; the one measuring and comparing things of which the other can form no conception, but in the attempt is utterly bewildered and lost.

*Magnitude of the universe.*

But as there are other globes like our earth, so too there are other worlds like our solar system. There are self-luminous suns exceeding in number all computation. The dimensions of this earth pass into nothingness in comparison with the dimensions of the solar system; and that system, in its turn, is only an invisible point if placed in relation with the countless hosts of other systems which form, with it, clusters of stars. Our solar system, far from being alone in the universe, is only one of an extensive brotherhood, bound by common laws and subject to like influences. Even on the very verge of creation, where imagination might lay the beginning of the realms of chaos, we see unbounded proofs of order, a regularity in the arrangement of inanimate things, suggesting

*The infinity of worlds.*

to us that there are other intellectual creatures like us, the
tenants of those islands in the abysses of space.

Though it may take a beam of light a million of years to
bring to our view those distant worlds, the end is not yet.
Far away in the depths of space we catch the faint gleams
of other groups of stars like our own. The finger of a man
can hide them in their remoteness. Their vast distances from
one another have dwindled into nothing. They and their
movements have lost all individuality; the innumerable suns
of which they are composed blend all their collected light into
one pale milky glow.

Thus extending our view from the earth to the solar system, *Insignificance of man.*
from the solar system to the expanse of the group of stars to
which we belong, we behold a series of gigantic nebular creations rising up one after another, and forming greater and
greater colonies of worlds. No numbers can express them, for
they make the firmament a haze of stars. Uniformity, even
though it be the uniformity of magnificence, tires at last, and
we abandon the survey, for our eyes can only behold a boundless prospect, and conscience tell us our own unspeakable insignificance.

But what has become of the time-honoured doctrine of the *Triumphs of scientific truth.*
human destiny of the universe,—that doctrine for the sake of
which the controversy I have described in this chapter was
raised? It has disappeared. In vain was Bruno burnt and
Galileo imprisoned; the truth forced its way, in spite of all
opposition, at last. The end of the conflict was a total rejection of authority and tradition, and the adoption of scientific
truth.

# CHAPTER XXIII.

## THE EUROPEAN AGE OF REASON—(*Continued*).

### HISTORY OF THE EARTH.—HER SUCCESSIVE CHANGES IN THE COURSE OF TIME.

*Age of the earth.*

A VICTORY could not be more complete nor a triumph more brilliant than that which had been gained by science in the contest concerning the position of the earth. Though there followed closely thereupon an investigation of scarcely inferior moment,—that respecting the age of the earth,—so thoroughly was the ancient authority intellectually crushed, that it found itself incapable of asserting by force the Patristic idea that our planet is less than six thousand years old.

*The question is impersonally solved.*

Not but that a resistance was made. It was, however, of an indirect kind. The contest might be likened rather to a partisan warfare than to the deliberate movement of regular armies under recognized commanders. In its history there is no central figure like Galileo, no representative man, no brilliant and opportune event like the invention of the telescope. The question moves on to its solution impersonally. A little advance is made here by one, there by another. The war was finished, though no great battle was fought. In the chapter we are entering upon, there is therefore none of that dramatic interest connected with the last. Impersonally the question was decided, and therefore impersonally I must describe it.

*Oriental and Western doctrines of the age of the earth.*

In Oriental countries, where the popular belief assigns to the creation of man a very ancient date, and even asserts for some empires a duration of hundreds of thousands of years, no difficulty as respects the age of the earth was felt, there seeming to have been time enough for every event that human researches have detected to transpire. But in the West, where the doctrine that not only the earth, but the universe itself, was intended for man, has been carried to its consequences with exacting rigour, circumstances forbid us to admit that there was any needless delay between the preparation of the habitation and the introduction of the tenant. They also force upon us the conclusion that a few centuries constitute a very large portion of the time of human existence, since, if we adopt the doctrine of an almost limitless period, we should fall into a difficulty in explaining what has become of the countless myriads of generations in the long time so passed; and, considering that we are taught that the end of the world is at hand, and must be expected in a few years at the most, we might seem to arraign the goodness of God in this, that He has left to their fate immeasurably the larger proportion of our race, and has restricted His mercy to us alone, who are living in the departing twilight of the evening of the world.

But in this, as in the former case, a closer examination of the facts brings us to the indisputable conclusion that we have decided unworthily and untruly; that our guiding doctrine of the universe being intended for us is a miserable delusion; that the scale on which the world is constructed as to time answers to that on which it is constructed as to space; that, as respects our planet, its origin dates from an epoch too remote for our mental apprehension; that myriads of centuries have been consumed in its coming to its present state; that, by a slow progression, it has passed from stage to stage uninhabited, and for a long time uninhabitable by any living thing; that, in their proper order and in due lapse of time, the organic series have been its inhabitants, and of these a vast majority, whose numbers are so great that we cannot offer an intelligible estimate of them, have passed away and become extinct, and that finally, for a brief period, we have been its possessors.

*Correction of the European doctrine.*

Of the intentions of God it becomes us, therefore, to speak with reverence and reserve. In those ages when there was not a man upon the earth, what was the object? Was the twilight only given that the wolf might follow his flying prey, and the stars made to shine that the royal tiger might pursue his midnight marandings? Where was the use of so much that was beautiful and orderly, when there was not a solitary intellectual being to understand and enjoy? Even now, when we are so much disposed to judge of other worlds from their apparent adaptedness to be the abodes of a thinking and responsible order like ourselves, it may be of service to remember that this earth itself was for countless ages a dungeon of pestiferous exhalations and a den of wild beasts.

*It elevates rather than degrades the position of man.*

It might moreover appear that the conclusions to which we come, both as respects the position and age of the world, must necessarily have for their consequences the diminution and degradation of man, the rendering him too worthless an object for God's regard. But here again we fall into an error. True, we have debased his animal value, and taught him how little he is—how insignificant are the evils, how vain the pleasures of his life. But, as respects his intellectual principle, how does the matter stand? What is it that has thus been measuring the terrestrial world, and weighing it in a balance? What is it that has been standing on the sun, and marking out the orbits and boundaries of the solar system? What is it that has descended into the infinite abysses of space, examined the countless worlds that they contain, and compared and contrasted them together? What is it that has shown itself capable of dealing with magnitudes that are infinite, even of comparing infinites together? What is it that has not hesitated to trace things in their history through a past eternity, and been found capable of regarding equally the transitory moment and endless duration? That which is competent to do all this, so far from being degraded, rises before us with an air of surpassing grandeur and inappreciable worth. It is the soul of man.

*Relations of the earth in time.*

From the facts given in the last chapter respecting the relations of the earth in space, we are next led to her relations in time.

So long as science was oppressed with the doctrine of the human destiny of the universe, which, as its consequence, made this earth the great central body, and elevated man to anpreme importance, there was much difficulty in treating the problem of the age of the world. The history of the earth was at first a wild and fictitious cosmogony. Scientific cosmogony arose, not from any theological considerations, but from the telescopic ascertainment of the polar compression of the planet Jupiter, and the consequent determination by Newton that the earth is a spheroid of revolution. With a true cosmogony came a better chronology. The Patristic doctrine had been that the earth came into existence but little more than five thousand years ago, and to this a popular opinion long current was added, that its end might be very shortly expected. From time to time periods were set by various authorities determining the latter event, and, as true knowledge was extinguished, the year 1000 came to be the universally appointed date. In view of this, it was not an uncommon thing for persons to commence their testamentary bequests with the words, "In expectation of the approaching end of the world." But the tremendous moment passed by, and still the sun rose and set, still the seasons were punctual in their courses, and Nature wore her accustomed aspect. A later day was then predicted, and again and again disappointment ensued, until sober-minded men began to perceive that the Scriptures were never intended to give information on such subjects, and predictions of the end of the world fell into discredit, abandoned to the illiterate, whose morbid anticipations they still amuse.

*Anthropocentric ideas of the beginning and end of the world.*

As it was thus with the end of our planet, so it was as regards her origin. By degrees evidence began to accumulate casting a doubt on her recent date, evidence continually becoming more and more cogent. In no insignificant manner did the establishment of the heliocentric theory, aided by the discoveries of the telescope, assist in this result. As I have said, it utterly ruined past restoration the doctrine of the human destiny of the universe. With that went down all arguments which had depended on making man the measure of things. Ideas of unexpected sublimity as to the scale of magnitude on which the world is constructed soon enforced themselves, and proved to be the precursors of similar ideas as to time. At length it was perceived by those who were in the

*Rise of the doctrine of illimitable age.*

van of the movement that the Bible was never intended to deliver a chronological doctrine respecting the beginning any more than the end of things, and that those well-meaning men who were occupied in wresting it from its true purposes were engaged in an unhappy employment, for its tendency could be no other than to injure the cause they designed to promote. Nevertheless, so strong were the ancient persuasions, that it was not without a struggle that the doctrine of a long period forced its way—a struggle for the age of the earth, which, in its arguments, in its tendencies, and in its results, forcibly recalls the preceding one respecting the position of the earth; but, in the end, truth overrode all authority and all opposition, and the doctrine of an extremely remote origin of our planet ceased to be open to dispute.

In a scientific conception of the universe, illimitable spaces are of necessity connected with limitless time.

*Indications depending on the progressive motion of light.* The discovery of the progressive motion of light offered the means of an absolute demonstration of this connection. Rays emitted by an object, and making us sensible of its presence by impinging on the eye, do not reach us instantaneously, but consume a certain period in their passage.

If any sudden visible effect took place in the sun, we should not see it at the absolute moment of its occurrence, but about eight minutes and thirteen seconds later, this being the time required for light to cross the intervening distance. All phenomena take place in reality anterior to the moment at which we observe them by a time longer in proportion as the distance to be travelled is greater.

There are objects in the heavens so distant that it would take many hundreds of thousands of years for their light to reach us. Then it necessary follows, since we can see them, that they must have been created and must have been shining so long.

The velocity with which light moves was first determined by the Danish astronomer Römer from the eclipses of Jupiter's satellites, November, 1675. It was, therefore, a determination of the rate for reflected solar light in a vacuum, and gave 198,000 miles in a second. In 1727, Bradley determined it for direct stellar light by his great discovery of the aberration of the fixed stars. More recently, the experiments of M. Foucault and those of M. Fizeau, by the aid of rotating mirrors or wheels, have confirmed these astronomical observations, Fizeau's determination of the velocity approaching that of Römer. Probably, however, the most correct is that of Struve, 191,515 miles per second.

This astronomical argument, which serves as a general introduction, is strengthened by numerous physical and physiological facts. But of the different methods by which the age of the earth may be elucidated, I shall prefer that which approaches it through the phenomena of heat. Such a manner of viewing the problem has led to its determination in the minds of many thinking men. *Investigation of the age of the earth through the phenomena of heat.*

As correct astronomical ideas began to prevail, it was perceived that all the heat now on the surface of our planet is derived from the sun. Through the circumstance of the inclination of her axis of rotation to the plane of her annual motion, or through the fact of her globular form occasioning the presentation of different parts of her surface, according to their latitudes, with more or less obliquity, and hence the reception of less or more of the rays, there may be local and temporary variations. But these do not affect the general principle that the quantity of heat thus received must be the same from year to year. *Astronomical heat alone on the earth's surface.*

This thermometric equilibrium not only holds good for the surface, it may also be demonstrated for the whole mass of the planet. The day has not shortened by the $\frac{1}{100}$ of a second since the time of Hipparchus, and therefore the decrease of heat cannot have been so much as the $\frac{1}{170}$ of a Fahrenheit degree, on the hypothesis that the mean dilatation of all terrestrial substances is equal to that of glass, $\frac{1}{10000}$ for one degree. If a decline had taken place in the intrinsic heat of the earth, there must have been a diminution in her size, and, as a necessary consequence, the length of the day must have become less. The earth has therefore reached a condition of equilibrium as respects temperature. *The equilibrium of interior heat.*

A vast body of evidence has, however, come into prominence, *Its ancient decline.*

establishing with equal certainty that there was in ancient times a far higher temperature in the planet; not a temperature concerned with a fraction of a degree, but ranging beyond the limits of our thermometric scale. The mathematical figure of the earth offers a resistless argument for its ancient liquefied condition—that is, for its originally high temperature. But how is this to be co-ordinated with the conclusion just mentioned? Simply by the admission that there have elapsed prodigious, it might almost be said limitless periods. As thus the true state of affairs began to take on a shape, it was perceived that the age of the earth is not a question of authority, not a question of tradition, but a mathematical problem sharply defined: to determine the time of cooling of a globe of known diameter and of giving conductibility by radiation in a vacuum.

*Necessity of a long time.*

In such a state of things, what could be more unwise than to attempt to force opinion by the exercise of authority? How unspeakably mischievous had proved to be a like course as respects the globular form of the earth, which did not long remain a mere mathematical abstraction, but was abruptly brought to a practical issue by the voyage of Magellan's ship. And on this question of the age of the earth it would have been equally unwise to become entangled with or committed to the errors of Patristicism,—errors arising from well-meant moral considerations, but which can never exert any influence on the solution of a scientific problem.

*Indications of the interior heat of the earth.*

One fact after another bearing upon the question gradually emerged into view. It was shown that the diurnal variations of temperature—that is, those connected with night and day—extend but a few inches beneath the surface, the seasonal ones, connected with winter and summer, to many feet; but beyond this was discovered a stratum of invariable temperature, beneath which, if we descend, the heat increases at the rate of 1° Fahr. for every fifty or seventy feet. The uniformity of this rate seemed to imply that, at depths quite insignificant, a very high temperature must exist. This was illustrated by such facts as that the water which rushes up from a depth of 1701 feet in the Artesian well of Grenelle has a temperature of 82° Fahr. The mean temperature of Paris being about

51° Fahr., these numbers give a rate of 1° for every fifty-eight feet. If, then, the increase of heat is only 100° per mile, at a depth of less than ten miles everything must be red-hot, and at thirty or forty in a melted state. It was by all admitted that the rise of temperature with the depth is not at all local, but occurs in whatever part of the earth the observation may be made. The general conclusion thus furnished was reinforced by the evidence of volcanoes, which could no longer be regarded as merely local, depending on restricted areas for the supply of melted material, since they are found all over the land and under the sea, in the interior of continents and by the shores, beneath the equator and in the polar regions. It had been estimated that there are probably two thousand aerial or subaqueous eruptions every century. Some volcanoes, as Ætna, have for thousands of years poured forth their lavas, and still there is an unexhausted supply. Everywhere a common source is indicated by the rudely uniform materials ejected. The fact that the lines of volcanic activity shift pointed to a deep source; the periodic increments and decrements of force bore the same interpretation. They far transcend the range of history. The volcanoes of central France date from the Eocene period; their power increased in the Miocene, and continued through the Pliocene; those of Catalonia belong to the Pliocene, probably. Coupled with volcanoes, earthquakes, with their vertical, horizontal, and rotary vibrations, having a linear velocity of from twenty to thirty miles per minute, indicated a profound focus of action. The great earthquake of Lisbon was felt from Norway to Morocco, from Algiers to the West Indies, from Thuringia to the Canadian lakes. It absolutely lifted the whole bed of the North Atlantic Ocean. Its origin was in no superficial point.

A still more universal proof of a high temperature affecting the whole mass of the interior of the globe was believed to be presented in the small mean density of the earth, a density not more than 5·66 times that of water, the mean density of the solid surface being 2·7, and that of the solid and sea-surface together 1·6. But this is not a density answering to that which the earth should have in virtue of the

*Proof from the mean density.*

attraction of her own parts. It implied some agent capable of rarefying and dilating, and the only such agent is heat. Although the law of the increase of density from the upper surface to the centre is unknown, yet a comparison of the earth's compression with her velocity of rotation demonstrated that there is an increasing density in the strata as we descend. The great fact, however, which stands prominently forth is the interior heat.

Not only were evidences thus offered of the existence of a high temperature, and, therefore, of the lapse of a long time by the present circumstances of the globe; every trace of its former state, duly considered, yielded similar indications, the old evidence corroborating the new. And soon it appeared that this would hold good whether considered in the inorganic or organic aspect.

*Inorganic proofs of a former high temperature.*

In the organic, what other interpretation could be put on the universal occurrence of igneous rocks, some in enormous mountain-ranges, some ejected from beneath, forcing their tortuous way through the resisting superincumbent strata; veins of various mineral constitution, and, as their relations with one another showed, veins of very different dates? What other interpretation of layers of lava in succession, one under another, and often with old disintegrated material between? What of those numerous volcanoes which have never been known to show any signs of activity in the period of history, though they sometimes occur in countries like France, pre-eminently historic? What meaning could be assigned to all those dislocations, subsidences, and elevations which the crust of the earth in every country presents, indications of a loss of heat, of a contraction in diameter, and its necessary consequence, fracture of the exterior consolidated shell along lines of least resistance? And though it was asserted by some that the catastrophes of which these are the evidences were occasioned by forces of unparalleled energy and incessant operation,—unparalleled when compared with such terrestrial forces as we are familiar with,—that did not, in any respect, change the interpretation, for there could have been no abrupt diminution in the intensity of those forces, which, if they had lessened in power, must have passed through a long, a gradual decline. In that very decline there thus spontaneously came forth evidences of a long lapse of time. The whole course of Nature satisfies us how gradual and deliberate are her proceedings; that there is no abrupt boundary between the past and the present, but that the one insensibly shades off into the other, the present springing gently and imperceptibly out of the past. If volcanic phenomena and all kinds of igneous manifestations,—if dislocations, injections, the intrusion of molted material into strata were at one time more frequent, more violent,—if, in the old times, mundane forces possessed an energy which they have now lost, their present diminished and deteriorated condition, coupled with the fact that for thousands of years, throughout the range of history, they have been invariably such as we find them now, should be to us a proof how long, how very long ago those old times must have been.

*These necessarily imply long time.*

Thus, therefore, was perceived the necessity of co-ordinating the scale of time with the scale of space, and such views of the physical history of the earth were extended to celestial bodies which were considered as having passed through a similar course. In one, at least, this assertion was no mere matter of speculation, but of actual observation. The broken surface of the moon, its volcanic cones and craters, its mountains, with their lava-clad sides and ejected blocks glistening in the sun, proved a succession of events like those of the earth, and demonstrated that there is a planetary as well as a terrestrial geology, and that in our satellite there is evidence of a primitive high temperature, of a gradual decline, and, therefore, of a long process of time. Perhaps, also, considering the rate of heat-exchange in Venus by reason of her proximity to the sun, the pale light which it is said has been observed on her non-illuminated part is the declining trace of her own intrinsic temperature, her heat lasting until now.

*Support from astronomical facts.*

If astronomers sought in systematic causes an explanation of these facts,—if, for instance, they were disposed to examine how far changes in the obliquity of the ecliptic were connected therewith,—it was necessary at the outset to concede that the

*Astronomical facts imply slow secular changes.*

scale of time on which the event proceeds is of prodigious duration, this secular variation observing a slow process of only 45″·7 in a century; and hence, since the time of Hipparchus, two thousand years ago, the plane of the ecliptic has approached that of the equator by only a quarter of a degree. Or if, again, they look to a diminishing of the eccentricity of the earth's orbit, they were compelled to admit the same postulate, and deal with thousands of centuries. Under whatever aspect, then, the theory was regarded, if once a former high temperature was admitted, and the fact coupled therewith that there has been no sensible decline within the observation of man, whether the explanation was purely geological or purely astronomical, the motion of heat in the mass of the earth is so slow, yet the change that has taken place is so great, the variations of the contemplated relations of the solar system so gradual—under whatever aspect and in whatever way the fact was dealt with,—there arose the indispensable concession of countless centuries.

To the astronomer such a concession was nothing extraordinary. It is not because of the time required that he entertains any doubt that the sun and his system accomplish a revolution round a distant centre of gravity in nineteen millions of years, or that the year of $\epsilon$ Lyræ is half a million of ours. He looks forward to that distant day when Sirius will disappear from our skies, and the Southern Cross be visible, and Vega the polar star. He looks back to the time when $\gamma$ Draconis occupied that conspicuous position, and the builders of the great pyramid, B.C. 3970, gave to its subterranean passage an inclination of 26° 15′, corresponding to the inferior culmination of that star. He tells us that the Southern Cross began to be invisible in 52° 30′ N., 2000 years before our era, and that it had previously attained an altitude of more than 10°. When it disappeared from the horizon of the countries on the Baltic, the pyramid of Cheops had been erected more than a thousand years.

Proofs of time from aqueous effects.

We must pass by a copious mass of evidence furnished by aqueous causes of change operating on the earth's surface, though these add very weighty proof to the doctrine of a long period. The filling up of lakes, the formation of deltas, the cutting power of running water, the deposit of travertines, the denudation of immense tracts of country, the carrying of their detritus into the sea, the changes of shores by tides and waves, the formation of strata hundreds of miles in length, and the embedding therein of fossil remains in numbers almost beyond belief, furnished many interesting and important facts. Of these not a few presented means of computation. It would not be difficult to assign a date for such geographical events as the production of the Caspian and Dead Seas from an examination of the sum of saline material contained in their waters or deposited in their bed, with the annual amount brought into them by their supplying rivers. Such computations were executed as respects the growth of Lower Egypt and the backward cutting of Niagara Falls, and, though they might be individually open to criticism, their mutual accordance and tendency furnished an evidence that could not be gainsaid. The continual accumulation of such evidence ought not to be without its weight on those who are still disposed to treat slightingly the power of geological facts in developing truth.

To such facts were added all those, with which volumes might be filled, proving the universality of the movements of the solid crust of the earth,—strata once necessarily horizontal, now inclined at all angles, strata unconformable to one another,—a body of evidence most copious and most satisfactory, yet demonstrating from the immensity of the results how slowly the work had gone on. *And from the movements of the earth's crust.*

How was it possible to conceive that beds many hundred feet in thickness should have been precipitated suddenly from water? The mechanical condition implied slow disintegration and denudation in other localities to furnish material; their contents showed no trace of violence; they rather proved the deposition to have occurred in a tranquil and quiet way. What interpretation could be put upon facts continually increasing in number like those observed in the south-east of England, where freshwater beds a thousand feet thick are covered by other beds a thousand feet thick, but of marine origin? What upon those in the north of England, where masses once uplifted a thousand feet above the level, and, at the time of their elevation, presenting abrupt precipices and cliffs of that height, as is proved by the fractures and faults of the existing strata, have been altogether removed, and the surface left plain? In South Wales there are localities where 11,000 feet in thickness have been bodily carried away. Whether, therefore, the strata that have been formed, and which remain to strike us with astonishment at their prodigious mass, were considered; or those that have been destroyed, not however without leaving unmistakable traces of themselves; the processes of wearing away to furnish material as well as the accumulation, of necessity required the lapse of long periods of time. The undermining of cliffs by the beating of the sea, the redistribution of sands and mud at the bottom of the ocean, the washing of material from hills into the lowlands by showers of rain, its transport by river courses, the disintegration of soils by the influence of frost, the weathering of rocks by carbonic acid, and the solution of limestone by its aid in water,—these are effects which, even at the quickest, seem not to amount to much in the course of the life of a man. A thousand years could yield but a trifling result.

We have already alluded to another point of view from which these mechanical effects were considered. The level of the land and sea has unmistakably changed. There are mountain eminences ten or fifteen thousand feet in altitude in the interior of continents over which, or through which, shells and other products of the sea are profusely scattered. And though, considering the proverbial immobility of the solid land and the proverbial instability of the water, it might at first be supposed much more likely that the sea had subsided than that the land had risen, a more critical examination soon led to a change of opinion. Before our eyes, in some countries, elevations and depressions are taking place, sometimes in a slow, secular manner, as in Norway and Sweden, that peninsula on the north rising, and on the south sinking, at such a rate that, to accomplish the whole seven hundred feet of movement, more than twenty-seven thousand years would be required if it had always been uniform as now. Elsewhere, as on the south-western coast of South America, the movement is paroxysmal, the shore line lifting for hundreds of miles instantaneously, and then pausing for many years. In the Morea also, range after range of old sea-cliffs exist, some of them more than a thousand feet high, with terraces at the base of each; but the Morea has been well known for the last twenty-five centuries, and in that time has undergone no material change. Again, in Sicily, similar interior sea-cliffs are seen, the rubbish at their bases containing the bones of the hippopotamus and mammoth, proofs of the great change the climate has undergone since the sea washed those ancient beaches. Italy, pre-eminently the historic country, in which, within the memory of man, no material change of configuration has taken place, since the Pleistocene period, very late geologically speaking, has experienced elevations of fifteen hundred feet. The seven hills of Rome are of the Pliocene, with fluviatile deposits and recent terrestrial shells two hundred feet above the Tiber. There intervened between the older Pliocene and the newer a period of enormous length, as is demonstrated by the accumulated effects taking place in it, and indeed the same may be said of every juxtaposed pair of distinctly-marked strata. It demanded an inconceivable time for beds once horizontal at the bottom of the sea to be tilted to great inclinations; it required also the enduring exertion of a prodigious force. Ascent and descent may be detected in strata of every age; movements sometimes paroxysmal, but more often of a tranquil and secular kind. The coal-bearing strata, by gradual submergence, attained in South Wales a thickness of 12,000 feet, and on the American continent, in Nova Scotia, a total thickness of 14,570 feet; the uniformity of the process of submergence and its slow steadiness is indicated by the occurrence of erect trees at different levels: seventeen such repetitions may be counted in the thickness of 4515 feet. The age of the trees is proved by their size, some being four feet in diameter. Round them, as they gradually went down with the subsiding soil, calamites grew at one level after another. In the Sydney coal-field fifty-nine fossil forests thus occur in superposition.

Such was the conclusion forcing itself from considerations

298                  *Proof from Organic Remains.*

**Organic proofs of a former high temperature.**

connected with inorganic nature. It received a most emphatic endorsement from the organic world, for there is an intimate connection between the existence and well-being both of plants and animals, and the heat to which they are exposed. Why is it that the orange and lemon do not grow in New York? What is it that will inevitably ensue if these exotics be exposed to the cold of one of its winters? What is it that must take place if, in Florida or other of the Southern States, a season of unusual rigour should occur? Does not heat thus confine within a fixed boundary the spread of those plants? And so, again, how many others there are which grow luxuriantly with us, but are parched up and killed if fortuitously carried beneath a hot tropical sun. To every one there is a climate which best suits the condition of its life, and certain limits of heat and cold beyond which its existence is not possible.

**Boundary of organisms by heat.**

If the mean annual heat of the earth's surface were slowly to rise, and, in the course of some centuries, the temperature now obtaining in Florida should obtain in New York, the orange and lemon would certainly be found there. With the increasing heat those plants would commence a northward march, steadily advancing as opportunity was given. Or, if the reverse took place, and for any reason the heat of the torrid zone declined until the winter's cold of New York should be at last reached under the equator, as the descent went on the orange and lemon would retreat within a narrower and narrower region, and end by becoming extinct, the conditions of their exposure being incompatible with the continuance of their life. From such considerations it was therefore seen that not only does heat arrange the limits of the distribution of plants, erecting round them boundaries which, though invisible, are more insuperable than a wall of brass, it also regulates their march, if march there is to be,—nay, even controls their very existence, and to genera and species and individuals appoints a period of duration.

**Animals localised as well as plants.**

Such observations apply not alone to plants; the animal kingdom offers equally significant illustrations. Why does the white bear enjoy the leaden sky of the pole and his native iceberg? Why does the tiger restrict himself to the jungles of

India? Can it be doubted that, if the mean annual temperature should decline, the polar bear would come with his iceberg to corresponding southern latitudes, or, if the heat should rise, the tiger would commence a northward journey? Does he not, indeed, every summer penetrate northward in Asia as far as the latitude of Berlin, and retire again as winter comes on? Why is it that, at a given signal, the birds of passage migrate, pressed forward in the spring by the heat, and pressed backward in the autumn by the cold? The annual migration of birds illustrates the causes of geological appearances and extinctions. Do we not herein recognize the agent that determines animal distribution? We must not deceive ourselves with any fancied terrestrial impediment or restraint. Let the heat rise but a few degrees, and the turkey-buzzard, to whose powerful wing distances are of no moment and the free air no impediment, would be seen hovering over New York; let it fall a few degrees, and he would vanish from the streets of Charleston; let it fall a little more, and he would vanish from the earth. Shell-fish, once the inhabitants of the British seas, retired during the glacial period to the Mediterranean, and with the returning warmth have gone back northward again.

Animals are thus controlled by heat in an indirect as well as a direct way. Indirectly; for, if their food be diminished, they must seek a more ample supply; if it fails, they must perish. Doubtless it was insufficient food, as well as the setting in of a more rigorous climate, that occasioned the destruction of the mastodon giganteus, which abounded in the United States after the drift period. Such great elephantine forms could not possibly sustain themselves against the rigours of the winters, nor could they find a sufficient supply of food for a considerable portion of the year. The disappearance of animals from the face of the earth was, as Palæontology advanced, ascertained to have been a determinate process, a condition of their existence, and either inherent in themselves or dependent on the surrounding circumstances. It was proved that the forms now existing are only an insignificant part of the countless tribes that had lived. The earth has been the theatre of a long succession of appearances and removals, of

*Control of animals by food.*

**Nature of creations and extinctions.**

creations and extinctions, reaching to the latest times. In the Pleistocene of Sicily, $\frac{7}{12}$ of the fossil shells are extinct; in the bone-caverns of England, out of thirty-seven mammals eighteen are extinct. But judging, from what may be observed of the duration of races contemporary with us, that their life is prolonged for thousands of years, successive generations of the same species in a long order replacing their predecessors before final removal occurs, this again resistlessly brought forward the same conclusion to which all the foregoing facts had pointed, that there have transpired since the introduction of animal life upon this globe very long periods of time.

Through the operation of this law of extinction and of creation, animated nature, both on the continents and in the seas, has undergone a marvellous change. In the lias and oolitic seas, the Enaliosauria, Cetiosauria, and Crocodilia dominated, as the Delphinidæ and Balænidæ do in ours; the former have been eliminated, the latter produced. Along with the cetaceans came the soft-scaled Cycloid and Ctenoid fishes, orders which took the place of the Ganoids and Placoids of the Mesozoic times. One after another successive species of air-breathing reptiles have been created, continued for their appointed time to exist, and then died out. The developement has been, not in the descending, but in the ascending order; the Amphitheria, Spalacotheria, Triconodon of the Mesozoic times were substituted by higher tertiary forms. Nor have these mutations been abrupt. If mammals are the chief characteristic of the Tertiary ages, their first beginnings are seen far earlier; in the triassic and oolitic formations there are a few of the lower orders struggling, as it were, to emerge. The aspect of animated nature has altogether changed. Nor does the camelopard wander over Europe as he did in the Miocene and Pliocene times; no more are great elephants seen in the American forests, the hippopotamus in England, the rhinoceros in Siberia. The hand of man has introduced upon the Western continent the horse of the Old World; but the American horse, that ran on those great plains contemporary with the megatherium and megalonyx, has for tens of thousands of years been extinct. Even the ocean and the rivers are no exception to these changes.

What, then, is the manner of origin of this infinite succession of forms? It is often sufficient to see clearly a portion of a plan, to be able to determine with some degree of certainty the general arrangement of the whole; it is often sufficient to know with precision a part of the life of an individual, to guess with probable accuracy his action in some forthcoming event, or to determine the share he has borne in affairs that are past. It is enough to appreciate thoroughly the style of a master, to ascertain without doubt the authenticity of an imputed picture. And so, in the affairs of the universe, it is enough to ascertain the manner of operation of a part, in order to settle the manner of operation of the whole. When, therefore, it was perceived how the disappearance of vanishing forms from the surface of the globe is accomplished—that it is not by a sudden and grand providential intervention—that there is no visible putting forth of the Omnipotent hand, but slowly and silently, yet surely, the ordinary laws of Nature are permitted to take their course—that heat, and cold, and want of food, and dryness, and moisture, in the end, as if by an irresistible destiny, accomplish the event, it seemed to indicate that, as regards the introduction of new-comers, a suitableness of external conditions had called them forth, as an unsuitableness could end them. Changes in the constitution of the air or its pressure, in the composition of the sea or its depth, in the brilliancy of light or the amount of heat, in the inorganic material of a medium, will modify old forms into new ones, or compel their extinction. Birth and death go hand in hand; creation and extinction are inseparable. The variation of organic form is continuous; it depends upon an orderly succession of material events; appearances and eliminations are managed upon a common principle; they stand connected with the irresistible course of great mundane changes. It was impossible that geologists could reach any other conclusion than that such phenomena are not the issue of direct providential interventions, but of physical influences. The procession of organic life is not a motley march; it follows the procession of physical events; and, since it is impossible to re-establish a sameness of physical conditions that have once come to an end, or reproduce the

*Creations and extinctions by law.*

order in which they have occurred, it of necessity follows that no organic form can reappear after it has once died out: once dead, it is clean gone for ever.

*Interstitial molecular creations.*

In the course of the life of individual man, the parts that constitute his system are undergoing momentary changes; those of to-day are not the same as those of yesterday, and they will be replaced by others to-morrow. There have been, and are every instant, interstitial deaths of all the constituent portions, and an unceasing removal of those that have performed their duty. In the stead of departing portions, new ones have been introduced, interstitial births and organizations perpetually taking place. In physiology it became no longer a question that all this proceeds in a determinate way under the operation of principles that are fixed, of laws that are invariable. The alchemists introduced no poetical fiction when they spoke of the microcosm, asserting that the system of man is emblematical of the system of the world. The intercalation of a new organic molecule in a living being answers to the introduction of a new form in the universal organic series. It requires as much power to call into existence a living molecule as to produce a living being. Both are accomplished upon the same principle, and that principle is not an incessant intervention of a supernatural kind, but the operation of unvarying law. Physical agents, working through physical laws, remove in organisms such molecules as have accomplished their work and create new ones; and physical agents, working through physical laws, control the extinctions and creations of forms in the universe of life. The difference is only in the time. What is accomplished in the one case in the twinkling of an eye, in the other may demand the lapse of a thousand centuries.

The variation of organic forms, under the force of external circumstances, is thus necessary to be understood in connection with that countless succession of living beings demonstrated by geology. It carries us, in common with so much other evidence, to the lapse of a long time. Nor are such views as those to which we are thus constrained inconsistent with the admission of a Providential guidance of the world. Man, however learned and pious he may be, is not always a reliable interpreter of the ways of God. In deciding whether any philosophical doctrine is consistent or inconsistent with the Divine attributes, we are too prone to judge of those attributes by our own finite and imperfect standard, forgetting that the only test to which we ought to resort is the ascertainment if the doctrine be true. If it be true, it is in unison with God. Perhaps some who have rejected the conception of the variation of organic forms, with its postulate limitless duration, may have failed to remember the grandeur of the universe and its relations to space and to time; perhaps they do not recall the system on which it is administered. Like the anthropomorphite monks of the Nile, they conceive of God as if he was only a very large man; else how could it for a moment have been doubted that it is far more—I use the expression reverently—in the style of the great Constructor to carry out his intentions by the summary operations of law? It might be consistent with the weakness and ignorance of man to be reduced to the necessity of personal intervention for the accomplishment of his plans, but would not that be the very result of such ignorance? Does not absolute knowledge actually imply procedure by preconceived and unvarying law? Is not momentary intervention altogether derogatory to the thorough and absolute sovereignty of God? The astronomical calculation of ancient events, as well as the prediction of those to come, is essentially founded on the principle that there has not in the times under consideration, and that there will never be in the future, any exercise of an arbitrary or overriding will. The corner-stone of astronomy is this, that the solar system, nay even the universe, is ruled by necessity. To operate by expedients is for the creature, to operate by law for the Creator; and so far from the doctrine that creations and extinctions are carried on by a foreseen and predestined ordinance—a system which works of itself without need of any intermeddling—being an unworthy, an ignoble conception, it is completely in unison with the resistless movements of the mechanism of the universe, with whatever is orderly, symmetrical, and beautiful upon earth, and with all the dread magnificence of the heavens.

*Defence of the process of all things by law.*

It was in Italy that particular attention was first given to

304                                Palæontology.

**Historical sketch of early Palæontology.**

organic remains. Leonardo da Vinci asserts that they are real shells, or the remains thereof, and hence that the land and sea must have changed their relative position. At this time fossils were looked upon as rare curiosities, no one supposing that they were at all numerous, and many were the fantastic hypotheses proposed to account for their occurrence. Some referred them to the general deluge mentioned in Scripture; some to a certain plastic power obscurely attributed to the earth; some thought that they were engendered by the sunlight, heat, and rain. To Da Vinci is due the first clear assertion of their true nature, that they are actually the remains of organic beings. Soon the subject was taken up by other eminent Italians. Fracastor wrote on the petrifactions of Verona; Scilla, a Sicilian, on marine bodies turned into stone, illustrating his work by engravings. Still later, Vallisneri, 1721, published letters on marine bodies found in rocks, attempting by their aid to determine the extent of the marine deposits of Italy. These early cultivators of geology soon perceived the advantage to be gained by the establishment of museums and the publication of catalogues. The first seems to have been that of John Kentman, an example that was followed by Calceolarius and Vallisneri. Subsequently Fontanelle proposed the construction of charts in accordance with fossil remains; but the principle involved was not applied on the great scale as a true geological test until introduced by Smith in connection with the English strata.

**The preorganic time.**

To Steno, a Dane, is due the recognition of preorganic in contradistinction to organic rocks, a distinction the terms of which necessarily involve the idea of time. Soon it became generally recognised that the strata in which organic remains occur are of a later date than of those devoid of them, the preorganic rocks demonstrating a preorganic time. Moreover, as facts were developed, it was plain that there are essential differences in the relations of fossils, and that, though in Italy the same species of shells may occur in the mountains that occur in the adjacent seas, this was very far from being the case uniformly elsewhere. At length the truth began to emerge, that in proportion as the strata under examination are of an older date, so are the differences between their organic remains and existing species more marked. It was also discovered that the same species often extended superficially over immense districts, but that in a vertical examination one species after another rapidly appears in a descending order—an order which could be verified in spite of the contortions, fractures, and displacements of the strata. A very important theoretical conclusion was here presented; for the rapid succession of essentially different organic forms, as the rocks were older, was clearly altogether inconsistent with one catastrophe, as the universal deluge, to which it had been generally referred. It was plain that the thickness of the strata in which they were enveloped, and the prodigious numbers in which they occurred, answered in some degree to the period of life of those fossils, since every one of them, large or small, must have had its time of birth, of maturity, and of death. When, therefore, it could be no longer doubted that strata many hundreds of feet in thickness were crowded with such remains, it became altogether out of the question to refer their entombment to the confusion of a single catastrophe, for everything indicated an orderly and deliberate proceeding. Still more cogent did this evidence become when, in a more critical manner, the fossils were studied, and some strata were demonstrated to be of a freshwater and others of a marine origin, the one interalated with the other like leaves in a book. To this fact may be imputed the final overthrow of the doctrine of a single catastrophe, and its replacement by a doctrine of periodical changes. *Insufficiency of a single catastrophe.*

From these statements it will therefore be understood that, commencing with the first appearance of organization, an orderly process was demonstrated from forms altogether unlike those with which we are familiar, up to those at present existing, a procedure conducted so slowly that it was impossible to assign for it a shorter duration than thousands of centuries. Moreover, it seemed that the guiding condition which had controlled this secular march of organization was the same which still determines the possibility of existence and the distribution of life. The succession of organic forms indicates a clear rela- *The orderly progression of organization.*

tion to a descending temperature. The plants of the earliest times are plants of an ultratropical climate, and that primitive vegetation seemed to demonstrate that there had been a uniform climate—a climate of high temperature—all over the globe. The coal-beds of Nova Scotia exhibited the same genera and species as those of Europe; and so well marked was the botanical connection with the declining temperature in successive ages, that attempts were made to express eras by their prevailing organisms; thus Brongniart's division is, for the Primary strata, the Age of Acrogens; the Secondary, exclusive of the Cretaceous, the Age of Gymnogens; the third, including the Cretaceous and Tertiary, the Age of Angiosperms. It is to be particularly remarked that the Cretaceous flora, in the aggregate, combines the antecedent and succeeding periods, proving that the change was not by crisis or sudden catastrophe, but that the new forms rose gently among the old ones. After the Eocene period, dicotyledonous angiosperms became the prevalent form, and from that date to the Pleistocene the evidences of a continued refrigeration are absolute.

*Climates in time and in place.*

As thus an examination was made from the most ancient to the later ages, indications were found of a climate arrangement more and more distinct—in the high latitudes, from the ultratropical through the tropical, the temperate, down to the present frigid state; in lower latitudes the declining process stopping short at an earlier point. It therefore appeared that there has been a production of climates both in an order of time and in an order of locality, the greatest change having occurred in the frigid zone, which has passed through all mean temperatures, an intermediate change in the temperate, and a minimum in the torrid zone. The general effect has thus been to present a succession of surfaces on the same planet adapted to a varied organization, and offering a more magnificent spectacle than if we were permitted to inspect many different planets; for in them there might be no necessary connection of their forms of life, but in this there is, so that, were our knowledge of Comparative Physiology more perfect, we might amuse ourselves with intercalating among the plant and animal organisms familiar to us hypothetical forms that would make the series complete, and verify our principles by their subsequent discovery in the deep strata of the earth.

Does not this progression of life in our planet suggest a like progression for the solar system, which in its aggregate is passing in myriads of years through all organic phases? May we not also, from our solar system, rise to a similar conception for the universe?

There are two very important considerations, on which we must dwell for the complete understanding of the consequences of these changes:—1st. The mechanism of the declining temperature; 2nd. Its effect in the organic world.

1st. A uniformly high temperature could never be manifested all over the surface of our planet through any heating influence of the sun. A high and uniform temperature unerringly points to an internal cause; and the gradual appearance of climates manifesting a relatively increasing power of the sun, indicates the slow diminution of that internal heat. But this is precisely the conclusion which was come to from a contemplation of the earth from a purely physical point of view. So long as its intrinsic heat overpowered that derived from the sun, it was not possible that anything answering to climates could be established; and, until a certain degree of cooling by radiation had been accomplished, the heat must have been comparatively uniform in all latitudes; but, that point gained, there necessarily ensued an arrangement of zones of different temperatures, or, in other words, climates appeared, the process being essentially slow, and becoming slower as the loss of heat went on. Finally, when loss of heat from the earth ceased, an equilibrium was reached in the climate arrangement as we now find it. Thus purely physical as well as geological considerations brought philosophers on this point to the same conclusion—that conclusion which has been so often repeated—very long periods of time.

*The nature of terrestrial declining temperature.*

2nd. As to the effect on the organic world. Nothing can live at a temperature higher than the boiling-point of water, for the condition of life implies that there shall circulate from part to part of a living mechanism a watery liquid, sap, or blood. From this it necessarily follows that a planet, the

*Consequent effect on the Flora and Fauna.*

temperature of which is above a certain limit, must necessarily have a lifeless surface; and this seemed to be the interpretation of that preorganic time to which we have referred. Moreover, when the temperature suitably descends so as to come within the limit at which life is possible, its uniformity over the surface of a planet will produce a sameness in the organization. It would be an identity if heat were the only regulating condition of life. At this stage of things, the solar heat overpowered, and a sensibly uniform temperature in all latitudes existing, still the only possible organic forms are those consistent with a high temperature, uniformity in the physical condition impressing a general uniformity in the aspect of life geographically. But the moment that climate arrangement has become possible, variety of organic form becomes possible. Now also ensues another all-important result—geographical distribution. Both of plants and animals, those whose vital conditions are inconsistent with the occurring change must retire from the affected locality. In plants this retrocession is brought to pass by the gradual sickening and death of individuals, or the impossibility of reproduction; in animals there is added thereto, because of their power of locomotion, voluntary retirement, at least in the case of individuals, and immobility in the species is corrected by locomotion in the individual. The affected region has become unsuitable, cheerless, uncomfortable; they abandon it; and as the boundary they thus, in the one case, cannot, and in the other will not overpass, advances, so do they recede before it. If the change was abrupt, or took place by a sudden crisis, there would seem to be no other possible event than an overcrowding of the unaffected region and a desolation of the part that had varied. But, since a developing cell under a new condition produces a new form, and since the physical change is taking place with extreme slowness, the appearance of modified structures ensues. And thus, by decline of temperature, two distinct results are accomplished—the production of organic forms in an order of succession, new ones replacing the old, as if they were transmutations of them, and geographical distribution.

In my 'Physiology' I have endeavoured to explain in detail

*Production and distribution of new organisms.*

the principles here set forth. I have endeavoured to show that the aspect of sameness presented by an animal or plant is no proof of unchangeability. Those forms retain in our times their special aspect because the conditions of the theatre in which they live do not change; but let the mean temperature rise, let the sun-rays become brighter, change the composition of the air, and forthwith the world of organization would show how profoundly it was affected. Nor need such changes, in one sense, be more than insignificant to produce prodigious results. Thus the air contains only $\frac{1}{1000}$ of its volume of carbonic acid gas. That apparently trifling quantity taken away, in an instant the whole surface of the earth would become a desolate waste, without the possibility of vegetable life.

*Delusive nature of organic equilibrium.*

As physical geology advanced, the Coal period was perceived to be the chief epoch in the history of our planet. Through a slow decline of temperature, a possibility had gradually been attained, so far as the condition of heat was concerned, for a luxuriant vegetable growth. All that prodigious mass of carbon now found in the earth in various forms of coal existed as carbonic acid in the atmosphere. The proportion of free oxygen was less than at present by a volume equal to the excess of carbonic acid. A change in the constitution of this primeval atmosphere was occasioned by the action of the light; for, under the influence of the sun-rays, plants decompose carbonic acid, appropriating its carbon, and, for the most part, setting the oxygen free. The quantity of carbon which can thus be condensed for the use of a plant, and, indeed, every such decomposing action by light, is directly proportionate to the quantity of light consumed, as experiments which I have personally made have proved. For the production of so great a weight of combustible matter a very long period of time was necessarily required, that the sun might supply the necessary luminous influence.

*The Coal period.*

*Effects of light on the atmosphere,*

For age after age the sunbeams continued their work, changing the mechanical relations and composition of the atmosphere, the constitution of the sea, and the appearance of the surface of the earth. There was a prodigious growth of ferns, lepidodendra, equisetaceæ, coniferæ. The percentage of oxy-

*And also on the sea.*

gen in the air continually increased, that of carbonic acid continually declined; the pressure of the air correspondingly diminished, partly because of the replacement of a heavy gas by a lighter one, and partly because of the general decline of temperature slowly taking place, which diminished the absolute volume of vapour. The sea, in its deepest abysses, was likewise affected by the sunlight; not directly, but in an indirect way; for, as the removal of carbonic acid from the atmosphere went on, portions of that gas were perpetually surrendered by the ocean in order to maintain a diffusion-equilibrium between its dissolved gas and the free gas of the air. And now no longer could be held in transparent solution by the water those great quantities of carbonate of lime which had once been concealed in it, the deposit of a given weight of coal in the earth being inevitably followed by the deposit of an equivalent weight of carbonate of lime in the sea. It might have taken place as an amorphous precipitate; but the probabilities were that it would occur, as in fact it did, under forms of organization in the great limestone strata coeval with and posterior to the coal. The air and the ocean were thus suffering an invisible change through the disturbing agency of the sun, and the surface of the solid earth was likewise undergoing a more manifest, and, it may be said, more glorious alteration. Plants, in wild luxuriance, were developing themselves in the hot and dank climate, and the possibility was now approaching for the appearance of animal types very much higher than any that had yet existed. In the old heavy atmosphere, full of a noxious gas, none but slowly-respiring cold-blooded animals could maintain themselves; but after the great change in the constitution of the air had been accomplished, the quickly-respiring and hot-blooded forms might exist. Hitherto the highest advancement that animal life could reach was in batrachian and lizard-like organisms; yet even these were destined to participate in the change, increasing in magnitude and vital capacity. The pterodactyl of the chalk, a flying lizard, measures nearly seventeen feet from tip to tip of its wings. The air had now become suitable for mammals, both placental and implacental, and for birds. One after another, in their

*Cold-blooded animals succeeded by hot.*

due order, appeared the highest vertebrates: marine, as the cetacean; aerial, as the bat; and in the terrestrial, reaching, in the Eocene, quadrumanous animals, but not, until long after the Pliocene, man.

Although the advancement of geology may hereafter lead to a correction of some of the conclusions thus attained to respecting the first dates of different organic forms, and carry them back to more ancient times, yet it is scarcely likely that any material modification of their order of occurrence will ever be made. Birds, mammals, reptiles, fishes, and invertebrates may each be detected in earlier strata; even for some of those formations now regarded as non-fossiliferous, organisms may be found; but it is not at all probable that the preponderance of reptiles will ever cease to be the essential characteristic of the Secondary rocks, or that of mammals of the Tertiary, or that a preceding period of vast duration, in which the type of life had been the invertebrate, will ever be doubted. Nothing, probably, will ever be discovered to invalidate the physical conclusion that, while there was an excess of carbonic acid in the air, the Flora would tend to be Cryptogamic and Gymnospermic, and that there would be a scarcity of monocotyledons and dicotyledonous angiosperms in the coal; nothing to disprove the fact that the animals were slow-breathing and cold-blooded; and that it was not until after the oxygen of the air had increased and the mean temperature had declined that birds made their appearance. Though both placental and marsupial animals may hereafter be found earlier than the Stonesfield slate; though wood and herb-eating beetles, grasshoppers, dragon-flies, and May-flies may be found beneath the lias, and scorpions and cockroaches beneath the coal; though also beneath the coal, salamanders and sauroid batrachians, of which the archegosaurus is an example, may occur; though reptiles, as the telerpeton, may be found deeper than the old red sandstone; yet the connection between aerial constitution and form of life will never be shaken. Still will remain the facts that the geographical distribution of types was anterior to the appearance of existing species; that organisms first appeared in a liquid medium, primitively marine, the alluviatile, and at last

*The dates of organisms may change, but the order not.*

terrestrial; that Radiates, Mollusks, Articulates, Vertebrates, were all at first aquatic, and that the Radiates have ever remained so; that the plane of greatest vital activity has ever been the sea-level, where the earth and air touch each other; that the order of individual developement is the order of mundane developement. Still will remain the important conclusions that the mammalian Fauna has diverged more rapidly than the testaceous; that hot-blooded animals have not had that longevity of species which has been displayed by the cold, just as we observe in the individual the possibility of muscular contraction by a given galvanic force lasts much longer in the latter than in the former; that if the hot-blooded tribes have thus a briefer duration, they enjoy a compensation in the greater energy of their life—perhaps this being the cause and that the effect; that, notwithstanding the countless forms exhibited by species, their duration is so great that they outlive vast changes in the topographical configuration of countries—the Fauna of some countries having been in existence before those countries themselves; that the plan of individual developement has ever been as it is now, and that sameness of external influence produces similarity of organization.

*The doctrines of catastrophes and uniformity.*
In its early history, theoretical geology presented two schools,—one insisting on a doctrine of catastrophes, one on a doctrine of uniformity. The former regarded those changes which have manifestly taken place in the history of our planet as having occurred at epochs abruptly. To this doctrine the prevailing impression that there had been providential interventions lent much force. The other school, reposing on the great principle of the invariability of the laws of Nature, insisted that affairs had always gone on at the same rate and in the same way as they do now. Hence it maintained an opposition to the catastrophists, and in this, it may be said, was actually not true to its own principles. Any doctrine of uniformity, rightly considered from its most general point of view, includes an admission of catastrophes. Numerous illustrations of this truth spontaneously suggest themselves. A tower, the foundations of which are slowly yielding, may incline more and more for many centuries, but the day must come in which

it will fall at last. In the uniformity of the disturbance a catastrophe was eventually involved. And thus, in what has been said respecting geological events, though they are spoken of as proceeding quietly and with uniformity, it may be understood that sudden crises are also contemplated. Moreover, they who adopt the doctrine of uniformity in an absolute sense must pay a due regard to the variations in intensity of physical acts which their own principles imply. The uniform cooling of a hot body actually means a cooling at first fast, and then slower and slower; and invariability of chemical change actually implies more violent and summary modifications at a high temperature than at one which is low.

But, though it may at first sight have appeared that an admission of the doctrine of catastrophes was in harmony with a providential government of the world, and that the emergence of different organic forms in successive ages was a manifestation of creative intervention, of which it was admitted that as many as from twelve to twenty, if not more, successive instances might be recognized, we may well congratulate ourselves that those important doctrines rest upon a far more substantial basis. Rightly considered, the facts lead to a very different conclusion. Physiological investigations have proved that all animals, even man, during the process of developement, pass in succession through a definite cycle of forms. Starting from a simple cell, form after form, in a definite order, is assumed. In this long line of advance the steps are ever, in all individuals, the same. But no one would surely suppose that the changed aspect at any moment presented is due to a providential interposition. On the contrary, it is the inevitable result of what has been taking place under the law of developement, and the sure precursor of what is about to follow. In the organic world, the successive orders, and genera, and species are the counterparts of these temporary embryonic forms of the individual. Indeed, we may say of those successive geological beings that they are mere embryos of the latest,—embryos that had gained a power of reproduction. How shall we separate the history of the individual from the history of the whole? Do not the fortunes and way of pro-

*[margin: Successive forms assumed by man.]*

*[margin: But they are rigidly determined by law.]*

*Individual and race development conducted in the same way.*

gress of the one follow the fortunes and way of progress of the other? If, in a transitory manner, these forms are assumed in the individual, equally in a transitory manner are they assumed by the race. Nor would it be philosophical to suppose that the management in the one instance differs from the management in the other. If the one is demonstrably the issue of a law in action, so must the other be too. It does not matter that the entire cycle is passed through by the individual in the course of a few months, while in the race it demands ages. The standard of time that ought to be applied is the respective duration of life. In man it is much if he attains to threescore years and ten; but the entire period of human record, embracing several thousand years, offers not a single instance of the birth, maturity, and death of a species. They, therefore, who think they find in the successive species that have in an orderly manner replaced each other in the life of the earth the sure proof of Divine intervention, would do well to determine at what point the production of such forms by law ceases, and at what point their production by the immediate act of God begins. Their task will be as hard as to tell where one colour in the rainbow ends and where the next commences. They will also do well to remember that, in great mundane events, the scale of time is ample, and that there may be no essential difference between a course that is run over in a few days and one that requires for its completion thousands of centuries.

*Catastrophes disproved by the coexistence of types.*

The coexistence of different types in the organic series was the incontrovertible fact by which was demonstrated the gradual passage from form to form without catastrophes, the argument relied upon gathering strength from such circumstance as these, that even the fossil shells of the modern Italian tuffs which are not extinct exhibit a slight want of correspondence when compared with those now inhabiting the Mediterranean, some of the old ones being twice and a half as large as the present, and that there is a numerical passage from strata containing seventy per cent. of recent shells to those that are altogether recent, or contain one hundred per cent. This is manifestly indicative of a continual impression bringing on a corresponding modelling. It is the proof of a slow merging into, or of a measured assumption of, the new form—a transition, for the completion of which probably a very long time is required. That the existing reindeer is found in the same fluviatile deposits with an extinct hippopotamus seemed certainly to prove that there was a condition of things in which the co-life of those animals was possible in the same locality, and that, as the physical causes slowly changed, the one might be eliminated and the other might be left. That the regulating conditions were altogether physical was obvious from such facts as that in the bone-caves of Australia all the mammals are marsupial, and in the pampas of South America they are allied to such forms as are indigenous, armadilloes, sloths, etc., showing the tokens of lineage or hereditary transmission. For still more remote times numerous instances of a similar nature were detected; thus, throughout the whole Secondary period, the essential characteristic was the wonderful developement of reptile life, while in the Tertiary it was the developement of mammals. But the appearance of mammals had commenced long before that of reptiles had ceased. Indeed, the latter event is incomplete in our times; for though the marine Saurians have been almost entirely removed, the fluviatile and terrestrial ones maintain themselves, though diminished both in species and individuals. Now such an overlapping of reptiles and mammals was altogether irreconcilable with the doctrine of a crisis or catastrophe, and, in fact, it demonstrated the changing of organisms in the changing of physical states.

Cuvier maintained the doctrine of the permanence of animal species from the considerations that the oldest known do not appear to have undergone any modification, and that every existing one shows a resistance to change. If his observations are restricted to periods not exceeding human history, they may perhaps be maintained; but that duration cannot be looked upon as more than a moment in the limitless progress we are considering, and it was in this view that Cuvier's doctrine proved to be incapable of defence. What does it signify if our domestic animals show no variations when compared with the corresponding images depicted on the hieroglyphic monuments of Egypt, or with the descriptions left by ancient

*Cuvier's doctrine of permanence of species.*

*Imperfection of evidence in its support.*

authors? Evidence of that kind is valueless. Does the geologist ask of the architect his opinion whether there have ever been upliftings and down-sinkings of the earth? If he did, would not every structure in Europe be brought forward as an evidence that nothing of the kind had ever occurred? A leaning tower, or a church with inclining walls in Italy, might pass for nothing; the Pyramids would testify that Egypt itself had never undergone any disturbance—they remain solid on their bases, undisturbed. But what is the weight of all this when placed in opposition with the mass of evidence offered by inclined and fractured strata? And yet such is precisely the proof offered in behalf of the permanence of animals. The facts with which the zoologist deals, like those on which the architect depends, are insufficient for the purpose—they are wanting in extent of time. There have been movements in the crust of the earth, though every building in the world may be perpendicular; there have been transformations of organisms, though for four thousand years there may have been no perceptible change.

*Control of organisms by physical conditions.*  If ever there had been a universal creation of all possible organic forms or combinations, forthwith vast numbers of them must have disappeared, every type being eliminated which was not in correspondence with the external conditions or with the medium in which it was placed. If the medium or the physical conditions underwent a variation, a corresponding variation in the forms that could by possibility exist must ensue, and, from a thorough study of those not eliminated, the physical conditions might be ascertained; and conversely, from a thorough knowledge of the physical conditions, the forms that could escape elimination might be designated. The facts on which Cuvier rested did not demonstrate what he supposed. His immobility of species was no consequence of an innate or intrinsic resistance possessed by them, but merely an illustration that external physical agents had not undergone any well-marked variation in the time with which he was concerned.

*Nature of variation of physical conditions.* What is here meant by variation in physical forces or conditions is not any intrinsic change in their nature, but the varied manner in which they may work by interfering with one another, or experiencing declines of intensity. From the fact that we may read in the fixed stars, through the progressive motion of light, the history of a million of past years, we may be sure that the forces of nature have undergone no intrinsic change; that light was propagated at the same rate, was capable of producing the same optical and chemical effects, and varied in its intensity by distance, as it does now; that heat determined corporeal magnitudes. These are things that in their nature are absolutely unchangeable. Always, as now, the freezing of water, and its boiling under a given pressure, must have been the same; there must have been a thermometric zero of life and an upward limit, no organic process ever going on below 32° Fahrenheit or above 212° Fahrenheit.

But out of this invariability of natural cause variations in their condition of action arise, and it is these that affect organic forms. Of such forms, some become at length incapable of maintaining themselves in the slow progress of change; others acclimate, or accommodate, or suit themselves thereto by undergoing modifications, and this was at last discerned to be the true explanation of extinctions and appearances, events taking place very slowly in untold periods of time, and rather by imperceptible degrees than by a sudden catastrophe or crisis. *Effect thereof on organisms.*

The doctrine of the transmutation of species has met with no little resistance. They who have refused to receive it as one of the truths of Nature have perhaps not given full weight to physiological evidence. When they ask, Has any one ever witnessed such an event as the transmutation of one species into another? has any experimenter ever accomplished it by artificial means? they do not take a due account of time. In the Fables it is related that when the flowers were one evening conversing, "Our gardener," said the rose to the lily, "will live for ever. I have not seen any change in him. The tulip, who died yesterday, told me that she had remarked the same thing; she believed that he must be immortal. I am sure that he never was born." *Transmutation of species.*

Two modes have been presented by which we may conceive of the influence of physical agents upon organic forms. Their long persistent action upon the individual may give rise to *Two modes of action.*

modifications, developing one part, stunting another; and such variations, being transmitted in an hereditary way, may become firmly fixed at last. Thus a given plant may, in the course of ages, under the influence of unremittingly acting physical conditions, undergo a permanent change, and a really new plant arise as soon as, through the repetitions of successive generations, the modifications have become so thorough, so profound, as to be capable of transmission with certainty. Perhaps this is what has taken place with many of our kitchen-garden plants, of which the special varieties may be propagated by seeds. But there is another mode by which that result may be reached, even if we decline the doctrine of St. Augustine, who, in his work 'De Civitate Dei,' shows how islands may be peopled with animals by "spontaneous generation." All organic forms originally spring from a simple cell, the developement of which, as indicated by the final form attained, is manifestly dependent on the physical conditions it has been exposed to during it course. If those conditions change, that final form must change correspondingly; and in this manner, since all organic beings come from the same starting-point,—the same cell, as has been said, which helplessly submits to whatever impression may be put upon it,—the issue is the same as though a transformation or transmutation had occurred, since the descendant is not like its ancestors. Such a manner of considering these changes is in harmony with our best physiological knowledge, since it does not limit itself to a small portion of the life of an individual, but embraces its whole cycle or career. For the more complete examination of this view I may refer to the second chapter of the second book of my 'Physiology.'

*Problem of the modification of forms.* But here has arisen the inquiry, Does the modification of organic forms depend exclusively on the impressions of external influences, or is it due to a nisus or force of developement residing in the forms themselves?

Whether we consider the entire organic series in its succession, or the progress of an individual in his developement, the orderly course presented might seem to indicate that the operation is taking place under a law,—an orderly progression being always suggestive of the operation of law. But a philosophical caution must, however, be here exercised; for deceptive appearances may lead us into the error of imputing to such a law, impressed by the Creator on the developing organism, that which really belongs to external physical conditions, which, on their part, are following a law of their own. What is here meant may be illustrated by the facts that occur on the habitable surface of a planet suffering a gradual decline of heat. On such a surface a succession of vegetable types might make its appearance, and, as these different types emerged or were eliminated, we might speak of the events as creations and extinctions, and therefore as the acts of God. Or, in the second place, we might refer them to an intrinsic force of developement imparted to each germ, which reached in due season its maximum, and then declined and died out; and, comparing each type with its preceding and succeeding ones, the interrelation might be suggested to us of the operation of a controlling law. Or, in the third place, we might look to the external physical condition—the decline of heat—itself taking place at a determinate rate under a mathematical law, and drawing in its consequences the organic variations observed. *Three solutions of it.*

Now the first of these explanations in reality means the arbitrary and unchallengeable will of God, who calls into existence, and extinguishes according to his sovereign pleasure, whatever he pleases; the orderly progression we notice becoming an evidence that his volitions are not erratic, but are according to pure reason. The second implies that there has been impressed upon every germ a law of continuous organic variation,—it may have been through the arbitrary fiat of God. The third implies that the successive types owe their appearance and elimination to a physical influence, which is itself varying under a strict mathematical necessity; for the law of cooling, which the circumstances force on our attention, is such a strict mathematical necessity.

If at this point we balance the probabilities of these three explanations, we shall perhaps find ourselves biassed toward the last, as physiologists have been, because of its rigorous scientific aspect, and should not be surprised to find it sup- *Their relative probability.*

ported by an array of facts depending on the principle that the appearance of new forms does not observe a certain inevitable order, or stand in a certain relation to time. From individual developement it might seem as if the advancing procession of an organism is such that specific forms ever appear in a certain order one after another, and at certain intervals; but the fallacy of such a conclusion is apparent when we attend to the orderly procedure of the physical conditions to which the developing organism is exposed. The passing through a given form at a given epoch is due to the relation being to space and its conditions, not to time. And so in the life of the earth, if developement were according to time, we should have an orderly succession of grades as the earth grew older, and in all localities, at a given moment, the contemporary organisms would be similar; but if it were according to space, that rigorous procedure would not occur; in its stead we should have a broken series, the affiliation being dependent on the secularly continuous variation of the physical condition.

*Developement is in place, not in time.*

Now this was discovered to be the case. For instance, throughout the northern hemisphere, during the Tertiary period, an extinct placental Fauna was contemporaneous with an extinct marsupial Fauna in Australia. If the developement was proceeding according to time, by an innate nisus, and not according to external influences, the types for the same epoch in the two hemispheres should be the same; if under external influences, irrespective of time, they should be, as they were found to be, different.

If true-going clocks, which owe their motion to their own interior mechanism, were started in all countries of the earth at the same instant, they would strike their successive hours simultaneously. But sun-dials, which owe their indications to an exterior cause, would in different longitudes tell different times, or, when the needful light was absent, their shadows would altogether fail. They count no hours but those that are serene.

As to the vegetable kingdom, the principles that hold for the animal again apply. At a very early period, even before the deposit of the coal, all the distinct forms of vegetable tissue were in existence, and nothing to prevent, so far as time was concerned, their being united together all over the world into similar structural combinations. And, in truth, as the botany of the Coal period proves, there was a far more extensive sameness than we see at present, simply because the distribution of heat was more uniform and climates were less marked. But from this point the diversity of form in climate distribution becomes more and more conspicuous, though we must descend, perhaps as late as the Wealden, before we discover any flowering plants, except Gymnosperms, as Conifers and Cycads. All this is what might be expected on the doctrine of external influence, but not on the doctrine of an innate and interior developemental force.

If, at this stage, attention is once again turned to the animal kingdom, we find our opinion confirmed. The diminution of carbonic acid in the atmosphere, the deposit of coal in the earth, the precipitation of carbonate of lime in the sea, the disengagement of an increased quantity of oxygen in the air, and the reduction of atmospheric pressure,—different effects contemporaneously occurring,—were soon followed by the consequence which they made possible,—the appearance of hot-blooded mammals. Perhaps those first arising might, like our hibernators, lead a sluggish existence, with imperfect respiration; but as the media improved and the temperature declined, more vigorous forms of life emerged, though we have probably to descend to the Tertiary epoch before we meet with birds, which of all animals have the most energetic respiration, and possess the highest heat. Cold and hot blooded mammals.

As with the atmosphere, so with the sea. Variations in its composition must control the organisms it contains. With its saline constituents its life must change. Before the sunlight had removed from the atmosphere so much of its carbonic acid, decomposing it through the agency of plants, the weight of carbonate of lime held in solution by the highly-carbonated water was far greater than was subsequently possible, and the occurrence of limestone became a necessary event. With such a disturbance in the composition of the sea-water, its inhabiting organisms were necessarily disturbed. The organisms of the sea.

And so again, subsequently, when the solar heat began to preponderate on the surface over the subsiding interior heat, the constitution of the sea-water, as respects its salinity, was altered through difference of evaporation in different latitudes—an effect inevitably making a profound impression on marine animal life.

*Nature of hereditary transmission.* Supported by the facts that have been mentioned respecting the later fossils of Australia and Brazil, and their analogy to forms now existing in those countries, much stress was laid on the hereditary transmission of structure, and hence the inference was drawn that such examples are of a mixed nature, depending in part on external agency, in part on an interior developemental force. From marsupial animals, marsupials will issue; from placental ones, those that are placental. But here, perhaps, an illustration drawn from the inorganic kingdom may not be without interest and use. Two pieces of carbonate of lime may be rolling among the pebbles at the bottom of a brook, one perpetually splitting into rhomboids, the other into arragonitic prisms. The fragments differ from one another not only thus in their crystalline form, but in their physical qualities, as density and hardness, and in their optical qualities also. We might say that the calc-spar crystals gave birth to calc-spar crystals, and the arragonitic to arragonite; we might admit that there is an interior propensity, an intrinsic tendency to produce that result, just as we say that there is a tendency in the marsupial to engender a marsupial; but, if, in our illustration, we look for the cause of that cause, we find it in a physical impression long antecedently made, that the carbonate of lime, crystallizing at 212° Fahr., produces arragonite, and, at a lower temperature, calc-spar; and that the physical impression thus accomplished, though it may have been thousands of years ago, was never cast off, but perpetually manifested itself in all the future history of the two samples. That which we sometimes speak of as hereditary transmission, and refer to an interior property, peculiarity, or force, may be nothing more than the manifestation of a physical impression long antecedently made.

In the last place, the idea of an intrinsic force of developement is in connection with time and a progression, and only comes *The broken organic chain.* into prominence when we examine a limited portion or number of the things under consideration. The earth, though very beautiful, is very far from being perfect. The plants and animals we see are only the wrecks of a broken series, an incomplete and therefore unworthy testimonial of the Almighty power. We should judge very inadequately of some great author if only here and there a fragmentary paragraph of his work remained; and so, in the book of organization, we must combine what is left with what we can recover from past ages and buried strata before we can rise to a comprehension of the grand argument, and intelligibly grasp the whole work.

Of that book it is immaterial to what page we turn. It *Enormous age of the earth.* tells us of effects of such magnitude as imply prodigiously long periods of time for their accomplishment. Its moments look to us as if they were eternities. What shall we say when we read in it that there are fossiliferous rocks which have been slowly raised ten thousand feet above the level of the sea so lately as since the commencement of the Tertiary times; that the Purbeck beds of the upper oolite are in themselves the memorials of an enormous lapse of time; that, since a forest in a thousand years can scarce produce more than two or three feet of vegetable soil, each dirt-bed is the work of hundreds of centuries? What shall we say when it tells us that the delta of the Mississippi could only be formed in many tens of thousands of years, and yet that is only as yesterday when compared with the date of the inland terraces; that the recession of the Falls of Niagara from Queenstown to the present site consumed thirty thousand years; that if the depression of the carboniferous strata of Nova Scotia took place at the rate of four feet in a century, there were demanded 375,000 years for its completion—such a movement in the upper direction would have raised Mont Blanc; that it would take as great a river as the Mississippi two millions of years to convey into the Gulf of Mexico as much sediment as is found in those strata? Such statements may appear to us, who with difficulty shake off the absurdities of the Patristic chronology, wild and impossible to be maintained, and yet they are the conclusions that the most learned and profound geologists draw from their reading of the book of Nature.

*Summary as respects the world in time.*

Thus, as respects the age of the earth and her relations in time, we approach the doctrine of the Orientals, who long ago ascertained that the scales of time and of space correspond to each other. More fortunate than we, they had but one point of resistance to encounter, but that resistance they met with dissimulation, and not in an open way. They attempted to conceal the tendency of their doctrine by allying or affiliating it with detected errors. According to their national superstition, the earth is supported on the back of an elephant, and this on a succession of animals, the last of which is a tortoise. It is not to be supposed that the Brahmans, who wrote commentaries on the Surya Siddhanta, should for a moment have accepted these preposterous delusions—that was impossible for such great geometers; yet led, perhaps, by a wish to do nothing that might disturb public feeling, they engaged in the hopeless task of showing that their profound philosophical discoveries were not inconsistent with the ancient traditions; that a globular and revolving earth might be sustained on a descending succession of supporting beasts. But they had the signal advantage over us, that those popular traditions conceded to them that limitless time for which we have had to struggle.

*The life of the universe.*

The progression of life on the surface of our planet is under the guidance of preordained and resistless law,—it is affiliated with material and correspondingly changing conditions. It suggests that the succession of organic forms which, in a due series, the earth's surface in the long lapse of time has presented, is the counterpart of a like progress which other planets in the solar system exhibit in myriads of years, and leads us to the conception of the rise, developement, and extinction of a multiplicity of such living forms in other systems,—a march of life through the universe, and its passing away.

*Multiplicity of worlds implies succession of worlds.*

Magnitudes and times therefore go parallel with one another. With the abandonment of the geocentric theory, and of the doctrine of the human destiny of the universe, have vanished the unworthy hypotheses of the recent date of creation and the approaching end of all things. In their stead are substituted more noble ideas. The multiplicity of worlds in infinite space leads to the conception of a succession of worlds in infinite time. This existing universe, with all its splendours, had a beginning, and will have an end; it had its predecessors, and will have its successors; but its march through all its transformations is under the control of laws as unchangeable as destiny. As a cloud, which is composed of myriads of separate and isolated spherules of water, so minute as to be individually invisible, on a summer's afternoon changes its aspect and form, disappearing from the sky, and being replaced in succeeding hours by other clouds of a different aspect and shape, so the universe, which is a cloud of suns and worlds, changes in the immensity of time its form and fashion, and that which is contemporary with us is only an example of countless combinations of a like kind, which in ancient times have one after another vanished away. In periods yet to come the endless succession of metamorphoses will still go on, a series of universes to which there is no end.

## CHAPTER XXIV.

### THE EUROPEAN AGE OF REASON—(Continued).

#### THE NATURE AND RELATIONS OF MAN.

*The apparent position of man on the heliocentric theory.*

WHEN the ancient doctrine of the plurality of worlds was restored by Bruno, Galileo, and other modern astronomers, the resistance it encountered was mainly owing to its anticipated bearing on the nature and relations of man. It was said, if round our sun, as a centre, there revolve so many planetary bodies, experiencing the changes of summer and winter, day and night—bodies illuminated by satellites, and perhaps enjoying twilight and other benefits such as have been conferred on the earth—shall we not consider them the abodes of accountable, perhaps of sinful, beings like ourselves? Nay more, if each of the innumerable fixed stars is, as our sun, a central focus of light, attended by dark and revolving globes, is it not necessary to admit that they also have their inhabitants? But among so many families of intelligent beings, how is it that we, the denizens of an insignificant speck, have alone been found worthy of God's regard?

It was this reasoning that sustained the geocentric theory, and made the earth the centre of the universe, the most noble of created things; the sun, the moon, the stars being only ministers for the service of man.

*The fallacy of objections to that theory.*

But, like many other objects urged in that memorable conflict, this was founded on a misconception, or rather, on imperfect knowledge. There may be an infinity of worlds placed under the mechanical relations alluded to, but there may not be one among them that can be the abode of life. The physical conditions under which organization is possible are so numerous and so strictly limited, that the chances are millions to one against their conjoined occurrence.

In a religious point of view, we are greatly indebted to Geology for the light it has cast on this objection. It has taught us that during inconceivable lapses of time our earth itself contained no living thing. These were those preorganic ages to which reference was made in the last chapter. Then, by slow degrees, as a possibility of existence occurred, there gradually emerged one type after another. It is as but yesterday that the life of man could be maintained. *Evidence furnished by Geology.*

Only in the presence of special physical conditions can an animal exist. Even then it is essentially ephemeral. The life of it, as a whole, depends on the death of its integrant parts. In a waterfall, which maintains its place and appearance unchanged for many years, the constituent portions that have been precipitated headlong glide finally and for ever away. For the transitory matter to exhibit a permanent form, it is necessary that there should be a perpetual supply and also a perpetual removal. So long as the jutting ledge over which the waters rush, and the broken gulf below that receives them, remain unchanged, the cataract presents the same appearance. But variations in them mould it into a new shape; its colour changes with a clear or a cloudy sky; the rainbow seen in its spray disappears when the beams of the sun are withdrawn. *The transitory nature of living forms.*

So in that collection of substance which constitutes an animal; whatever may be its position, high or low, in the realm of life, there is a perpetual introduction of new material and a perpetual departure of the old. It is a form, rather than an individual, that we see. Its permanence altogether depends on the permanence of the external conditions. If they change, it also changes, and a new form is the result.

An animal is therefore a form through which material substance is visibly passing, and suffering transmutation into new products. In that act of transmutation force is disengaged. That which we call its life is the display of the manner in which the force thus disengaged is expended. *Characteristics of animal life.*

A scientific examination of animal life must include two

*Matter and force.*  primary facts. It must consider whence and in what manner the stream of material substance has been derived, in what manner and whither it passes away. And since force cannot be created from nothing, and is in its very nature indestructible, it must determine from what source that which is displayed by animals has been obtained, in what manner it is employed, and what disposal is made of it eventually.

*Force is derived from the sun.*  The force thus expended is originally derived from the sun. Plants are the intermedium for its conveyance. The inorganic material of a saline nature entering into their constitution is obtained from the soil in which they grow, as is also, for the most part, the water they require; but their organic substance is derived from the surrounding atmosphere, and hence it is strictly true that they are condensations from the air.

*Mode in which plants obtain material substance.*  These statements may be sufficiently illustrated, and the relation between plants and animals shown, by tracing the course of any one of the ingredients entering into the vegetable composition, and derived, as has been said, from the air. For this purpose, if we select their chief solid element, carbon, the remarks applicable to the course it follows will hold good for other accompanying elements. It is scarcely necessary to embarrass the brief exposition of vegetable life now to be given by any historical details, since these will come with more propriety subsequently. It is sufficient to mention that the chemical explanations of vegetable physiology rest essentially on the discovery of oxygen gas by Priestley, of the constitution of carbonic acid by Lavoisier, and of water by Cavendish and Watt.

*Action of a plant on the air.*  While the sun is shining, the green parts of plants, especially the leaves, decompose carbonic acid, one of the ingredients of the atmospheric air. This substance is composed of two elements, carbon and oxygen; the former is appropriated by the plant, and enters into the composition of elaborated or descending sap, from which forthwith organic products, such as starch, sugar, wood-fibre, acids, and bases, are made. The other element, the oxygen, is for the most part refused by the plant, and returns to the air. As the process of decomposition goes on, new portions of carbonic acid are presented through mechanical movements, the trembling of the leaf, breezes, and currents rising from the foliage warmed by the solar beams giving place to other cool currents that set in below.

The action of a plant upon the air is therefore the separation of combustible material from that medium. Carbon is thus obtained from carbonic acid; hydrogen from water. Plant life is chemically an operation of reduction, for in like manner ammonia is decomposed into its constituents, which are nitrogen and hydrogen; and sulphuric and phosphoric acids, which, like ammonia, may have been brought into the plant through its roots in the form of salt bodies, are made to yield up the oxygen with which they had been combined, and their sulphur and phosphorus, combustible elements, are appropriated.

Every plant, from the humblest moss to the oak of a thousand years, is thus formed by the sun from material obtained from the air,—combustible material once united with oxygen, but now separated from that body. It is of especial importance to remark that in this act of decomposition, force, under the form of light, has disappeared, and become incorporated with the combustible, the organizing material. This force is surrendered again, or reappears, whenever the converse operation, combination with oxygen, occurs. *Composition and resolution of matter and force.*

Vegetable products thus constitute a magazine in which force is stored up and preserved for any assignable time. Hence they are adapted for animal food and for the procuring of warmth. The heat evolved in the combustion of coal in domestic economy was originally light from the sun appropriated by plants in the Secondary geological times, and locked up for untold ages. The sun is also the source from which was derived the light obtained in all our artificial operations of burning gas, oil, fat, wax, for the purposes of illumination.

My own experiments have proved ('Physiology,' p. 401) that it is the light of the sun, in contradistinction to the heat, which occasions the decomposition of carbonic acid, furnishing carbon to plants and oxygen to the atmosphere. But such is the relation of the so-called imponderable principles of chemistry to each other, and their mutual convertibility, that that *Correlation of physical forces.*

which has disappeared in performing its function as light may reappear as heat or electricity, or in the production of some mechanical effect.

*The nature of food.*  Food is used by all animals for the sake of the force it thus contains, the remark applying to the carnivora as well as the herbivora. In both cases the source of supply is the vegetable kingdom, indirectly or directly. The plant is thus indispensable to the animal. It is the collector and preserver of that force the expenditure of which constitutes the special display of animal life.

From this point of view, animals must therefore be considered as machines, in which force, obtained as has been described, is utilized. The food they take, or the tissue that has been formed from it, is acted upon by the air they breathe, and undergoes partial or total oxidation, and now emerges again, in part as heat, in part as nerve-force, in some few instances in part as light or electricity, the force that originally came from the sun.

*Cycle through which matter and force pass.*  There is, therefore, a cycle or revolution through which material particles suitable for organization incessantly run. At one moment they exist as inorganic combinations in the air or the soil, then as portions of plants, then as portions of animals, then they return to the air or soil again to renew their cycle of movement. The metamorphoses feigned by the poets of antiquity have hence a foundation in fact, and the vegetable and animal, the organic and inorganic worlds are indissolubly bound together. Plants are reducing, animals oxidizing, machines. Plants form, animals destroy.

Thus, by the light of the sun, the carbonic acid of the atmosphere is decomposed,—its oxygen is set free, its carbon furnished to plants. The products obtained serve for the food of animals, and in their systems the carbon is reoxidized by the air they respire, and, resuming the condition of carbonic acid, is thrown back into the atmosphere in the breath, ready to be decomposed by the sunlight once more, and run through the same cycle of changes again. The growth of a plant and the respiration of an animal are dependent on each other.

Material particles are thus the vehicles of force. They undergo no destruction. Chemically speaking, they are eternal. And so, likewise, force never deteriorates or becomes lessened. It may assume new phases, but it is always intrinsically unimpaired. The only changes it can exhibit are those of aspect and of distribution: of aspect, as electricity, affinity, light, heat; of distribution, as when the diffused aggregate of many sunbeams is concentrated in one animal form.

It is but little that we know respecting the mutations and distribution of force in the universe. We cannot tell what becomes of that which has characterized animal life, though of its perpetuity we may be assured. It has no more been destroyed than the material particles of which such animals consist. They have been transmuted into new forms—it has taken on a new aspect. The sum total of matter in the world is invariable; so, likewise, is the sum total of force.

These conclusions resemble in many respects those of the philosophy of Averrhoes, but they are free from the heresy which led the Lateran Council, under Leo X., to condemn the doctrines of the great Spanish Mohammedan. The error of Averrhoes consisted in this, that he confounded what is here spoken of under the designation of force with the psychical principle, and falsely applied that which is true for animals to the case of man, who is to be considered as consisting of three essentially distinct parts,—a material body, upon which operate various physical forces, guided and controlled by an intelligent soul.

In the following paragraphs the distinction here made is brought into more striking relief.

The station of any animal in the organic series may be determined from the condition of its nervous system. To this observation man himself is not an exception. Indeed, just views of his position in the world, of the nature of his intellect and mental operations, cannot be obtained except from the solid support afforded by Anatomy. The reader has doubtless remarked that, in the historical sketch of the later progress of Europe given in this book, I have not referred to metaphysics, or psychology, or mental philosophy. Cultivated as they have been, it was not possible for them to yield any other result than they did among the Greeks. A lever is no mechanical power unless it has a material point of support. It is only through the physical that the metaphysical can be discovered.

*Necessity of recurring to Anatomy and Physiology.*

An exposition of the structure, the physical forces, and the intellectual operations of man must be founded on anatomy. We can only determine the methods of action from the study of the mechanism, and the right interpretation of that mechanism can only be ascertained from the construction of its parts, from observations of the manner in which they are developed, from comparisons with similar structures in other animals, not rejecting even the lowest, and from an investigation of their habits and peculiarities. Believing that, in the present state of science, doctrines in psychology, unless they are sustained by evidence derived from anatomy and physiology, are not to be relied on, I have not thought it necessary to devote much space to their introduction. They have not taken a part in the recent advances of humanity. They belong to an earlier social period, and are an anachronism in ours. I have referred to these points heretofore in my work on 'Physiology,' and perhaps shall be excused the following extract (p. 259):—

*Solution of psychological questions.*

"The study of this portion of the mechanism of man brings us therefore in contact with metaphysical science, and some of its fundamental dogmas we have to consider. Nearly all philosophers who have cultivated in recent times that branch of knowledge, have viewed with apprehension the rapid advances of physiology, foreseeing that it would attempt the final solution of problems which have exercised the ingenuity of the last twenty centuries. In this they are not mistaken. Certainly it is desirable that some new method should be introduced, which may give point and precision to whatever metaphysical truths exist, and enable us to distinguish, separate, and dismiss what are only vain and empty speculations.

*Uncertainty of metaphysics.*

"So far from philosophy being a forbidden domain to the physiologist, it may be asserted that the time has now come when no one is entitled to express an opinion in philosophy except he has first studied physiology. It has hitherto been to the detriment of truth that these processes of positive investigation have been repudiated. If from the construction of the human brain we may demonstrate the existence of a soul, is not that a gain? for there are many who are open to arguments of this class on whom speculative reasoning or a mere dictum falls without any weight. Why should we cast aside the solid facts presented to us by material objects? In his communications throughout the universe with us, God ever materializes. He equally speaks to us through the thousand graceful organic forms scattered in profusion over the surface of the earth, and through the motions and appearances presented by the celestial orbs. Our noblest and clearest conceptions of His attributes have been obtained from these material things. I am persuaded that the only possible route to truth in mental philosophy is through a study of the nervous mechanism. The experience of 2500 years, and the writings of the great metaphysical intellects attest, with a melancholy emphasis, the vanity of all other means.

"Whatever may be said by speculative philosophers to the contrary, the advancement of metaphysics is through the study of physiology. What sort of a science would optics have been among men who had purposely put out their own eyes? What would have been the progress of astronomy among those who disdained to look at the heavens? Yet such is the preposterous course followed by the so-called philosophers. They have given us imposing doctrines of the nature and attributes of the mind in absolute ignorance of its material substratum. Of the great authors who have thus succeeded one another in ephemeral celebrity, how many made themselves acquainted with the structure of the human brain? Doubtless some had been so unfortunate as never to see one! Yet that wonderful organ was the basis of all their speculations. In voluntarily isolating themselves from every solid fact which might serve to be a landmark to them, they may be truly said to have sailed upon a shoreless sea from which the fog never lifts. The only fact they teach us with certainty is, that they know nothing with certainty. It is the inherent difficulty of their method that it must lead to unsubstantial results. What is

*Necessity of the interpretation of structure.*

not founded on a material substratum is necessarily a castle in the air."

*Intellectual relations of man depend on his nervous system.*

Considering thus that scientific views of the nature of man can only be obtained from an examination of his nervous system, and that the right interpretation of the manner of action of that system depends on the guiding light of comparative anatomy and physiology, I shall, in the following exposition, present the progress of discovery on those principles.

*The rudimentary nervous system is automatic.*

In those low tribes of life which show the first indications of a nervous system, its operation is purely mechanical. An external impression, as a touch, made upon animals of that kind, is instantly answered to by a motion which they execute, and this without any manifestation of will or consciousness. The phenomenon is exactly of the same kind as in a machine, of which, if a given lever is touched, a motion is instantly produced.

*Two elementary forms of nerve matter.*

In any nervous system there are two portions anatomically distinct. They are—1st, the fibrous; 2nd, the vesicular. It may be desirable to describe briefly the construction and functions of each of these portions. Their conjoint action will then be intelligible.

*Structure of a nerve fibre.*

1st. A nerve fibre consists essentially of a delicate thread—the axis filament, as it is called—enveloped in an oil-like substance, which coagulates or congeals after death. This, in its turn, is enclosed in a thin investing sheath or membranous tube. Many such fibres bound together constitute a nerve.

*Function of a nerve-fibre is conduction.*

The function of such a nerve fibre is indisputably altogether of a physical kind, being the conveyance of influences from part to part. The axis filament is the line along which the translation occurs, the investing material being for the purpose of confining or insulating it, so as to prevent any lateral escape. Such a construction is the exact counterpart of many electrical contrivances, in which a metallic wire is coated over with sealing-wax or wrapped round with silk, the current being thus compelled to move in the wire without any lateral escape. Of such fibres, some convey their influences to the interior, and hence are called centripetal; some convey them to the exterior, and hence are called centrifugal. No anatomical difference in the structure of the two has, however, thus far been discovered. As in a conducting wire the electrical current moves in a progressive manner with a definite velocity, so in a nerve filament the influence advances progressively at a rate said to be dependent on the temperature of the animal examined. It seems in the cold-blooded to be much slower than in the hot. It has been estimated in the frog at eighty-five feet in a second; in man, at two hundred feet,—an estimate probably too low.

The fibres thus described are of the kind designated by physiologists as the cerebro-spinal; there are others, passing under the name of the sympathetic, characterized by not possessing the investing medullary substance. In colour they are yellowish-grey; but it is not necessary here to consider them further.

2nd. The other portion of the nervous structure is the vesicular. As its name imports, it consists of vesicles filled with a grey granular material. Each vesicle has a thickened spot or nucleus upon it, and appears to be connected with one or more fibres. If the connection is only with one, the vesicle is called unipolar; if with two, bipolar; if with many, multipolar or stellate. Every vesicle is abundantly supplied with blood. *Structure of a nerve vesicle.*

As might be inferred from its structure, the vesicle differs altogether from the fibre in function. I may refer to page 268 of my 'Physiology' for the reasons which have led to the inference that these are contrivances for the purposes of permitting influences that have been translated along or confined within the fibre to escape and diffuse themselves in the grey granular material. They also permit influences that are coming through many different channels into a multipolar vesicle to communicate or mix with one another, and combine to produce new results. Moreover, in them influences may be long preserved, and thus they become magazines of force. Combined together, they constitute ganglia or nerve-centres, on which, if impressions be made, they do not necessarily forthwith die out, but may remain gradually declining away for a long time. Thus is introduced into the nervous mechanism the element of *Function of a nerve vesicle.*

time, and this important function of the nerve vesicle lies at the basis of memory.

*Physiological condition of nerve action is nerve waste.*

It has been said that the vesicular portion of the nerve mechanism is copiously supplied with blood. Indeed the condition indispensably necessary for its functional activity is waste by oxidation. Arterial vessels are abundantly furnished to ensure the necessary supply of aerated blood, and veins to carry away the wasted products of decay. Also, through the former, the necessary materials for repair and renovation are brought. There is a definite waste of nervous substance in the production of a definite mechanical or intellectual result,—a material connection and condition that must never be overlooked. Hence it is plain that unless the repair and the waste are synchronously equal to one another, periodicities in the action of the nervous system will arise, this being the fundamental condition connected with the physical theories of sleep and fatigue.

The statements here made rest upon two distinct forms of evidence. In part they are derived from an interpretation of anatomical structure, and in part from direct experiment, chiefly by the aid of feeble electrical currents. The registering or preserving action displayed by a ganglion may be considered as an effect, resembling that of the construction known as Ritter's secondary piles.

*Reflex action of the nervous system.*

It will not suit my purpose to offer more than the simplest illustration of the application of the foregoing facts. When an impression, either by pressure or in any other way, is made on the exterior termination of a centripetal fibre, the influence is conveyed with a velocity such as has been mentioned into the vesicle to which that fibre is attached, and thence, going forth along the centrifugal fibre, may give rise to motion through contraction of the muscle to which that fibre is distributed. An impression has thus produced a motion, and to the operation the designation of reflection is commonly given. This reflection takes place without consciousness. The three parts—the centripetal fibre, the vesicle, and the centrifugal fibre—conjointly constitute a simple nervous arc.

A repetition of these arcs, each precisely like all the others, constitutes the first step toward a complex nervous system.

Their manner of arrangement is necessarily subordinated to the general plan of construction of the animals in which they occur. Thus, in the Radiata it is circular; in the Articulata, linear, or upon an axis. But, as the conditions of life require consentaneousness of motion in the different parts, these nerve arcs are not left isolated or without connection with each other. As it is anatomically termed, they are commissured, nerve fibres passing from each to its neighbours, and each is thus brought into sympathy with all the others. *Gradual complexity of the nervous system.*

The next advance is a very important one, for it indicates the general plan on which the nervous system is to be developed: it is the dedication of special nerve arcs for special duties. Thus, in the higher articulata and mollusca there are such combinations expressly for the purpose of respiration and deglutition. Their action is altogether of the reflex kind; it takes place without consciousness. These ganglia are commissured for the sake of sympathetic action, and frequently several of them coalesce for the sake of package. *First appearance of special ganglia.*

This principle of dedication to special uses is carried out in the introduction of ganglia intended to be affected by light, or sounds, or odours. The impressions of those agencies are carried to the ganglion by its centripetal fibres. Such ganglia of special action most commonly coalesce together, forming nervous masses of conspicuous size; they are always commissured with those for ordinary motions, the action being reflex, as in the preceding case, though of a higher order, since it is attended with consciousness.

Such being the elementary construction of a nervous system, it is plain that animal tribes in which it exists in no higher degree of complexity must be merely automata. In this remark insects must be included, for the instinct they display is altogether of a mechanical kind, and, so far as they are concerned, without design. Their actions are uniformly alike; what one does under given circumstances, under the same circumstances another will certainly do. They are incapable of education, they learn nothing by experience, and the acts they are engaged in they accomplish as well at the first trial as ever after. *They are automatic mechanisms.*

Of parts like those thus described, and of others of a higher order, as will be presently seen, is the most complex nervous system, even that of man, composed. It might, perhaps, be expected that for the determination of the duty of each part of such complex systems the physiologist must necessarily resort to experiment, observing what functions have been injured or destroyed when given portions have been removed by his knife. At the best, however, evidence of that kind must be very unsatisfactory on account of the shock the entire system receives in vivisections, and, accordingly, artificial evidence can, for the most part, be used only in a corroborative way. But, as Cuvier observed, the hand of Nature has prepared for us these very experiments without that drawback. The animal series, as we advance upward from its lowest member, proves to us what is the effect of the addition of new parts in succession to a nervous system, as also does any individual thereof in its successive periods of developement. It is one of the most important discoveries of modern physiology that, as respects their nervous system, we can safely transfer our reasonings and conclusions from the case of the lowest to that of the highest animal tribes.

*First introduction of governing ganglia.*

The articulata present structures and a mode of action illustrating in a striking manner the nervous system of man. Lengthwise upon their ventral region is laid a double cord, with ganglia, like a string of beads; sometimes the cords are a little distance apart, but more generally they coalesce, each pair of ganglia being fused into one. To every segment of the body a pair is supplied, each pair controlling its own segment, and acting toward it automatically, each also acting like any of the others. But in the region of the head there is a special pair, the cephalic ganglia, receiving fibres from the eyes and other organs of sense. From them proceed filaments to the ventral cord, establishing communications with every segment. So every part has two connections, one with its own ventral ganglia, and one with the cephalic.

*But thus far actions are only instinctive.*

It is not difficult to determine experimentally the functions of the ventral ganglia and those of the cephalic. If a centipede be decapitated, its body is still capable of moving, the motion being evidently of a reflex kind, originating in the pressure of the legs against the surface on which they rest. The ventral cord, with its ganglia, is hence purely an automatic mechanism. But if, in making the decapitation, we leave a portion of the body in connection with the head, we recognize very plainly that the cephalic ganglia are exercising a governing power. In the part from which they have been cut off the movement is forward, regardless of any obstacle; in that to which they are attached there are modifications in the motions, depending on sight or other special senses; obstacles are avoided, and a variety of directions pursued. Yet still the actions are not intelligent, only instinctive. The general conclusion therefore is, that the cephalic ganglia are of a higher order than the ventral, the latter being simply mechanical, the former instinctive; but thus far there is no trace of intelligence.

In man these typical parts are all present, and discharge the functions specified. His spinal cord answers to the ventral cord of the articulata. It has its lateral communications in the same way, and each segmental portion presents the same reflex action. Toward its upper part it dilates to form the medulla oblongata, sending forth nerves for respiration and deglutition. Of these the action is still reflex, as is proved by the involuntary movements of respiration and deglutition. A portion of food being placed in the pharynx, contraction instantly occurs, the will having no kind of control over the act of swallowing. Above or in front of this enlargement is a series of ganglia, to which converge the nerves of special sense—of hearing, sight, smell; these are, therefore, the equivalents of the cephalic ganglia of insects, their function being also the same. In the lowest vertebrata, as in the amphioxus, the nervous system consists of nothing more. It may therefore be said to have only two parts—the cord and the sensory ganglia, and to have two functions—the automatic, attributable to the former, and the instinctive, attributable to the latter.

But as we advance from the low vertebrata upward in the animal scale, we begin to detect new organs; on the medulla oblongata a cerebellum, and on the sensory ganglia a cerebrum. From this moment the animal displays reasoning powers, its

*Nervous anatomy of vertebrata, as man.*

*Their automatic apparatus.*

*Their instinctive apparatus.*

*Their intellectual apparatus.*

intelligence becoming more strikingly marked as the developement of the new organs is greater.

*Functions of the brain.* It remains to determine with exactness the function of one of these new parts, the cerebrum; the other portion, the cerebellum, being of minor interest, and connected probably with the locomotive apparatus. For the same reason it is unnecessary to speak of the sympathetic nerve, since it belongs to the apparatus of organic life. Confining our attention, therefore, to the true brain, or cerebrum, we soon recognize that the intelligence of an animal is, in a general manner, proportional to the relative size of this organ as compared with the sensory ganglia. *Its relations to the instinctive and automatic portions.* We are also struck with the fact that the cerebrum does not send forth to other portions any independent fibres of its own, nor does it receive any from them, its only means of communication being through the parts that have been described,—that is to say, through the sensory and automatic apparatus. The cerebrum is therefore a mechanism of a higher order, and its relationship with the thalami optici and corpora striata indicate the conditions of its functions. It can only receive impressions which have come through them, and only act upon the body through their intermedium. *Its secondary and tertiary lobes.* Moreover, as we ascend the animal scale, we find that these cerebral parts not only increase in size, but likewise, in their turn, give rise to offshoots; secondary lobes emerging posteriorly on the primary ones, and, in due season, tertiary lobes posteriorly on the secondary. To these in human anatomy, the designations of anterior, middle, and posterior lobes have been respectively given. In proportion as this developement has proceeded, the intellectual qualities have become more varied and more profound.

*Action of the spinal cord alone.* The relation of the cerebrum to the cranio-spinal axis is manifested by the circumstance that the latter can act without the former. In sleep the cerebrum is, as it were, torpid, but respiration, deglutition, and other reflex actions go on. If we touch the palm of a sleeping infant our finger is instantly grasped. *Conjoint action of the brain and cord.* But, though the axis can work without the cerebrum the cerebrum cannot work without the axis. Illustrations of these truths may be experimentally obtained. An animal from which the cerebrum has been purposely removed may be observed to perform actions automatic and instinctive, but never intelligent; and that there is no difference between animals and man in this respect is demonstrated by the numerous instances recorded in the works of medicine and surgery of injuries by accident or disease to the human nervous system, the effects corresponding to those artificially produced in experiments on animals. This important observation moreover shows that we may with correctness use the observations made on animals in our investigations of the human system.

Thus, then, the matter stands. In the nervous system of man our attention is especially demanded by three essentially distinct parts—the spinal cord, the sensory ganglia, and the cerebrum. Of the first, the spinal cord, the action is automatic; by its aid we can walk, without bestowing a thought on our movements, from place to place; by it we swallow involuntarily; by it we respire unconsciously. The second portion, the sensory ganglia, is, as we have seen, the counterpart of the cephalic ganglia of the invertebrata; it is the place of reception of sensuous impressions and the seat of consciousness. To these ganglia instinct is to be referred. Their function is not at all impaired by the cerebrum superposed upon them. The third portion, the cerebrum, is anatomically distinct. It is the seat of ideas. It does not directly give rise to motions, being obliged to employ for that purpose its intermediate automatic associated apparatus. In this realm of ideas thoughts spring forth suggestively from one another in a perpetual train or flux, and yet the highest branch of the nervous mechanism still retains traces of the modes of operation of the parts from which it was developed. Its action is still often reflex. Reason is not always able to control our emotions, as when we laugh or weep in spite of ourselves, under the impression of some external incident. Nay more, the inciting cause may be, as we very well know, nothing material,—nothing but a recollection, an idea,—and yet it is enough. But these phenomena are perhaps restricted to the first or anterior lobes of the brain, and, accordingly, we remark them most distinctly in children and in animals. As the second and third lobes begin to exercise their power, such effects are brought under control.

*[margin: Three distinct parts of the nervous system of man. They are the automatic, the instinctive, the intellectual. Dominating control of the latter.]*

There is, therefore, a regular progression, a definite improvement in the nervous system of the animal series, the plan never varying, but being persistently carried out, and thus offering a powerful argument for relationship among all those successively improving forms, an observation which becomes of the utmost interest to us in its application to the vertebrata. In the amphioxus, as has been said, the cranio-spinal axis alone exists; the Cyclostome fishes are but a step higher. In fishes the true cerebrum appears at first in an insignificant manner, a condition repeated in the early embryonic state both of birds and mammals. An improvement is made in reptiles, whose cerebral hemispheres are larger than their optic lobes. As we advance to birds, a further increase occurs; the hemispheres are now of nearly sufficient dimensions to cover those ganglia. In the lower mammalia there is another step, yet not a very great one. But from the anterior lobes, which thus far have constituted the entire brain, there are next to be developed the middle lobes. In the Rodentia the progress is still continued, and in the Ruminantia and Pachydermata the convolutions have become well marked. In the higher carnivora and quadrumana the posterior or tertiary lobes appear. The passage from the anthropoid apes to man brings us to the utmost developement thus far attained by the nervous system. The cerebrum has reached its maximum organization by a continued and unbroken process of developement.

This orderly developement of the nervous system in the animal series is recognized again in the gradual developement of the individual man. The primitive trace, as it faintly appears in the germinal membrane, marks out the place presently to be occupied by the cranio-spinal axis, and that point of developement gained, man answers to the amphioxus. Not until the twelfth week of embryonic life does he reach the state permanently presented by birds; at this time the anterior lobes are only perceptible. In four or six weeks more the middle lobes are evolved posteriorly on the anterior, and finally, in a similar manner, the tertiary or posterior ones are formed. And thus it appears that, compared with the nervous system of other animals, that of man proceeds through the same predetermined succession of forms. Theirs suffers an arrest, in some instances at a lower, in some at a higher point, but his passes onward to completion.

But that is not all. The biography of the earth, the life of the entire globe, corresponds to this progress of the individual, to this orderly relation of the animal series. Commencing with the oldest rocks that furnish animal remains, and advancing to the most recent, we recognize a continual improvement in construction, indicated by the degree of advancement of the nervous system. The earliest fishes did not proceed beyond that condition of the spinal column which is to be considered as embryonic. The Silurian and Devonian rocks do not present it in an ossified state. The fishes, up to the Carboniferous epoch, had a heterocercal tail, just as the embryos of osseous fishes of the present time have up to a certain period of their life. There was therefore an arrest in the old extinct forms, and an advance to a higher point in the more modern. The buckler-headed fishes of the Devonian rocks had their respiratory organs and much of their digestive apparatus in the head, and showed an approximation to the tadpoles or embryos of the frog. The crocodiles of the oolite had biconcave vertebræ, like the embryos of the recent ones which have gained the capability of making an advance to a higher point. In the geological order, reptiles make their appearance next after fishes, and this is what we should expect on the principle of an ascending nervous developement. Not until long after come birds, later in date and higher in nervous advancement, capable not only of instinct, but also of intelligence. Of mammals, the first that appear are what we should have expected—the marsupials; but, among the tertiary rocks, very many other forms are presented, the earlier ones, whether herbivorous or carnivorous, having a closer correspondence to the archetype than the existing ones, save in their embryonic states, the analogies occurring in such minor details as the possession of forty-four teeth. The biography of the earth is thus, on the great scale, typical of individual life, even that of man, and the succession of species in the progress of numberless ages is the counterpart of the transmutation of an indivi-

*It occurs again in the entire life of the globe.*

*Absolute necessity of admitting transmutation of forms.*

dual from form to form. As in a dissolving view, new objects emerge from old ones, and new forms spontaneously appear without the exercise of any periodical creative act.

*Life of man from infancy to maturity in accordance with his anatomy*

For some days after birth the actions of the human being are merely reflex. Its cranio-spinal axis alone is in operation, and thus far it is only an automaton. But soon the impressions of external objects begin to be registered or preserved in the sensory ganglia, and the evidences of memory appear. The first token of this is perhaps the display of an attachment to persons, not through any intelligent recognition of relationship, but merely because of familiarity. This is followed by the manifestation of a liking to accustomed places and a dread of strange ones. At this stage the infant is leading an instinctive life, and has made no greater advance than many of the lower mammals; but they linger here, while he proceeds onward. He soon shows high powers of memory, the exercise of reason in the determinations of judgment, and in the adaptation of varied means to varied ends.

Such is therefore the process of developement of the nervous system of man; such are the powers which consequently he successively displays. His reason at last is paramount. No longer are his actions exclusively prompted by sensations; they are determined much more by ideas that have resulted from his former experiences. While animals which approach him most closely in construction require an external stimulus to commence a train of thought, he can direct his mental operations, and in this respect is parted from them by a vast interval. The states through which he has passed are the automatic, the instinctive, the intellectual; each has its own apparatus, and all at last work harmoniously together.

*Every person consists of two lateral individuals.*

But besides this superposition of an instinctive apparatus upon an automatic one, and an intellectual upon an instinctive, the nervous system consists of two equal and symmetrical lateral portions, a right half and a left. Each person may be considered as consisting in reality of two individuals. The right half may be stricken with palsy, the left be unimpaired; one may lose its sight or hearing, the other may retain them. These lateral halves lead independent lives. Yet, though independent in this sense, they are closely connected in another. The brain of the right side rules over the left half of the body, that of the left side rules over the right of the body. On the relationships and antagonisms of the two halves of the cerebro-spinal system must be founded our explanations of the otherwise mysterious phenomena of double and alternate life; of the sentiment of pre-existence; of trains of thought, often double, but never triple; of the wilful delusions of castle-building, in which one hemisphere of the brain listens to the romance suggestions of the other, though both well know that the subject they are entertaining themselves with is a mere fiction. The strength and precision of mental operations depend as much upon the complete equivalency of the two lateral halves as upon their absolute developement. It is scarcely to be expected that great intellectual indications will be given by him, one of whose cerebral hemispheres is unequal to the other. But for the detailed considerations of these topics I may refer the reader to my work on 'Physiology.' He will there find the explanation of the nature of registering ganglia; the physical theory of memory; the causes of our variable psychical powers at different times; the description of the ear as the organ of time; the eye as the organ of space; the touch as that of pressures and temperatures; the smell and taste as those for the chemical determination of gases and liquids. *Consequences of this doublences of construction.*

From a consideration of the construction, developement, and action of the nervous system of man, we may gain correct views of his relations to other organic beings, and obtain true psychical and metaphysical theories. There is not that homogeneousness in his intellectual structure which writers on those topics so long supposed. It is a triple mechanism. A gentle, a gradual, a definite developement reaches its maximum in him without a breach of continuity. Parts which, because of their completion, are capable of yielding in him such splendid results, are seen in a rudimentary and useless condition in organisms very far down below. On the clear recognition of this rudimentary, this useless state, very much depends. It indicates the master-fact of psychology—the fact that Averrhoes overlooked—that, while man agrees with inferior beings in *Conclusions from the foregoing anatomical facts.* *Man a member of the animal series.*

the type of his construction, and passes in his developement through transformations analogous to theirs, he differs from them in all this, that he alone possesses an accountable, an immortal soul. It is true that there are some which closely approach him in structure, but the existence of structure by no means implies the exercise of functions. In the still-born infant, the mechanism for respiration, the lungs, is completed; but the air may never enter, and the intention for which they were formed never be carried out.

*His life and that of the planet alike.* Moreover, it appears that the order of developement in the life of individual man and the order of developement in the life of the earth are the same, their common features indicating a common plan. The one is the movement of a few hours, the other of myriads of ages. This sameness of manner in their progression points out their dependence on a law immutable and universal. The successive appearance of the animal series in the endless course of time has not, therefore, been accidental, but as predetermined and as certain as the successive forms of the individual. In the latter we do not find any cause of surprise in the assumption of states ever increasing in improvement, ever rising higher and higher toward the perfection destined to be attained. We look upon it as the course of nature. Why, then, should we consider the extinctions and creations of the former as offering anything unaccountable, as connected with a sudden creative fiat or with an arbitrary sentence of destruction?

*Progress of humanity is according to law.* In this book I have endeavoured to investigate the progress of humanity, and found that it shows all the phases of individual movement, the evidence employed being historical, and therefore of a nature altogether different from that on which our conclusions in the collateral instances rest. It may serve to assure us that the ideas here presented are true when we encounter, at the close of our investigation, this harmony between the life of the individual, the life of society, and the life of the earth.

Is it probable that the individual proceeds in his movement under law, that the planet also proceeds in its movement under law, but that society does not proceed under law?

Man, thus, is the last term of an innumerable series of organisms, which, under the domination of law, has, in the lapse of time, been evolving. Law has controlled the inorganic world, and caused the earth to pass through various physical conditions, gently and continuously succeeding one another. The plastic forms of organic beings have been modelled to suit those changing conditions. The invariability of that law is indicated by the numberless ages through which it has been maintained, its universality by its holding good in the life of the meanest individual. *Eternity and universality of that law.*

But it is only a part of sociology that we have considered, and of which we have investigated the developement. In the most philosophical aspect the subject includes comparative as well as human sociology. For, though there may not be society where actions are simply reflex, there is a possibility of it where they are instinctive, as well as where they are intellectual. Its essential condition being intercommunication, there are necessarily modifications depending respectively on touch or upon the higher and more delicate senses. That is none the less society which, among insects, depends upon antennal contacts. Human society, founded on speech, sight, hearing, has its indistinct beginnings, its rudiments, very low down in the animal scale, as in the bell-like note which some of the nudibranchiate gasteropoda emit, or the solitary midnight tapping with which the death-watch salutes his mate. Society resting on instinct is characterized by immobility; it is necessarily unprogressive. Society resting on intellect is always advancing. *Comparative sociology.*

But, for the present, declining this general examination of sociology, and limiting our attention strictly to that of humanity, we cannot fail to be struck with the fact that in us the direction of evolution is altogether toward the intellectual, a conclusion equally impressed upon us whether our mode of examination be anatomical or historical. Anatomically we find no provision in the nervous system for the improvement of the moral, save indirectly through the intellectual, the whole aim of developement being for the sake of intelligence. Historically, in the same manner, we find that the intellectual has *The aim of Nature is not at moral, but intellectual developement.*

always led the way in social advancement, the moral having been subordinate thereto. The former has been the mainspring of the movement, the latter passively affected. It is a mistake to make the progress of society depend on that which is itself controlled by a higher power. In the earlier and inferior stages of individual life we may govern through the moral alone. In that way we may guide children; but it is to the understanding of the adult that we must appeal. A system working only through the moral must sooner or later come into an antagonism with the intellectual, and, if it does not contain within itself a means of adaptation to the changing circumstances, must in the end be overthrown. This was the grand error of the Roman system, which presided while European civilization was developing. It assumed as its basis a uniform, a stationary, psychological condition in man. Forgetting that the powers of the mind grow with the possessions of the mind, it considered those who lived in past generations as being in no respect mentally inferior to those who are living now, though our children at sixteen may have a wider range of knowledge than our ancestors at sixty. That such an imperfect system could exist for so many ages is a proof of a contemporary condition of undeveloped intellect, just as we see that the understanding of a child does not revolt against the moral suasion, often intrinsically feeble, through which we attempt to influence him. But it would be as unphilosophical to treat with disdain the ideas that have served for a guide in the earlier ages of European life, as to look with contempt on the motives that have guided us in youth. Their feebleness and incompetency is excused by their suitability to the period of life to which they are applied.

But whoever considers these things will see that there is a term beyond which the application of such methods cannot be extended. The head of a family would act unwisely if he attempted to apply to his son at twenty-one the methods he had successfully used at ten; such methods could be only rendered effective by a resort to physical compulsion. A great change in the intervening years has taken place, and ideas once intrinsically powerful can exert their influence no more.

The moral may have remained unchanged; it may be precisely as it was—no better, no worse; but that which has changed is the understanding. Reasoning and inducements of an intellectual kind are now needful. An attempt to persist in an absolute system by constraint would only meet with remonstrance and derision.

If it is thus with the individual, so it is likewise with humanity. For centuries nations may live under forms that meet their requirements, forms suitable to a feeble state; but it is altogether illusory to suppose that such an adaptedness can continue for ever. A critical eye discerns that the mental features of a given generation have become different from those of its ancestors. New ideas and a new manner of action are the tokens that a modification has silently taken place. Though after a short interval the change might not amount to much, in the course of time there must inevitably be exhibited the spectacle of a society that had outgrown its forms, its rules of life. *And the same holds good for humanity.*

Wherever, then, such a want of harmony becomes perceptible, where the social system is incompatible with the social state, and is in effect an obsolete anachronism, it is plainly unphilosophical and unwise to resort to means of compulsion. No matter what the power of governments or of human authorities may be, it is impossible for them to stop the intellectual advancement, for it forces its way by an organic law over which they have no kind of control.

Astronomers sometimes affirm that the sun is the cause, directly or indirectly, of all the mechanical movements that take place upon the earth. Physiologists say that he is the generator of the countless living forms with which her surface is adorned. *Summary of the investigation of the position of man.*

If the light, the warmth, and other physical influences of the sun could be excluded, there would be a stagnant and icy sea encircling silent and solitary shores. But the veil once withdrawn, or the influences permitted to take effect, this night and stillness would give place to activity and change. In the morning beams of the day, the tropical waters, expand- *Influence of the sun on inorganic nature.*

ing, would follow from east to west the course of the sun, each renewed dawn renewing the impulse, and adding force to the gentle but resistless current. At one place the flowing mass would move compactly; at another, caught by accidentally projecting rocks, it would give off little eddies, expending their share of its force; or compressed in narrow passages, it would rush impetuously along. Upon its surface myriads of momentary ripples would play, or opposing winds, called into existence by similar disturbances in the air, would force it into waves, making the shores resound with their breaking surge. Twice every day, under the conjoint influences of the sun and the moon, as if the inanimate globe itself were breathing, the tide would rise and fall again upon the bosom of the deep.

The eddy, the ripple, the wave, the current, are accidental forms through which the originally imparted force is displayed. They are all expending power. Their life, if such a term can be used, is not the property of themselves, but of the ocean to which they belong.

*And on organic nature.* Influences which thus metaphorically give life to the sea, in reality give life to the land. Under their genial operation a wave of verdure spreads over the earth, and countless myriads of animated things attend it, each like the eddies and ripples of the sea, expending its share of the imparted force. The life of these accidental forms, through which power is being transposed, belongs, not to itself, but to the universe of which it is a part.

*Nature of animals.* Of the waves upon the ocean there may not be two alike. The winds, the shores, their mutual interferences, a hundred extraneous influences, mould them into their ephemeral shapes. So those collections of matter of which animated things consist offer a plastic substance to be modified. The number of individuals counts like the ripples of the sea.

*They constitute a series.* As external circumstances change, animated forms change with them, and thus arises a series of which the members stand in a connected relation. The affiliated sequence of the external circumstances is represented in the affiliated succession of living types. From parts, or from things already existing, new parts and new things emerge, the new not being added or juxtaposed to the old, but evolved or developed from it. From the homogeneous or general, the heterogeneous or special is brought forth. A new member, fashioned in secrecy and apart, is never abruptly engrafted on any living thing. New animal types have never been suddenly located among old ones, but have emerged from them by process of transmutation. As certainly as that every living thing must die, so must it reach perfection by passing through a succession of subordinate forms. An individual, or even a species, is only a zoological phase in a passage to something beyond. An instantaneous adult, like an immortal animal, is a physiological impossibility.

This bringing forth of structure from structure, of function from function, incidentally presents, upon the whole, an appearance of progressive improvement, and for such it has been not unfrequently mistaken. Thus, if the lowest animals, which move by reflex action, instantly but unconsciously, when an impression is made upon them, be compared with the higher ones, whose motions are executed under the influence of antecedent impressions, and are therefore controlled by ideas, there seems to have been such an improvement. Still, however, it is altogether of a physical kind. Every impression of which the dog or elephant is conscious implies change in the nerve centres, and these changes are at the basis of the memory displayed by those animals. Our own experience furnishes many illustrations. When we gaze steadfastly on some brightly-illuminated object, and then close or turn aside our eyes, a fading impression of the object at which we have been looking still remains; or when a spark is made to revolve rapidly, we think we see a circle of fire, the impression upon the retina lasting until the spark has completed its revolution. In like manner, though far more perfectly, are impressions registered or stored up in the sensory ganglia, the phantoms of realities that have once been seen. In those organs countless images may thus be superposed.

*The doctrine of progressive improvement.*

Man agrees with animals thus approaching him in anatomical construction in many important respects. He, too, represents a continuous succession of matter, a continuous expen-

*Analogies between animals and man.*

diture of power. Impressions of external things are concealed in his sensory ganglia, to be presented for inspection in subsequent times, and to constitute motives of action. But he differs from them in this, that what was preparatory and rudimentary in them is complete and perfect in him. From the instrument of instinct there has been developed an instrument of intellection. In the most perfect quadrupeds, an external stimulus is required to start a train of thought, which then moves on in a determinate way, their actions indicating that, under the circumstances, they reason according to the same rules as man, drawing conclusions more or less correct from the facts offered to their notice. But, the instrument of intellection completed, it is quickly brought into use, and now results of the highest order appear. The succession of ideas is under control; new trains can be originated not only by external causes, but also by an interior, a spontaneous influence. The passive has become active. Animals remember, man alone recollects. Everything demonstrates that the development and completion of this instrument of intellection has been followed by the superaddition of an agent or principle that can use it.

*Points of distinction between them.*

There is, then, a difference between the brutes and man, not only as respects constitution, but also as repects destiny. Their active force merges into other mundane forces and disappears, but the special principle given to him endures. We willingly persuade ourselves that this principle is actually personified, and that the shades of the dead resemble their living forms. To Eastern Asia, where philosophy has been accustomed to the abstract idea of force, the pleasures we derive from this contemplation are denied, the cheerless doctrine of Buddhism likening the life of man to the burning of a lamp, and death to its extinction. Perceiving in the mutation of things, as seen in the narrow range of human vision, a suggestion of the variations and distribution of power throughout nature, it rises to a grand, and, it must be added, an awful conception of the universe.

*The human soul.*

But Europe, and also the Mohammedan nations of Asia, have not received that view with approbation. To them there is an individualized impersonation of the soul, and an expectation of its life hereafter. The animal fabric is only an instrument for its use. The eye is the window through which that mysterious principle perceives; through the ear are brought to its attention articulate sounds and harmonies; by the other organs the sensible qualities of bodies are made known. From the silent chambers and winding labyrinths of the brain the veiled enchantress looks forth on the outer world, and holds the subservient body in an irresistible spell.

This difference between the Oriental and European ideas respecting the nature of man reappears in their ideas respecting the nature of the world. The one sees in it only a gigantic engine, in which stars and orbs are diffusing power and running through predestined mutations. The other, with better philosophy and a higher science, asserts a personal God, who considers and orders events in a vast panorama before Him.

*Extension of these views to the nature of the world.*

# CHAPTER XXV.

## THE EUROPEAN AGE OF REASON—(*Continued*).

### THE UNION OF SCIENCE AND INDUSTRY.

*Analogies between the Age of Reason in Europe and in Greece.*

THE Age of Reason in Europe presents all the peculiarities of the Age of Reason in Greece. There are modern representatives of King Ptolemy Philadelphus among his furnaces and crucibles; of Hipparchus cataloguing the stars; of Aristyllus and Timochares, with their stone quadrants and armyls, ascertaining the planetary motions; of Eratosthenes measuring the size of the earth; of Herophilus dissecting the human body; of Archimedes settling the laws of mechanics and hydrostatics; of Manetho collating the annals of the old dynasties of Egypt; of Euclid and Apollonius improving mathematics. There are botanical gardens and zoological menageries like those of Alexandria, and expeditions to the sources of the Nile. The direction of thought is the same; but the progress is on a greater scale, and illustrated by more imposing results. The exploring voyages to Madagascar are replaced by circumnavigations of the world; the revolving steam-engine of Hero by the double-acting engine of Watt; the great galley of Ptolemy, with its many banks of rowers, by the ocean steamship; the solitary watch-fire on the Pharos by a thousand lighthouses, with their fixed and revolving lights; the courier on his Arab horse by the locomotive and electric telegraph; the scriptorium in the Serapion, with its shelves of papyrus, by countless printing-presses; the 'Almagest' of Ptolemy by the 'Principia' of Newton; and the Museum itself by English, French, Italian, German, Dutch, and Russian philosophical societies, universities, colleges, and other institutions of learning.

So grand is the scale on which this cultivation of science has been resumed, so many are those engaged in it, so rapid is the advance, and so great are the material advantages, that there is no difficulty in appreciating the age of which it is the characteristic. The most superficial outline enables us to recognize at once its resemblance to that period of Greek life to which I have referred. To bring its features into relief, I shall devote a few pages to a cursory review of the progress of some of the departments of science, selecting for the purpose topics of general interest. European progress in the acquisition of knowledge.

First, then, as respects the atmosphere, and the phenomena connected with it.

From observations on the twilight, the elasticity of aerial bodies, and the condensing action of cold, the conclusion previously arrived at by Alhazen was established, that the atmosphere does not extend unlimitedly into space. Its height is considered to be about forty-five miles. From its compressibility, the greater part of it is within a much smaller limit; were it of uniform density, it would not extend more than 29,000 feet. Hence, comparing it with the dimensions of the earth, it is an insignificant aerial shell, in thickness not the eightieth part of the distance to the earth's centre, and its immensity altogether an illusion. It bears about the same proportion to the earth that the down upon a peach bears to the peach itself. The atmosphere.

A foundation for the mechanical theory of the atmosphere was laid as soon as just ideas respecting liquid pressures, as formerly taught by Archimedes, were restored, the conditions of vertical and oblique pressures investigated, the demonstration of equality of pressure in all directions given, and the proof furnished that the force of a liquid on the bottom of a vessel may be very much greater than its weight.

Such of these conclusions as were applicable were soon transferred to the case of aerial bodies. The weight of the atmosphere was demonstrated, its pressure illustrated and measured; then came the dispute about the action of pumps, and the over- Its mechanical relations.

throw of the Aristotelian doctrine of the horror of a vacuum.
Coincidently occurred the invention of the barometer, and the
proof of its true theory, both on a steeple in Paris and on a
mountain in Auvergne. The invention of the air-pump, and
its beautiful illustrations of the properties of the atmosphere,
extended in a singular manner the taste for natural philosophy.

*Its chemical relations.*

The mechanics of the air was soon followed by its chemistry.
From remote ages it had been numbered among the elements,
though considered liable to vitiation or foulness. The great
discovery of oxygen gas placed its chemical relations in their
proper position. One after another, other gases, both simple
and compound, were discovered. Then it was recognized that
the atmosphere is the common receptacle for all gases and
vapours, and the problem whether, in the course of ages, it
has ever undergone change in its constitution arose for solution.

*The antagonism of animals and plants.*

The negative determination of that problem, so far as a few
thousand years were concerned, was necessarily followed by a
recognition of the antagonism of animals and plants, and their
mutually balancing each other; the latter accomplishing their
duty under the influence of the sun, though he is a hundred
millions of miles distant. From this it appeared that it is not
by incessant interventions that the sum total of animal life is
adjusted to that of vegetable, but that, in this respect, the
system of government of the world is by the operation of natural causes and law,—a conclusion the more imposing since it
contemplates all living things, and includes even man himself. The detail of these investigations proved that the organic
substance of plants is condensed from the inorganic air to
which that of all animals returns, the particles running in
ever-repeating cycles, now in the air, now in plants, now in
animals, now in the air again; the impulse of movement being
in the sun, from whom has come the force incorporated in
plant tissues, and eventually disengaged in our fires, shining
in our flames, oppressing us in fevers, and surprising us in
blushes.

Organic disturbances by respiration and the growth of plants being in the lowest stratum of the air, its uniformity of composition would be impossible were it not for the agency of the winds and the diffusion of gases, which it was found would take place under any pressure. The winds were at length properly referred to the influence of the sun, whose heat warms the air, causing it to ascend, while other portions flow in below. The explanation of land and sea breezes was given, and in the trade-wind was found a proof of the rotation of the earth. At a later period followed the explanation of monsoons in the alternate heating and cooling of Asia and Africa on opposite sides of the line, and of tornadoes, which are disks of air rotating round a translated axis with a diameter of one hundred or one hundred and fifty miles, the axis moving in a curvilinear track with a progressive advance of twenty or twenty-five miles an hour, and the motions being in opposite directions on opposite hemispheres of the globe.

*The winds; their origin and nature.*

The equatorial calms and trade-winds accounted for on physical principles, it was admitted that the winds of high latitudes, proverbially uncertain as they are, depend in like manner on definite causes.

With these palpable movements there are others of a less obvious kind. Through the air, and by reason of motions in it, sounds are transmitted to us.

The Alexandrian mathematicians made sound a favourite study. Modern acoustics arose from the recognition that there is nothing issuing from the sounding body, but that its parts are vibrating and affecting the medium between it and the ear. Not only by the air-pump, but also by observations in the rare atmosphere of the upper regions, it was shown that the intensity of sound depends upon the density. On the top of a mountain the report of a pistol is no louder than that of a cracker in the valley. As to the gradual propagation of sounds, it was impossible to observe fire-arms discharged at a distance without noticing that the flash appears longer before the report in proportion as the distance is greater. The Florentine academicians attempted a determination of the velocity, and found it to be 1148 feet in a second. More accurate and recent experiments made it 1089·42 feet at the freezing-point

*Of sounds; their velocity.*

of water; but the velocity, though independent of the density, increases with the temperature at the rate of 1·14 foot for each degree. For other media the rate is different; for water, about 4687 feet in a second, and in cast-iron about 10½ times greater than in air. All sounds, irrespective of their note or intensity, move at the same velocity, the medium itself being motionless in the mass. No sound can pass through a vacuum. The sudden aerial condensation attending the propagation of a sound gives rise to a momentary evolution of heat, which increases the elasticity of the air, and hence the velocity is higher than 916 feet in a second, otherwise the theoretical rate.

*Acoustic phenomena.* Turning from soniferous media to sounding bodies, it was shown that the difference between acute and grave sounds depends on the frequency of vibration. The ear cannot perceive a sound originating in less than thirty-two vibrations in a second, nor one of more than 24,000. The actual number of vibrations in a given note was counted by means of revolving wheels and other contrivances. I have not space to relate the investigation of many other acoustic facts, the reference of sounds to phases of condensation, and rarefaction in the elastic medium taking place in a normal direction; the affections of note, intensity, quality; the passage in curved lines and around obstacles; the production of sympathetic sounds; nodal points; the effect of reeds; the phenomena of pipes and flutes, and other wind instruments; the various vibrations of solids, as bells; or of membranes, as drums; visible acoustic lines; the reflection of undulations by surfaces of various forms; their interferences, so that, no matter how intense they may be individually, they can be caused to produce silence; nor of whispering galleries, echoes, the nature of articulate sounds, the physiology of the vocal and auditory organs of man, and the construction of speaking machines.

*The ocean; its size.* Like the air, the ocean, which covers three-fourths of the earth's surface, when reduced to a proper standard of measure, loses very much of its imposing aspect. The varnish that covers a twelve-inch globe represents its relative dimension not inadequately.

On the theory of gravitation, the tides of the ocean were ex- *Tides and currents.* plained as depending on the attractive force of the sun and moon. Its currents, in a general manner, are analogous to those of the air. They originate in the disturbing action of solar heat, the temperature of the sea varying from 85° in the torrid zone to the freezing-point as the poles are approached. Its specific gravity at the equator is estimated at 1·028; but this density necessarily varies with the rate at which superficial evaporation takes place; the pure vapour rising, leaves a more concentrated salt solution. The effect is therefore, in some degree, to counteract the expansion of the water by warmth, for the sun-rays, being able to penetrate several feet below the surface, correspondingly raise the temperature of that portion, which expands and becomes lighter; but, simultaneously, surface-evaporation tends to make the water heavier. Notwithstanding this, currents are established through the preponderance of the dilatation, and of them the Gulf Stream is, to us, the most striking example.

The physical action of the sun-rays in occasioning currents *Effects of* operates through the expansion of water, of which warm por- *ocean streams.* tions ascend to the surface, colder portions from beneath setting in to supply their place. These currents, both hot and cold, are affected by the diurnal rotation of the earth, the action being essentially the same as that for the winds. They exert so great an influence as conveyers of heat as to disturb the ordinary climate relation depending on the sun's position. In this way the Gulf Stream, a river of hot water in a sea of cold, as soon as it spreads out on the surface of the Atlantic in higher latitudes, liberates into the air the heat it has brought from the torrid zone; and this, being borne by the south-west wind, which blows in those localities for the greater part of the year to the westerly part of the European continent, raises by many degrees the mean annual temperature; thus not only regulating the distribution of animals and plants, but also influencing human life and its pursuits, making places congenial that would otherwise be inclement, and even facilitating the progress of civilization. Whatever, therefore, can affect the heat, the volume, the velocity, the direction of such a stream, at once produces important consequences in the organic world.

*Physical and chemical relations of water.* The Alexandrian school had attained correct ideas respecting the mechanical properties of water as the type of liquids. This knowledge was, however, altogether lost in Europe for many ages, and not regained until the time of Stevinus and Galileo, who recovered correct views of the nature of pressure, both vertical and oblique, and placed the sciences of hydrostatics and hydrodynamics on proper foundations. The Florentine academicians, from their experiments on water enclosed in a globe of gold, concluded that it is incompressible; an error subsequently corrected, and its compressibility measured. The different states in which it occurs, as ice, water, steam, were shown to depend altogether on the amount of latent heat it contains. Out of these investigations originated the invention of the steam-engine, of which it may be said that it has revolutionized the industry of the world. Soon after the explanation of the cause of its three states followed the great discovery that the opinion of past ages respecting its elementary nature is altogether erroneous. It is not a simple element, but is composed of two ingredients, oxygen and hydrogen, as was rigorously proved by decomposing and forming it. By degrees, more correct views of the nature of evaporation were introduced; gases and vapours were found to coexist in the same space, not because of their mutual solvent power, but because of their individual and independent elasticity. The instantaneous formation of vapours in a vacuum showed that the determining condition is heat, the weight of vapour capable of existing in a given space being proportional to the temperature. More scientific views of the nature of maximum density were obtained, and on these principles was effected the essential improvement of the low-pressure steam-engine—the apparent paradox of condensing the steam without cooling the cylinder.

*Clouds and their nomenclature.* In like manner much light was cast on the meteorological functions of water. It was seen that the diurnal vaporization from the earth depends on the amount of heat received, the vapour rising invisibly in the air till it reaches a region where the temperature is sufficiently low. Their condensation into vesicles of perhaps ṭ...; of an inch in diameter ensues, and of myriads of such globules a cloud is composed. Of clouds, notwithstanding their many forms and aspects, a classification was given,—cirrus, cumulus, strata, etc. It was obvious why some dissolve away and disappear when they encounter warmer or drier spaces, and why others descend as rain. It was shown that the drops cannot be pure, since they come in contact with dust, soluble gases, and organic matter in the air. Sinking into the ground, the water issues forth as springs, contaminated with whatever is in the soil, and finds its way, through streamlets and rivers, back to the sea, and thus the drainage of countries is accomplished. Through such a returning path it comes to the receptacle from which it set out; the heat of the sun raised it from the ocean, the attraction of the earth returns it thereto; and, since the heat-supply is invariable from year to year, the quantity set in motion must be the same. Collateral results of no little importance attend these movements. Every drop of rain falling on the earth disintegrates and disturbs portions of the soil; every stream carries solid matter into the sea. It is the province of geology to estimate the enormous aggregate of detritus, continents washed away and new continents formed, and the face of the earth remodelled and renewed. *The return of water to the sea.*

The artificial decomposition of water constitutes an epoch in chemistry. The European form of this science, in contradistinction to the Arabian, arose from the doctrine of acids and alkalies, and their neutralization. This was about A.D. 1614. It was perceived that the union of bodies is connected with the possession of opposite qualities, and hence was introduced the idea of an attraction of affinity. On this, the discovery of elective attraction followed. Then came the recognition that this attraction is connected with the opposite electrical states, chemistry and electricity approaching each other. A train of splendid discoveries followed; metals were obtained light enough to float in water, and even apparently to accomplish the proverbial impossibility of setting it on fire. In the end it was shown that the chemical force of electricity is directly propor- *Progress of chemistry.*

*Attraction. The elements.* — tional to its absolute quantity. Better views of the nature of chemical attraction were attained, better views of the intrinsic nature of bodies. The old idea of four elements was discarded, as also the Saracenic doctrine of salt, sulphur, and mercury. The elements were multiplied, until at last they numbered more than sixty. Alchemy merged into chemistry through the theory of phlogiston, which accounted for the change that metals undergo when exposed to the fire on the principle that something was driven off from them,—a something that might be restored again by the action of combustible bodies. It is remarkable how adaptive this theory was. It was found to include the cases of combustive operations, the production of acids, the breathing of animals. It maintained its ground even long after the discovery of oxygen gas, of which one of the first names was dephlogisticated air.

*Theory of phlogiston.*

*Introduction of the balance into chemistry.* — But a false theory always contains within itself the germ of its own destruction. The weak point of this was, that when a metal is burnt, the product ought to be lighter than the metal, whereas it proves heavier. At length it was detected that what the metal had gained the surrounding air had lost. This discovery implied that the balance had been resorted to for the determination of weights and for the decision of physical questions. The reintroduction of that instrument,—for, as we have seen, it had ages before been employed by the Saracen philosophers, who used several different forms of it,—marked the epoch when chemistry ceased to be exclusively a science of quality, and became one of quantity.

*Theory of oxygen and the nomenclature.* — On the ruins of the phlogistic theory arose the theory of oxygen, which was sustained with singular ability. Its progress was greatly facilitated by the promulgation of a new nomenclature in conformity to its principles, and of remarkable elegance and power. In the course of time it became necessary, however, to modify the theory, especially by deposing oxygen from the attitude of sovereignty to which it had been elevated, and assigning to it several colleagues, such as chlorine, iodine, etc. The introduction of the balance was also followed by important consequences in theoretical chemistry, among which pre-eminently was the establishment of the laws of combinations of bodies.

Extensive and imposing as is the structure of chemistry, it is very far from its completion. It is so surrounded by the scaffolding its builders are using, it is so deformed with the materials of their work, that its true plan cannot yet be made out. In this respect it is far more backward than astronomy. It has, however, disposed of the idea of the destruction and creation of matter. It accepts without hesitation the doctrine of the imperishability of substance; for, though the aspect of a thing may change through decompositions and recombinations, in which its constituent parts are concerned, every atom continues to exist, and may be recovered by suitable processes, though the entire thing may have seemingly disappeared. A particle of water raised from the sea may ascend invisibly through the air, it may float above us in the cloud, it may fall in the rain-drop, sink into the earth, gush forth again in the fountain, enter the rootlets of a plant, rise up with the sap to the leaves, be there decomposed by the sunlight into its constituent elements, its oxygen and hydrogen; of these and other elements, oils, and acids, and various organic compounds may be made; in these, or in its undecomposed state, it may be received in the food of animals, circulate in their blood, be essentially concerned in acts of intellection executed by the brain, it may be expired in the breath. Though shed in the tear in moments of despair, it may give birth to the rainbow, the emblem of hope. Whatever the course through which it has passed, whatever mutations it has undergone, whatever the force it has submitted to, its elementary constituents endure. Not only have they not been annihilated, they have not even been changed; and in a period of time, long or short, they find their way as water back again to the sea from which they came.

Discoveries in electricity not only made a profound impression on chemistry, they have taken no insignificant share in modifying human opinion on other very interesting subjects. In all ages the lightning had been looked upon with superstitious dread. The thunderbolt had long been feigned to be the especial weapon of Divinity. A like superstitious sentiment had prevailed respecting the northern lights, universally regarded in those countries in which they display themselves as glimpses of the movements of the angelic hosts, the banners and weapons of the armies of Heaven. A great blow against superstition was struck when the physical nature of these phenomena was determined. As to the connection of electrical science with the progress of civilization, what more needs to be said than to allude to the telegraph?

*Theories of electricity.*

It is an illustration of the excellence and fertility of modern methods that the phenomena of the attraction displayed by amber, which had been known and neglected for two thousand years, in one tenth of that time led to surprising results.

*Electrical phenomena.*

First it was shown that there are many other bodies which will act in like manner; then came the invention of the electrical machine, the discovery of electrical repulsion, and the spark; the differences of conductibility in bodies; the two apparent species of electricity, vitreous and resinous; the general law of attraction and repulsion; the wonderful phenomena of the Leyden phial and the electric shock; the demonstration of the identity of lightning and electricity; the means of protecting buildings and ships by rods; the velocity of electric movement—that immense distances can be passed through in an inappreciable time; the theory of one fluid and that of two; the mathematical discussion of all the phenomena, first on one and then on the other of these doctrines; the invention of the torsion balance; the determination that the attractive and repulsive forces follow the law of the inverse squares; the conditions of distribution on conductors; the elucidation of the phenomena of induction. At length, when discovery seemed to be pausing, the facts of galvanism were announced

*Voltaic electricity.*

in Italy. Up to this time it was thought that the most certain sign of the death of an animal was its inability to exhibit muscular contraction, but now it was shown that muscular movements could be excited in those that were dead and even mutilated. Then followed quickly the invention of the Voltaic

*Results of the discovery of Galvani.*

pile. Who could have foreseen that the twiching of a frog's leg in the Italian experiments would establish beyond all question the compound nature of water, separating its constituents from one another? would lead to the deflagration, and dissipation in a vapour, of metals that could hardly be melted in a furnace? would show that the solid earth we tread upon is an oxide? yield new metals light enough to swim upon water, and even seem to set it on fire? produce the most brilliant of all artificial lights, rivalling, if not excelling, in its intolerable splendour, the noontide sun? would occasion a complete revolution in chemistry, compelling that science to accept new ideas, and even a new nomenclature; that it would give us the power of making magnets capable of lifting more than a ton, and cast a light on that riddle of ages, the pointing of the mariner's compass north and south, and explain the mutual attraction or repulsion of magnetic needles? that it would enable us to form exquisitely in metal casts of all kinds of objects of art, and give workmen a means of gilding and silvering without risk to their health? that it would suggest to the evil-disposed the forging of bank-notes, the sophisticating of jewellery, and be invaluable in the uttering of false coinage? that it would carry the messages of commerce and friendship instantaneously across continents or under oceans, and "waft a sigh from Indus to the pole"?

Yet this is only a part of what the Italian experiment, carried out by modern methods, has actually done. Could there be a more brilliant exhibition of their power, a brighter earnest of the future of material philosophy?

As it had been with amber, so with the magnet. Its properties had lain uninvestigated for two thousand years, except in China, where the observation had been made that its qualities may be imparted to steel, and that a little bar or needle so prepared, if floated on the surface of water or otherwise suspended, will point north and south. In that manner the magnet had been applied to the navigation of ships, and in journeys across the trackless deserts. The first European magnetical discovery was that of Columbus, who observed a line of no variation west of the Azores. Then followed the detection of the dip, the demonstration of poles in the needle, and of the law of attraction and repulsion; the magnetic voyage undertaken by the English government; the construction of general variation charts; the observation of diurnal

*Discoveries in magnetism.*

variation; local perturbations; the influence of the Aurora, which affects all the three expressions of magnetical power; the disturbance of the horary motion, simultaneously over thousands of miles, as from Kazan to Paris. In the mean time, the theory of magnetism improved as the facts came out. Its germ was the Cartesian vortices, suggested by the curvilinear forms of iron filings in the vicinity of magnetic poles. The subsequent mathematical discussion was conducted upon the same principles as in the case of electricity.

*Electro-magnetism.* Then came the Danish discovery of the relations of electricity and magnetism, illustrated in England by rotatory motions, and in France adorned by the electrodynamic theory, embracing the action of currents and magnets, magnets and magnets, currents and currents. The generation of magnetism by electricity was after a little delay followed by its converse, the production of electricity by magnetism; and thermoelectric currents, arising from the unequal application or propagation of heat, were rendered serviceable in producing the most sensitive of all thermometers.

*Of light and optics.* The investigation of the nature and properties of light rivals in interest and value that of electricity. What is this agent, light, which clothes the earth with verdure, making animal life possible, extending man's intellectual sphere, bringing to his knowledge the forms and colours of things, and giving him information of the existence of countless myriads of worlds? What is this light, which, in the midst of so many realities, presents him with so many delusive fictions, which rests the coloured bow against the cloud—the bow once said, when men transferred their own motives and actions to the Divinity, to be the weapon of God?

*Optical discoveries.* The first ascertained optical fact was probably the propagation of light in straight lines. The theory of perspective, on which the Alexandrian mathematicians voluminously wrote, implies as much; but, agreeably to the early methods of philosophy, which was inclined to make man the centre of all things, it was supposed that rays are emitted from the eye and proceed outwardly, not that they come from exterior objects and pass through the organ of vision interiorly. Even the great geometer Euclid treated the subject on that erroneous principle; an error corrected by the Arabians. In the mean time the law of reflection had been discovered; that for refraction foiled Alhazen, and was reserved for a European. Among natural optical phenomena the form of the rainbow was accounted for, notwithstanding a general belief in its supernatural origin. Its colours, however, could not be explained until exact ideas of refrangibility, dispersion, and the composition of white light were attained. The reflecting telescope was invented; the recognized possibility of achromatism led to an improvement in the refractor. A little previously the progressive motion of light had been proved, first for reflected light by the eclipses of Jupiter's satellites, then for the direct light of the stars. A true theory of colours originated with the formation of the solar spectrum; that beautiful experiment led to the discovery of irrationality of dispersion and the fixed lines. The phenomena of refraction in the case of Iceland spar were examined, and the law for the ordinary and extraordinary rays given. At the same time the polarization of light by double refraction was discovered. A century later it was followed by polarization by reflection and single refraction, depolarization, irised rings, bright and black crosses in crystals, and unannealed or compressed glass, the connection between optical phenomena and crystalline form, uniaxial crystals giving circular rings and biaxial oval ones, and circular and elliptical polarization. *Colours and white light.*

The beautiful colours of soap-bubbles, at first mixed up with those of striated and dotted surfaces, were traced to their true condition—thickness. The determination of thickness of a film necessary to give a certain colour was the first instance of exceedingly minute measures beautifully executed. These soon became connected with fringes in shadows, and led to ascertaining the length of waves of light.

Meantime more correct ideas respecting vision were obtained. Alhazen's explanation of the use of the retina and lens was adopted. This had been the first truly scientific investigation in physiology. The action of the eye was reduced to that of the camera-obscura described by Da Vinci, and the *Vision; the functions of the eye.*

old notion of rays issuing therefrom finally abandoned. It had held its ground through the deceptive illustration of the magic lantern. Of this instrument the name indicates the popular opinion of its nature. In the stories of necromancers and magicians of the time are to be found traces of applications to which it was insidiously devoted,—the raising of the dead, spectres skipping along the ground or dancing on the walls and chimneys, pendulous images, apparitions in volumes of smoke. These early instruments were the forerunners of many beautiful inventions of later times,—the kaleidoscope, producing its forms of marvellous symmetry; the stereoscope, aided by photography, offering the very embodiment of external scenery; the achromatic and reflecting telescope, to which physical astronomy is so greatly indebted; and the achromatic microscope, now working a revolution in anatomy and physiology.

*Optical instruments.*

In its theory optics has presented a striking contrast to acoustics. Almost from the very beginning it was recognized that sound is not a material substance emitted from the sounding body, but only undulations occurring in the air. For long, optics failed to reach an analogous conclusion. The advancement of the former science has been from the general principle down to the details, that of the latter from the details up to the general principle.

*The undulatory theory.*

That light consists of undulations in an elastic medium was first inferred in 1664. Soon after, reflection, refraction, and double refraction were accounted for on that principle. The slow progress of this theory was doubtless owing to Newton's supremacy. He gave a demonstration in the second book of the 'Principia' (Prop. 42) that such motions must diverge into the unmoved spaces, and carried popular comprehension with him by such illustrations as that we hear sounds though a mountain interpose. It was thought that the undulatory theory was disposed of by such facts as the impossibility of seeing through a crooked pipe, though we can hear through it; or that we cannot look round a corner, though we can listen round one.

The present century finally established it through the discovery of interference, the destruction of the emission theory being inevitable when it was shown that light, interfering under certain circumstances with light, may produce darkness, as sound added to sound may produce silence,—results arising from the action of undulating motion. The difficulties presented by polarization were not only removed, but that class of phenomena were actually made a strong support of the theory. The discovery that two pencils of oppositely polarized light would not interfere, led at once to the theory of transverse vibrations. Great mathematical ability was now required for the treatment of the subject, and the special consideration of many optical problems from this new point of view, as for example, determining the result of transverse vibrations coming into a medium of different density in different directions. As the theory of universal gravitation had formerly done, so now the undulatory theory began to display its power as a physical truth, enabling geometers to foresee results, and to precede the experimenter in conclusions. Among earlier results of the kind was the prediction that both the rays in the biaxial crystal topaz are extraordinary, and that circular polarization might be produced by reflection in a rhomb of glass. The phenomena of depolarization offered no special difficulty; and many new facts, as those of elliptic polarization and conical refraction, have since illustrated the power of the theory.

Light, then, is the result of ethereal undulations impinging on the eye. There exists throughout the universe and among the particles of all bodies an elastic medium, the ether. By reason of the repulsion of its own parts it is uniformly diffused in a vacuum. In the interior of refracting media it exists in a state of less elasticity compared with its density than in *vacuo*. Vibrations communicated to it in free space are propagated through such media by the ether in their interior. The parts of shining bodies vibrate as those of sounding ones, communicating their movement to the ether, and giving rise to waves in it. They produce in us the sensation of light. The slower the vibration, the longer the wave; the more frequent, the shorter. On wave-length colour depends. In all

*The ether and its movements.*

cases the vibrations are transverse. The undulatory movement passes onward at the rate of 192,000 miles in a second. The mean length of a wave of light is 0·0000219 of an inch; an extreme red wave is twice as long as an extreme violet one. The yellow is intermediate. The vibrations which thus occasion light are, at a mean, 555 in the billionth of a second. As with the air, which is motionless when a sound passes through it, the ether is motionless, though traversed by waves of light. That which moves forward is no material substance, but only a form, as the waves seen running along a shaken cord, or the circles that rise and fall, and spread outwardly when a stone is thrown into water. The wave-like form passes onward to the outlying spaces, but the water does not rush forward. And as we may have on the surface of that liquid waves the height of which is insignificant, or those which, as sailors say, are mountains high in storms at sea, their amplitude thus differing, so in the midst of the ether difference of amplitude is manifested to us by difference in the intensity or brilliancy of light.

*The human eye: its capabilities.* The human eye, exquisitely constructed as it is, is nevertheless an imperfect mechanism, being limited in its action. It can only perceive waves of a definite length, as its fellow organ, the ear, can only distinguish a limited range of sounds. It can only take note of vibrations that are transverse, as the ear can only take note of those that are normal. In optics there are two distinct orders of facts,—the actual relations of light itself, and the physiological relations of our organ of vision, with all its limitations and imperfections. Light is altogether the creation of the mind. The ether is one thing, light is another, just as the air is one thing and sound another. The ether is not composed of the colours of light, any more than the atmospheric air consists of musical notes.

*Chemical influence of light.* To the chemical agency of light much attention has in recent times been devoted. Already, in photography, it has furnished us an art which, though yet in its infancy, presents exquisite representations of scenery, past events, the countenances of our friends. In an almost magical way it evokes invisible impressions, and gives duration to fleeting shadows.

Moreover, these chemical influences of light give birth to the whole vegetable world, with all its varied charms of colour, form, and property, and, as we have seen in the last Chapter, on them animal life itself depends.

The conclusions arrived at in optics necessarily entered as fundamental ideas in thermotics, or the science of heat; for radiant heat moves also in straight lines, undergoes reflection, refraction, double refraction, polarization, and hence the theory of transverse vibrations applies to it. Heat is invisible light, as light is visible heat. Correct notions of radiation originated with the Florentine academicians, who used concave mirrors; and, in the cold-ray experiment, masses of ice of five hundred pounds' weight. The refraction of invisible heat was ascertained in consequence of the invention of the thermo-electric pile. Its polarization and depolarization soon followed. Already had been demonstrated the influence of the physical state of radiant surfaces, and that the heat comes also from a little depth beneath them. The felicitous doctrine of exchanges of heat imparted true ideas of the nature of calorific equilibrium and the heating and cooling of bodies, and offered an explanation of many phenomena, as, for instance, the formation of dew. This deposit of moisture occurs after sunset, the more copiously the clearer the sky; it never appears on a cloudy night; it neither ascends from the ground like an exhalation, nor descends like a rain. It shows preferences in its manner of settling, being found on some objects before it is on others. All these singular peculiarities were satisfactorily explained, and another of the mysteries, the unaccountable wonders of the Middle Ages, brought into the attitude of a simple physical fact.

It is impossible, in a limited space, to relate satisfactorily what has been done respecting ignition, the production of light by incandescence, the accurate measurement of the conductibility of bodies, the determination of the expansions of solids, liquids, gases, under increasing temperature, the variations of the same substance at different degrees, the heat of fluidity and elasticity, and specific heat, or to do justice to the great improvements made in all kinds of instruments,—ba-

**Physical instruments.**  lances, thermometers, contrivances for linear and angular measures, telescopes, microscopes, chronometers, aerostats, telegraphs, and machinery generally. The tendency in every direction has been to practical applications. More accurate knowledge implies increasing power, greater wealth, higher virtue. The morality of man is enhanced by the improvement of his intellect and by personal independence. Our age has become rational, industrial, progressive. In its great physical inventions Europe may securely trust. There is nothing more to fear from Arabian invasions or Tartar irruptions. The hordes of Asia could be swept away like chaff before the wind. Let him who would form a correct opinion of the position of man in the present and preceding phases of his progress reflect on the losses of Christendom in Asia and Africa, in spite of all the machinery of an Age of Faith, and the present security of Europe from every barbarian or foreign attack.

**Effect of mechanical inventions.**

From almost any of the branches of industry facts might be presented illustrating the benefits arising from the application of physical discoveries. As an example, I may refer to the cotton manufacture.

**Illustration from the cotton manufacture.**  In a very short time after the mechanical arts were applied to the manufacture of textile fabrics, so great was the improvement that a man could do more work in a day than he had previously done in a year. That manufacture was moreover accompanied by such collateral events as actually overturned the social condition throughout Europe. These were such as the invention of the steam-engine, the canal system, the prodigious developement of the iron manufacture, the locomotive, and railroads; results not due to the placemen and officers to whom that continent had resigned its annals, whose effigies encumber the streets of its cities, but to men in the lower walks of life. The assertion is true that James Watt, the instrument maker, conferred on his native country more solid benefits than all the treaties she ever made and all the battles she ever won. Arkwright was a barber, Harrison a carpenter, Brindley a millwright's apprentice.

By the labours of Paul or of Wyatt, who introduced the

operation of spinning by rollers, a principle perfected by Arkwright; by the rotating carding-engine, first devised by Paul; by the jenny of Highs or Hargreaves; the water-frame; the mule invented by Crompton,—so greatly was the cotton manufacture developed as to demand an entire change in the life of operatives, and hence arose the factory system. At a critical moment was introduced Watt's invention, the steam-engine. His first patent was taken out in 1769, the same year that Arkwright patented spinning by rollers. Watt's improvement chiefly consisted in the use of a separate condenser, and the replacement of atmospheric pressure by that of steam. Still, it was not until more than twenty years that this engine was introduced into factories, and hence it was not, as is sometimes supposed, the cause of their wonderful increase. It came, however, at a fortunate time, nearly coincident with the invention of the dressing-machine by Radcliffe and the power-loom by Cartwright. *[margin: Development of the cotton manufacture in England. The steam-engine of Watt.]*

If the production of textile fabrics received such advantages from mechanics, equally was it favoured by chemistry in the discovery of bleaching by chlorine. To bleach a piece of cotton by the action of the air and the sun required from six to eight months, and a large surface of land must be used as a bleach-field. The value of land in the vicinity of great towns presented an insuperable obstacle to such uses. By chlorine the operation could be completed in the course of a few hours, and in a comparatively small building, the fibre being beautifully and permanently whitened. Nor were the chemical improvements restricted to this. Calico-printing, an art practised many thousand years ago among the Egyptians, was perfected by the operation of printing from cylinders. *[margin: Bleaching by chlorine. Calico-printing by cylinders.]*

It deserves to be remarked that the cotton manufacture was first introduced into Europe by the Arabs. Abderrahman III., A.D. 930, caused it to be commenced in Spain; he also had extensive manufactures of silk and leather, and interested himself much in the culture of the sugar-cane, rice, the mulberry. One of the most valuable Spanish applications of cotton was in the invention of cotton-paper. The Arabs were also the authors of the printing of calicoes by wooden blocks, a great improvement on the old Indian operation of painting by hand.

*Extent of the cotton manufacture.*

We may excuse the enthusiastic literature of the cotton manufacture its boasting, for men had accomplished works that were nearly God-like. Mr. Baines, writing in 1833, states that the length of yarn spun in one year was nearly five thousand millions of miles, sufficient to pass round the earth's circumference more than two hundred thousand times,—sufficient to reach fifty-one times from the earth to the sun. It would encircle the earth's orbit eight and a half times. The wrought fabrics of cotton exported in one year would form a girdle for the globe passing eleven times round the equator, more than sufficient to form a continuous sheet from the earth to the moon. And if this was the case thirty years ago, by what illustrations would it be possible to depict it, now (1859) when the quantity of cotton imported by England alone is more than twelve hundred millions of pounds?

*Improvements in locomotion.*

But such a vast developement in that particular manufacture necessarily implied other improvements, especially in locomotion and the transmission of intelligence. The pedlar's pack, the pack-horse, and the cart became altogether inadequate, and, in succession, were replaced by the canal system of the last century, and by the steamboats and railroads of this.

*Brindley's canals.*

The engineering triumphs of Brindley, whose canals were carried across valleys, over or through mountains, above rivers, excited unbounded admiration in his own times, and yet they were only the precursors of the railway engineering of ours. As it was, the canal system proved to be inadequate to the want, and oaken railways, which had long been used in quarries and coalpits, with the locomotive invented by Murdoch in 1784, were destined to supplant them. It does not fall within

*Stephenson's locomotive.*

my present purpose to relate how the locomotion of the whole civilized world was revolutionized, not by the act of some mighty sovereign or soldier, but by George Stephenson, once a steam-engine stoker, who, by the invention of the tubular boiler and the ingenious device of blowing the chimney instead of the fire, converted the locomotive of the last century, which, at its utmost speed, could only travel seven miles an hour, into the locomotive of this, which can accomplish seventy. I need not dwell on the collateral improvements, the introduction of iron for rails, metallic bridges, tubular bridges, viaducts, and all the prodigies of the existing system of railway engineering.

*The railway system.*

It is not only on account of the gigantic nature of the work it has to execute that the machinery employed in the great manufactures, such as those of cotton and iron, is so worthy of our admiration; improvements as respects the correctness, and even the elegance of its own construction, attract our attention. It has been truly said of steam-engines that they were never properly made until they made themselves. In any machine, the excellence of its performance depends on the accuracy of its construction. Its parts must be made perfectly true, and, to work smoothly, must work without error. To accomplish such conditions taxed to its utmost the mechanical ingenuity of the last century; and, indeed, it was not possible to reach perfect success so long as the hand alone was resorted to. Work executed by the most skilful mechanic could be no more than approximately correct. Not until such machines as the sliding rest and planing engine were introduced could any approach to perfection be made. Improvements of this nature reacted at once on the primary construction of machinery, making it more powerful, more accurate, more durable, and also led to the introduction of greater elegance in its planning or conception, as any one may see who will compare the clumsy, half-wood half-metal machinery of the last century with the light and tasteful constructions of this.

*Improvement in the construction of machinery.*

While thus the inventive class of men were gratifying their mental activity, and following that pursuit which has ever engrossed the energetic in all ages of the world,—the pursuit of riches; for it was quickly perceived that success in this direction was the high-road to wealth, public consideration, and honour,—the realization of riches greater than the wildest expectations of the alchemists, there were silently and in an unobserved manner great social and national results arising. The operative was correct enough in his conclusion that ma-

*Social changes effected by machinery.*

chinery was throwing him out of work, and reflecting persons were right enough in their belief that this extensive introduction of machines was in some way accomplishing a disorganization of the social economy. Doubtless, for the time being, the distress and misery were very severe; men were compelled to starve or to turn to new avocations; families were deprived of their long-accustomed means of support; such must necessarily be the incidents of every great social change, even though it be a change of improvement. Nor was it until the new condition of things had passed through a considerable advance that its political tendency began to be plainly discerned. It was relieving the labourer from the burden of his toil, supplanting manual by mechanical action. In the cotton-mill, which may be looked upon as the embodiment of the new system and its tendencies, the steam-engine down below was doing the drudgery, turning the wheels and executing the labour, while the operatives above, men, women, and children, were engaged in those things the engine could not accomplish,—things requiring observation and intelligent action. Under such a state it was not possible but that a social change should ensue, for relief from corporeal labour is always followed by a disposition for mental activity; and it was not without a certain degree of plausibility that the philanthropist, whose attention was directed to this subject, asserted that the lot of the labouring man was no better than it had been before: he had changed the tyrant, but had not got rid of the tyranny; for the demands of the insatiate, inexorable, untiring steam-engine must be without delay satisfied; the broken thread must be instantly pieced; the iron fingers must receive their new supply; the finished work must be forthwith taken away.

*Life in the mill.*

*Intellectual activity.*

What was thus going on in the mill was a miniature picture of what was going on in the state. Labour was comparatively diminishing, mental activity increasing. Throughout the last century the intellectual advance is most significantly marked, and surprising is the contrast between the beginning and the close. Ideas that once had a living force altogether died away, the whole community offering an exemplification of the fact that the more opportunity men have for reflection the more they will think. Well, then, might those whose interests lay in the perpetuation of former ideas and the ancient order of things look with intolerable apprehension on what was taking place. They saw plainly that this intellectual activity would at last find a political expression, and that a power, daily increasing in intensity, would not fail to make itself felt in the end.

In such things are manifested the essential differences between the Age of Faith and the Age of Reason. In the former, if life was enjoyed in calmness, it was enjoyed in stagnation, in unproductiveness, and in a worthless way. But how different in the latter! Everything is in movement. So many are the changes we witness, even in the course of a very brief period, that no one, though of the largest intellect, or in the most favourable position, can predict the future of only a few years hence. We see that ideas which yesterday served us as a guide die to-day, and will be replaced by others, we know not what, to-morrow. *Difference between past and present ages.*

In this scientific advancement, among the triumphs of which we are living, all the nations of Europe have been engaged. Some, with a venial pride, claim for themselves the glory of having taken the lead. But perhaps each of them, if it might designate the country—alas! not yet a nation—that should occupy the succeeding post of honour, would inscribe Italy on its ballot. It was in Italy that Columbus was born; in Venice, destined one day to be restored to Italy, newspapers were first issued. It was in Italy that the laws of the descent of bodies to the earth and of the equilibrium of fluids were first determined by Galileo. In the cathedral of Pisa that illustrious philosopher watched the swinging of the chandelier, and observing that its vibrations, large and small, were made in equal times, left the house of God, his prayers unsaid, but the pendulum clock reinvented. To the Venetian senators he first showed the satellites of Jupiter, the crescent form of Venus, and, in the garden of Cardinal Baudini, the spots upon the sun. It was in Italy that Sanctorio invented the thermometer; that Torricelli constructed the barometer and demonstrated the pressure of the air. It was there that Castelli laid the foundation of hydraulics and discovered the laws of the flowing of water. There, too, the first Christian astronomical observatory was established, and there Stancari counted the number of vibrations of a string emitting musical notes. There Grimaldi discovered the diffraction of light, and the Florentine academicians showed that dark heat may be reflected by mirrors across space. In our own times Melloni furnished the means of proving that it may be polarized. The first philosophical societies were the Italian; the first botanical garden was established at Pisa; the first classification of plants given by Cæsalpinus. The first geological museum was founded at Verona; the first who cultivated the study of fossil remains were Leonardo da Vinci and Fracasta. The great chemical discoveries of this century were made by instruments which bear the names of Galvani and Volta. Why need I speak of science alone? Who will dispute with that illustrious people the palm of music and painting, of statuary and architecture? The dark cloud which for a thousand years has hung over that beautiful peninsula is fringed with irradiations of light. There is not a department of human knowledge from which Italy has not extracted glory, no art that she has not adorned.

*Causes of her depression.* Notwithstanding the adverse circumstances in which she has been placed, Italy has thus taken no insignificant part in the advancement of science. I may, at the close of a work of which so large a portion has been devoted to the relation of her influences, political and religious, on the rest of Europe, be perhaps excused the expression of a hope that the day is approaching in which she will, with Rome as her capital, take that place in the modern system to which she is entitled. The course of centuries has proved that her ecclesiastical relation with foreign countries is incompatible with her national life. It is that, and that alone, which has been the cause of all her ills. She has asserted a jurisdiction in every other government; the price she has paid is her own unity. The first, the all-important step in her restitution is the reduction of the Papacy to a purely religious element. Her great bishop must no longer be an earthly prince. Rome, in her outcry for the preservation of her temporal possessions, forgets that Christian Europe has made a far greater sacrifice. It has yielded Bethlehem, Gethsemane, Calvary, the Sepulchre, the Mount of the Ascension. That is a sacrifice to which the surrender of the fictitious donations of barbarian kings is not to be compared.

## CHAPTER XXVI.

### CONCLUSION.—THE FUTURE OF EUROPE.

General summary of the work.

A PHILOSOPHICAL principle becomes valuable if it can be used as a guide in the practical purposes of life. The object of this book is to impress upon its reader a conviction that civilization does not proceed in an arbitrary manner or by chance, but that it passes through a determinate succession of stages, and is a developement according to law.

Individual and social life have been considered;

For this purpose, we considered the relations between individual and social life, and showed that they are physiologically inseparable from one another, and that the course of communities bears an unmistakable resemblance to the progress of an individual, and that man is the archetype or exemplar of society.

And the intellectual history of Greece;

We then examined the intellectual history of Greece—a nation offering the best and most complete illustration of the life of humanity. From the beginnings of its mythology in old Indian legends and of its philosophy in Ionia, we saw that it passed through phases like those of the individual to its decrepitude and death in Alexandria.

And the history of Europe.

Then, addressing ourselves to the history of Europe, we found that, if suitably divided into groups of ages, these groups, compared with each other in chronological succession, present a striking resemblance to the successive phases of Greek life, and therefore to that which Greek life resembles—that is to say, individual life.

For the sake of convenience in these descriptions we have

assumed arbitrary epochs, answering to the periods from infancy to maturity. History justifies the assumption of such periods. There is a well-marked difference between the aspect of Europe during its savage and mythologic ages; its changing, and growing, and doubting condition during the Roman republic and the Cæsars; its submissive contentment under the Byzantine and Italian control; the assertion of its manhood, and right of thought, and freedom of action which characterize its present state—a state adorned by great discoveries in science, great inventions in art, additions to the comforts of life, improvements in locomotion, and the communication of intelligence. Science, capital, and machinery conjoined are producing industrial miracles. Colossal projects are undertaken and executed, and the whole globe is literally made the theatre of action of every individual. *The contrasts its ages display.*

Nations, like individuals, are born, proceed through a predestined growth, and die. One comes to its end at an early period and in an untimely way; another, not until it has gained maturity. One is cut off by feebleness in its infancy, another is destroyed by civil disease, another commits political suicide, another lingers in old age. But for every one there is an orderly way of progress to its final term, whatever that term may be.

Now, when we look at the successive phases of individual life, what is it that we find to be their chief characteristic? Intellectual advancement. And we consider maturity to be reached when intellect is at its maximum. The earlier stages are preparatory; they are wholly subordinate to this. *The object of developement is intellect.*

If the anatomist is asked how the human form advances to its highest perfection, he at once disregards all the inferior organs of which it is composed, and answers that it is through provisions in its nervous structure for intellectual improvement; that in succession it passes through stages analogous to those observed in other animals in the ascending scale, but in the end it leaves them far behind, reaching a point to which they never attain. The rise in organic developement measures intellectual dignity. *It is the same in individual life.*

In like manner, the physiologist, considering the vast series *And in the animal series,* of animals now inhabiting the earth with us, ranks them in the order of their intelligence. He shows that their nervous mechanism unfolds itself upon the same plan as that of man, and that, as its advancement in this uniform and predetermined direction is greater, so is the position attained to higher.

*And in the general life of the globe.* The geologist declares that these conclusions hold good in the history of the earth, and that there has been an orderly improvement in intellectual power of the beings that have inhabited it successively. It is manifested by their nervous systems. He affirms that the cycle of transformation through which every man must pass is a miniature representation of the progress of life on the planet. The intention in both cases is the same.

*Succession of automatism, instinct, and intelligence.* The sciences, therefore, join with history in affirming that the great aim of nature is intellectual improvement. They proclaim that the successive stages of every individual, from its earliest rudiment to maturity—the numberless organic beings now living contemporaneously with us, and constituting the animal series—the orderly appearance of that grand succession which, in the slow lapse of time, has emerged,—all these three great lines of the manifestation of life furnish not only evidences, but also proofs of the dominion of law. In all those three lines the general principle is to differentiate instinct from automatism, and then to differentiate intelligence from instinct. In man himself the three distinct modes of life occur in an epochal order through childhood to the most perfect state. And this holding good for the individual, since it is physiologically impossible to separate him from the race, what holds good for the one must also hold good for the other. Hence man is truly the archetype of society. His developement is the model of social progress.

*The object of social developement.* What, then, is the conclusion inculcated by these doctrines as regards the social progress of great communities? It is that all political institutions—imperceptibly or visibly, spontaneously or purposely—should tend to the improvement and organization of national intellect.

The expectation of life in a community, as in an individual, increases in proportion as the artificial condition or laws under which it is living agree with the natural tendency. Existence may be maintained under very adverse circumstances for a season; but, for stability, and duration, and prosperity, there must be a correspondence between the artificial conditions and the natural tendency.

Europe is now entering on its mature phase of life. Each of its nations will attempt its own intellectual organization, and will accomplish it more or less perfectly, as certainly as that bees build combs and fill them with honey. The excellence of the result will altogether turn on the suitability and perfection of the means.

*Application of these principles to Europe.*

There are historical illustrations which throw light upon the working of these principles. Thus, centuries ago, China entered on her Age of Reason, and instinctively commenced the operation of mental organization. What is it that has given to her her wonderful longevity? What is it that ensures the well-being, the prosperity of a population of three hundred and sixty millions—more than one-third of the human race—on a surface not by any means as large as Europe? Not geographical position; for, though the country may in former ages have been safe on the East by reason of the sea, it has been invaded and conquered from the West. Not a docility, want of spirit, or submissiveness of the people, for there have been bloody insurrections. The Chinese empire extends through twenty degrees of latitude; the mean annual temperature of its northern provinces differs from that of the southern by twenty-five degrees of Fahrenheit. Hence, with a wonderful variety in its vegetation, there must be great differences in the types of men inhabiting it. But the principle that lies at the basis of its political system has confronted successfully all these human varieties, and has outlived all revolutions.

*Example offered by China.*

The organization of the national intellect is that principle. A broad foundation is laid in universal education. It is intended that every Chinese shall know how to read and write. The special plan then adopted is that of competitive examinations. The way to public advancement is open to all. Merit, real or supposed, is the only passport to office. Its

*She has organized her public intellect.*

degree determines exclusively social rank. The government is organized on mental qualifications. The imperial constitution is imitated in those of the provinces. Once in three years public examinations are held in each district or county, with a view of ascertaining those who are fit for office. The bachelors, or those who are successful, are triennially sent for renewed examination in the provincial capital before two examiners deputed from the general board of public education. The licentiates thus sifted out now offer themselves for final examination before the imperial board at Pekin. Suitable candidates for vacant posts are thus selected. There is no one who is not liable to such an inquisition. When vacancies occur they are filled from the list of approved men, who are gradually elevated to the highest honours.

*And obtains stability for her institutions.*
It is not because the talented, who, when disappointed, constitute in other countries the most dangerous of all classes, are here provided for, that stability of institutions has been attained, but because the political system approaches to an agreement with that physiological condition which guides all social developement. The intention is to give a dominating control to intellect.

*Imperfection of the method she employs.*
The method through which that result is aimed at is imperfect, and consequently an absolute coincidence between the system and the tendency is not attained, but the stability secured by their approximation is very striking. The method itself is the issue of political forms through which the nation for ages has been passing. Their insufficiency and imperfections are incorporated with and reappear in it.

*Its literary basis inadequate.*
To the practical eye of Europe a political system thus founded on a literary basis appears to be an absurdity. But we must look with respect on anything that one-third of mankind have concluded it best to do, especially since they have consistently adhered to their determination for several thousand years. Forgetting that herein they satisfy an instinct of humanity which every nation, if it lives long enough, must feel, Europe often asserts that it is the competitive system which has brought the Chinese to their present state, and made them a people without any sense of patriotism or honour,

without any faith or vigour. These are the results, not of their system, but of old age. There are octogenarians among us as morose, selfish, and conceited as China.

The want of a clear understanding of our relative position vitiates all our dealings with that ancient empire. The Chinese has heard of our discordant opinions, of our intolerance toward those who differ in ideas from us, of our worship of wealth, and the honour we pay to birth; he has heard that we sometimes commit political power to men who are so little above the animals that they can neither read nor write; that we hold military success in esteem, and regard the profession of arms as the only suitable occupation for a gentleman. It is so long since his ancestors thought and acted in that manner that he justifies himself in regarding us as having scarcely yet emerged from the barbarian stage. On our side, we cherish the delusion that we shall, by precept or by force, convert him to our modes of thought, religious or political, and that we can infuse into his stagnating veins a portion of our enterprise.  *Relative position of Europe and China.*

A reliable account of the present condition of China would be a valuable gift to philosophy, and also to statesmanship. On a former page I have remarked (Vol. I. p. 11) that it demands the highest policy to govern populations living in great differences of latitude. Yet China has not only controlled her climatic strands of people, she has even made them, if not homogeneous, yet so fitted to each other that they all think and labour alike. Europe is inevitably hastening to become what China is. In her we may see what we shall be like when we are old.  *What China has really accomplished.*

A great community, aiming to govern itself by intellect rather than by coercion, is a spectacle worthy of admiration, even though the mode by which it endeavours to accomplish its object is plainly inadequate. Brute force holds communities together as an iron nail binds pieces of wood by the compression it makes—a compression depending on the force with which it has been hammered in. It also holds more tenaciously if a little rusted with age. But intelligence binds like a screw. The things it has to unite must be carefully  *Difference in government by force and intelligence.*

adjusted to its thread. It must be gently turned, not driven, and so it retains the consenting parts firmly together.

Notwithstanding the imperfections of a system founded on such a faulty basis, that great community has accomplished what many consider to be the end of statesmanship. I have already (p. 133 of this volume) quoted the remark of Machiavelli, that, "as to governments, their form is of very little moment, though half-educated people think otherwise. The great end of statesmanship should be permanence, which is worth everything else, being far more valuable than freedom." But permanence is only, in an apparent sense, the object of good statesmanship; progression, in accordance with the natural tendency, is the real one. The successive steps of such a progression follow one another so imperceptibly that there is a delusive appearance of permanence. Man is so constituted that he is never aware of continuous motion. Abrupt variations alone impress his attention.

Forms of government, therefore, are of moment, though not in the manner commonly supposed. Their value increases in proportion as they permit or encourage the natural tendency for developement to be satisfied.

*A similar example in the case of Italy.*
While Asia has thus furnished an example of the effects of a national organization of intellect, Europe, on a smaller scale, has presented an illustration of the same kind. The Papal system opened, in its special circumstances, a way for talent. It maintained an intellectual organization for those who were within its pale, irrespective of wealth or birth. It was no objection that the greatest churchman frequently came from the lowest walks of life. And that organization sustained it in spite of the opposition of external circumstances for several centuries after its supernatural and ostensible basis had completely decayed away.

*Approach of Europe to universal education.*
Whatever may be the facts under which, in the different countries of Europe, such an organization takes place, or the political forms guiding it, the basis it must rest upon is universal, and, if necessary, compulsory education. In the most enlightened places the movement has already nearly reached that point. Already it is an accepted doctrine that the state

has rights in a child as well as its parent, and that it may insist on education; conversely also, that every child has a claim upon the government for good instruction. After providing in the most liberal manner for that, free countries have but one thing more to do for the accomplishment of the rest.

That one thing is to secure intellectual freedom as completely as the rights of property and personal liberty have been already secured. Philosophical opinions and scientific discoveries are entitled to be judged of by their truth, not by their relation to existing interests. The motion of the earth round the sun, the antiquity of the globe, the origin of species, are doctrines which have had to force their way in the manner described in this book, not against philosophical opposition, but opposition of a totally different nature. And yet the interests which resisted them so strenuously have received no damage from their establishment beyond that consequent on the discredit of having so resisted them. *Necessity of intellectual freedom.*

There is no literary crime greater than that of exciting a social, and especially a theological odium against ideas that are purely scientific, none against which the disapproval of every educated man ought to be more strongly expressed. The republic of letters owes it to its own dignity to tolerate no longer offences of that kind.

To such an organization of their national intellect, and to giving it a political control, the countries of Europe are thus rapidly advancing. They are hastening to satisfy their instinctive tendency. The special form in which they will embody their intentions must, of course, depend to a great degree on the political forms under which they have passed their lives, modified by that approach to homogeneousness which arises from increased intercommunication. The canal system, so wonderfully developed in China, exerted no little influence in that respect,—an influence, however, not to be compared with that which must be the result of the railway system of Europe. *The future course of Europe.*

In an all-important particular the prospect of Europe is bright. China is passing through the last stage of civil life *Its hopefulness compared*

2 c 2

[with that of China] in the cheerlessness of Buddhism; Europe approaches it through Christianity. Universal benevolence cannot fail to yield a better fruit than unsocial pride. There is a fairer hope for nations animated by a sincere religious sentiment, who, whatever their political history may have been, have always agreed in this, that they were devout, than for a people who dedicate themselves to a selfish pursuit of material advantages, who have lost all belief in a future, and are living without any God.

I have now come to the end of a work which has occupied me for many years, and which I submit, with many misgivings as to its execution, to the indulgent consideration of the public. These pages will not have been written in vain if the facts they present impress the reader, as they have impressed the author, with a conviction that the civilization of Europe has not taken place fortuitously, but in a definite manner, and under the control of natural law; that the procession of nations does not move forward like a dream, without reason or order, but that there is a predetermined, a solemn march, in which all must join, ever moving, ever resistlessly advancing, encountering and enduring an inevitable succession of events; that individual life and its advancement through successive stages is the model of social life and its secular variations.

I have asserted the control of natural law in the shaping of human affairs—a control not inconsistent with free-will any more than the unavoidable passage of an individual as he advances to maturity and declines in old age is inconsistent with his voluntary actions; that higher law limits our movements to a certain direction, and guides them in a certain way. As the Stoics of old used to say, an acorn may lie torpid in the ground, unable to exert its living force, until it receives warmth, and moisture, and other things needful for its germination; when it grows, it may put forth one bud here and another bud there; the wind may bend one branch, the frost blight another; the innate vitality of the tree may struggle against adverse conditions or luxuriate in those that are congenial; but whatever the circumstances may be, there is an overruling power for ever constraining and modelling it. The acorn can only produce an oak.

The application of this principle to human societies is completely established by a scientific study of their history; and the more extensive and profound that study, the better shall we be able to distinguish the invariable law in the midst of the varying events. But that once thoroughly appreciated, we have gained a philosophical guide for the interpretation of the past acts of nations, and a prophetic monitor of their future, so far as prophecy is possible in human affairs.

391

# INDEX.

Abba Oumma, a distinguished Jewish physician, i. 330.
Abbot Arnold, his sanguinary order at the capture of Beziers, ii. 59.
Abderrahman slain at the battle of Tours, ii. 21.
Abderrahman III., description of the Court of, ii. 31.
Introduces cotton manufacture into Spain, ii. 273.
Abderrahman Sufi improves the photometry of the stars, ii. 41.
Abdallah penetrates Africa as far as Tripoli, i. 323.
Abdalmalek invades Africa, i. 323.
Abdulmalek, his scrupulous integrity in regard to the church of Damascus, i. 327.
Abelard, Peter, his character and doctrines, ii. 10.
Abkah, his temporary success in subjugating Africa, i. 322.
Aboul Wefa discovers the variation of the moon, i. 315.
Abraham Ibn Sahal, obscene character of the songs of, ii. 31.
Absorption of the soul of man, the Veda doctrine of, i. 52.
Abu-Bekr, the successor of Mohammed, and first Khalif, i. 322.
Abul Casem, a Moorish writer of the tenth century on trade and commerce, ii. 42.
Abul Hassan, an Arab astronomer, ii. 40.
Abu Othman, a Moorish writer on zoology, ii. 37.
Acacius, Bishop of Constantinople, excommunicates Felix, the Bishop of Rome, i. 312.

Academies, accusation of heresy against the Italian, ii. 207.
Foundation of modern kurned, ii. 277.
Academy, Old, founded by Plato, i. 163.
Middle, founded by Arcesilaus, i. 163.
New, founded by Carneades, i. 163.
Fourth, founded by Philo of Larissa, i. 101.
Fifth, founded by Antiochus of Ascalon, i. 164.
Acherusian Cave, superstitiously believed to lead to hell, i. 31.
Achilles, spear of, preserved as a relic, i. 49.
Puzzle, advanced by Zeno the Eleatic as one of four arguments against the possibility of motion, i. 117.
Acoustics, discoveries in, and phenomena of, ii. 258.
Adrian, Pope, incurs the displeasure of Charlemagne in consequence of selling his vassals as slaves, i. 362.
Adriatic Sea, North, change of depth in, 29.
Æneas Sylvius becomes Pope Pius II., i. 280.
His remark on the Council of Basle, ii. 97.
On the state of faith, ii. 100.
On Christendom, ii. 100.
Aerial martyrs, account of, i. 114.
Æschylus condemned to death for blasphemy, but saved by his brother Aminias, i. 17.
Æsculapius, the father of Greek medicine, i. 582.
Affinity, first employed in its modern acceptation by Albertus Magnus, ii. 110.

Africa, circumnavigation of, by the ships of Pharaoh Necho, i. 74.
  Conquered by the Arabs, i. 323.
  Effects of the loss of, on Italy, i. 340.
  Circumnavigation of, by Vasco de Gama, ii. 103.
Age of the earth, problem of, ii. 281.
  Proofs of, ii. 323.
Age of Faith, Greek, i. 138.
  Its problems, i. 213.
  European, i. 216.
  In the East, i. 318.
  In the West, i. 330; ii. 1, 20, 75, 102.
  Its literary condition, ii. 124.
  Results of, in England, ii. 222.
  Contrast of, and age of Reason, ii. 377.
Age of Greek decrepitude, i. 200.
Age of Inquiry, European, its solutions, i. 210.
  History of, i. 232, 258.
Age of Reason, European, its problems, i. 213.
  Approach of, ii. 117, 185.
  History of, ii. 245, 284.
Age of Reason, Greek, i. 160.
Ages, duration of Greek, i. 215.
Ages, of life of man, i. 14.
  Of intellectual progress of Europe, i. 11.
  Algazzali's, of life of man, ii. 50.
  Each has its own logic, ii. 187.
Agriculture in a rainless country, i. 81.
Aiznadin, battle of, i. 324.
Air, modern discoveries of the relations of, i. 97.
Aix-la-Chapelle, adorned by Charlemagne, i. 363.
Al Abbas, a Moorish writer on botany, ii. 37.
Alaric, capture of Rome by, i. 291.
Albategnius discovers the motion of the sun's apogee, i. 315.
  Determines the length of the year, ii. 40.
Al Beithar, a Moorish writer on botany, ii. 37.
Albertus Magnus, power imputed to, ii. 112.
  His extensive acquirements, ii. 118.
Alberuni, a Moorish writer on gems, ii. 37.
Albigensian revolt, ii. 142.
Albucasis, a skilful surgeon of Cordova, ii. 38.
Alby, edict of Council of, against the Jewish physicians, ii. 121.
Al-Cawther, river of, mentioned in the Koran, i. 336.
Alchemists, Saracenic, i. 398.

Alchemists, minor, of England, France, and Germany, ii. 151.
Alchemy, theory and object of, i. 395.
Alemanni, Christianized at the beginning of the sixth century, i. 354.
Alexander, Bishop of Constantinople, his controversy with Arius, i. 276.
Alcuin, a Benedictine monk, founded the University of Paris, i. 425.
Alexander II. excommunicates the Bishop of Milan, ii. 10.
Alexander IV., Pope, he endeavours to destroy the "Everlasting Gospel," ii. 78.
Alexander of Aphrodisias, his principles and tendencies, i. 261.
Alexander the Great, his invasion of Persia, i. 166.
  His character, i. 168.
Alexandria, foundation of, i. 167.
  Political state of, i. 195.
  Decline of the school of, i. 199.
  Description of, i. 312.
  Its capture, i. 324.
"Alexiad" of Anna Comnena, ii. 67.
Algazzali, his writings and doctrines, ii. 48.
Alhakem, Khalif, his extensive library, ii. 31.
Alhasen discovers atmospheric refraction, ii. 40.
  Review of, ii. 44.
  His conclusions on the extent of the atmosphere confirmed, ii. 338.
Ali, believed by the Shiites to be an incarnation of God, i. 336.
  His patronage of literature carried out by his successors, ii. 24.
Alturations, employed by Hipparchus in making a register of the stars, i. 197.
Alliacus, Cardinal, the five memoirs of, ii. 246.
Almagest, of Ptolemy, description of i. 197.
  Translated by Averrhoes, ii. 61.
Almaimon, his letter to the Emperor Throphilus, ii. 38.
  Determines the obliquity of the ecliptic, ii. 30.
  Also the size of the earth, ii. 40.
  His accuracy confirmed by the measurements of Fernel, ii. 217.
Almansor patronises learned men irrespective of their religious opinions, i. 325.
Alps, upheaval of, i. 29.
Al-Sirat bridge, spoken of in the Koran, i. 335.

Alwalid I., Khalif, prohibits the use of Greek, i. 328
Amadeus, elected "Pope Felix V.," ii. 100.
Amber brought from the Baltic, i. 44.
Supposed by Thales to possess a living soul, i. 92.
Its electrical power imputed to a soul residing in it, i. 96.
Study of its phenomena has led to important results, ii. 361.
Ambrose of Milan converts St. Augustine, i. 295.
Apology for the impostures practised by, i. 303.
Ambrose Paré lays the foundation of modern surgery, ii. 275.
America, persecutions practised in, ii. 113.
Discovery of, ii. 158.
Where name first occurs, ii. 159.
Crime of Spain in, ii. 182.
Antiquity of its civilization, ii. 184.
America, United States of, separation of Church and State in, ii. 198, 220.
Opportune occurrence of the Revolution, ii. 116.
Culmination of the Reformation in, ii. 220.
American tragedy, ii. 161.
Ammon, St., wonder related of, i. 415.
Ammonius Saccas, reputed author of the doctrines of Neo-Platonism, i. 201.
Amrou, the Mohammedan general, takes Alexandria, i. 323.
Amulets, whence their supposed power derived, i. 302.
Anabaptists, number of, put to death, ii. 220.
Analogy of Greek and Indian philosophy, i. 201.
Analysis, higher, commencement of the, i. 129.
Political dangers of, i. 131.
Anaxagoras condemned to death for impiety, i. 47.
His doctrines, i. 102.
Persecution and death of, i. 100.
Anaximander of Miletus, his doctrines, i. 102.
Originates cosmogony and biology, i. 102.
Anaximenes of Miletus holds the doctrine that air is the first principle, i. 94.
Anchorets, number of, i. 421.
Animals, Veda doctrine of use of, i. 57.
Are localized as well as plants, ii. 298.
Order of succession of, ii. 310.

Animals, cold and hot-blooded, ii. 321.
Characteristics of, ii. 327.
In lower tribes of, the movements are automatic, ii. 337.
Their instinctive and intellectual apparatus, ii. 339.
Their nature, ii. 350.
Analogy between, and Man, ii. 351.
Anselm, Archbishop of Canterbury, takes part in the dispute between the realists and nominalists, ii. 11.
Anthropocentric stage of thought, i. 34.
Ideas, prominence of, i. 61.
Ruin of, ii. 270.
Philosophy, review of, ii. 278.
Anthony, St., a grazing hermit, i. 415.
Delusions of, i. 418.
Antimony, its uses, and origin of its name, ii. 152.
Antiochus of Ascalon, founder of the fourth Academy, ii. 164.
Antiochus, King of Syria, cedes his European possessions to Rome, i. 239.
Antisthenes, founder of the Cynical School, i. 113.
Antonina, wife of Belisarius, her cruel treatment of Sylverius, i. 314.
Antoninus, Marcus Aurelius, Emperor, his acknowledgments to Epictetus, i. 251.
Antonio de Dominis, outrage on the body of, ii. 212.
Apennines, upheaval of, i. 31.
Apocalypse, comments on, ii. 26.
Apollonius Pergæus, the writings of, i. 188.
His geometry underrated by Patricians, i. 360.
Apollonius of Tyana aids in the introduction of Orientalism, i. 201.
Wonders related of, i. 111.
Aquinas, Thomas, a Dominican, the rival of Duns Scotus, ii. 14.
Sojourns with Albertus Magnus, ii. 112.
Arabian, influence, importance of, 373.
Sorcery, i. 379.
School system, ii. 31.
Practical science, ii. 37.
Medicine and surgery, ii. 38.
Astronomy, ii. 39.
Practical art, ii. 41.
Commerce, ii. 42.
Numerals, ii. 47.
Arabs cultivate learning, i. 325.
Rapidity of their intellectual development, i. 326.
Invade Spain, ii. 27.

Arabs, civilisation and refinement of Spanish, ii. 29.
Introduce the manufacture of cotton into Europe, ii. 272.
Invent cotton paper, and the printing of calico by wooden blocks, ii. 173.
Arantius, a distinguished anatomist, ii. 175.
Arcesilaus, founder of the Middle Academy, i. 163.
Archimedes, the writings of, i. 188.
His mechanical inventions held in contempt by Patristicism, i. 300.
Aretinus, his poems held in veneration, i. 42.
Arddha Chiddi, the founder of Buddhism, life of, i. 83.
Argonautic voyage, object of, i. 39.
Its real nature, i. 41.
Ariminium, Council of, i. 280.
Aristarchus attempts to ascertain the sun's distance, i. 194.
Aristippus, the founder of the Cyrenaic School, i. 113.
Aristotle keeps a druggist's shop in Athens, i. 124, 386.
Biography of, i. 170.
His works translated into Arabic, i. 301.
Aristotelism compared with Platonism, i. 172.
Arithmetic, Indian, ii. 30.
Arius, his heresy, i. 276.
His death, i. 278.
Political results of his heresy, i. 316.
Arnold of Brescia, murder of, ii. 24.
Arnold de Villa Nova, biographical sketch of, ii. 120.
Art, Black, i. 313.
Artesian Wells, ii. 200.
Articulata, anatomy of, ii. 338.
Asclepions, effect of the destruction of, i. 376.
Nature and organization of, i. 382.
Asellius discovers the lacteals, ii. 270.
Asoka, King, patronizes Buddhism, i. 94.
Aspasia, history of, significant, 127.
Astrolabe, known to the Saracens, ii. 40.
Astronomical refraction, understood by Alhazen, ii. 44.
Astronomy, primitive, i. 37.
Passes beyond the fetich stage, i. 86.
Of Eratosthenes, i. 193.
How she takes her revenge on the Church, i. 350.
The intellectual impulse makes its attack through, ii. 122.

Astronomy affords illustration of the magnitude and age of the world, ii. 270.
Athanasius rebels against the Emperor Constantine, i. 280.
First introduces monasticism into Italy, i. 121.
Athene, statues of, i. 42.
Athens, her progress in art, i. 127.
Athens, her philosophy, i. 128.
Her fall, ii. 105.
Atlantic, first voyage across, ii. 167.
Atmosphere, height of, determined by Alhazen, ii. 44.
Effects of light on, i. 300.
The phenomena and properties of, i. 355.
Atomic theory, suggested by Democritus, i. 120.
Attalus, King of Pergamus, effect of his bequests to Rome, i. 239.
Attila, king of the Huns, " the scourge of God," invades Africa, i. 340.
Augsburg, Diet of, ii. 205.
Augustine, St., causes Pelagius to be expelled from Africa, i. 291.
Writes the "City of God," i. 292.
Character of that work, i. 294.
Denies the possibility of the Antipodes, i. 303.
His notion of the Virgin, i. 351.
On spontaneous generation, ii. 318.
Auricular confession, introduction of, ii. 63.
" Auricula Fili," Papal bull of, ii. 81.
Australian, how affected by physical circumstances, i. 26.
Avenzoar, a Moorish writer on pharmacy, ii. 37.
Averrhoes, of Cordova, the chief commentator on Aristotle, ii. 37.
His theory of the soul, ii. 188.
Confounded force with the psychical principle, ii. 301.
His erroneous view of man, ii. 315.
Avicenna, the geological views of, i. 310.
A physician and philosopher, ii. 37.
Avignon, Papacy removed to, ii. 83.
Voluptuousness of, ii. 92.
Papacy leaves, i. 93.
Azof, Sea of, dependency of the Mediterranean, i. 57.

Babylonian, extent of, astronomical observations, i. 187.
Astronomy, i. 193.
Captivity ended by Gregory XI., ii. 93.

Bacon, Lord, nature of his philosophy, ii. 360.
Bacon, Roger, titles of his works, ii. 117.
Is the friend of the Pope, ii. 123.
His history and his discoveries, ii. 140.
Baconian philosophy, its principles understood and carried into practice eighteen hundred years before Bacon was born, ii. 170.
Bactrian empire, European ideas transmitted through, i. 43.
Badbee, John, the second English martyr, denies transubstantiation, ii. 161.
Bagdad, Khalifs of, patronise learning, i. 325.
Its university founded by the Khalif Al Raschid, i. 301.
Baghavat Gita, i. 61.
Baines on the extent of the cotton manufacture, ii. 375.
Bajazet, defeats Sigismund, King of Hungary, at the battle of Nicopolis, ii. 102.
"Balance of Wisdom," probably written by Alhazen, ii. 43.
Balboa discovers the Great South Sea, ii. 160.
Ball, John, his preaching an index of the state of the times, ii. 111.
Balthazar Cossa, Pope John XXIII., ii. 95.
Barbarians, Northern, their influence on civilisation in Italy, i. 404.
Barbarossa, Frederick, surrenders Arnold of Brescia to the Church, ii. 24.
Barsumas assists in the murder of the Bishop of Constantinople, i. 283.
Basil Valentine introduces antimony, ii. 160.
Basil, St., Bishop of Cæsarea, founder of the Basilean order of monks, i. 424.
Basle, Council of, i. 99.
Bavarians Christianized, i. 334.
"Beatific Vision," questioned by John XXII., ii. 91.
Beecher introduced the phlogistic theory, ii. 276.
Bechil, the discoverer of phosphorus, i. 379.
Belgrade, taken by Soliman the Magnificent, ii. 104.
Belisarius reconquers Africa, i. 317.
Captures Rome, i. 310.
Benedict, St., miracles related of, i. 423.
Benedictines, their numbers, i. 425.

Benedetto Gaetani, Cardinal, his participation in causing the abdication of Peter Morrone, Celestino V., ii. 77.
Ben Ezra, his numerous acquirements, ii. 110.
Berengar of Tours, opinions of, ii. 9.
Many of his doctrines embraced by Wickliffe, ii. 96.
Berkeley, his doctrine on the existence of matter, i. 221.
Bernard of Clairvaux stimulates the second Crusade, ii. 21.
Bernard, St., attacks Abelard, ii. 10.
Bernardini, Peter, the father of St. Francis, ii. 61.
Bertha, Queen of Kent, assists in the conversion of England to Christianity, i. 355.
Beziers, the capture of, by Abbot Arnold, ii. 60.
Council of, opposes the Jewish physicians, ii. 131.
Bible, translated into Latin by Jerome, i. 290.
Its superiority to the Koran, i. 333.
Translated into English by Wickliffe, ii. 96.
Its character and general circulation, ii. 218.
Biology originates with Anaximander, i. 102.
Birds, migration of, i. 0.
Bishops, rivalries of the three, i. 289.
Their fate, i. 207.
Accusation of House of Commons against the English, ii. 227.
Their reply, ii. 221.
Black Art sprang from Chaldee notions, i. 392.
Black Sea, a dependency of the Mediterranean, i. 27.
Bleaching by chlorine, ii. 373.
Blood admixture, effect of, i. 18.
Degeneration, its effect, ii. 134.
Bodin's, 'De Republica,' i. 0.
Boccacce, obtains a professorship for Leontius Pilatus, ii. 188.
Boethius falls a victim to the wrath of Theodoric, i. 312.
His character, i. 318.
Boilman, Tom, origin of the nickname, ii. 230.
Boniface VIII., Pope, "Benedetto Gaetani," his quarrel with the Colonna, ii. 78.
Boniface of Savoy, Archbishop of Canterbury, his rapacity, ii. 73.

Boniface, an English missionary of the seventh century, i. 356.
Books, longevity of, ii. 195.
Borelli on circular motion, ii. 263.
 Applies mathematics to muscular movement, ii. 277.
Boyle improves the air-pump, ii. 278.
Bradley determines the velocity of direct stellar light, ii. 280.
Brahman, how regarded according to the Institutes of Menu, i. 60.
 Attempted to reconcile ancient traditions with modern philosophical discoveries, ii. 324.
Brain, functions, ii. 310.
Breakspear, Nicholas, afterwards Pope Adrian IV., ii. 21.
Brown, discoverer of the quinary arrangement of flowers, ii. 278.
Brindley, a millwright's apprentice, ii. 372.
 His engineering triumph in the construction of canals, ii. 374.
Bruchion, the library in, i. 307.
Bruno, Giordano, teaches the heliocentric theory, ii. 349.
 Is burnt as a heretic, ii. 250.
Brutes, why supposed by Diogenes to be incapable of thought, i. 97.
Buddhism, its rise, i. 62.
 The organization of, i. 64.
 Its fundamental principle, i. 65.
 Its views of the nature of man, i. 66.
 Philosophical estimate of, i. 68.
Bulgarians converted by a picture, i. 356.
Bunsen, his estimate of Eusebius's chronology, i. 192.
Bunyan, John, his writings surpass those of St. Augustine, i. 295.
 His twelve years' imprisonment for preaching, ii. 235.
 Probable source of much of the machinery of the Pilgrim's Progress, ii. 240.
Burnet's 'Sacred Theory of the Earth,' ii. 277.
Byzantine system adopted in Italy, i. 332.
 Government persecutes the Nestorians and Jews, i. 374.
 Suppression of medicine, i. 375.

Cabanis, quoted on the influence of the Jews, ii. 110.
Cabot, Sebastian, rediscovers Newfoundland, and attempts to find a north-west passage to China, ii. 169.
Cabral discovers Brazil, ii. 161.
Cadesia, effect of the battle of, i. 328.
Cæsalpinus first gives a classification of plants, ii. 378.
Cæsar becomes master of the world, i. 240.
Calico printing, antiquity of the art, and how improved, ii. 373.
Caligula, Emperor, an adept in alchemy, i. 395.
Calixtus III., Pope, issues his fulminations against Halley's comet, ii. 216.
Callimachus, author of a treatise on birds, and a poet, 195.
Callisthenes accompanies Alexander the Great in his campaigns, i. 157.
 Is hanged by his orders; transmits to Aristotle records of astronomical observations, i. 187.
Calvin establishes a new religious sect, ii. 205.
 Causes Servetus to be burnt as a heretic, ii. 219.
Calydonian boar, hide of, preserved as a relic, i. 49.
Cambyses conquers Egypt, i. 75, 180.
Canal of Egypt, reopened by Necho, i. 74.
 A warning from the oracle of Amun causes Necho to stop the construction of, i. 89.
 Cleared again from sand, i. 315.
Canals the precursors of railways, ii. 374.
 Of China, their influence, ii. 387.
Cannibalism of Europe, i. 31.
Canons, some at, the King of Germany seeking pardon of the Pope, ii. 14.
Canons of Epicurus, imperfection of, i. 161.
Cape of Good Hope, doubled by Vasco de Gama, ii. 162.
 First made known in Europe by the Jews, ii. 170.
Caracalla, alluded to in the reply of the Christians to the Pagans, i. 292.
Carat, its derivation and signification, ii. 42.
Carneades, the founder of the New Academy, his doctrines, i. 183.
Carthage, description of, i. 124.
 Its conquest contemplated by Alexander the Great, i. 168.
 Most effectually controlled by invading Africa, i. 237.
 Heraclius contemplates making it the metropolis of the Eastern empire, i. 318.

*Index.* 397

Carthage stormed and destroyed by Hassan, i. 322.
Carthaginian commerce, nature and extent of, i. 105.
"Carolinian Books" published by Charlemagne, against image worship, i. 361.
Caspian and Dead Seas, level of, i. 205.
Castelli assists in the verification of the laws of motion, ii. 262.
   Creates hydrostatics, ii. 270.
   Lays the foundation of hydraulics, ii. 277.
Casuistry, development of, ii. 63.
Catalogue of stars contained in the Almagest of Ptolemy, i. 198.
Catasterisms of Eratosthenes, i. 190.
Catastrophe, insufficiency of a single, ii. 305.
   Doctrine of, ii. 312.
Cato causes Carneades to be expelled from Rome, i. 104.
Celibacy of clergy insisted on by the monks, i. 415.
   Necessity of, ii. 15.
Celt, sorcery of the, i. 32.
Cerebral sight, important religious result of, i. 418.
Cerinthus, his opinion of the nature of Christ, i. 262.
Chadijah, the wife of Mohammed, i. 320, 326.
Chakia Mouni, meaning of the name, i. 63.
   The founder of Buddhism, i. 331.
Chalcedon, Council of, i. 288.
   It determines the relation of the two natures of Christ, i. 290.
Chaldee notions give rise to the black art, i. 393.
Châlons, battle of, i. 310.
Charlemagne, his influence in the conversion of Europe, i. 353.
   Disapproves of idolatry, i. 357.
   Developes the policy of his father Pepin, i. 360.
   Is crowned Emperor of the West, i. 361.
   The immorality of his private life, i. 363.
Charles Martel gains the battle of Tours, i. 358.
   His relations to the Church, i. 359.
   Pope Gregory III. seeks his aid, i. 412.
Charms, the source of their supposed power, i. 392.
Chemistry, fetichism of, i. 90.
   Pythagorean, i. 111.
   Scientific, cultivated by the Arabs, i. 307.

Chemistry, progress of, ii. 361.
Childeric II. permitted to retain his title, i. 358.
   Deposed and shut up in the convent of St. Omer, i. 360.
China, her policy, ii. 343.
Chinese Buddhism, i. 68, 70.
Chosroes II., his successes, i. 318.
   The effect of his wars on commerce, i. 320.
Christian reply to the accusation of the Pagans, i. 292.
Christianity, influence of Roman, i. 231.
   Debased in Rome, i. 256.
   Distinction between, and ecclesiastical organizations, i. 258.
   Its first organization, i. 260.
   Three modifications of, i. 262.
   Judaic, i. 262.
   Gnostic, i. 264.
   Platonic, i. 264.
   Spreads from Syria, i. 265.
   Antagonizes imperialism, i. 266.
   Its persecutions, i. 268.
   Hellenized, i. 281.
   Paganization of, i. 298.
   Expelled from Palestine, Asia Minor, Egypt, and Carthage, i. 321.
   Paganisms of, i 340.
   Allied to art, i. 349.
Chronology of Eratosthenes, i. 192.
Church, Greek and Latin, i. 282.
   Effects of union of, and State, i. 369.
   What she had done, ii. 141.
   Services, their influence on the people, ii. 196.
   Separation of, and State, ii. 220.
Cicero, his opinions and principles, i. 219.
Cimbri, cause of their invasion, i. 29.
Cipher, its derivation and meaning, ii. 80.
   Alluded to by Emperor Otho, ii. 47.
Circle, the quadrature of, treated by Archimedes, i. 189.
Circumnavigation of Africa, why undertaken by the Egyptian Kings, i. 74.
   Its repetition contemplated by Alexander, i. 168.
   Of the earth, ii. 107.
   Results of, ii. 108.
Circumstances, how far man is the creature of, i. 378.
Clement, of Alexandria, his invective against the corruptions of Christianity, i. 318.
Clement V., Pope, takes up his residence at Avignon, ii. 83.
Cleomedes, an astronomer of Alexandria i. 197.

Cleopatra, the last of the Ptolemies, i. 193.
  Is presented with one of the Alexandrian libraries, i. 307.
Clergy, responsible for the massacre at Thessalonica, i. 343.
  Support the delusion of supernaturalism, ii. 101.
  American, ii. 241.
  English, accused by the Commons, ii. 227.
  Discipline Act, ii. 229.
  Degraded condition of the lower, in England, ii. 234.
"Clericis Laicos," bull issued by Pope Boniface, ii. 78.
Clermont, Council of, authorizes the First Crusade, ii. 21.
Climacus, John, author of "Ladder of Paradise," ii. 60.
Climates, in time and place, ii. 306.
Clotilda, Queen of the Franks, counsels her husband Clovis, i. 355.
Clouds and their nomenclature, ii. 300.
Cnidus, medical school of, i. 385.
Coal period, ii. 320.
  Its botany, ii. 320.
Cochlea, its function, i. 5.
Cobham, Lord, executed for heresy and treason, ii. 96.
Coenobitism succeeds Eremitism, i. 421.
Coffee-houses, their political and social importance, ii. 212.
Coinage, its adulteration, i. 244.
Coiter creates pathological anatomy, ii. 276.
Cold, influence of, on man, i. 27.
Colleges founded by the Jews, i. 391; ii. 117.
Colonial system, origin of Greek, i. 123.
Colonies, Greek, necessarily weak, i. 100.
  Philosophical influence of, 123.
Colonnas, their quarrel with Pope Boniface, ii. 78.
Colossus of Rameses II., its great antiquity, i. 83.
Colours of rainbow, ii. 307.
Columban, a missionary of the sixth century, i. 356.
Columbus, his early life, ii. 155.
  Is confuted by the Council of Salamanca, ii. 156.
  His voyage across the Atlantic, ii. 157.
  Discovery of America, ii. 158.
Commerce, development of Mediterranean, i. 43.
  Favourable to the spread of new ideas, i. 122.

Commerce, many of the devices of modern, known to the Carthaginians, i. 128.
Communities, nature of progress of, i. 12.
Comnena, Anna, "Alexiad" of, ii. 67.
Condranya, aqueduct of, ii. 181.
Condillac, his theory of memory and comparison, i. 225.
Canon of Alexandria, i. 188.
Constance, Council of, ii. 90.
Constantine, the Great, the success of his policy, i. 269.
  Influence of the reign of, i. 269.
  Removes the metropolis, i. 270.
  His tendencies to Paganism, i. 271.
  His relations to the Church, i. 272.
  His policy, i. 272.
  Conversion and death, i. 274.
  Attempts to check the Arian controversy, i. 277.
  Denounces Arius as a heretic, i. 278.
Constantine Pope, an usurper, his cruel treatment, i. 307.
Constantine Copronymus, his iconoclastic policy, i. 407.
Constantine Palæologus, the last of the Roman Emperors, ii. 108.
Constantinople, Council of, i. 407.
  Determines that Son and Holy Spirit are equal to the Father, i. 280.
  The seventh general, held at, i. 407.
  Sack of, ii. 64.
  Its literature, ii. 66.
  Siege of, by the Turks, ii. 104.
  Fall of, ii. 105.
Convocation, charges against, ii. 228.
Copais, tunnel of, i. 80.
Copernican system condemned by the Inquisition, ii. 244.
  Theory of, rectified, ii. 239.
Copernicus, the works of, ii. 247.
  His doctrine, ii. 248.
Copronymus the Iconoclast, i. 407.
Cordova, description of, ii. 20.
Corinth, mechanical art reached its perfection in, i. 127.
  Her fall, ii. 105.
Cosmas Indicopleustes, his argument against the sphericity of the earth, ii. 155.
Cosmo de' Medici, ii. 187.
Cosmogony, originates with Anaximander, i. 102.
  Of Anaxagoras, i. 104.
  Of Pythagoras, i. 111.
Cotton manufacture, ii. 372.
Councils, their object and nature, i. 229.
  Are not infallible, i. 287.

Creations and extinctions, cause of, ii. 300.
Criterion of truth, existence of, doubted by Anaxagoras, i. 105.
One of the problems of Greek philosophy, i. 221.
Remarks on, i. 225.
A practical one exists, i. 228.
Criticism, effect of philosophical, i. 44.
Rise of, ii. 185.
Effect of, on literature and religion, ii. 218.
Cross, the true, discovered, i. 292.
Crotona, a Greek colonial city, i. 107.
Its extent, i. 124.
Crusades, origin of, ii. 20.
The first, ii. 21.
Political result of, ii. 22.
In the South of France, ii. 60.
Effect of, ii. 131.
Ctesiphon, the metropolis of Persia, sack of, i. 325.
Cuvier, his doctrine of the permanence of species, ii. 315.
His remark on vivisection, ii. 338.
Cuzco, the metropolis of Peru, description of, ii. 170.
Cycle of life, i. 220.
Cyclopean structures, i. 30.
Cynical school, i. 143.
Cyprian, his complaints against the clergy and confessors, i. 317.
Cyprian, St., his remarks at the Council of Carthage, i. 282.
Cyprus taken by the Saracens, i. 325.
Cyrenaic school, i. 143.
Cyril, St., his acts, i. 310.
An ecclesiastical demagogue, i. 380.

Daillé, his estimate of the Fathers, ii. 219.
Damascus taken, i. 324.
Damascus, riots at the election of, i. 283.
Damiani, Peter, his charges against the priests of Milan, ii. 7.
Death, interstitial, i. 13.
"Defender of Peace," nature of the work, ii. 90.
Deification, John Erigena on, ii. 9.
Deity, anthropomorphic ideas of, in the Koran, i. 342.
Delos, a slave market, i. 238.
Deluges, ancient, i. 24.
Delusions, of the sense, i. 223.
Created by the mind, i. 118.
Demetrius Phalereus, his instructions to collect books, i. 182.
Demetrius Poliorcetes quoted, i. 160.
Democritus asserts the unreliability of knowledge, i. 120.

Descartes, his theory of clear ideas, 224.
Introduces the theory of an ether and vortices, ii. 275.
Desert, influences of the, i. 6.
Destiny, Democritus's opinion of, i. 121.
Stoical doctrine of, i. 172.
Deucalion, deluge of, i. 40.
Dew, the nature of, ii. 371.
Diaphragm of Dicæarchus, i. 191.
Didymus, wonderful taciturnity related of, i. 415.
Diocles, a writer on hygiene and gymnastics, i. 380.
Diocletian, state of things under, 267.
Diogenes of Apollonia develops the doctrines of Anaximenes, i. 85.
Diogenes of Sinope extends the doctrines of Cynicism, i. 144.
Dioscorus, Bishop of Alexandria, deposed by the Council of Chalcedon, i. 288.
Djafar, or Geber, an Arabian chemist, describes nitric acid and aqua regia, i. 348.
Djondesabour, medical college of, founded by the Nestorians and Jews, i. 341.
Patronized by the Khalif Al Raschid, i. 301.
Docetæ, their ideas of the nature of Christ, i. 201.
Dogmatists, their theory of the treatment of disease, i. 388.
Dominic, St., wonders related of, ii. 61.
Dominicans, they oppose Galileo, ii. 251.
Donatists recalled from banishment by Constantine, i. 273.
Drama, an index of national mental condition, ii. 211.
Draper's Physiology quoted, on cerebral sight, i. 119.
On the benefits conferred by the Church, ii. 141.
On the necessity of resorting to anatomy and physiology, ii. 332.
Dreams, Algazzali's view of their nature, ii. 40.
Druids, i. 233.
Du Molay, burnt at the stake, ii. 88.
Duns Scotus, John, a Franciscan monk, the rival of Thomas Aquinas, ii. 14.
Duverney on the sense of hearing, ii. 277.

Ear, i. 5.
Earth, globular form of, implied by the voyage of Columbus, ii. 159.

Earth, globular form of, proved by its shadow in eclipses of the moon, ii. 107.
  Is not the immovable centre of the universe, ii. 216.
  Age of, ii. 268.
  Its slow cooling, ii. 290.
  Mean density of, ii. 291.
  Movement in the crust of, ii. 295.
  Development of life on, ii. 343.
Earthquakes, ii. 291.
Easter, dispute respecting, i. 282.
Ebn Djani, physician to the Sultan Saladin, and author of a work on the medical topography of Alexandria, ii. 120.
Ebionites, their doctrine of our Saviour's lineage, i. 203.
Ebn Junis, a Moorish astronomer, ii. 39.
  Astronomical table of, ii. 41.
Ebn Zohr, competitor of Raschi, ii. 119.
Ecclesiasticism, its decline, ii. 138.
  Its downfall, ii. 274.
Eclipse, solar, predicted by Thales, i. 83.
Ecliptic, discovery of obliquity of, falsely imputed to Anaximenes, i. 85.
  Determined with accuracy by Almaimon, ii. 89.
  Slow process of its secular variation, ii. 294.
Ecstasy, i. 247.
Edessa, church of, re-built by Maowiyah for his Christian subjects, i. 327.
Edward I., of England, compels the clergy to pay taxes, ii. 211.
Egypt, conquest of, by Cambyses, i. 75.
  Antiquity of civilization in, i. 77.
  Pre-historic Life of, i. 77.
  Influence of, on Europe, i. 78.
  Antiquity of its monarchy, i. 80.
  Geological age of, i. 81.
  Geography and topography of, i. 82.
  Roman annexation of, i. 240.
Egyptian ports opened, i. 75.
Theology, i. 84.
Elcano, Sebastian de, the Lieutenant of Magellan, ii. 168.
Eleatic philosophy, i. 113.
  Influence of the school, i. 213.
Electricity, discoveries in, ii. 304.
Electro-magnetism, ii. 304.
Elixir of Life, i. 356.
  Effect of the search for, on medicine, i. 400.
Eloquence, Parliamentary, decline of its power, ii. 138.
Elphinstone, quotation from, i. 61.
Elysium, i. 31.
Emanation, doctrine of, i. 213.

Empedocles, biography of, i. 118.
Empirics, their doctrine, i. 392.
England, conversion of, i. 315.
  Policy of an Italian town gave an impress to its history, ii. 16.
  Its social condition, ii. 222.
  Condition of, at the suppression of the monasteries, ii. 223.
  Backward condition of, ii. 226.
  State of, at the close of the seventeenth century, ii. 241.
Ephesus, Council of, called "Robber Synod," ii. 226.
  Determines that the two natures of Christ make but one person, ii. 280.
Epictetus, his doctrines, i. 251.
Epicureans, modern, i. 162.
Epicurus, the doctrine of, i. 160.
  His irreligion, i. 162.
Epicycles and eccentrics, Hipparchus's theory of, i. 198.
Epochs of individual life, i. 14.
  Of national life, i. 14.
Eratosthenes, the writings and works of, i. 180.
Erasmus becomes alienated from the Reformers, ii. 218.
  Wonderful popularity of his "Colloquies," ii. 231.
Eremitism, its modifications, i. 420.
Eusebius, his contempt of philosophy, i. 304.
Erigena, John, a Pantheist employed by the Archbishop of Rheims, ii. 9.
Essenes, a species of the first hermits among the Jews, i. 112.
Ether, movements of, ii. 369.
Ethical philosophy, i. 138.
  Its secondary analysis, i. 162.
Ethics of Plato, i. 152.
Ethical element, definition of, and conditions of change in, i. 11.
Eucharist, difference of opinion about, ii. 204.
Euclid, of Alexandria, his various works, i. 188.
  His reply to Ptolemy Philadelphus, i. 187.
Euclid, of Megara, an imitator of Socrates, i. 143.
Eugenius IV., Pope, dethroned by the Council of Basle, ii. 121.
Eumenes, King of Pergamus, establishes a second library in Alexandria, i. 207.
Eunapius, his opinion of Plotinus, i. 295.
Eunostos, harbour of, connected by a canal with Lake Mareotis, i. 312.

Euripides tainted with heresy, i. 17.
Europe, description of, i. 22.
  Greatest elevation of, above the sea, i. 22.
  Vertical displacement of, i. 28.
  Conversion of, i. 354.
  Psychical change in, i. 351.
  Social condition of, after Charlemagne, i. 366.
  Barbarism of, ii. 20.
  Future of, ii. 380.
European, climate, modification of Asiatic intruders by, i. 32.
  Old religion, i. 233.
  Priesthood, i. 233.
  Slave-trade, i. 362.
Eusebius perverts chronology, i. 192.
  Is deposed, i. 287.
  His apology for the Fathers, i. 301.
  His chronology subverts that of Manetho and Eratosthenes, i. 348.
  His admission of his own want of truthfulness, i. 349.
Eustachius distinguished by his dissections, ii. 278.
Eutychianism, i. 287.
"Everlasting Gospel," i. 76.
Existence depends on physical conditions, i. 7.
Extinction of species, cause of, i. 7.
Extinctions and creations, law of, ii. 380.
Eye, arranged on refined principles of optics, i. 5.
  Functions of, ii. 357.
  Capabilities of the human, ii. 370.

Fabricius ab Aquapendente discovers the valves in the veins, ii. 276.
Fairies destroyed by tobacco, ii. 122.
Faith, two kinds of, ii. 187.
Fallopius distinguished by his dissections, ii. 275.
Fasting, continued, its effect on the mind, i. 117.
Faustus, his accusation to Augustine, i. 299.
Felix V., Pope, abdicates, ii. 109.
Fernel establishes the true nature of syphilis, ii. 224.
  Measures the size of the earth, ii. 248.
Fetiches supposed a panacea, 376.
Fetichism displaced by star-worship, i. 3.
  Difficulty of early cultivators of philosophy to emerge from, i. 95.
Feudal system, how it originated, i. 365.
Fire, asserted by Heraclitus to be the first principle, i. 99.

Fire, liquid or Greek, used by the Arabs, i. 307.
Fireworks used by the Arabs, i. 307.
Flagellants, their origin, ii. 73.
Flavanus, Bishop of Constantinople, deposed, i. 287.
Florence, the Academy of Athens revived in the Medicean gardens of, ii. 168.
Florentine Academicians erroneously suppose water to be incompressible, ii. 360.
  Originate correct notions of the radiation of heat, ii. 371.
  Show that dark heat may be reflected by mirrors, ii. 378.
Florentius, a priest, attempts to poison St. Benedict, i. 121.
Food, location of animals controlled by, ii. 331.
  Its nature, ii. 330.
Force, animal, its source, ii. 329.
Formosus, Pope, converted the Bulgarians, i. 350.
Forms, contrasted with law, i. 21.
  Introduction of, personified, i. 35.
  Fictitious permanence of, successive, i. 191.
Fracasta, an early cultivator of fossil remains, ii. 378.
Francis, St., his early life, ii. 61.
  Placed by the lowest of his order in the stead of our Saviour, ii. 80.
Franciscans, higher English, their opposition to Pope Boniface, ii. 80.
Franks christianized at the end of the fifth century, i. 354.
Fratricelli, their affirmation, i. 271.
  Burned by the Inquisition for heresy, ii. 76.
Frederick II., Emperor of Germany, birth of, ii. 23.
  His Mohammedan tendencies, ii. 64.
Free trade, its effects, i. 217.
Freewill not inconsistent with the doctrine of law, i. 20.

Galen, his opinions, i. 251.
  His division of physicians into two classes, i. 389.
Galileo, the historical representative of the intellectual impulse, ii. 130.
  Invents the telescope, ii. 252.
  Astronomical discoveries of, ii. 253.
  Is condemned by the Inquisition, ii. 254.
  Publishes 'The System of the World,' ii. 255.

Galileo, his degradation and punishment, ii. 258.
His death, ii. 257.
His three laws of motion, ii. 261.
Rediscovers the mechanical properties of fluids, ii. 300, 377.
Geber, or Djafar, the alchemist, discovers nitric acid and aqua regia, i. 388.
Gelmius, his fearless address to the Emperor, i. 312.
Geminus, an Alexandrian astronomer, i. 157.
Genoa, her commerce, ii. 153.
Genseric, King of the Vandals, invited by Count Boniface into Africa, i. 310.
Invited to Rome, i. 310.
Geocentric theory, its adoption by the Church, ii. 216.
Important result of its abandonment, ii. 324.
Geographical discovery, effects of, i. 42.
Geography, primitive, i. 37.
Its union with the marvellous, i. 40.
Of Ptolemy, i. 158.
End of Patristic, ii. 159.
Geological movements of Asia, i. 28.
Geology, ii. 284.
Evidence furnished by, as to the position of man, ii. 327.
Gepidæ, converted in the fourth century, i. 351.
Gerbert, life of, ii. 3.
His Saracen education, ii. 4.
His ecclesiastical advancement, ii. 5.
Becomes Pope Sylvester II., ii. 6.
Is the first to conceive of a European crusade, ii. 20.
Said to have introduced a knowledge of the Arabic numerals into Europe, ii. 17.
Germans not prone to idolatry, i. 404.
Insist on a reform in the Papacy, ii. 2.
Gesner, Luther's opinion of the manner of his death, ii. 112.
Leads the way to zoology, ii. 275.
Gilbert proposed to determine the longitude by magnetic observations, ii. 163.
Adopts the views of Copernicus, ii. 252.
Publishes his book on the magnet, ii. 275.
Gilbert of Ravenna elected antipope, ii. 14.
Gisella, Queen of Hungary, assists in the conversion of her subjects to Christianity, i. 358.

Glass, its rate of dilatation by heat, ii. 289.
Globes, used by the Saracens, ii. 40.
Gobi, dry climate of, i. 22.
Character of its botany, i. 24.
Was once the bed of a sea, i. 27.
Gold, ancient value of, i. 211.
Potable, attempts to make, i. 388.
Problem of, solved by Djafar, i. 390.
Gotama, the founder of Buddhism, life of, i. 63.
Goths become permanently settled in the Eastern empire, i. 280.
Adopt the Byzantine system, i. 339.
Have possession of Italy, i. 310.
Date of their conversion, i. 354.
Gotschalk, his persecution, ii. 8.
Graaf, a physiologist, i. 277.
Greece, Roman invasion of, i. 239.
Greek mythology, i. 36.
Transformations of, i. 41.
Cause of its destruction, i. 42.
Secession of literary men and philosophers, i. 44.
Movements repeated in Europe, i. 51.
Philosophy, origin of, i. 61.
Summary of, i. 135.
Its four grand topics, i. 216.
Fire, i. 307.
Learning, revival of, ii. 188.
Cause of dislike of, ii. 190.
Gregory II., Pope, defends image-worship, i. 441.
Gregory III., Pope, defies the emperor, i. 412.
Gregory VI., Pope, purchases the Papacy, i. 371.
Gregory VII., his policy, ii. 15.
Gregory IX., Pope, excommunicates Frederick II., i. 65.
Gregory XI., Pope, restores the Papacy to Rome, ii. 63.
Gregory XII., Pope, deposed by the Council of Pisa, ii. 94.
Gregory the Great, his history, i. 345.
Burns the Palatine Library, i. 347.
Attempts to reconvert England, i. 355.
Gregory of Nazianzum, his opinion of Councils, i. 282.
Grew discovers the sexes of plants, ii. 276.
Grimaldi discovers the diffraction of light, ii. 378.
Grostête, Robert, Bishop of Lincoln, the result of his inquiry into the emoluments of foreign ecclesiastics, ii. 53.
Makes a speaking head, ii. 112.

Grotius, his opinion of the Reformation, ii. 210.
Guido, a Benedictine monk, the inventor of the scale of music, i. 425.
Gulf Stream, its influence on the western countries of Europe, i. 24; ii. 352.
Gunpowder, its composition given by Marcus Græcus, i. 327.

Hades, i. 38.
 Origin of the Greek, i. 88.
Hadrian IV., Nicholas Breakspear, ii. 21.
Hallam, his opinion of Leonardo da Vinci quoted, ii. 200.
Halley's comet, how described and regarded, ii. 218.
Hallucination, fasting a frequent cause of, i. 417.
Hannina, the earliest Jewish physician, i. 380.
Haroun, a physician of Alexandria, the first to describe the smallpox, i. 380.
Haroun-al-Raschid, Khalif, sends Charlemagne the keys of our Saviour's sepulchre, i. 362.
 Places all his public schools under John Masué, i. 381.
 Patronizes a medical college and founds a university, i. 381.
 Causes Homer to be translated into Syriac, ii. 38.
Harpalus, employed by Alexander in his scientific undertakings, i. 168.
Harvey discovers the circulation of the blood, ii. 276.
Hasan takes Carthage by storm, i. 322.
Heart, constructed upon the principles of hydraulics, i. 5.
Heat, central, of, over life, i. 8.
 Distribution of, in Europe, i. 25.
 Sources of, i. 62.
 Boundary of organisms by, ii. 208.
 Decline of, in the earth, ii. 307.
 Properties of, ii. 371.
Helena, the mother of Constantine the Great, superintends the building of monumental churches, i. 281.
 The influence she exercised in the religion of the world, i. 355.
 Her benevolence in founding hospitals, i. 375.
 Adopts image-worship, i. 403.
Heliocentric theory, its meaning, ii. 216.
 Resistless spread of, ii. 263.
Heming introduced street-lamps in England, ii. 231.
Henry the Fowler asserts the power of the monarchical principle, i. 255.

Henry V., Emperor of Germany, his resistance to the Popes, ii. 22.
Henry VIII., King of England, had personal reasons for discontent, ii. 210.
 The instrument, not the author, of the revolution, ii. 230.
Heraclitus, his philosophical system, i. 92.
Heraclius, Emperor, resists the second Persian attack, i. 316.
 His contemplated abandonment of Constantinople, i. 318.
 Defeated at the battle of Aisnadin, i. 321.
 The effect on commerce of his long wars, i. 320.
Hercules, legend of, i. 35.
Heresy, Pelagian, i. 281.
 Nestorian, i. 285.
 Eutychian, i. 287.
 Followed the spread of literature, ii. 67.
Heretics, burning of, by the Inquisition, ii. 72.
Hermits, their origin, i. 413.
 Aerial, i. 414.
 Grazing, i. 415.
 Their numbers, i. 421.
Hero, the inventor of the first steam-engine, i. 192.
Herodotus, i. 17.
Herschels, their discoveries, ii. 267.
Hesiod extends the theogony of Homer, i. 41.
Hessians, period of their conversion, i. 355.
Hiero's crown gives origin to hydrostatics, i. 182.
Hieroglyphics, their origin and value, i. 70.
Hilarion, a hermit of the fourth century, i. 413.
 Said to be the first to establish a monastery, i. 420.
Hilary, Bishop of Arles, his contumacy denounced, i. 282.
Hildebrand brought on an ecclesiastical reform, ii. 3.
 His difficulty in reconciling the dogmas of the Church with the suggestions of reason, ii. 12.
 Becomes Pope Gregory VII., ii. 15.
Hindu polytheism, i. 32.
 Philosophy, i. 53.
Hipparchus, the writings of, i. 190.
Hippocrates, his opinion of Democritus, i. 131.
 Review of, i. 382.

Historians, secession of, from the public faith, i. 17.
Hobbes, his philosophical opinions, i. 224.
Holy places, loss of, ii. 130.
Homer, theogony of, extended by Hesiod, i. 11.
Homeromeros, i. 101.
Honorius passes a law against concubinage among the clergy, i. 318.
Honorius III. compels Frederick II. to marry Yolinda de Lusignan, ii. 66.
Hooke, his paper to the Royal Society on circular motion, ii. 263.
 Determines the essential conditions of combustion, ii. 270.
Hormisdas, Pope, policy pursued by, i. 311.
Horner's observation on the rate of the mud deposit of the Nile, i. 81.
Hosius, of Cordova, sent to Alexandria, i. 277.
Houris of Paradise, i. 336.
Humboldt pays a tribute to Eratosthenes, i. 191.
 His remarks on the movement of Jupiter's satellites, ii. 259.
Hume, his doctrine of mind and matter, i. 225.
Huss, John, martyrdom of, ii. 97.
 Adopts the theological views of Wickliffe, ii. 111.
Hydrometer improved by Alhazen, ii. 40.
Hyksos, old empire of Egypt invaded and overthrown by the, i. 72.
Hypatia lectures on philosophy in Alexandria, i. 312.
 Murdered by Cyril, i. 313.
Hypocrisy, organization of, i. 52.

Iamblicus, a wonder-worker, i. 308.
Iconoclasm, i. 363.
Ideal theory, Plato's, i. 147.
 Criticism on, i. 150.
Illiberis, Council of, condemns the worship of images, i. 362.
Images, bleeding and winking, i. 401.
Image-worship resisted by Charlemagne, i. 301.
 Fostered by the Empress Helena, i. 400.
 In the West, i. 401.
"Imitation of Christ," tendency of, ii. 101.
Immortality, double, implied by Plato's doctrine, i. 155.
Impulses, two, against the Church, ii. 127.

Incandescence, the production of light by, ii. 371.
Incarnations, divine, necessary consequence of the belief of, i. 87.
Incas, the ancestors of one of the orders of nobility among the Peruvians, ii. 178.
Incombustible men, i. 397.
Index Expurgatorius, promulgated by Paul IV., ii. 208.
Indian, American, i. 25.
Indo-Germanic invasion, i. 30.
Inductive philosophy founded by Aristotle, i. 171.
Indulgences, nature of, ii. 201.
Innocent I., Pope, settles the Pelagian controversy in favour of the African bishops, i. 285.
Innocent III., Pope, his interference in behalf of temporary political interests, ii. 51.
 His death, ii. 60.
 Prohibits the study of science in the schools of Paris, ii. 71.
Innocent IV., Pope, excommunicates Frederick, ii. 68.
Innocent VIII., Pope, his bull against witchcraft, ii. 113.
Inquisition, its origin, ii. 60.
 Attempts to arrest the intellectual revolt, ii. 72.
 Its sacrifices, ii. 181.
 Its effect on Protestantism in Spain and Italy, ii. 211.
Insane, Diogenes' view of the, i. 97.
Insect, an automatic mechanism, ii. 347.
Institutes of Menu, i. 69.
Intellect, the primal, Anaxagoras's view of, i. 101.
Intellectual class, the true representation of a community, i. 13.
 Despair, ii. 60.
 Impulse makes its attack through astronomy, ii. 121.
 Developement the aim of nature, ii. 317.
Interstitial death, i. 13.
 Creations, ii. 302.
Investiture, the conflict on, ii. 16.
Invisible, localization of the, i. 31.
Ionian philosophy, puerilities of, i. 101.
Irene, the Empress, puts out her son's eyes, i. 363.
 Her superstitious cruelty, i. 401.
Iris, its function, i. 5.
Isis, her worship, i. 182.
Isothermal lines, i. 24, 25.
Israfil, the angel, i. 335.

Italian Christianity, boundaries of, ii. 1.
 System, its movements, ii. 110.
Italy, relations of, ii. 123.
 Degraded state of, ii. 123.
 Immorality of, ii. 132.
 Cause of her degradation, ii. 130.
 Scientific contributions of, ii. 377.
 Causes of her depression, ii. 378.

James I., his proceedings against witchcraft, ii. 111.
Jason, the voyage of, i. 32.
Jaxartes, its drying up, i. 28.
Jerome of Prague, his martyrdom, ii. 98.
Jerome, St., denounces Pelagius, i. 284.
 Translates the Bible into Latin, i. 286.
 His equivocal encomiums on marriage, i. 318, 415.
Jerusalem, position of, i. 74.
 Bishops of, i. 263.
 Church of, i. 282.
 Fall and pillage of, i. 318, 324.
 Capture of, ii. 21.
 Surrender of, to Frederick II., ii. 66.
Jesuits, the Order of, instituted, ii. 211.
 The extent of their influence, ii. 211.
 Causes of their suppression, ii. 216.
Jewish physicians, their writings, ii. 116.
Jewish-Spanish physicians, writings of, ii. 119.
Jews, conversion of, i. 262.
 Are the teachers of the Saracens, i. 373.
 Influence of supernaturalism on the, ii. 110.
 Medical studies among, ii. 117.
 Expulsion of, from France, ii. 122.
 Their geographical knowledge and its results, ii. 170.
John of Damascus takes part in the Iconoclastic dispute, ii. 60.
John, King of England, is excommunicated by Pope Innocent III., ii. 52.
John, Pope, died in prison, i. 343.
John VIII., Pope, pays tribute to the Mohammedans, i. 368.
John XVI., Antipope, cruel and ignominious treatment of, i. 370.
John XXII., Pope, the practical character of his policy, ii. 80.
Joshua ben Nun, a professor at Bagdad, i. 391.
Journalism is gradually supplanting oratory, ii. 108.
Judgment, future, according to the Egyptian theology, i. 87.

Judgment, future, according to the Koran, i. 335.
 Right of individual, asserted by Luther, ii. 203.
Jugurthine War, i. 240.
Julian, Emperor, attempts the restoration of paganism, i. 301.
Justinian closes the philosophical schools in Athens, i. 282.
 His re-conquest of Africa, i. 317.
 Effect of his wars, i. 310.
 Conquers Italy, i. 311.
Justin Martyr, his illustrations of his idea of the divine ray, i. 265.

Kaleidoscope, an optical instrument, ii. 368.
Kaled, the "Sword of God," defeats Heraclius at the battle of Aiznadin, i. 324.
Kalid, a Jewish physician, i. 390.
Kant, his philosophical doctrines, i. 225.
Kempis, Thomas à, author of the "Imitation of Christ," ii. 191.
Kepler, the effect of the discovery of his laws, i. 1.
 His work prohibited by the Inquisition, ii. 251.
 His mode of inquiry, ii. 257.
 Discovery of his laws, ii. 258.
 Cause of his laws, ii. 265.
Kiersi, Council of, quotation from, i. 358.
Kirk's lambs, ferocity of, ii. 230.
Koran, passages from the, i. 321.
 Review of the, i. 334.

Labarum, story of, believed, i. 290.
Lactantius, his argument against the globular form of the earth, i. 301.
"Ladder of Paradise," ii. 56.
Langton, Stephen, Magna Charta originates from his suggestion, ii. 52.
Languages, modern, their effects, ii. 186.
Languedoc, light literature of, ii. 33.
Laplace discovers the cause of the irregularity of the moon's motion, ii. 264.
 On some of the phenomena of the solar system, ii. 272.
Lapland, cause of the contentment and inferiority of, i. 12.
Lateran Council, second, vests the elective power to the Papacy in the Cardinals, ii. 14.
 Third, defines the new basis of the Papal system, ii. 17.
 Fourth, establishes the necessity of auricular confession, ii. 62.

Latin, the use of, as a sacred language, required by the Church, ii. 182.
Lavaur, massacre of, ii. 60.
Law, the world ruled by, I. 19.
   Succession of affairs determined by, i. 379.
   Eternity and universality of, ii. 317.
Lawyers, their agency first recognized, ii. 70.
   Their power antagonistic to the ecclesiastical, ii. 80.
   Their opposition to supernaturalism, ii. 102.
Leaning towers, I. 20.
Leaves of plants, their action, ii. 328.
Legends of Western Saints, i. 423.
Legion, Roman, how constructed, i. 243.
Leibnitz, his doctrine of the mind, i. 224.
   His contribution to geology, ii. 277.
Leif, the first discoverer of America, ii. 159.
Lentulus, spurious letter of, to the Roman senate, i. 350.
Leo III., Pope, crowns Charlemagne in St. Peter's, i. 301.
   Assaulted by the nephews of Adrian, i. 302.
Leo the Chazar continues an Iconoclastic policy, i. 443.
Leo the Great, i. 311.
Leo the Isaurian, the founder of a new dynasty at Constantinople, i. 405.
   Publishes an edict prohibiting the worship of images, i. 400.
Leo X., Pope, exposed to obloquy, ii. 207.
   His character, ii. 202.
   Is reported to have contracted syphilis, ii. 225.
Leontius Pilatus, description of, by Boccaccio, ii. 188.
Lesches, poems of, i. 40.
Levites, their manner of healing, i. 380.
Lewenhoeck discovers spermatozoa, ii. 277.
Liberty not appreciated in India, i. 59.
   Mental, when maintained, ii. 221.
Libraries, Alexandrian, size of, i. 182.
   Establishment of, i. 107.
Licinius neutralizes the policy of Constantine, i. 260.
Life, individual, is of a mixed kind, i. 2.
   Social, its nature, i. 2.
   First opinion of savage, I. 3.
   Variable rapidity of, i. 18.
Light, velocity of motion of, ii. 271, 288.
   Proves the age of the world, ii. 289.
   White, ii. 317.
   Chemical influences of, ii. 370.

Limestone deposited from the sea, ii. 310.
Lipari, the crater of, supposed to be the opening into hell, i. 343, 346.
Lippershey first constructs a telescope, ii. 252.
Lisbon, the great earthquake of, ii. 201.
Listening contrasted with reading, ii. 198.
Lister, author of a synopsis of shells, ii. 276.
   Ascertains the continuity of strata, ii. 277.
Literary men, their influence, ii. 145.
Literature, spread of gay, from Spain, ii. 57.
   Profligate character of, in England, ii. 237.
Lithotomy, new operations for, by the Alexandrian surgeons, i. 188.
Livy, writings of, vindictively pursued by Gregory the Great, i. 317.
Locke, his theory of the sources of ideas, i. 224.
Locomotion, followed by mental development, ii. 116, 132.
   Provisions for, show the social condition of a nation, ii. 231.
Locomotives, invented by Murdock, ii. 371.
Logic, Aristotle's, i. 172.
   Character of mediæval, ii. 108.
   Each age of life has its own, ii. 187.
"Logos," Philo's idea of the, i. 202.
   Justin Martyr's idea of the, i. 263.
Lombards, converted at the beginning of the sixth century, i. 354.
London, condition of, towards the close of the seventeenth century, ii. 231.
Lorenzo de' Medici, his patronage of literature and philosophy, ii. 189.
Loretto, miracle of, ii. 77.
Louis XIV., his order in council punishing sorcery, ii. 111.
Louis, St., his character, ii. 71.
Lucius Apuleius, i. 204.
Lucretius, the irreligious nature of his poem, i. 249.
Luitprand captures Ravenna, i. 410.
Luther, experiences of, ii. 113.
   The revolt of, ii. 144.
   History of, ii. 202.
   Excommunication of, ii. 203.
   Looked upon with contempt by the Italians, ii. 209.
Lyceum, Aristotle founds a school in, i. 171.
Lyons, Council of, ii. 69.

Macaulay, Lord, has taken too limited a view of the Reformation, ii. 243.
Macedonian campaign opens a new world to the Greeks, i. 12.
Its ruinous effects on Greece, i. 166.
Its effect on intellectual progress, i. 181.
Macedonius, Bishop of Constantinople, his heresy, i. 280.
Machiavelli, the principles of, ii. 133.
His 'History of Florence,' ii. 131.
Machinery, social changes effected by, ii. 375.
Magellan, his great voyage, ii. 165.
Magic and necromancy, Plotinus resorts to, i. 208.
Magic lantern, ii. 368.
Magna Charta originates from a suggestion of Stephen Langton, ii. 52.
Magnet, supposed by Thales to have a living soul, i. 86.
Magnetic variation, discovery of the line of, ii. 158.
Erroneously supposed by Columbus to be immovable, ii. 160.
Magnetism, discoveries in, ii. 365.
Maimonides, his life and writings, ii. 120.
Malpighi devotes himself to botany, ii. 276.
Applies the microscope to anatomy, ii. 277.
Man the archetype of society, i. 2.
Controlled by physical agents, i. 9.
Variations of, i. 10.
First form of, according to Anaximander, i. 102.
Nature and development of, i. 226.
His race connections, i. 227.
Apparent position of, on the heliocentric theory, ii. 326.
Marco Polo, ii. 109.
Marcus Græcus gives the composition of gunpowder, i. 397.
Marcotis, Lake, i. 312.
Mariner's compass introduced by the Arabs, ii. 42.
Marozia, her infamy and cruelty, i. 389.
Marriage, compulsory in the time of Augustus, i. 215.
Sinfulness of, according to the principles of the monks, i. 413.
Marsilio, his work 'The Defender of Peace,' ii. 93.
Marsilius Ficinus, the Platonist, ii. 187.
Masud, John, the Nestorian, superintendence of schools entrusted to, by Haroun al Raschid, i. 302, 381; ii. 36.

Matilda, Countess, aids Gregory VII., ii. 16.
Calumniated by the married clergy, ii. 17.
Matter, its indestructibility, ii. 362.
Maximus Tyrius, i. 251.
Maximum of certainty, i. 229.
Max Muller on language, i. 31.
Mayow on respiration, ii. 277.
Mechanical invention, effect of, ii. 373.
Medicine, Byzantine, suppression of, i. 375.
Origin of Greek, i. 382.
Egyptian, i. 386.
Alexandrian, i. 387.
Mediterranean Sea, its dependencies and extent, i. 27.
Propriety of its name, i. 27.
Wonders of, i. 30.
Trade of, ii. 153.
Megaric school, i. 143.
Melissus, of Samos, an Eleatic, i. 118.
Melloni first polarizes light, ii. 378.
Mendicant Orders, establishment of, ii. 60.
Menu, institutes of, i. 50.
Extract from, i. 216.
Metaphysics, Aristotle's, i. 172.
Uncertainty of, ii. 332.
Meteoric stone, boasted prediction of fall of, i. 100.
Mexico, social condition of, ii. 170.
Michael, the stammerer, his incredulity and profanity, i. 409.
Middle Ages, their condition, i. 131.
Migration of birds, i. 8.
Milan, Bishop of, excommunicated, ii. 16.
Milky way, as explained by the Pythagoreans, i. 112.
Mill life, ii. 378.
Milton, his 'Paradise Lost' a Manichæan composition, ii. 237.
In favour of the Copernican system, ii. 252.
Miracle cure, i. 370.
Plays, ii. 234.
Missionaries, Irish and British, i. 358.
Mithridates, King of Pontus, studies poisons and antidotes, i. 388.
Moawiyah, Khalif, sends his lieutenant against Africa, i. 323.
Rebuilds the church of Edessa, i. 327.
Morris, Lake, i. 62.
Moestlin quoted in favour of the Copernican system, ii. 257.
Mohammed subject to delusions, i. 113, 320.

Mohammed, history of, i. 319.
Mohammed II., ii. 101.
Mohammedanism, causes of the spread of, i. 320.
   Popular, i. 331.
   Sects of, i. 338.
   Arrest of, in Western Europe, ii. 28.
   Literature of, ii. 33.
   Uniformly patronized physical science, ii. 117.
Monasteries, condition of Europe at the suppression of, ii. 223.
Monasticism, amelioration of, i. 420.
   Spread of, from Egypt, i. 421.
Monks, African and European, i. 230.
   Labours and successes of, i. 354.
   Their origin and history, i. 412.
   Differences of Eastern and Western, i. 422.
   Their intellectual influence, i. 426.
Monotheism preceded by imperialism, i. 218.
Romm, its boundaries, i. 253.
Montanus, the pretended Paraclete, i. 282.
Moon, variations of, discovered by Aboul Wefa, i. 315.
   Volcanic action in, ii. 293.
Moors boast of an Arab descent, i. 327.
Moral plays, ii. 210.
Moslems, their creed, ii. 35.
Motion, the three laws of, ii. 201.
Muggleton, Lewis, his doctrines, ii. 232.
Murdock invents the locomotive, ii. 274.
Musa completes the conquest of Africa, i. 323.
   Arrested at the head of his army, i. 324.
Museum of Alexandria, i. 181.
   Its studies arranged in four faculties, i. 186.
Music, scale of, invented by Guido, i. 423.
Mycenæ, gate of, i. 20.
Mythology, Greek, origin of, i. 32.

Napier invents and perfects logarithms, ii. 270.
Narses, the eunuch, sent by Justinian against Rome, i. 311.
Nations, progress of, like that of individuals, i. 13.
   Secular variations of, i. 15.
   Death of, i. 16.
   Are only transitional forms, i. 17.
Nearchus, an intimate friend of Alexander the Great, i. 168.
Nebulæ, existence of, ii. 273.
Nebular hypothesis, ii. 272.

Necromancy, Alexandrian, i. 202.
Neo-Platonism, its origin imputed to Ammonius Saccas, i. 204.
Nervous System, general view of, ii. 331.
   Three distinct parts of human, ii. 311.
Nestorians, their origin, i. 288.
   Early cultivate medicine, i. 375.
   Their history and progress, i. 380.
New academy founded by Carneades, i. 163.
Newspapers, their origin, ii. 198.
   When first regularly issued in England, ii. 212.
   Were first issued in Italy, ii. 277.
Newton, quotation from 'Principia' of, i. 117.
   Availed himself of the doctrines of Hipparchus, ii. 197.
   Under no obligation to Bacon, ii. 251.
   Publication of the 'Principia' of, ii. 263.
   His mathematical learning and experimental skill, ii. 270.
Niagara Falls furnish proof of time from effect produced, ii. 295.
   Prove the enormous age of the earth, ii. 323.
Nicæa, Council of, summoned by Constantine, i. 277.
   Second council of, summoned by Irene, i. 418.
Nicene Creed, i. 278.
Nicholas V. a patron of art, ii. 107.
Nicomedia, church of, destroyed, i. 263.
Niebuhr, his opinion of the Greek account of the Persian war, i. 126.
Nile, inundations of, i. 82.
Nirvana, the end of successive existences in the Buddhist doctrine, i. 67, 222.
Nitria, why well adapted for monks, i. 421.
Nogaret, William de, the legal adviser of Boniface, ii. 81.
   Advises King Philip the Fair, ii. 88.
Nomades, Asiatic, i. 23.
Nominalism, doctrine of, sprang from scholastic philosophy, ii. 11.
Norman invasion of England favoured by Pope Gregory VII., ii. 16.
Norway, depth of rain in, i. 21.
   Elevation and depression in level of, ii. 286.
Norwegians, diet of, accounted for, i. 26.
Novatus the heretic, i. 275.
Numa introduces Pythagorean rites among the Romans, i. 109.

Number the first principle according to the Pythagorean philosophy, i. 101.
Numenius, a Trinitarian, i. 204.
Numerals, Arabic, derived from the Hindus, ii. 30.
　Introduced into different countries, ii. 47.

Oaks, objects of adoration among the German nations, i. 211.
Obelisks, Egyptian, prodigious height of, i. 72.
Observatories first introduced into Europe by the Arabs, ii. 40.
Ocean, its size, ii. 358.
Octave, the grand standard of harmonical relation among the Pythagoreans, i. 112.
Oliva, John Peter, his comment on the Apocalypse, ii. 76.
Olympian duties, their nature, i. 48.
Omar, Khalif, takes Jerusalem, i. 324.
　His behaviour contrasted with that of the Crusaders, ii. 22.
Opinion and Reason, Parmenides's work on, i. 110.
Optics, discoveries in, ii. 360.
Oratory supplanted by journalism, ii. 194.
Orchomenos, ruins of, i. 30.
Orders, monastic, rise and progress of, i. 421.
Orestes compelled to interfere to stop a riot in Alexandria, i. 311.
Organ, the, invented by Sylvester, a Benedictine monk, i. 425.
Organisms, permanence of, due to external conditions, i. 8.
　Control of physical agents over, i. 9.
　Dates of various, ii. 311.
Orpheus, legend of, i. 35.
Osiris, daily ceremony before tomb of, i. 85.
　One of the divinities of the Egyptian theology, i. 86.
　Site of temple of, given to the church, i. 304.
Osporco changes his unseemly name into Sergius, ii. 139.
Ostrogoth monarchy overthrown, i. 311.
Otho III., Emperor, contemplates a reform in the Church, and is poisoned by Stephania, ii. 6.
Otranto taken by the Mohammedans, ii. 103.
Otto, Guericke, invented the air-pump, ii. 276.
Oxus, its drying up, i. 29.

Pacific Ocean crossed, ii. 166.
Paganism, attitude of, i. 260.
　Death-blow given to, by Theodosius, i. 302.
Pagans, accusation of, against the Christians, i. 301.
Painting and sculpture, relation of the Church to, i. 350.
Palæontology, historical sketch of early, ii. 304.
Palatine library burnt by Gregory the Great, i. 317.
Pandataria, Sylverius banished to, i. 344.
Pantheism, theology of, India overlaid with, i. 58.
　Adopted by Parmenides, i. 110.
　Greek, i. 217.
Papacy, history of, i. 281.
　Consolidation of its power in the West, i. 351.
　Signal peculiarity of, i. 367.
　Human origin of, i. 372.
Paper, invention of, ii. 195.
Pappus, an Alexandrian geometrician, i. 199.
Parabolani diverted from their original intent by Cyril, i. 311, 375.
"Paraclete," doctrines of faith discussed in the, ii. 10.
Paradise spoken of with clearness by Mohammed, i. 332.
Parliament, its accusation against the clergy, ii. 227.
Parma, John of, the General of the Franciscans, ii. 75.
Parmenides, doctrines of, i. 110.
Pascal, his views of humanity, ii. 17.
　The influence of his writings, ii. 270.
Path-zone, i. 22.
Patricians, introduction of, i. 303.
　Doctrines of, i. 305.
　Conflict of, with philosophy, i. 306.
　Decline of, ii. 125.
　End of geography of, ii. 159.
　Ethnical ideas of, ii. 160.
　End of, ii. 210.
Paulus Æmilius, his severity, i. 211.
Pausanias, i. 126.
Pelagian controversy, its effect on Papal superiority, i. 281.
Pelagius, his doctrines, i. 281, 355.
Peruncci, the Veda doctrine of, i. 57.
Pendulum first applied to clocks by the Moors, ii. 40.
Pepin, the son of Charles Martel, i. 359.
Pergamus, library of, transferred to Egypt, i. 207.
Pericles embraces obnoxious opinions, i. 18.

Pericles, his the age of improvement in architecture and oratory, i. 127.
Perictione, the reputed mother of Plato, i. 110.
Periodicities, human cause of, i. 8.
Peripatetics, their philosophy, i. 173.
Persecutions, moral effects of, ii. 219.
Persepolis, burning of, by Alexander the Great, i. 168.
Perses, revolt of, i. 239.
Persia, Greek invasion of, i. 106. Subdued by Othman III., i. 325.
Persian invasion of Europe, i. 125. Attack on the Byzantine system, i. 318.
Personified forms introduced, i. 35.
Perturbations, astronomical, accounted for, ii. 265.
Peru, its coast a rainless district, i. 82. A description of, ii. 174.
Peter d'Apono, the alchemist, the wonders imputed to him, ii. 112.
Peter de Bruçys, his martyrdom, ii. 58.
Peter the Hermit, ii. 21, 131.
Peter Morrone becomes Celestine V., i. 77.
Peter the Venerable, his acquirements, ii. 11.
Peter's pence, ii. 52.
Petrarch, his opinion of Avignon, ii. 82. His zeal for learning, ii. 180.
Pharaoh Necho, his ships first double the Cape of Good Hope, ii. 162.
Philadelphus Ptolemy, i. 181.
Philæ, mysterious temple of, i. 85.
Philip the Fair protects the Colonnas, ii. 78.
Philiston, a writer on regimen, i. 366.
Philo the Jew thinks he is inspired, i. 203.
Compares the mind to the eye, i. 227.
Philo of Larissa, founder of the fifth academy, i. 194.
Philosopher's stone, i. 396.
Philosophers, persecution of, i. 301. The revolt of, ii. 145.
Philosophical criticism, effect of, i. 44. Schools, Indian, i. 62. Principles, application of, i. 230.
Philosophy, peripatetic, i. 173. Greek, end and summary of, i. 210. Greek and Indian, the analogy between, i. 229. Reappearance of, ii. 2.
Phlogiston, theory of, ii. 302.
Phoceans built Marseilles, i. 41.
Phocas quoted on Constantinople, ii. 50.
Phœnicians, enterprise of, i. 43.

Phosphorus discovered by Achild Bechil, i. 359.
Photius, his two works, ii. 56.
Photography, ii. 370.
Physical instruments, improvements in, ii. 372.
Physicians, classes of, i. 386. Jewish, i. 389. Oppose supernaturalism, ii. 109. Are disliked by the Church, ii. 117.
Physics of Zeno, i. 178.
Physiology, its phases the same as those of physics, i. 8. Of Plato, i. 151. Of Aristotle, i. 155.
Piccolomini lays the foundation of general anatomy, ii. 278.
Pietro de Vinea undertakes to poison Frederick II., ii. 69.
Pinzons, of Palos, assist Columbus, ii. 157.
Pisa, Council of, deposes the rival Popes, ii. 91. The first botanical gardens established at, ii. 278.
Plagues, mortality of ancient, i. 212.
Plants, effect of seasons on, i. 8. Their dependence on the air, i. 98; ii. 323.
Plateas, fabulous number slain at battle of, i. 125.
Plater first classified diseases, ii. 275.
Plato, his profound knowledge of human nature, i. 50. His doctrines, i. 148.
Platonism, Plutarch leans to, i. 204. Reappearance of, in Europe, ii. 187.
Plays, miracle, moral, real, ii. 210.
Pleiades, a nickname given to seven Alexandrian poets, i. 195.
Plotinus, writings of, i. 205, 322.
Plutarch leans to platonizing Orientalism, i. 204.
Poggio Bracciolini quoted, ii. 98.
Polarization of light lends support to the undulatory theory, ii. 369.
Pole star, ii. 271.
Polycrates, Bishop of Ephesus, opposes Victor, Bishop of Rome, i. 282.
Polygamy, institutions of, i. 321. Secured the conquest of Africa, i. 321. Its influence in consolidating the conquests of Mohammedanism, i. 322.
Polytheism, its antagonism to science, i. 40. Slowness of its decline, i. 40.
Pontifical power sustained by physical force, i. 280.

Popes, biography of, i. 367.
  Had no faith in the result of the Crusades, ii. 22.
Porphyry, his writings, i. 297, 392.
Porsenna takes Rome, i. 237.
Posidonius, i. 228.
Praxagoras wrote on the pulse, i. 386.
Pre-existence, Plato's notion of, i. 154.
Press, liberty of, secured, ii. 242.
"Principia," Newton's, quotation from, i. 115.
  Publication of, ii. 263.
  Its incomparable merit, ii. 267.
Printing, invention of, ii. 102.
  Effects of, ii. 104.
Problems of Greek philosophy, i. 210.
Proclus burns Vitalian's ships, i. 208.
  His theology, i. 201.
Procopius, the historian, secretary to Bellsarius, ii. 56.
Profatius, a Jew, appointed regent of the faculty of Montpellier, ii. 121.
Prosper Albinus writes on diagnosis, ii. 275.
Protestant, origin of the name, ii. 205.
Provincial letters of Pascal, influence of, ii. 270.
Psammetichus overthrows the ancient policy of Egypt, i. 71.
"Psammites," a work of Archimedes, i. 189.
Psychology, origin of, i. 97.
  Solution of questions of, ii. 332.
Ptolemies, political position of, i. 180.
  Biography of, i. 194.
Ptolemy, his "Syntaxis," i. 197.
Puffendorf, author of the "Law of Nature and Nations," ii. 270.
Pulpit, influence of, affected by the press, ii. 190.
  Decline of eloquence of, ii. 108.
  Its relation to the drama, ii. 211.
  State of, an index of the mental condition of a nation, ii. 241.
Punic wars, results of, i. 238.
Puranas, i. 61.
Pyramids of Egypt, size of, i. 72.
  The Great, its antiquity and wonders, i. 77.
  What they have witnessed, i. 80.
  Their testimony unreliable as to the age of the world, ii. 316.
Pyrrho, the founder of the Sceptics, i. 158.
Pyrrhus, the Epirot, i. 237.
Pythagoras, biography of, i. 100.
  The service he rendered us, i. 224.

Quintus Sextius, i. 250.

Quipus, a Peruvian instrument for enumeration, ii. 180.
Quito, why it was regarded as a holy place, ii. 189.

Rab, a Jewish anatomist, i. 389.
Rabanus, a Benedictine monk, sets up a school in Germany, i. 425.
Rabbis cultivate medicine, ii. 118.
Radbert, his views on transubstantiation, ii. 10.
Railways, ii. 375.
Rain, quantity of, in Europe, i. 21.
  Maximum points of, i. 21.
Rainless countries, agriculture in, i. 81.
  Of the West, i. 82.
  Peru one, ii. 171.
Rainless days, number of, i. 24.
  Influence of, i. 26.
Rameses II., his policy, i. 71.
Raschi, his varied acquirements, ii. 119.
Ravenna, Gerbert appointed Archbishop of, ii. 6.
Ray leads the way to comparative anatomy, ii. 278.
Raymond Lully, said to have been compelled to make gold for Edward II., ii. 131.
Raymond de Pennaforte compiles a lie of Decretals, ii. 67.
Reading, its advantage over listening, ii. 108.
Realism, its origin, ii. 11.
Reason, Algazzali's doctrine of the unreliability of, ii. 49.
Reductio ad absurdum introduced by Zeno, i. 117.
Reflection, Democritus's view of, 120.
Reflex action, ii. 336.
Reformation attempted in Greece, i. 48.
  Influences leading to, ii. 185.
  Dawn of the, ii. 199.
  In Switzerland, ii. 201.
  Organization of, ii. 205.
  In Italy, ii. 200.
  Arrest of, ii. 208.
  Counter, ii. 213.
  Culmination of, in America, ii. 220.
Relics, age of, i. 40.
  Worship of, i. 402.
Reminiscence, Plato's doctrine of, i. 148.
Republic of Plato, i. 153.
Revolution, French, ii. 145.
Rhacotis, Alexandria erected on the site of, i. 186.
Rhazes discovers sulphuric acid, i. 300.
Rhazes, a Moorish writer on botany, ii. 37.

Rheims, Gerbert appointed Archbishop of, ii. 5.
Rhodes raised from the sea, i. 29.
Rhodians, maritime code of, i. 43.
Richard I., of England, treacherously imprisoned, ii. 25.
His treatment by Saladin contrasted with that he received from a Christian prince, ii. 131.
Rienzi, a demagogue, ii. 92.
Rig Veda, asserted to have been revealed by Brahma, i. 55.
"Robber Synod," the Council of Ephesus, i. 287.
Roderic, King of the Goths, ii. 27.
Roderigo de Triana, the first of Columbus's crew to descry land, ii. 158.
Roman power, influence of, i. 62.
Christianity, influence of, on the people, i. 234.
History, importance of, i. 221.
Power, triple form of, i. 235.
First theocracy and legends, i. 236.
History, early, i. 236.
Slave laws, atrocity of, i. 241.
Slave system, social effects of, 242.
Depravity, i. 244.
Women, their dissoluteness, i. 245.
Ethnical element disappears, i. 247.
Conquest, effects of, i. 248.
Rome, cause of permanence of, i. 11.
Unpitying tyranny of, i. 259.
Fall and sack of, by Alaric, i. 291.
Fall and pillage of, by the Vandals, i. 340.
Progress of, to supremacy, i. 311.
Relations of, to Constantinople, i. 342.
Three pressures upon, ii. 1.
Pillaged, sacked, and fired by Henry, ii. 10.
Immoralities of, brought to light by the Crusades, ii. 132.
Its geological peculiarities, ii. 297.
Römer, his estimate of the velocity of light confirmed, ii. 280.
Roscelin of Compiègne, an early advocate of Nominalism, ii. 11.
Ruysch improves minute anatomy, ii. 277.

Sacramentarians separate from the Lutherans, ii. 215.
Sahara Desert affects the distribution of heat in Europe, i. 23.
Saladin retakes Jerusalem, ii. 25.
His noble behaviour to Richard I., ii. 131.
Salamanca, Columbus confuted by the Council of, ii. 156.

Salamanca, Council of, its reply when urged to teach physical science, ii. 269.
Sampson, Agnes, burnt for witchcraft, ii. 114.
Samuel, an accomplished Jewish physician, i. 389.
Sanctorio lays the foundation of modern physiology, ii. 276.
Invents the thermometer, ii. 277.
Sanscrit vocabulary, i. 31.
Saracens, their policy, i. 326.
Cause of their check in the conquest of France, i. 358.
Are taught by the Nestorians and Jews, i. 373.
They dominate in the Mediterranean, i. 411.
Their chemistry, medicine, and surgery, ii. 38.
Their philosophy, ii. 48.
Early cultivators of astronomy, ii. 150.
Sardica, council of, i. 281.
Satan, notion of, had become debased, i. 103.
Santree, William, the first English martyr, ii. 98.
Saviour, in Koran never called Son of God, i. 312.
Model of, eventually received, i. 350.
Scandinavian geological motion, i. 29.
Discovery of America, ii. 159, 170.
Sceptics, rise of, i. 158.
Schism, causes of the great, ii. 93.
Scholastic philosophy, rise of, ii. 11.
Theology, rise of, ii. 12.
Schools, philosophical Greek, merely points of reunion, i. 107.
The Megaric, Cyrenaic, and Cynical, i. 112.
Science, Alexandrian, suppressed, i. 311.
Sculpture, relation of Church to, i. 354.
Sea of Azof, a dependency of the Mediterranean, i. 27.
Seasons, effect of, on animals and plants, i. 6.
Sebastian de Elcano, the lieutenant of Magellan, ii. 168.
Secular, geological movement of Europe and Asia, i. 27.
Inequalities of satellites, ii. 268.
Semicircular canals, their function, i. 5.
Seneca, the influence of his writings accounted for, i. 250.
Sens, Council of, report of, to Rome, ii. 10.
Sensation, Democritus confounds it with thought, i. 120.

Senses, Algazzali's doctrine of the unreliability of, ii. 41.
Septuagint Bible, the translators of, entertained by Ptolemy Philadelphus, i. 144.
Serapion, causes of its umbrage to Archbishop Theophilus, i. 298.
Destruction of, i. 300.
Serapis, establishment of the worship of, i. 182.
Description of the temple of, i. 308.
Statue of, destroyed, i. 300.
Temple of, used for a hospital, i. 388.
Servetus, the burning of, by Calvin, ii. 219.
Almost detected the circulation of the blood, ii. 276.
Servile rebellion in Sicily, i. 240.
Seville, tower of, an observatory built by the Arabs, ii. 40.
Shakspeare, quotation from, i. 201.
His position with regard to English literature, ii. 241.
Shepherds, the, their exertions in behalf of King Louis, ii. 75.
Shiites, one of the seventy-three Mohammedan sects, i. 336.
Sigismund, Emperor, his treacherous conduct to John Huss, ii. 98.
Silver, its comparative value in Rome, i. 244.
Simon Magus, an Oriental magician, wonders related of, ii. 111.
Simony, organization of, ii. 94.
Sirius, its supposed influence on the waters of the Nile, i. 86.
Slave system, Roman, i. 241.
Slavery under Charlemagne, i. 302.
Recognized in certain cases in Mexico, ii. 171.
Slavians converted by Greek missionaries, i. 356.
Smyrna, Erasistratus established a school there, i. 388.
Snow, distribution of, in Europe, i. 25.
Snowy days, number of, at various places, i. 25.
Social war, important results of, i. 240.
Eminence, no preservative from social delusion, ii. 111.
Society, the intellectual class the true representative of a community, i. 13.
Sociology, comparative, ii. 317.
Socrates, Aristophanes excites the people against, i. 15.
His mode of teaching, and his doctrines, i. 138.
Character of, Athens, i. 141.
"The Mad," i. 115.

Solar system proves the existence of law, i. 4.
Soliman the Magnificent takes Belgrade, ii. 105.
Sonnites, one of the seventy-three Mohammedan sects, i. 336.
Sopater accused of magic, and decapitated, i. 300.
Sophists, their doctrines, i. 130.
Their influence, i. 213.
Sorcery, intermingling of magic and, i. 301.
Introduction of European, ii. 112.
Soul, Indian ideas of the, i. 66.
Purification of, i. 68.
Diogenes's opinion of that of the world, i. 95.
Plato's doctrine of the triple constitution of, i. 150.
Greek problem as to the nature of, i. 213.
As to the immortality and absorption of, i. 221.
The human, ii. 352.
Sound, nature and properties of, ii. 357.
Spain, Roman annexation of, i. 239.
Arab invasion of, ii. 27.
Literature of, ii. 34.
Crimes of, ii. 102.
Sparta, Lycurgus abolished private property in, i. 124.
Spartacus, the gladiator, i. 240.
Species, Cuvier's doctrine of the permanence of, ii. 315.
Opposition to the doctrine of transmutation of, ii. 317.
Specific gravity, Alhazen's tables of, closely approach our own, ii. 46.
Sphærus, the Stoic, fraud practised on, i. 184.
Spheres, music of, a belief entertained by the Pythagoreans, i. 112.
Sphinxes, one of the wonders of ancient Egypt, i. 72.
Spinal cord, its separate and conjoint action, ii. 340.
Spires, first Diet of, ii. 205.
Spirit, in chemistry, had at first a literal meaning, i. 391.
Spiritualists, their devout regard for the "Everlasting Gospel," ii. 76.
Spontaneous generation, Anaximander's doctrine of, i. 102.
Anaxagoras's doctrine of, i. 105.
Stage, state of, an index of the mental condition of a nation, ii. 241.
Stancari first counted the vibrations of a string emitting musical notes, ii. 378.

Stars, multiple, i. 4.
   Coloured light of double, ii. 268.
   Our cluster of, how divided, ii. 271.
Star-worship, fetichism displaced by, i. 3.
   The philosophy of, i. 80.
Steam-engine first invented by Hero, i. 376.
   The nature of Watt's improvement in, ii. 373.
Steno first recognizes the twofold division of rocks, ii. 304.
Stephania, wife of Crescentius, poisons Otho III., ii. 6.
Stephanus, a grammarian of Constantinople, ii. 58.
Stephen II., Pope, consecrates Charlemagne, i. 300.
Stephen III., Pope, urges Charlemagne against the Lombards, i. 300.
Stephenson, George, his improvement in the locomotive, and its results, ii. 374.
Stercoraists, their doctrines, ii. 9.
Stereoscope an optical instrument, ii. 368.
Stevinus, his mechanical works, ii. 260.
   Revives correct views of the mechanical properties of water, ii. 300.
Stigmata, marks miraculously impressed on the body of St. Francis, ii. 62.
Stilicho, a Goth, compels Alaric to retreat, and Rhadogast to surrender, i. 291.
   Is murdered by the Emperor, his master, i. 291.
Stoicism, its intention, i. 177.
Stoics, exoteric philosophy of, i. 170.
Struve, his estimate of the velocity of light, ii. 269.
Stylites, St. Simeon, an aerial martyr of the fifth century, i. 411.
Success too often the criterion of right, i. 321.
Sun, agency of, i. 99.
   Aristarchus's attempts to ascertain the distance of, i. 194.
   The source of force, ii. 328.
   Influence of, on organic and inorganic nature, ii. 349, 350.
Sun-dials, invention of, wrongfully ascribed to Anaximander, i. 103.
Supererogation, the theory of, ii. 201.
Supernatural appearances, cause of, i. 410.
Supernaturalism, its adoption by the age of faith, ii. 108.
   Overthrow of, in France, ii. 122.

Superstitions, disappearance of, i. 247.
Swammerdam applies dissection to the natural history of insects, ii. 270.
Sweden, change of level in, ii. 316.
Sybaris a luxurious Italiot city, i. 124.
Sylverius, Pope, deposed by the Emperor's wife Theodora, i. 343.
Sylvester, a Benedictine monk, invents the organ, i. 426.
Sylvester II., Pope, is believed to have made a speaking head, 
Symmachus, Pope, falls a victim to the wrath of Theodoric, the Gothic king, i. 313.
"Syntaxis," the great work of Ptolemy, i. 197.
Syphilis, moral state of Europe indicated by the spread of, ii. 224.
Syria, importance of conquest of, to the Arabs, i. 325.

Tacitus, his testimony to the depraved state of Roman morality, i. 240.
Tarasius created Patriarch by Irene, i. 408.
Tarik lands at Gibraltar, so called in memory of his name, ii. 27.
Tartars, why they prefer a milk diet, i. 25.
Tartarus, one of the two divisions of hell, according to Anaximenes, i. 31.
Taxation, amount of Roman, i. 213.
Taylor, Jeremy, his testimony as to the authority of the Fathers, ii. 219.
Telescope, invention of, ii. 262, 362.
Temperature, life can only be maintained within a narrow range, i. 7.
Templars, apostacy, arrest, and punishment of, ii. 87, 88, 89.
Tensons, or poetic disputations, originated among the Arabs, ii. 33.
Tertullian, his letter to Scapula, i. 267.
   Denounces the Bishop of Rome as a heretic, i. 282.
   Denies the Scripture authority for certain observances, i. 318.
   His impression of the personal appearance of the Saviour, i. 350.
Testimony, human, value of, ii. 114.
Tetractys, the number "ten," why so called, i. 101.
Tezcuco, description of, ii. 171.
Thabor, mysterious light of, ii. 57.
Thales, philosophy of, i. 96.
Thaumasius, the name of Ammonius changed to, i. 311.
Theatre, the English, ii. 237.

Thebit Ben Corrah determines the length of the year, ii. 44.
Theodora, Empress, restores image-worship, i. 400.
Theodoric, the Ostrogoth, effect of the conquest of Italy by, i. 312.
The change in his policy, i. 313.
Theodorus, Bishop, his tongue cut out, i. 364.
Theodosius, an Alexandrian geometrician, i. 199.
Theodosius, Emperor, fanaticism of, i. 303.
His cruel vengeance at Thessalonica, i. 303.
His acts, i. 307.
Orders the Serapion to be torn down, i. 305.
Theon, an Alexandrian geometrician, and father of Hypatia, i. 199, 312.
Theophilus, Archbishop of Alexandria, his character, i. 307.
Cause of his umbrage at the Serapion, i. 308.
Persecutions of, i. 309.
Theophilus, Bishop of Antioch, first introduced the word "Trinity," i. 261.
Theophilus, Emperor, image-worship restored at his death, i. 402.
His surly and insolent reply to Al-maimon, ii. 30.
Theoria, its meaning as employed by John Erigena, ii. 0.
Therapeutæ, early Egyptian hermits, i. 413.
Thermotics, science of heat, ii. 371.
Thessalonica, massacre at, i. 303.
Thomas à Kempis, the reputed author of "The Imitation of Christ," ii. 191.
Thought, confounded with sensation by Democritus, i. 120.
Variation of human, ii. 199.
Thucydides, his secret disbelief of the Trojan war, i. 47.
Thuringians converted in the seventh and eighth centuries, i. 351.
Tides and currents explained on the theory of gravitation, ii. 359.
Time, nothing absolute in, i. 17.
Torricelli, weight of atmosphere understood before, ii. 45.
Hydrostatics created by, ii. 270.
Constructs the barometer, and demonstrates the pressure of the air, ii. 277.
Toscanelli, a Florentine astronomer, and friend of Columbus, ii. 156.

Toscanelli constructs his gnomon in the Cathedral of Florence, ii. 216.
Tours, battle of, i. 359.
Trade-wind, under the dominion of law, i. 4.
Transformation, the world is undergoing unceasing, i. 55.
Transitional forms, nature of, i. 11.
Transmigration of souls, the Veda doctrine of, i. 87.
The Buddhist doctrine of, i. 87.
The Pythagorean doctrine of, does not imply the absolute immortality of the soul, i. 112.
Plato's doctrine of, i. 150.
Transmission, hereditary, nature of, i. 122.
Transmutation of metals, i. 305.
Alhazen's doctrine of, ii. 46.
Of species, doctrine of, has met with opposition, i. 317.
Transubstantiation a twin-sister of transmutation, i. 300.
The doctrine of, first attacked by the new philosophers, ii. 9.
The Italian doctrine of, rejected by the German and Swiss reformers, ii. 201.
Tribonian suspected of being an atheist, i. 318.
Trinitarian disputes had their starting point in Alexandria, i. 146.
Trinity, the Indian doctrine of, i. 61.
The Egyptian doctrine of, i. 87.
Is assumed in the doctrine of Numenius, i. 204.
The word does not occur in the Scriptures, i. 261.
Triumvirate, the First, usurps the power of the senate and people, i. 210.
Trojan war, various views entertained about, i. 48.
Horse, superstitious notions of the, i. 49.
Troubadours use the Langue d'Oc in the north of France, ii. 68.
Trouvères use the Langue d'Oïl in the south of France, ii. 58.
Tupac Yupanqui, Inca, quoted, ii. 178.
Turkish invasion, effect of, ii. 1181.
Turks, their origin and progress, ii. 102.
Tutching, his severe and prolonged punishment, ii. 236.
Tycho makes a new catalogue of the stars, ii. 275.
Tympanum, its function, i. 5.
Types, Platonic, i. 118.
Tyre, fall of, i. 70.
Tyrians, their enterprise, i. 43.

Ulphilas invents an alphabet for the Goths, i. 350.
"Unam Sanctam," the bull of, issued by Pope Boniface, ii. 81.
Under-world, primitive notions respecting, i. 38.
Undulatory theory of light, ii. 368.
Uniformity, doctrine of, ii. 312.
Unity of mankind, i. 10.
   Religious, implies tyranny to the individual, ii. 221.
Universe, unchangeability of, taught by Anaxagoras, i. 103.
   Its magnitude, ii. 282, 321.
Unreliability of sense, Zeno's illustration of, i. 118.
Urban II. institutes the Crusades, ii. 20.
Urban VI., his cruelty to his cardinals and bishops, ii. 95.

Valentinian issues an edict denouncing the contumacy of Hilary, i. 280.
   Is a Nicenist, i. 301.
Valerius, Count, the Pelagian question settled through his influence, i. 285.
Vallisneri, an Italian geologist of the eighteenth century, ii. 301.
Vault, attack, i. 316.
Vandals converted in the fourth century, i. 351.
Van Helmont introduced the theory of vitality into medicine, ii. 276.
Variation of organic forms, i. 8.
   Man not exempt from law of, i. 9.
   Human, best seen when examined on a line of the meridian, i. 10.
   The political result of human, i. 11.
Varolius, a distinguished anatomist, ii. 275.
Varro, Terentius, his scepticism, i. 219.
Vasco de Gama doubles the Cape of Good Hope, ii. 162.
Vatican library founded by Nicholas V., ii. 107.
Vedaism, the adoration of nature, its doctrines, i. 51.
   Its changes, i. 60.
Vedic doctrines, minor, i. 58.
Venice, commercial rivalry between, Genoa and, ii. 164.
   Takes the lead in the publication of books, ii. 144.
Venus, light of the planet, ii. 283.
Verona, Fracastor wrote on the petrifactions found at, ii. 301.
   The first geological museum established at, ii. 378.
Vesicles, nerve, structure and functions of, ii. 335.

Victor, Bishop of Rome, requires the Asiatic bishops to conform to his view respecting Easter, i. 242.
   Denounces the life of Pope Benedict IX. as foul and execrable, i. 371.
Vienne, Council of, ii. 80.
Vieta improves algebra, and applies it to geometry, ii. 271.
Vigilius purchases the Papacy for two hundred pounds of gold, i. 344.
Vinci, Leonardo da, his contributions to science, ii. 280.
   First asserts the true nature of fossil remains, ii. 301, 378.
   Compares the action of the eye to that of a camera obscura, ii. 367.
Virgin Mary, worship of, i. 287.
   Various art types of the, i. 351.
Visconti, Barnabas, irreverence of, ii. 93.
Visigoths, spread of, through Greece, Spain, Italy, i. 291.
Vision, correct ideas respecting, ii. 367.
Vitello publishes a treatise on optics in the sixteenth century, ii. 216.
Vocabulary, Indo-Germanic, i. 30.
Volcanoes, ii. 291.
Volta, indebtedness of chemistry to, ii. 378.
Voltaic electricity, ii. 361.
Voyages, minor, ii. 162.
Vulgate becomes the ecclesiastical authority of the West, i. 286.
   Jealous fears of Rome respecting the authority of, ii. 140.

Wales, South, thickness of coal-bearing strata in, ii. 297.
Walter the Penniless, one of the first Crusaders, ii. 22.
War, effect of, on the low Arab class, i. 329.
   Moral state of Europe indicated by the usages of war, ii. 225.
War system, Roman, i. 243.
Water, importance of, in Egypt, i. 91.
   The curious treatise of Zosimus on the virtues and composition of, i. 307.
   Physical and chemical relation of, ii. 360.
Watt, James, has revolutionized the industry of the world, i. 376.
   His discovery of the constitution of water, ii. 328.
   His invention of the steam-engine, ii. 372, 373.
Week, origin of the, i. 342.

Warping statues, held in superstitious veneration by the vulgar, i. 49.
Western empire becomes extinct, i. 210.
Westphalia, Peace of, the culmination of the Reformation, ii. 206.
Whewell, his testimony to the incomparable merit of Newton's "Principia," ii. 267.
Wickliffe, translates the Bible, ii. 06. The revolt of, ii. 143.
Willis, his researches on the brain and nervous system, ii. 277.
William of Champeaux opens a school of logic in Paris, ii. 12.
William, Lord of Montpellier, his edict respecting the practice of medicine, ii. 120.
William de Nogaret assists King Philip against Pope Boniface II., ii. 81. Also against the Templars, ii. 88.
William de Plaisian prefers a long list of charges against Pope Boniface, ii. 81.
Winking pictures held in superstitious veneration by the vulgar, i. 49.
Witchcraft, introduction of European, ii. 118.
Women, condition of, in India, i. 69. "Sub-introduced," i. 248. Exerted extraordinary influence in the conversion of Europe, i. 355.
Woodward improves mineralogy, ii. 277.
Worms, synod of, ii. 17.
World, to determine the origin and manner of production of, the first object of Greek philosophy, i. 210. Hindu doctrine of the absorption of, i. 210. Moral, is governed by principles analogous to those which obtain in the physical, i. 337. Expected end of, i. 366. Anthropocentric ideas of the beginning of, ii. 287.

Worlds, infinity of, ii. 282. Succession of, ii. 324.

Xantippe, the wife of Socrates, her character unfairly judged of, i. 141.
Xenophanes, the representative of a great philosophical advance, i. 113.
Xerxes, his exploits exaggerated, i. 125.
Ximenes, Cardinal, burns Arabic manuscripts, ii. 172.

Year, length of, determined by Albategnius and Thebit Ben Corrah, ii. 141.
Yezad, Khalif, origin of Iconoclasm imputed to, i. 400.
Yolinda de Lusignan, Frederick compelled to marry her by Honorius III., ii. 66.
York, Archbishop of, excommunicated, ii. 73.
Yucay, the site of the national palace of Peru, ii. 177.

Zachary, Pope, enters into an alliance with King Pepin, i. 352.
Zaryab, the musician, honour paid him by the Khalif Abderrahman, ii. 33.
Zedekias, physician to Charles the Bald, fabulous story of, ii. 118.
Zehra, splendour and magnificence of the palace and gardens of, ii. 31.
Zemzem, a well, one of the fictions of popular Mohammedanism, i. 331.
Zeno the Eleatic, the doctrines of Parmenides carried out by, i. 117.
Zeno the Stoic, rival of Epicurus, i. 176.
Ziska, John, desecration of the body of, ii. 144.
Zosimus, Pope, annuls the decision of Innocent I., and declares the opinion of Pelagius to be orthodox, i. 285.
Zosimus the Panopolitan, describes the process of distillation, i. 308.
Zuinglius, the leader of the Swiss reformation, ii. 201.

THE END.

www.ingramcontent.com/pod-product-compliance
Lightning Source LLC
Chambersburg PA
CBHW051741300426
44115CB00007B/650